The Paradox of Plenty

Studies in International Political Economy
Stephen D. Krasner and Miles Kahler, General Editors
Ernst B. Haas, Consulting Editor

The Paradox of Plenty

Oil Booms and Petro-States

Terry Lynn Karl

UNIVERSITY OF CALIFORNIA PRESS
Berkeley · *Los Angeles* · *London*

University of California Press
Berkeley and Los Angeles, California

University of California Press, Ltd.
London, England

© 1997 by
The Regents of the University of California

Karl, Terry Lynn, 1947–
    The paradox of plenty : oil booms and petro-states / Terry Lynn
Karl.
        p.   cm.—(Studies in international political economy ; v.
26)
    Includes bibliographical references and index.
    ISBN 0-520-07168-9 (cloth : alk. paper).—ISBN 0-520-20772-6
(pbk. : alk. paper)
    1. Petroleum industry and trade—Venezuela.   2. Venezuela—
Economic conditions—1958–   3. Venezuela—Foreign economic
relations.   4. Organization of Petroleum Exporting Countries.
5. Economic development.   6. Democracy.   I. Title.   II. Series.
HD9574.V42K37   1997
338.2'7282'0987—dc21   96-53044
                                                   CIP

Printed in the United States of America
9 8 7 6 5 4 3 2 1

To my parents and Philippe

Contents

Figures and Tables

FIGURES

TABLES

TABLES IN STATISTICAL APPENDIX

Preface

"Don't study OPEC," Juan Pablo Pérez Alfonzo told me when I sought out the founder of the Organization of Petroleum Exporting Countries (OPEC) in his home in Caracas, Venezuela, during the height of the 1970s oil boom. "It is boring. Study what oil is doing to Venezuela, what oil is doing to *us.*" At the very moment that the coffers of OPEC governments overflowed and gasoline consumers waited in long lines in the United States and Europe, the man whose idea had reshaped the international system mused over the impact of the most dramatic price rise in history. Stopping several times to admire the 1930s Mercedes that he still drove, one of the world's first conservationists—who believed early on that a depletable resource should have exceptionally high market value (and that cars should be built to last forever!)—offered some parting and remarkably prophetic words: "Ten years from now, twenty years from now, you will see. Oil will bring us ruin."

Those words were the origin of this book, which seeks to explain a puzzle: after benefiting from the largest transfer of wealth ever to occur without war, why have most oil-exporting developing countries suffered from economic deterioration and political decay? In the midst of two massive booms that seemed to create the opportunity for "politics without limits," why did different oil-exporting governments operating in distinctive contexts choose common development paths, sustain similar trajectories, and produce generally perverse outcomes? That countries as dissimilar in their regime types, social structures, geostrategic locations, cultures, and sizes as Venezuela, Iran, Nigeria, Algeria, and

Indonesia should demonstrate a strikingly similar conjuncture suggests some form of overarching determinism. To anticipate my argument, the experience of these countries provides evidence that a common condition reduces the range of decision-making, rewards some decisions and forms of behavior more than others, and shapes the preferences of officials in a manner that is not conducive to successful development.

Identifying how this common condition arises lies at the heart of understanding diverse development paths. Nonetheless, while it is well understood that countries vary in their ability to adapt their economic and political institutions to fit changing circumstances, explanations for these variations are still elusive. Most economic analyses, by taking political institutions as given, have not been able to provide satisfactory explanations for the different development trajectories of countries, while some political approaches, by vacillating between ignoring economics altogether and subjecting all behavior to microeconomic analyses alone, have also failed to come up with convincing interpretations for the perpetuation of successful or unsuccessful development paths. Paying special attention to the complex historical interaction between economic development and political institutions is required; thus this book uses a political-economy approach to explain why policymakers make the choices they do, what alternatives are available to them, why some paths look more attractive (to them) than others, and how preference structures are established in the first place.

My central contention is that frameworks for decision-making, that is, the incentive structures embedded in the institutions of a particular political economy, hold the key to understanding different development trajectories. Above all else, these incentives are the reflection and product of power relations, either actual or anticipated, at a given point in time; they cannot be attributed primarily to either belief systems or preferences, although both may play a role. They tend to persist even when power relations and their accompanying ideologies have begun to change, and they cannot be changed at will—even when there is widespread understanding that they are sub-optimal or outright should be altered. In developing countries, it is the interaction between this framework for decision-making and the leading export sector, *not* the properties of a commodity per se, that determines whether a particular product is a blessing or a curse.

Thus far there is no detailed and compelling account of just how these frameworks for decision-making are created and reproduced through the combination of politics and economics. I seek to fill that gap. In doing so, I adopt an eclectic approach, borrowing from a range of sectoral, Marxist, dependency, rational-choice, organizational, and staple theories without fully espousing any of them. I explicitly reject the notions that efficiency is the rule for markets or other institutions in many developing countries, that a rationality assumption in which individuals understand their self-interest and act accordingly is necessarily the best way to understand human behavior, and that states are the central culprit where poor development outcomes are found—fundamental assumptions of most economists and some political scientists. Instead, I show that efficiency is often a code word to mask new power arrangements, that some players may act in their own self-interest but only by raising the overall cost of a country's transformation, and that states and markets are mutually constitutive such that the reform of one necessarily involves the transformation of the other.

Finally, in trying to discover why a pattern is repeated in a number of different countries, I reaffirm the importance of comparative case-study methodologies while arguing for the necessity to move beyond the confines of area studies by taking a cross-regional perspective. Once incentives structures are in place, the elaborate games between organized interests, bureaucrats, leading government officials, and other actors who choose to target the state may be modelled schematically, but only detailed case studies can illustrate how frameworks for decision-making are constructed, the power relations they embody at a particular point in time, and why they vary—which is the key to understanding different development trajectories. In this study, examining whether these frameworks form a generalizable pattern across a set of countries is best done through inter-regional comparison. As a specialist in Latin America, I have been fortunate to be able to draw on the previous work of knowledgeable scholars of Europe, Africa, Asia, and the Middle East for this task.

I am especially grateful to the many people who have supported me since the beginning of this project. To this day I still benefit from everything that I learned from my adviser and friend, Richard Fagen, and from my other (then) Stanford professors, Alexander George, Nannerl Keohane, and Robert Keohane. Fernando Henrique Cardoso, Albert Hirschman, Guillermo O'Donnell, and Philippe Schmitter have given me constant intellectual inspiration (even before I met them) and, along with Carmen Diana Deere, David Collier, and Stephen Krasner, have lent me invaluable support.

The rigors of fieldwork in Venezuela were eased by a number of colleagues and friends: Gene Bigler, Sergio Bitar, Robert Bond, Fernando Coronil, Andrés Duarte, Carmen García, Miriam Kornblith, Joseph Mann, Moises Naím, Marisela Padron, Julie Skurski, and Andrés Stambouli. I am grateful to the late Juan Pablo Pérez Alfonzo, Juan Carlos Rey, Luis Esteban Rey, and José Augustín Silva Michelena, the many Venezuelans who gave unsparingly of their time through interviews, and the Centro de Estudios de Desarrollo and the Instituto de Estudios Superiores de Administración for their institutional support. Special acknowledgement is reserved for Robert Bottome, whose generosity in sharing his vast knowledge of Venezuela still amazes.

I have benefited greatly from the comments of Larry Diamond, Peter Evans, Nina Halpern, Oscar Munoz, Douglas North, Claus Offe, John Ruggie, Michael Shafer, Dorothy Solinger, Barbara Stallings, and several anonymous reviewers. I am especially fortunate to have had excellent advice, critiques, and research assistance from my (now former) students: Delia Boylan, Andrew Gould, Gregory Greenway, Philip Oxhorn, Kenneth Roberts, Cynthia Sanborn, and Elisabeth Wood. Elizabeth Jusino, Honora Lundin, and Patricia Van Ness helped to prepare various stages of the manuscript. Naomi Schneider and Rose Anne White at the University of California Press and freelance editor Pamela Fischer gave invaluable editorial assistance.

Fellowships from the Social Science Research Council, Fulbright-Hays, and the Institute for the Study of World Politics supported my research in Venezuela. Subsequent research assistance was provided by the Tinker Foundation through grants to the Center for Latin American Studies at Harvard and Stanford.

Some contributions lay beyond the academic enterprise. Fond acknowledgments go to Susan Adelman, Karen Bernstein, Kathy Brady, Harold Kahn, Ethel Klein, Douglas Murray, Marc Schmitter, Monika Schmitter, and Regina Segura, who should know why.

I owe my greatest debt to my parents, Irene and Michael Karl, who are teachers and scholars themselves, and to Philippe Schmitter, whose love and support (plus unrelenting red pen) are inadequately reflected in these pages. This book is dedicated to them.

PART ONE

Commodities, Booms, and States

"Grant me this boon then," Midas cried eagerly, "that whatever I touch may turn to gold."

"So be it!" laughed the god. . . .

And Midas left his presence exulting to know that henceforth his wealth was boundless.

The Myth of King Midas

ONE

The Modern Myth
of King Midas

*Structure, Choice,
and the Development Trajectory
of States*

1973. In the Middle East, it was the era of the "Great Civilization"; in
Latin America, the epoch of "La Gran Venezuela." That year the members of the Organization of Petroleum Exporting Countries (OPEC)
succeeded in bringing about the most radical transfer of wealth ever to
occur without war. By seizing the institutional capacity to set prices for
oil and by nationalizing their domestic production, these countries,
which had been virtual case studies of foreign domination in the past,
finally appeared to gain control over their primary natural resource.
Petroleum prices soared overnight—from $3 to $10 per barrel, eventually reaching a whopping $40 per barrel in the spot market after the
second oil boom of 1980. In the brief period from 1970 to 1974 alone,
government revenues of OPEC nations leapt *elevenfold*. Money poured
into their national treasuries at an unprecedented rate. "More money,"
one finance minister reminisced, "than we ever in our wildest dreams
thought possible."[1]

The petrodollar deluge gave rise to new aspirations—for prosperity,
national greatness, equity, and autonomy—in short, for a future that
looked markedly different from the oil dependence of the past. Leaders
of oil countries believed that they would finally be able to "sow the
petroleum"—that is, redirect the capital accumulation from oil into
other productive activities. New revenues from petroleum would provide the resources necessary to "catch up" to the developed world while
simultaneously bringing political stability and a better life for their people. As Venezuelan President Carlos Andrés Pérez explained (interview,

Caracas, March 1979): "One day you Americans will be driving cars with bumpers made from our bauxite, our aluminum, and our labor. And we will be a developed country like you."

But less than a decade later, even before oil prices began their dramatic plunge in 1983, these dreams lay shattered. The exporting countries were plagued by bottlenecks and breakdowns in production, capital flight, drastic declines in the efficiency of their public enterprises, double-digit inflation, and overvalued currencies. Even the doubling of oil prices once again in 1980 failed to pull them out of their developmental doldrums. Their problems were subsequently exacerbated by a sharp decline of petroleum prices throughout the 1980s, which rapidly transformed their expectations of unparalleled prosperity into little more than a painful memory. Led by governments that seemed incapable of sound economic management or planning, most of the oil-exporting nations found their economic performance and their oil and debt dependence worse than in the pre-bonanza years. By the 1990s, they even faced the denationalization of their oil industries as they actively sought new forms of participation from the foreign oil companies they had once rejected.

Political turmoil accompanied this poor economic record. In the earliest and most dramatic case, the Shah of Iran was overthrown in 1979 in an Islamic revolution that bitterly criticized the rapid industrialization and Westernization characteristic of his "Great Civilization." Nigeria oscillated between military and civilian rule without being able to consolidate either. One-party domination was shaken in Mexico. By the 1990s, once stable Algeria teetered on the brink of civil war, while Venezuela, Latin America's second oldest democracy, struggled desperately to preserve its competitive party system. Indeed, less than two decades after the oil price increase, all major oil-producing developing countries except Indonesia and the scarcely populated Arab nations experienced serious disorganization in their state bureaucracies and severe disruption in their political regimes. Just as gold had once tainted King Midas's life, oil seemed to "petrolize" the economy and polity of these countries. "It is the devil's excrement," OPEC's founder, Juan Pablo Pérez Alfonzo, observed. "We are drowning in the devil's excrement." [2]

What happened? Is black gold an unmitigated development "good," as has been commonly believed, or is it the "devil's excrement"? Why have oil exporters apparently been unable to translate their fabulous windfalls into self-sustaining, equitable and stable development paths? Are their disappointing outcomes the result of coincidental but similar decision errors in each country, or can they be attributed to an overriding structural determinism linked to petroleum that inevitably produces economic deterioration and political decay? In sum, what is the impact of oil booms on oil-exporting countries?

THE DUTCH DISEASE:
THE INADEQUACY OF ECONOMIC EXPLANATIONS

Economists have come closest to finding answers to these questions. Not dazzled by the occasionally laudatory studies of "bonanza development,"[3] they argue that the so-called Dutch Disease, a process whereby new discoveries or favorable price changes in one sector of the economy—for example, petroleum—cause distress in other sectors—for example, agriculture or manufacturing—provides a powerful explanation for the poor performance of oil exporters.[4] Persistent Dutch Disease provokes a rapid, even distorted, growth of services, transportation, and other nontradeables while simultaneously discouraging industrialization and agriculture—a dynamic that policymakers seem incapable of counteracting (Corden 1982, Timmer 1982, Roemer 1983, Neary and van Wijnbergen 1986).

The Dutch Disease is especially negative when combined with other barriers to long-term productive activity characterized by the exploitation of exhaustible resources (Hotelling 1931, Robinson 1989). Beginning with Adam Smith ([1776] 1937, 399), economists have warned of the perils of mineral rents ("the income of men who love to reap where they never sowed"). These rents, they argue, too often foster persistent rent-seeking behavior and a bias toward unproductive activities, leading to poor development outcomes. Thus, when contrasting the Spanish obsession with gold and silver to the belief system of the Tartars, who, ignorant of the use of money, viewed cattle as the measure of value, Smith was not alone in concluding, "Of the two, the Tartar notion was perhaps the nearest to the truth."[5]

But such explanations, powerful though they are, cannot in themselves decipher the incongruity of poor development outcomes in rich oil states. They fail to capture the underlying political and institutional processes that set off economic laws and market forces in the first place and that subsequently form strong barriers to necessary readjustments. The Dutch Disease is not automatic. The extent to which it takes effect is the result largely of decision-making in the public realm. As Neary and van Wijnbergen (1986, 11) emphasize in their major study of this phenomenon, "In so far as one general conclusion can be drawn, it is that a country's economic performance following a resource boom depends to a considerable extent on the policies followed by its government." Yet, while noting that governments rarely exercise their influence wisely, they do not explain why.

The surprisingly unsuccessful outcomes of oil-exporting states cannot be fully understood separate from their institutional development. What are often seen by economists as strictly economic phenomena— the share of mineral rent, the type of links formed with other economic activities, the presence of boom-bust cycles, or even the Dutch Disease—have deep social and political roots. Commodities in themselves are not creative or destructive forces, and major explanatory power cannot be attributed to their peculiar character alone or even to the economic dynamics they encourage (McNally 1981). Petroleum, after all, is nothing but a black viscous material. Even rent, which is treated as a purely economic category in discussions of exhaustible resources, actually rewards the control of production, not the activity of the owner; in reality, it is income received through the exploitation of social, political, and legal privilege. Just as all narrowly economic activity is embedded in a web of social institutions, customs, beliefs, and attitudes, minerals too derive their economic significance from the social and political relations arising from their utilization.

Thus the fate of oil-exporting countries must be understood in a context in which economies shape institutions and, in turn, are shaped by them. Specific modes of economic development, adapted in a concrete institutional setting, gradually transform political and social institutions in a manner that subsequently encourages or discourages productive outcomes. Because the causal arrow between economic development and institutional change constantly runs in both directions, the accumulated outcomes give form to divergent long-run national trajectories. Viewed in this vein, economic effects like the Dutch Disease become *outcomes* of particular institutional arrangements and not simply causes of economic decline. This deeper explanation is revealed in the relentless interaction between a mode of economic development and the political and social institutions it fosters.

BEYOND STRUCTURE VERSUS AGENCY: EXAMINING THE STRUCTURATION OF CHOICE

By emphasizing the relationship between economic development and institutional change, rather than economic theories of raw materials alone, this book is rooted in the political-economy approaches of Karl Marx, Adam Smith, and the new institutional economists.[6] In its accent on the importance of the international oil industry as the catalyst for change, it draws inspiration from the Latin American dependency tradition[7] as well as the rapidly growing literature on sectoral approaches to development.[8] My study is different from these prior efforts, however, in its specific attention to the manner in which policy choices are structured. My claim is that dependence on a particular export commodity shapes not only social classes and regime types, as others have demonstrated so well, but also the very institutions of the state, the framework for decision-making, and the decision calculus of policymakers.

Briefly stated, my general argument is as follows. Commodity-led growth induces changes in prevailing notions of property rights, the relative power of interest groups and organizations, and the role and character of the state vis-à-vis the market. These institutional changes subsequently define the revenue basis of the state, especially its tax structure. How these states collect and distribute taxes, in turn, creates incentives that pervasively influence the organization of political and economic life and shapes government preferences with respect to public policies. In this manner, long-term efficiency in the allocation of resources is either helped or hindered, and the diverse development trajectories of nations are initiated, modified, or sustained.

Understanding this interaction between economic development and institutional change in oil-exporting countries is imperative for both theoretical and policy reasons. Oil price fluctuations in the international market since the 1970s are eloquent testimony to the significance of these countries. Oil prices rose sharply three times in the 1970s; two of these (the 1971 Libya jump and the 1979 Iran boom) were closely associated with a political crisis inside a major oil-exporting state. The market was disrupted and prices rose sharply again in 1990 as a result of Iraq's attempt to overcome its domestic crisis by invading neighboring Kuwait. Because the price of international oil is linked to the stability of oil-exporting countries, their internal dynamics have global implications—as the Gulf War illustrated so poignantly. Change inside a major exporter not only shapes and possibly immiserates the lives of its own people but can also reverberate powerfully throughout world markets and even threaten global peace. Yet, surprisingly, the impact of oil booms on the producer nations themselves and the implications for their future have been largely overlooked.[9]

The theoretical challenge posed by the performance of oil-exporting countries is equally compelling. How can a repeated pattern be explained when it occurs across countries as dissimilar in regime type, social structure, geostrategic location, culture, and size as Iran, Nigeria, Mexico, Algeria, and Venezuela? Why, in the midst of two booms, did different governments operating in distinctive contexts make choices that seem to have produced similar results? Behind this puzzle lies a central issue of political analysis: what influences the choices of public authorities and consequently the overall effectiveness of state policies? More specifically, to what extent are public policies, such as those adopted in the wake of a boom, the product of the unconstrained choices of decision-makers? To what extent can they be explained by structurally determined factors such as the organization of international markets, the peculiarities of class structures, or the existence of particular types of state institutions?

Framed in this way, an analysis of the experience of oil-exporting countries contributes to the critical debate over the relative merits of structural versus actor-centered approaches to political change. This debate revolves around different conceptions of explanation in the social sciences: at one extreme, Marxist structuralism or Parsonian functionalism presumes that decisions are determined largely independently of the choices of actors; at the other, many rational-choice theorists view decisions as relatively unconditioned by economic or social structures or other supra-individual entities. Structuralists insist on the importance of historically created constraints in determining the choices of actors, while rational-choice theorists believe that decisions are underdetermined. They emphasize the notion of contingency, meaning that outcomes depend less on objective conditions than on the subjective rules surrounding strategic choice or the qualities of specific leaders.

The extent to which voluntaristic choice is attributed to decision-makers separates these two approaches. Especially in the current intellectual climate, which is marked by the demise of socialist development models, the discrediting of Marxism, and attacks against the validity of dependency theories, structural approaches have been sharply and often correctly criticized for their systematic underestimation of human agency. Concomitantly, choice-based theorizing, which rests on notions of methodological individualism and rational self-interest, has come to dominate some political analysis, especially with regard to the United States. Central in this approach are not the constraints posed by international markets, the historic development of social classes, or particular patterns of state formation—which are viewed as mere parameters—but rather the specification of the preferences of individual policymakers.[10]

Such purely agency-based interpretations have gained credence in part because their emphasis on individual rationality resonates with the liberal tradition as well as with the less-constrained historical development trajectory of the United States. But scholars of developing countries have resisted these interpretations—and for good reason.[11] The central problem of development studies is explaining the emergence and persistence of radically different patterns of development and divergent levels of state performance. Observers seek to understand the relationship between economic growth and institutional change—that is, why industrialization is associated with strikingly disparate types of states and political regimes in different periods and regions. The most sophisticated theorists, especially North (1990), have helped to clarify why some countries seem to get on long-term productive development tracks while others, like Spain in the sixteenth century, fail to do so, and they amply demonstrate how, given suitable property rights, market forces can generate incentives for private decision-makers to promote the productive allocation of resources. But most rational-choice theorists have paid too little attention to the historical origins of institutions—that is, how institutions are actually created in a manner that subsequently reduces the range of decision-making, rewards some forms of behavior more than others, and shapes the preferences of policymakers in the future.

Furthermore, approaches that emphasize human choice to the detriment of structural factors cannot account for significant differences in the propensity of countries to adapt to changing circumstances. Too many theorists who emphasize choice have too often been blinded by an insistence on the supposed efficiency and rationality of institutions, especially private-property relations, to explain why detrimental development trajectories persist even in the face of international competitive pressures that ought to lead to their alteration. Even after recognizing that institutions making inefficient allocations may impose costs on the rest of society, they do not ask why rational political leaders might persistently engage in such behavior nor, more significantly, how they can get away with it—often for generations. But these questions cannot be ignored. They are the basis for understanding the relationship between economic development and "efficient" institutional change, the ability of governments to promote timely structural adjustments, the appropriate balance between public and private boundaries, and, ultimately, the rise and decline of nations.

This book addresses the debate over structure versus agency by emphasizing how choices are structured over time. In this sense, it unites structural and choice-based approaches by claiming that prior interactions of structure and agency create the institutional legacy that constrains choice down the road. It seeks to explain how these historical interactions construct the *range of choice* facing policymakers at a given moment, how this structuration is reproduced or modified, and why a particular range may be wide in some circumstances and quite narrow in others. Thus it problematizes the nature of choice, the identities of actors making such choices, and the way their preferences are formed within specific structures of incentives. Elsewhere I have called this approach "structured contingency" (Karl 1990).

Within this framework, decisions of policymakers are viewed as embedded in (and therefore shaped by) institutions that have been formed through constant interaction with organized groups, and domestic and international markets, and that are characterized by interlocking histories and shared meanings. As organizational theorists have demonstrated, policymakers are socialized and their preferences, values, and behaviors are shaped through their participation in these modern institutions (March and Olson 1984). Unlike microeconomic approaches, which understand bureaucratic (re)organization as the reflection of the preferences of competing politicians whose primary goals are getting and retaining office, the framework adopted here assumes a more interactive effect: while the preferences of policymakers may determine some of the parameters of institutions when they are being established, these same institutions, evolving over time, subsequently define the preferences of political actors rather than serving as mere constraints. Consequently, as we shall see, the preferences of policymakers may be strikingly similar in institutional contexts that seem different but actually resemble each other through a common structure of incentives.

Structured contingency does not argue that individual decisions made at particular points in time, or all observable political or economic phenomena, can be specifically and unambiguously linked to the presence of preexisting institutions. Instead it claims that historically created structures, while not determining which one of a limited set of alternatives decision-makers may choose, do in fact demarcate the types

of problems that arise and do define alternative solutions, thereby restricting or enhancing the choices available. Furthermore, institutional
structures may combine to produce a situation in which one path of
action becomes far more attractive or far less costly than another, and
thus they can define preferences by creating overwhelming incentives
for decision-makers to choose (or to avoid) a specific set of policies.

Nor should structured contingency be equated with inevitability—a
charge that is often leveled against structural approaches: decisions can
be made and alternatives can be chosen at every turn. Instead, the conception offered here is one of path dependence or, in David's words
(1989, 6), how "one damn thing follows another." David (1989, 1) has
noted that "systems possessing this property cannot shake off the effects
of past events, and do not have a limiting, invariant probability distribution that is continuous over the entire space." In more common par-
lance, the impact of decisions made in the past persists into the present
and defines the alternatives for the future. These decisions become em-
bodied in socioeconomic structures, political institutions, and rules that
subsequently mold the preferences and behaviors of individuals, thereby
enhancing (or reducing) the probability of certain outcomes. Because
these structures and institutions normally are altered incrementally and
at a slow pace, the notion of path dependence carries an implicit assumption of gradual change interrupted by sharp discontinuities
(Krasner 1988).[12] This is a key point. Trajectories can change, but these
changes are most frequently marked by "critical junctures"—the advent
of foreign domination, political regime change, war, an international
crisis, and so forth (Collier and Collier 1991). Otherwise, major
changes in direction do not arise easily.

Specifically, if the range of options available to decision-makers at a
given point in time is a function of institutions put in place in an earlier
period, then a type of "lock-in" can occur once a country sets down a
particular development path (David 1989): the framework for decision-
making is gradually restructured to reflect and even reinforce the initial
choice (North 1990). If the initial choice is effective and if the restructuring that occurs during critical junctures produces a framework that is
adaptable, with low barriers to change, then institutional development
subsequently can permit maximum space for human agency and the
pursuit of alternative courses of action. This is the result in "lucky"
countries—ones that can more easily than others adjust to changing
circumstances.

But there is another less historically fortunate result of restructuring the framework for decision-making. If it produces a rigidity in institutions, which are then characterized by high barriers to change and are led by organizations and interests with a powerful stake in the existing constraints, restructuring can reinforce the initial choice of a perverse development path by providing powerful incentives for its continued maintenance as well as real disincentives for change. Under these conditions, the probability is high that policymakers will be unwilling or unable to go "against the structural grain" (Fagen 1978) or may even be blind to the possibility of doing so. Inefficient institutions may simply never be questioned, or sufficient motivation may not exist to change them—even in the context of major disruptions. Countries in this mode cannot easily adjust to new circumstances or alter their development trajectories. Such is the case for oil-exporting countries.

An approach of this sort has important implications for the study of development. Because the structure of choice is seen not as merely parametric but rather as the heart of both stasis and change, identifying the "genesis, reproduction and consequences of various choice structures"[13] is essential for explaining different development trajectories. These structures of choice are not the same. The range of alternatives available to decision-makers is qualitatively different under varying circumstances—it may be quite wide in some cases and narrower in others. Examining policy choices without prior specification of this range runs the risk of producing epiphenomenal interpretations, while discovering how and why nations differ in their range of choice promises to reveal the roots of persistently divergent development paths.

COMMODITIES AND STATES: A SECTORAL APPROACH TO EXPLAINING DEVELOPMENT TRAJECTORIES

How are frameworks for decision-making created and reproduced in late-developing countries? I argue that determining the "structuring principle"[14] for these countries—that is, the appropriate starting point for identifying how ranges of choice are constructed—should begin with their leading sector. This means examining the export dependence that molds their economies, societies, and state institutional capacities, and that, in turn, is either reinforced or transformed by them. My effort to understand this set of interactions begins with differentiating the asset specificity, tax structure, and other features inherent in the exploitation of one particular commodity, petroleum.[15] It terminates by examining the state, where the impact of particular economic models and the organized interests they encourage occurs most fundamentally and is felt most persistently.

A central corollary of this argument is that countries dependent on the same export activity are likely to display significant similarities in the capacity of their states to guide development. In other words, countries dependent on mining should share certain properties of "stateness," especially their framework for decision-making and range of choice, even though their actual institutions are quite different in virtually all other respects. This should be true unless significant state building has occurred *prior* to the introduction of the export activity.

The specific mechanism for the creation of this institutional sameness lies in the origin of state revenues. It matters whether a state relies on taxes from extractive activities, agricultural production, foreign aid, remittances, or international borrowing because these different sources of revenues, whatever their relative economic merits or social import, have a powerful (and quite different) impact on the state's institutional development and its abilities to employ personnel, subsidize social and economic programs, create new organizations, and direct the activities of private interests. Simply stated, the revenues a state collects, how it collects them, and the uses to which it puts them define its nature. Thus it should not be surprising that states dependent on the same revenue source resemble each other in specific ways (and consequently so do the decisions made by their leaders).

What is surprising, however, given the significance of its fiscal base, is the dearth of systematic explorations of the relationship between the extractive capacities of the state and its own institutional formation. With the exception of Shafer's (1994) excellent study, the few that exist focus almost exclusively on Western Europe (North 1981, Webber and Wildavsky 1986). But most states in the periphery are distinguished from their European counterparts in one fundamental respect: as a result of their late insertion into the international economy, they generally rely on external rather than internal sources of revenue. Indeed, their tax base is quite distinctive in this respect. In contrast to the European experience of state building, they have grown dependent on revenues from the sale of their primary export commodities and, to a lesser extent, on external indebtedness, taxes on imported goods, or foreign aid. The consequence, to anticipate the argument of Chapter 3, is the absence of the coherent and highly institutionalized central bureaucracies that Eurocentric perspectives almost inevitably assume as points of departure. Therefore, constructs appropriate for understanding state formation and institutional capacity in the advanced industrialized world are less likely to apply to developing countries, and the absence of studies relating sources of revenue to stateness is felt more acutely.

This book attempts to redress this gap by demonstrating how the origin of a state's revenues influences the full range of its political institutions—the state, the regime, and the government. The analytical distinction between these three levels is important and should be specified at the outset. The *state* is defined, following Weber, as the permanent organizational structure within which binding collective choices are taken and implemented over a given territory. Consisting of bureaucracies, an institutionalized legal order, and formal and informal norms, it is ultimately the sole social institution that can make decisions effective by exercising legitimate force. The *regime* is the ensemble of patterns within the state determining forms and strategies of access to the process of decision-making, the actors who are admitted (or excluded) from such access, and the rules that determine how decisions may legitimately be made. It includes the method of selection of the government, forms of representation, and patterns of repression. The *government* consists of the actors (party politicians, civilian administrators, military administrators) who occupy dominant positions within the regime at any given moment in time.[16]

Dependence on a particular revenue base shapes all three levels of political domination in a distinctive manner and, in turn, is shaped by them. But it affects each level of political domination differently, sometimes bringing about alterations in state institutions without substantially changing regime arrangements and more often bringing about regime change without altering the nature of the state. Most enduringly, as we shall see in Chapter 3, such dependence molds the state, especially its *jurisdiction,* meaning its scope or degree of intervention in the economy, and its *authority,* meaning its ability to penetrate society and channel effectively the direction of change. Different sources of revenues from commodities have distinctive impacts on the scale of the state, its degree of centralization and decentralization, the coherence of public bureaucracies, the types of organizations adopted, the patterns of policymaking, and even its symbolic images. This "commodity state" underlies different regimes and governments, and, as we shall see, it can homogenize much of their behavior.

THE CASE OF OIL-EXPORTING COUNTRIES

Dependence on mineral rents produces a specific variant of the peripheral state, *mining states,* which have special difficulties in restructuring
their development trajectories. These states, as Shafer (1994) eloquently
points out, face great obstacles in attempting to exit from old patterns
and have low capacities to promote new ones. The high barriers to
change arising from their leading sector produce inertia: both organized
interests and state bureaucrats tend to fight to maintain the status quo
and to prevent modifications that might eclipse their standard operating
procedures. Although this essential conservatism characterizes institutions generally, mining states are an extreme case. In effect, they
embody a rigid framework of decision-making that, if not counter-
manded, contains strong incentives for maintaining the existing
mineral-based development model as well as disincentives for changing it.

This framework is reinforced by the inextricable link between power
and plenty in mining states. Because these states, not the private sector,
own the center of accumulation, extract or receive windfall revenues
from the international arena, benefit from rents, and provide the means
through which these rents enter the economy, they become the primary
object of rent-seeking behavior—even from inside their own institutions. Thus, economic rationality cannot be separated easily from political rationality, and the logic of rent seeking, the opposite of flexible
adjustment, may easily dominate both arenas. In addition, the fate of
their polities—be they authoritarian or democratic—is almost as closely
bound to economic performance as is the fate of polities in socialist
countries.

These obstacles to altering development trajectories are even more
pronounced in states dependent on petroleum than in other mining
states. Because rents are extraordinary in oil states, government officials
have additional capacity to extract unusually high income from their
resource without added investment. These rents, whatever their advantages, ultimately increase the difficulties of adjustment: they expand the
state's jurisdiction while simultaneously weakening its authority by
multiplying the opportunities for both public authorities and private
interests to engage in rent seeking. In this way, they have a direct impact
on the decisional framework of oil states. Even critical junctures that
may be sufficient to alter development trajectories in other contexts
do not have the same restructuring effect in these countries. Instead,

especially in periods of extraordinary windfall, the features characteristic of all mining states simply become exaggerated. Indeed, the institutional molding brought about by dependence on petrodollars is so overwhelming in oil-exporting countries that their states can appropriately be labeled *petro-states.*

To sum up the discussion thus far, similar disappointing macroeconomic and political outcomes in nations as widely disparate as Iran and Venezuela can be best explained as the result of a common condition created by the interaction of commodities, booms, and states. Oil booms seem to promise the opportunity for real choice and for the alteration of a development trajectory. But when they occur in countries with a legacy of oil-led development, especially a decision-making apparatus dependent on petrodollars, choice is in fact quite narrow. Regardless of the other alternatives available, booms generate powerful and even overwhelming incentives to sustain existing trajectories but on a grander, more accelerated, and ultimately unmanageable scale. Thus they are the catalyst for future trouble.

Specifically, the chapters ahead demonstrate the following claims:

1. *The "Petrolization" of the Policy Environment.* The production of oil for export produces a common set of policy problems for decision-makers in oil countries as well as a similar, though contradictory, environment for resolving them. This environment is characterized by unusually great opportunities for gain (and loss) on the international level and unusually strong impediments to development on the domestic level.

2. *Private Vested Interests as Barriers to Change.* Countries that export petroleum as their main economic activity generate specific types of social classes, organized interests, and patterns of collective action, both domestic and foreign, that are linked directly to the state and that benefit from oil rents. These classes and interests have strong reasons to reinforce petrolization as a means for realizing their demands.

3. *The Rentier State as a Barrier to Change.* Dependence on petroleum revenues produces a distinctive type of institutional setting, the petro-state, which encourages the political distribution of rents. Such a state is characterized by fiscal reliance on petrodollars, which expands state jurisdiction and weakens authority as other extractive capabilities whither. As a result, when faced with competing pressures, state officials become habituated to relying on the progressive substitution of public spending for statecraft, thereby further weakening state capacity.

4. *The Boom Effect.* Oil booms are likely to have pernicious effects in this context by dramatically exacerbating petrolization, reinforcing public and private oil-based interests, and further weakening state capacity. Thus they lead to economic decline and regime destabilization while creating the illusion that they are doing exactly the opposite.

PETRO-STATES AS UNITS OF ANALYSIS

Petroleum provides a particularly auspicious window for peering into the relationship between leading sectors and states. The exogenous shocks of 1973–1974 and 1979–1980 offer a critical juncture that facilitates the examination of constraints on choice because the effects of exploiting petroleum were especially dramatic and therefore easier to delineate than at other times. But the argument of this study is not intended to apply to all oil-producing countries. Here, *oil exporter* refers solely to those countries in which the high share of oil production in gross domestic product (GDP) and of oil exports in total exports places the petroleum sector at the center of economic accumulation. For classifying mineral economies of this sort, the World Bank uses guiding thresholds of approximately 10 percent of GDP and 40 percent of total merchandise exports (Nankani 1979, i). This definition effectively disqualifies developed countries like England, except for very brief moments in their history.

Furthermore, the empirical observations in this book, though relevant to all oil-exporting developing countries, are confined to one subset of these: the so-called *capital-deficient oil exporters.* This subset includes Mexico, Algeria, Indonesia, Nigeria, Venezuela, Iran, Trinidad-Tobago, Ecuador, Gabon, Oman, Egypt, Syria, and Cameroon. It excludes the capital-surplus countries of Saudi Arabia, Kuwait, Libya, Qatar, and the United Arab Emirates (UAE).[17] As Table 1 illustrates, these categories are generated by examining the relationship between the populations of these countries and their projected oil reserves prior to the 1973 boom.[18] Thus, the capital-deficient countries have relatively larger populations (column B) and smaller per capita reserves (column C) than do the capital-surplus countries. Table 1 also captures the strikingly lower GDP per capita (column D) of capital-deficient countries when compared with capital-surplus ones.

This distinction between types of oil exporters is critical to the analysis that follows in several ways. Capital-deficient oil exporters have a

TABLE I

CAPITAL-DEFICIENT AND CAPITAL-SURPLUS
OIL-EXPORTING COUNTRIES, 1973

	A Reserves (billion barrels)	B Population (millions)	C Reserves per Capita (billion barrels per million persons)	D GDP per Capita (U.S. dollars)	E Depletion Horizon (years)
Capital-Surplus Countries					
Kuwait	64.0	0.89	71.91	6,086	60.7
Libya	25.5	2.24	11.38	3,346	33.0
Saudi Arabia	132.0	6.76	19.53	1,618	48.8
Qatar	6.5	0.15	43.33	4,366	32.1
UAE	25.5	0.42	60.71	6,792	46.3
Iraq	31.5	10.41	3.03	517	45.7
Capital-Deficient Countries					
Algeria	7.6	15.77	0.48	514	20.2
Indonesia	10.5	123.80	0.08	126	22.1
Iran	60.0	31.23	1.92	820	27.4
Nigeria	20.0	61.71	0.32	271	27.4
Venezuela	14.0	11.28	1.24	1,509	11.4

SOURCES:

A: "Worldwide Report," *Oil and Gas Journal,* December 31, 1973, pp. 86–87.

B: International Monetary Fund (1988b, country tables). Figures are for 1973.

C: Calculated from A and B.

D: Calculated GDP, average exchange rate, and population figures in source for B. Figures do not reflect depreciation or purchasing-power parity.

E: Calculated from reserve and production figures in source for A.

larger skilled labor force and a more diversified economy than do their capital-surplus counterparts. They appear to be able to absorb all the oil revenues from their booms and in fact have generally been net importers of capital, except during the brief period from 1974 to 1976 (United Nations Commission on Trade and Development 1982, 48–54). Their less-populated counterparts, to the contrary, could not possibly absorb all their revenues and thus ran balance-of-payments surpluses until 1983, when oil prices fell sharply.

Moreover, although all oil-exporting developing countries are highly dependent on petroleum,[19] this dependence is felt more acutely in capital-deficient countries because their opportunities are so clearly bounded. Their ratio of population to proven reserves is relatively unfavorable, and estimates at the time of the 1973 boom showed (incorrectly) that their projected incomes could not carry the burden of development for more than several decades. As column E in Table 1

demonstrates, in 1973 most policymakers in capital-deficient countries
believed that they had only one or two decades of oil exploitation left![20]
This fear overrode any thoughts that the oil market itself might crash,
even for those few officials who were aware of the volatility of the market and the risks they might face in the future.

The threat of future limitations had several implications for behavior
in the 1973 boom. First, government preferences to diversify away from
petroleum were far greater in capital-deficient countries. Though these
countries were statistically less dependent on petroleum than the capital-surplus countries, where oil revenues made up almost half of earned
income, their governments viewed the petrodollars that constituted at
least a quarter of their income as the linchpin to successful diversification. They believed that their time horizon was far shorter than that of
other oil countries; they had to "sow the petroleum" before their reserves were depleted. Second, their "shortage" of petroleum meant that
they made decisions in the short term that had great significance for
their future development. In their view, there simply were no extra opportunities to squander. For these reasons, capital-deficient exporters
should be considered a group apart, and henceforth the terms *exporter*
and *producer* will refer only to them unless otherwise stated.

Finally, this study encompasses a subset of these capital-deficient oil
exporters chosen because of their larger share of world production: Algeria, Indonesia, Iran, Nigeria, and Venezuela. Norway is also included
for purposes of comparison with a developed country. Cameroon, Gabon, Ecuador, Syria, Oman, Egypt, and Trinidad-Tobago are excluded
because their share of world production is insignificant (less than 0.5
percent), and their inclusion would make this study unwieldy. Because
Mexico's boom occurred later than that of the OPEC countries and was
the result of discoveries rather than a price hike, its boom-bust cycle is
timed differently from that of the other capital-deficient oil exporters,
and it is not part of the same comparison set. Nonetheless, my argument
helps to explain Mexico's contemporary political and economic crisis,
and data on Mexico are included in the Statistical Appendix to illustrate
how similar its experience has been.

A RESEARCH DESIGN
FOR CROSS-REGIONAL COMPARISONS

This study employs several different variants of the comparative
method. Part I, "Commodities, Booms, and States," sets out the book's

general argument by asking John Stuart Mill's ([1843] 1967) classic question: how can the repeated occurrence of similar patterns across different countries be explained? Chapter 2 demonstrates that the outcomes in capital-deficient oil exporters are indeed surprisingly similar; it then compares their experience with that of Spain during the gold and silver boom of the sixteenth century as a heuristic device to facilitate finding answers to Mill's question. Instead of the more generally utilized "most-similar-systems" research design, I apply the method of agreement to highly contrasting cases. This method has the advantage of avoiding the overdetermination inherent in a most-similar-systems approach, which ultimately can inhibit the researcher from sorting out causal factors (Przeworski and Teune 1970). Chapter 3, the central theoretical chapter of the book, employs Mill's method of agreement by contending that the clue to the similarity in outcomes in oil-exporting countries must be the manner in which petroleum, their only fundamental commonality, transforms their institutional environment.[21]

Part II, "Democracy over a Barrel in Venezuela," relies on a detailed case study to illustrate the specific cause-and-effect links of the general argument regarding petro-states. Because my argument was induced largely from my understanding of the Venezuelan case, it should not be viewed as a "test." Though the conceptual framework of this part is designed for comparison with other cases in Chapter 9, the focus on one case is intended to provide the complexity and historical specificity regarding the institutional structuring of choice that are not possible in the rest of the book.

Venezuela is presented as a "crucial case" in several respects (Eckstein 1975). Prior to the sudden destabilization of its democracy in 1992, it seemed to possess many of the prerequisites for handling the challenge of an oil boom and therefore the greatest potential for effectively challenging the thesis developed here. As the oldest major oil exporter in the developing world (prior to Mexico's reentry into the international market), its state had been able to accumulate valuable experience in petroleum matters, unlike Nigeria or other relative newcomers. The founder of OPEC, it successfully wrested increasing shares of its global product from the international system, which permitted generally high growth rates. Industrialization produced a sizeable educated middle class, and its citizens enjoyed a competitive party system. Set apart thusly from its Middle Eastern and African oil-exporting counterparts, Venezuela seemed the most likely candidate to make productive use of its oil windfall.

In the Latin American context, Venezuela is a crucial case for another reason: it tests the contention that the export of petroleum contributes to a pattern of development that differs substantially from other development trajectories. In regional comparisons, Venezuela was a noted "outlier" prior to the 1990s; its generally strong growth and more than thirty-five-year-old democracy were the most striking signs of a path distinct from the uneven performances and bureaucratic authoritarian cycles of its Southern Cone neighbors. Most North American scholars have attributed this "exceptionalism" to strictly political factors: regular elections, viable political parties, and an unusual degree of statecraft characterized by pact making (Alexander 1964, Martz 1966, Martz and Myers 1977, Levine 1978, McCoy 1987). My argument rejects this explanation as incomplete, contending instead that the access to oil rents dispensed through the petro-state provides a more accurate explanation of Venezuela's unusual regime stability as well as its institutional fragility since 1989.

Chapter 4 explores the interaction between oil-led development and institutional change in Venezuela by analyzing the historical forging of its petro-state during the critical juncture provided by the entrance of foreign oil companies. Chapter 5 discusses the ramifications of the merging of this state with a "pacted democracy" during a second critical juncture of regime transition. Chapters 6 and 7 shift the level of analysis from the broader parameters of states, regimes, and economic models to government decision-making after the 1973 oil boom, emphasizing the manner in which the responses of the first Carlos Andrés Pérez administration were defined by the oil-forged institutions of the past. Chapter 8 returns to the structural level by examining the painful political and economic adjustments involved in the transition from a rentier to a post-rentier development model.

Part III, "The Impact of Oil Booms on Oil-Exporting Countries," examines the effect of booms in comparative perspective. Chapter 9 uses a combination of statistical data and structured-focused comparisons to explore similarities and variations in the economic and political outcomes of capital-deficient oil exporters. This chapter pays special attention to Indonesia, which performed significantly better on numerous indicators than its counterparts, and introduces the experience of one developed country, Norway, to illustrate the similarities and differences in the behavior of its policymakers. Chapter 10 concludes the book by reexamining the cases of both Spain and Venezuela, analyzing the significance of regime differences, and looking at the long-term effects of petroleum dependence on both economic outcomes and the structuration of choice.

One important advantage of this combined research design should be mentioned at the outset. In most existing studies, states in the developing world have been grouped for comparison by their geographical and cultural location or according to the level of development of their economies. Thus, customarily African or Latin American countries and, more recently, newly industrializing countries (NICs) are identified as relevant subsets for comparative analysis. An approach that examines similarities in highly contrasting cases necessarily moves scholarship beyond an area-studies focus. It has the advantage of encouraging new classificatory schemes for cross-regional comparison that may serve as a promising "theoretical map" for deriving distinctive new categories of states in the developing world. But even if these theoretical ambitions are not realized, cross-regional comparison is the most effective method for demonstrating why most oil exporters, though blessed when compared with "have-not" countries like El Salvador, may prove to be the modern counterparts of Midas.

TWO

Spanish Gold to Black Gold

Commodity Booms Then and Now

"Did I not tell you they are windmills!" Sancho cried, as he rushed to rescue Don Quixote's horse and broken lance from their encounter with "giants." If he were alive today, the founder of OPEC, Juan Pablo Pérez Alfonzo, might echo the words of Cervantes' famous character. Although considered a romantic visionary in his native Venezuela, Pérez Alfonzo was years ahead of his time in comprehending the false images projected by petroleum busts and booms. As early as 1959, when oil prices dropped sharply and exporters believed they would soon face disaster, he convinced reluctant governments that the moment was propitious for forming an organization of producers to protect the value of their resource. His idea came to fruition with OPEC's astonishing success a decade later.[1] But in 1976—in the midst of the oil exporters' wild euphoria over one of the greatest commodity booms in history—his vision once again differed from the norm. "Look at *us*," he warned. "We are having a crisis. . . . We are dying of indigestion" (interview, Caracas, summer 1976).

Pérez Alfonzo proved to be correct. By the mid-1980s, successful oil-led development appeared to be as illusory as the giants of Don Quixote's imagination. The optimism that followed the oil-price shocks of 1973–1974 and 1980 had turned to pessimism as oil exporters sought desperately to resolve the political and economic dilemmas created by soaring costs, declining commodity prices, and the manifestations of Dutch Disease. Their prevailing mood was captured in a World Bank study that concluded, "[The oil-exporting countries'] general goal of self-sustaining non-oil development is far from being attained" (Gelb 1984, 43). In perhaps the most pessimistic evaluation of their situation, one OPEC statesman remarked that history would show that oil-exporting countries "have gained the least, or lost the most, from the discovery and development of their resources" (Attiga 1981a, 7). While insufficient time has elapsed for such a definitive pronouncement, particularly in light of inadequate data about long-range development programs, most observers now agree that the medium-range prospects of most oil nations are not promising.

Why did the petroleum boom turn so quickly into a bust? This outcome is especially puzzling given the enormity of the boom itself. For most countries, the transfer of wealth in 1973 and again in 1980 produced greater revenues than those available to them over the entire past century. Yet their actual gains bore little relationship to the magnitude of this transfer. Whether the experience of these countries is likened to the illusory giants of Don Quixote, the ancient myth of King Midas, or the commodity booms of the past, the implications are the same: a sudden influx of great wealth is not always a development "good." Indeed, as Dutch Disease theorists have pointed out, foreign exchange—that most sought-after prize—can easily become a curse instead of a blessing.

The following account of the oil-exporting countries after the 1973 and 1980 booms shows most clearly their disappointing performance as a group as well as the surprising similarity of each state's overall response—regardless of its geographical location, culture, or regime type. To demonstrate that these results occurred even prior to the decline in petroleum prices, I emphasize especially the 1973 boom, the first and most important shock to these countries.

But the statistics presented provide few clues for understanding why the Dutch Disease occurred in the first place: why did all the oil exporters dramatically increase their public spending in a manner that was bound to set off this phenomenon? In order to examine this question, this chapter also presents an excursus on sixteenth-century Spain, a case with some striking parallels in a different setting. This historical analogy begins to illustrate how frameworks for decision-making can be restructured by mining rents, and thus it generates a valuable basis for explaining the institutional behavior of states in a boom.

THE "BOOM EFFECT": AN OVERVIEW

The huge windfall of 1973–1974 stunned the oil-exporting countries. After a slight decline in real terms throughout the 1960s, the price of petroleum quadrupled in 1973–1974, slowly increased from 1975 to 1978, then doubled once again in 1979–1981—this time peaking as high as $32.50 per barrel. Prices in the spot market reached $40.00 per barrel. (See Table A-1. Tables in the Statistical Appendix are referred to with the prefix "A" throughout the text.) This was one of the most remarkable international resource transfers in history—and it was sudden, immense, and unanticipated.

By any measure, the impact of this external shock was exceptional. Virtually overnight it transformed the economies and the states of exporting countries. The immediate effect of the price leap was a dramatic increase in the national savings of all exporters; national savings as a percentage of GDP more than doubled in Indonesia, Iran, and Nigeria between 1968 and 1974 (Nankani 1979, i). Countries like Venezuela and Algeria also registered a phenomenal leap in their acquired incomes. (See Table A-2.)

All oil-exporting states had the same response to the petrodollar influx: they massively increased their government expenditures. In each case, the rationale was similar. Governments believed that the removal of foreign-exchange constraints finally permitted them to take a "great leap forward" into the select category of NICs and that their relatively limited petroleum reserves meant they must move quickly. Since they now possessed a dramatically expanded revenue base, they could overcome the chief obstacles in their path to development by embarking on ambitious and expensive state-financed industrial programs. The boom raised widespread expectations of sowing the petroleum by diversifying their economies and improving the standard of living of their populations. Petrodollars, it was believed, provided the means to achieve material prosperity, autonomy, stability, and, in some cases, equity without the normal, painful tradeoffs that had wracked the rest of the Third World. State spending was the central component of this vision.[2]

And spend they did! In 1973–1974, Iran's government expenditures leapt a full 58.3 percent in real terms over the previous year; Venezuela's jumped 74.5 percent; and Nigeria's, 32.2 percent. (See Table A-3). Following the dominant development models of the time, all states embarked on huge state-led plans, financed through both petrodollars and foreign borrowing. Because they allocated the largest proportion of

their expenditures to hydrocarbon projects and import-substitution industrialization, the rate of growth of their capital expenditures was
higher than that of current expenditures. In one study based on a sample of seven oil-exporting countries (Algeria, Ecuador, Indonesia, Trinidad-Tobago, Nigeria, Venezuela, and Iran), Gelb (1984, 22–23) estimated that approximately half of the oil windfall was used for domestic
investment that, except in Venezuela, was overwhelmingly public. One-
quarter was saved abroad through the reduction of trade deficits, while
another quarter was consumed. Algeria was a notable exception here. It
invested the entire first oil windfall and borrowed abroad to finance a
small increase in public and private consumption; by 1977 its public investment rate had reached an astonishing 74 percent of nonmining GDP.

The abrupt flow of petrodollars into national treasuries, combined
with decisions to increase government spending, had a profound impact
on the state. Oil money was power, if only because it enhanced the
financial base of the public sector. In fact, it did much more. In a dynamic that will be explored in Chapter 3, windfall rents expanded the
jurisdiction of the state, which then grew even more as a result of conscious government policy. The public sector's economic role was transformed in the process. In addition to deepening its involvement in a
number of traditional activities, the state shifted into new arenas of
industrial production, often for the first time. This spending on industry
took different forms in different countries, but almost all exporting
states demonstrated a strong bias toward macroprojects in heavy industry. Given the dramatic growth of the state and this different industrial
role, the boom also forced each government to delineate new boundaries between its public and private spheres and to redefine rules for the
relationship of those spheres.

State spending had a multiplier effect. The new demand that it created encouraged the private sector to raise its own level of investment.
In part, this increase resulted from direct incentives to the private sector
through an increase in the granting of credits and in the money supply;
private-sector investment also increased because of indirect incentives
provided by the ripple effects of public spending. (See Tables A-4 and A-
5.) Wage levels also accelerated and quickly surpassed any gains in productivity. The rise in wages and the creation of new employment opportunities provoked tremendous demographic changes as waves of foreign
workers poured into oil countries. Between 2.5 and 3.5 million people
migrated into the Persian Gulf from Egypt, while up to 3 million Colom-
bians moved across the border into Venezuela (Amuzegar 1982, 824).

The results of increased spending were easily visible. If, on the one hand, the markets of oil countries became saturated with imported automobiles, video recorders, and name-brand whisky, on the other hand, significant national capital formation did take place. The ratio of investment to GDP—an important indicator of future prospects—doubled in Iran, Nigeria, and Venezuela. For most oil-exporting countries, government spending helped them to attain rapid growth in their non-oil economies (Amuzegar 1982, 52). As a group, including the capital-surplus countries, they averaged a 12 percent increase in the rates of growth of their non-oil sectors between 1974 and 1976—a figure that dropped to an average of 4.5 percent in 1980. Still, at its lowest, the growth rate of the non-oil sectors of these countries was higher than the estimated 3.5 percent average rate of growth for non-oil developing countries in 1980 (Amuzegar 1983, 51).

Spending produced other achievements. Public welfare improved through expanded goods and services, increased employment opportunities, and subsidized consumer necessities. Private consumption—one indication of the standard of living—rose at an average annual rate of 7 percent for all major oil countries from 1970 to 1979, almost twice as fast as the average rate of the previous decade and almost twice as much as in the low-income developing countries. In the Gulf, governments offered free medical care, free education, and generous pension plans. In Latin America, they embarked on programs of employment creation. Taxes were reduced and housing subsidized. In each country, middle classes made up of state employees, small shopkeepers, and skilled laborers grew rapidly, fostered by oil-fueled economic dynamism. Although figures on income distribution are scarce, observers generally agree that most groups improved their standard of living, even though the distribution of benefits was markedly unequal.[3]

The benefits of government spending, however, were quickly overwhelmed by the costs of an overheated economy. It did not take long for state expenditures to meet, and then surpass, the level of oil revenues. Although their rate of growth decelerated sharply, particularly as oil prices and exports began to stagnate, it was too late. By the late 1970s, record-high budget deficits and negative shifts in current-account balances appeared—a trend that was only temporarily offset by the second oil shock of 1979–1980 (Table A-6). In a mere four years, the capital-deficient oil exporters moved from a combined current-account surplus of almost $24 billion (1974) to a deficit of over $14 billion (1978) (Table A-7).

The manifestations of Dutch Disease exacerbated these unfavorable developments. First, imports soared because domestic production—hindered in part by supply rigidities, overloaded services, and bottlenecks—could not keep up with the rise in demand. Between 1974 and 1975, the combined imports of oil-exporting countries grew at an annual rate of 67 percent, an astounding figure, which dropped to an average of 16 percent from 1976 to 1978—the period of oil-price stagnation (Amuzegar 1983, 54).

Second, the real exchange rates of exporters appreciated, thus encouraging import dependence and discouraging local production. The extent of these currency shifts is revealed in Gelb's sample of seven capital-deficient exporters. These countries shared exchange rates that were 10 percent higher in 1974–1978 than their average 1970–1972 levels, 21 percent higher in 1979–1981, and almost 40 percent higher in 1982–1983 (Gelb 1984, 36). Because the oil sector is the basis for the value of their currencies, these currencies became overvalued with respect to non-oil activities—a dynamic that cheapened imports and undermined local production. In this way, the extensive reliance on imports, which was once aimed at plugging conjunctural gaps between demand and supply in the aftermath of the boom, became a semipermanent and ultimately expensive feature of oil economies.

Third, drastic declines in the efficiency of public services and public investment programs exacerbated these deficits. Congested ports and an overloaded infrastructure were unable to handle the huge increase of foreign trade in the wake of the boom, causing lag times of up to one year for badly needed imports and additional strains on the capacity to meet domestic demands. Delays of several years and tremendous cost overruns plagued most state macroprojects; Murphy (1983, 19) estimates that the average cost escalation of the largest projects was more than 100 percent. The long gestation period of these projects and their constant requirements for inputs fueled the inability of domestic output to match the rising higher national income. This discrepancy contributed to the growth of imports and a rise in domestic prices. As money grew tighter and the rate of importing was forced to slow down, some macroprojects were postponed, while others were set aside indefinitely or abandoned—the symbol of planning fiascoes and waste.

The result, of course, was inflation, as Table A-8 demonstrates, although individual exporters varied greatly in their performance. These price increases were small compared with the double- and triple-digit inflation that wracked other developing countries, but they had a strong impact on the oil exporters, which, as a group, were generally not used to dealing with rising prices. Inflation in turn provoked or exacerbated a number of structural distortions. Most states tried to reduce prices and spending by curtailing imports and implementing price controls, particularly in the agricultural sector. These policies brought about a further deterioration in the rural-urban terms of trade and eventually led to an increased reliance on imported food.

Because of inflation, subsidies for unprofitable firms and lower-income groups expanded rapidly. Between 1974 and 1978, they grew at a rate twice that of GDP (Gelb 1984, 36). These subsidies included low domestic oil prices (occasionally set at the cost of production so that the government was unable to derive significant revenues from fuel consumed at home), input or credit support for notoriously inefficient local industries, buffers for food costs, and public-works programs. Politically they proved to be extremely difficult to cut when oil revenues dropped, thus contributing to further inflationary pressures and the rise in government costs.

An astonishing growth in foreign debt, especially in the context of two massive booms, added to the woes of exporting countries. Calculating wrongly that petroleum would appreciate in value if left in the ground, governments utilized easily available and inexpensive credits to borrow heavily in the 1970s. Moreover, because the OPEC nations were considered particularly creditworthy during the recession years of that decade, money was literally thrust on them by foreign bankers. Thus, they ended up borrowing faster than other less developed countries (LDCs) experiencing real need. The statistics in Table 2 are

TABLE 2
INCREASE IN DEBT, INCREASE IN DEBT SERVICE, AND RATIO
OF DEBT SERVICE TO EXPORTS BY ECONOMIC CATEGORY,
LESS DEVELOPED COUNTRIES, 1970–1979

	Capital-Deficient Oil Exporters	Oil Importers[b]	All LDCs[b]
External debt (1979/1970), %	6.16	4.85	5.43
Debt service (1979/1970), %	10.16	5.96	7.20
Debt service/exports[a]	1.17	1.05	1.16

SOURCE: Calculated from Tables A-9, A-10, A-11.
[a] Ratio of aggregate debt service to aggregate export revenue for 1979 divided by that for 1970.
[b] Members of the World Bank only.

especially striking in this regard. Oil-exporting countries outpaced oil importers in borrowing—despite massive capital transfers from petroleum.[4]

The huge growth in debt can be seen in other statistics. Between 1976 and 1979, five countries accounted for over half of all LDC loans: three of them—Mexico, Venezuela, and Algeria—were oil exporters (Frieden 1991, 411). From 1976 to 1982, as oil revenues flowed in, the debt of both Nigeria and Venezuela rose by more than 45 percent per annum (calculated from Table A-9).[5] By 1980, capital-deficient oil exporters showed a combined debt of almost $100 billion, up from $19.5 billion before the first oil boom (Table A-9). Once their borrowing spree began, oil exporters became trapped in a debt spiral. By 1994, the total debt of the capital-deficient countries had reached $275 billion (Table A-9), and their debt service was $43.5 billion (Table A-10); their debt burden surpassed that of all LDC's as early as 1983 (Table A-11). This debt became a problem when oil exports failed to keep pace with rising interest rates or the rate of growth in borrowing. For countries like Nigeria and Venezuela, the emerging debt problem was compounded by their initial "great leap" into foreign borrowing, which led eventually to a bunching of expensive repayments as well as a new reliance on short-term loans.[6]

By the end of the 1970s—even before oil prices started to decline—oil-exporting countries faced debt, deficits, inflation, bottlenecks in production, cost overruns, and an inefficient and overloaded public sector. Disappointing growth rates cast doubt on the claim that these were merely adjustment costs to be born en route to modernization. Even though the domestic investment of oil exporters was considerably greater than that of middle-income energy-importing nations, this difference was barely reflected in comparable growth rates. Indeed, while growth rates were a high 5.6 percent (annual average) for oil countries as a whole, this performance fell short of the pre-boom figure of 9.0 percent and merely surpassed the 5.1 percent average of non-oil countries by a small margin. In fact, Gelb (1984, 26) estimates that overall growth rates were an average of 4.1 percent smaller over 1979–1981 than they would have been had these countries maintained their pre-boom, 1967–1972 growth rates.

More important, dependence on petroleum—the one fate exporters wanted to escape—increased markedly after the boom. In almost every case, the oil sector as a percentage of GDP grew significantly between 1973 and 1980, while agriculture, so vital to proclaimed goals of self-sufficiency, showed a significant decline (Amuzegar 1983, 52; Table A-12). In general, the share of manufacturing in the GDP barely increased; one simple measure of this share, the ratio of tradeables to nontradeables, decreased by at least 60 percent in Algeria, Indonesia, and Nigeria from 1965 to 1982 (Table A-12). These were disturbing signs for countries whose chief goal was to diversify their economies by sowing the oil.

By 1978, still under boom conditions, the oil-price hike showed clear signs of becoming a bust. Adverse economic developments had forced many of the oil exporters to contemplate austerity policies to slow down their overheated economies, ease bottlenecks, and lower inflation rates. But badly needed adjustment was postponed when oil prices shot up again as a result of the disruption in supply caused by the Iranian revolution. Even the six countries that had experienced current-account deficits in 1977–1978 recorded a new combined surplus of $12 billion in 1979–1980 (Amuzegar 1983, 53). Although some governments were initially more cautious this time, the second oil shock set off a new round of the boom effect.

The reprieve brought about by the second oil boom did not last long. Several factors—conservation efforts in the industrialized countries; the substitution of coal, nuclear power, and natural gas for oil; the entry of new exporters like Mexico, Norway, and Great Britain into the international market; and a prolonged recession in the industrial countries—pushed down the demand for petroleum. Because of their emerging role as the residual supplier of the world market, the decline in demand hit the OPEC nations harder than other major oil producers; their share of world oil output plummeted from 54 percent in 1973 to 32 percent a decade later.

The situation became critical as oil prices plunged from $32 per barrel in 1981 to approximately $13 in 1986 (Table A-1). By 1981, the rapidly deteriorating current-account balances of capital-deficient oil exporters reached an aggregate $5.68 billion deficit (Table A-7). Each country experienced a deceleration of non-oil growth, a decline in employment and wages, an increase in surplus capacity, and rapid capital flight. Meanwhile, inflationary and debt-repayment pressures climbed while oil prices dropped. In all cases but Algeria, the economy ceased to grow altogether.

The extent of this economic collapse is striking. Between 1981 and 1986, the total petroleum exports of oil-exporting countries dropped 39.4 percent, and government revenues declined or were stagnant

(Tables A-13 and A-2). Between 1980 and 1986, Venezuela's oil revenues dropped 64.5 percent, and Indonesia's, 76.1 percent, in real terms
(Table A-13). This drop had immediate consequences for government
expenditures, especially in Indonesia, Nigeria, and Venezuela (Table A-
3). Although the curtailment of spending enabled most countries (except Mexico and Nigeria) to gain some control over inflation, it also
brought about a significant new increase in foreign debt, which reached
record highs in all countries, especially Mexico, Nigeria, and Venezuela.
By 1988, the ratio of debt service to exports in the capital-deficient oil
exporters had reached a high of nearly 39 percent, compared with
nearly 20 percent for the ratio of aggregate debt service to aggregate
exports of all LDCs (Table A-11). In 1987, the ratio of debt to gross
national product (GNP) reached appalling highs of 65.3 percent in Venezuela and 112.8 percent in Nigeria (Table A-14). Perhaps most striking, although the aggregate GNP of all LDCs grew by approximately
14 percent between 1981 and 1986, the GNP of Indonesia, Venezuela,
and Nigeria plunged in a range from 20 to 50 percent in the same period
(calculated from Table A-15).

The abrupt ratcheting between abundance and stagnation profoundly affected oil states. True, most oil exporters were able to utilize
their newfound economic power to nationalize their oil industries or
extend the degree of national control over petroleum through renegotiated participation agreements.[7] But state expansion was no panacea for
discontent. The strain of managing large-scale investments and massive
distribution in an unpredictable stop-go economy, coupled with popular disillusionment with government performance, provoked crises. In
each country the shift from a boom mentality to austerity was politically painful and led to regime changes or important political shifts.
The direction was unpredictable: revolution in Iran, political liberaliza-
tion in Mexico, military coups in Nigeria, threatened civil war in Algeria, and a crisis of democracy in Venezuela. Only Indonesia, an exception that will be examined in Chapter 9, seemed more stable than its
counterparts. Despite these differences, it was clear that the oil boom
had turned into a common pattern of economic deterioration and political decay.

AN EXCURSUS ON SIXTEENTH-CENTURY SPAIN

Descriptions of the Dutch Disease notwithstanding, the explanation for
these common outcomes is not readily apparent. But comparative his-

torical analysis can provide some important clues. Only one boom in history—that resulting from the discovery of gold and silver in the Americas—rivals the 1973 and 1980 oil bonanzas in magnitude. Just as the redistribution of oil wealth marked a permanent shift in the dynamics of international capitalism, so the treasure exported into Spain changed the nature of international economic and political power in the sixteenth century. The expropriation of American bullion was the most spectacular single act of capital accumulation to that date, raising the mercantilist system, according to Adam Smith, "to a degree of splendor and glory which it could never otherwise have attained" (Smith [1776] 1937, 591). "In these golden years," John Maynard Keynes wrote, "modern capitalism was born" (1930, 159–163).

Of course, there are profound distinctions between Spain in the sixteenth century and the oil exporters today—beginning with the observation that the long-term decline of Spain, so poignant at the end of the Habsburg era, is by no means a given for the current oil exporters. Furthermore, these cases are set in different historical moments and involve different commodities. Spain was a dominant nation in the international system, while the oil exporters are in the semi-periphery. Regime types differed as did state objectives: the Spanish preoccupation with empire building through war has little in common with the current drive of oil exporters to sow their petroleum. Nevertheless, the commonalities are compelling and provide a unique opportunity to explore explanations for the behavior of states during booms.

The impact of the *siglo d'oro* on Spain—the country that directly appropriated the riches of the New World—is a parallel story of boom and decline, albeit in a different era and spread over a greater time period. Initially fueled by the riches of its colonies, Spain under the Habsburgs grew to encompass or influence southern Italy, Portugal, the Low Countries, and portions of present-day France and Germany. Yet even before the bullion influx began to slow down, the Spanish empire slowly slid into economic and political collapse. As early as 1588, when the rest of Europe moved lurchingly forward on a development path, Spain had begun to drop behind, with little prospect of recovering its position as a core actor in the world.[8] The lesson for the oil exporters is compelling: even Spain—then the leader of the world system—was unable to manage great wealth produced by mineral rents.

In its magnitude the bullion boom resembled that of black gold. From 1503 to 1595, American treasure poured into Europe in a steadily increasing stream. The first modest shipments included both gold and silver; by 1550 silver alone was being shipped. Hamilton (1934) describes two characteristics of the gold and silver boom that prefigure the petroleum boom. First, the boom was sustained over a significant duration of time, which, as we shall see, was also the case for oil. Second, within this sustained commodity boom, there were dramatic short booms, such as the tenfold increase of silver in 1571, the result of a new mercury amalgamation process used at the wealthy mines of Potosí. These short booms parallel the 1973 and 1980 price increases.

Gold and silver poured into Spanish institutional structures, which were somewhat comparable to those in oil-exporting countries centuries later. Most significantly, the state—powerful yet underdeveloped—was the initial recipient of the wealth from the New World. Just as oil became the property of the state through custom, tradition, or law, all treasure discovered in the colonies legally belonged to the Crown. Thus, the Spanish state, like its petroleum counterparts, lacked a fundamental distinction between its economic and its political role—a characteristic that would become critical to its ultimate destiny.

The state that received these revenues seemed strong. The bullion boom coincided with the powerful political marriage of Ferdinand and Isabella, which finally united the national territory and established the doctrine of *preeminencia real,* the absolute authority of the Crown. The Catholic Kings built an administrative system, formed a police force, subdued the towns through a series of royal appointments, domesticated the clergy, and even curbed the aristocracy. Ferdinand's subsequent success in seeking alliances with Germany, Italy, England, and the Netherlands warded off the French and ultimately won him the title of Holy Roman Emperor. These activities were carried out through warfare; by the mid-sixteenth century, 80 percent of the revenues of the Spanish state were spent on the military (Anderson 1979, 32). Later, Charles V continued to project the Habsburg monarchy in the international arena. From the outside, the Spanish state and monarchical regime appeared to be consolidated.

This impression of state strength, however, was deceptive, and revenues from the New World actually coincided with state building. Although Castile, Aragon, Catalonia, and Valencia had been fused through a dynastic marriage, the state itself was a fragile creation. It had never been knit into a unified entity at either the national or international level.[9] Each territory was compartmentalized and remained a separate administrative structure. In the process of state building, old institutions were not dismantled and replaced; instead, personnel appointed by the Crown were merely superimposed on the bureaucracies of the past. The Spanish state never had a common currency, tax system, or developed legal system, and it lacked the solid foundations of unification that marked other absolutist states in Europe.

Because power was centralized, the Spanish regime, like many of the oil-exporting countries, had few checks on its authority. The monarchy dominated all Spanish territories, particularly Castile, and thus state decisions remained relatively free of the influence of the Church, local aristocrats, the burghers, or peasants. The monarchy exercised its domination through an intricate arrangement of tradeoffs, ideological control, and repression. It consolidated the loyalty of the lesser aristocracy through political favoritism, especially by selling patents of nobility and ecclesiastical appointments. This practice dramatically expanded the size of a parasitic noble class—much to the dismay of the older aristocracy—while simultaneously siphoning off the most productive talent from business and commerce. The social pressure against a productive bourgeoisie and toward nobility, so graphically captured by Cervantes, was powerful: *el no vivir de rentas,* the saying went, *no es trato de nobles* (not to live from rents does not befit a nobleman) (Lynch 1965, 115).

These practices permeated other classes as well. The state bought the talents of those who might have become small entrepreneurs through the awarding of offices, establishing a pattern of *empleomania* that swelled the ranks of the public sector. Extreme inequality was one characteristic of this rentier mode; only 2 to 3 percent of the population owned 97 percent of the soil.

Not surprisingly, the economy was also undeveloped. Industry barely existed in the 1500s, and the only meaningful manufacturing sectors were textiles and shipbuilding (Larraz 1963, Mauro and Parker 1977). Although rural activity was far more important, the agrarian system was badly skewed, and Spain grew increasingly unable to produce its own food. (Vásquez de Prada 1978). By the time of the bullion boom, Spain could neither feed itself nor produce many of its necessary items. It depended on world trade, a tendency that would be badly exacerbated later.

What happened when precious metals flowed into these underdeveloped socioeconomic structures and weak state institutions? Because mercantilism was the dominant development paradigm of the time, the Habsburg monarchy made every effort to retain and then regulate bullion flows. It sought to increase the power of the state by encouraging the export of goods while banning exports of bullion on the assumption that there was a fixed quantity of wealth in the world. Even so, the firm belief in these tenets did not mean that the treasure from the Americas actually stayed in Spain (see Elliot 1970, 65).

Because a large percentage of American treasure initially accrued to the state, the monarchy adopted a pattern of behavior later adopted by the oil exporters: its goals became inflated, and its time horizons shortened. Charles V, Philip II, and their successors used their portions of precious metals to achieve the expansion and defense of empire. In twenty years, the Spanish army grew to fifteen times its original size, utilizing enormous revenues and creating a permanent need for more. Not surprisingly, the state's expenditures rose to meet and then surpass the level of its revenues.

As in the petroleum boom, the money that stayed in Spain provoked a feverish acceleration of the economy, a lightning growth of trade, and a spectacular industrial expansion. For a time, Seville became the bustling center of the world, a place on which "all European life and the life of the entire world could be said to have depended" (Chaunu 1959, quoted in Wallerstein 1974, 165). Wealth flowed to the cities of Valladolid, Cadiz, and Madrid, producing a visibly affluent elite. Although the distribution of wealth remained highly concentrated, the deluge of precious metals created a new social mobility within Spain and a generalized sense of prosperity.

The appearance of wealth, however, was deceptive. Prosperity masked the slow erosion of the country through excessive public spending abroad. The expansion of empire and the fateful series of European wars that followed were financially crippling, siphoning off the riches of the Americas because, quite simply, lack of money spelled military defeat. Given the overextension of the empire, it did not take long for adverse budgetary trends to reveal Spain's long-term fragility. In 1574, for example, Philip II spent twenty-two million florins even though the government's budget was only twelve million; over half of his expenditures went to support the Mediterranean fleet and the Army of Flanders (Parker 1972, 233–234).

This spending had a critical impact on the Spanish state. Because the supply of precious metals provided Habsburg absolutism with an enormous income outside the traditional orbit of revenues in Europe, regime goals soared beyond the normal royal ambitions and led to further spending. The monarchy began to overreach itself while simultaneously delaying the integration and administrative centralization of the state so essential to its imperial objectives. For example, it made no attempt to incorporate Castile into the other dominions because Castile's links to the Americas superseded and supplanted its relations with neighboring territories. As Anderson (1979, 71) writes, "[Huge quantities of silver] . . . meant that Absolutism in Spain could dispense with the slow fiscal and administrative unification which was a precondition of Absolutism elsewhere." In essence, precious metals replaced the crucial state building that other European entities engaged in during this same period.

State spending also produced one of the earliest examples of Dutch Disease. After an initial increase in industrial production due to rising demand (which still could never keep pace with the increase in money), Spanish output fell off, and money chased products from abroad. Accelerating inflation and Spain's overvalued currency encouraged imports. Silk and cotton, metallic articles, arms and utensils, books and paper began to pour in from the rest of Europe, often with the endorsement of the Crown. In 1548, the Cortes of Valladolid petitioned the Crown to permit the import of less expensive foreign goods to fight the rising cost of living; it also requested that the export of Castilian products be forbidden, even to the colonies in the New World. Their petitions were granted, and deindustrialization soon followed (Larraz 1963, 42–43). The effect on agriculture was equally devastating. Price controls put on grain to check inflation became a powerful disincentive to potential grain producers. By the 1570s, Spain had become incapable of meeting the national demand for food and was using the coin from the Americas to pay for imported grains.

A foreign-exchange factor exacerbated these tendencies in both agriculture and industry. The quantities of precious metals entering from the New World did not allow the Spanish currency to fluctuate with the elasticity that might have compensated for existing price differentials in the international system. This inflexibility ultimately encouraged imports and hurt exports as this overvalued currency priced Castilian goods out of the international market (Larraz 1963, 43). The end result, of course, was an adverse balance of payments. Inflation—the direct result of the entry of so much new bullion—also compounded Spain's problems. In one century, prices rose fivefold—a shocking phenomenon in a society accustomed to price stability.

By mid-century Spain had to make adjustments, just as did the oil exporters hundreds of years later. If the Crown wanted to protect its local industries from the competition of foreign goods, imports would have to be curbed. Yet this action could only exaggerate soaring inflation since the Spanish price structure had moved out of line with its neighbors'. If, however, protection were to be dropped in defiance of mercantilist thinking, other countries would gain access to the markets of Spain and its colonies, and the incomes of the Crown and the nobility would suffer. As the empire continued to expand from 1548 to 1558, the Crown vacillated between these alternatives, leading to a confused series of economic policies. Eventually protectionism was adopted. In order to retain the quantities of gold and silver entering Seville, Castile hid behind prohibitive tariffs that supported a noncompetitive industrial system and an agricultural system unable to feed its people (Larraz 1963, 24, 37).

As long as the country had the capacity to pay for its standard of living, the Habsburgs did not have to face these deep structural distortions. Yet Spain's capacity to pay had limits. In his noted study of the records of the Casa de Contratación, where precious metals entered Spain, Chaunu (1959, cited in Wallerstein 1974, 69) uncovered fifty years of revenue expansions, followed by minor recession, expansion, and, finally, deep recession. These patterns demonstrate that Charles V and his successor, Philip II, persistently ran out of revenues even before the flow of precious metals from the New World faltered at the end of the century and later ceased.

The alternative to mineral rents was taxation. As rents declined, rulers taxed Castile unmercifully to maintain their inflated aspirations, which contributed to the impoverishment of Spanish peasants because the largest burdens were placed on those least able to pay. In the face of soaring prices and taxes, it mattered little that wages doubled or tripled in the course of a century. Real wages actually dropped, squeezing urban and rural workers and causing widespread unemployment. By the 1590s, some farmers paid out over half their income in taxes, tithes, and seignorial dues; their level of taxation doubled between 1556 and 1584, a rate of increase faster than that in any other part of Europe (Mauro and Parker 1977, 58).

The failure to meet budgetary needs out of tax revenues exacerbated the Crown's dependence on its extraordinary income from American treasure and led to a new practice, foreign borrowing. Credit and the treasure from the Americas were deeply intertwined. Certain types of the king's expenditures—for example, the payments between countries or the wages of mercenaries—required actual coin, but precious metals could circulate only via long mule trains and convoys. Bankers eliminated this necessity to move great quantities of metals by issuing bills of exchange and credit—with interest. The era of Charles V thus became the age of the Fuggers as well, establishing a link between the monarchy and the banks that was to prove disastrous.[10]

A dangerous debt cycle began with Charles V's reign—one that would foreshadow the experience of the oil-exporting countries centuries later. The discovery of the wealth of the Americas permitted the king to resort to credit to buy the political support necessary to win the throne of the Holy Roman Emperor. But this election initiated an expensive habit of deficit financing that the Habsburg kings were never able to break. Over a period of thirty-seven years, Charles V, whose regular annual revenue as king of Spain was close to a million ducats a year, was able to borrow a full thirty-nine times that amount on the strength of the gold- and silver-backed credit of the Crown (Elliot 1963, vol. 1, 196–207, especially 203). In short, access to mineral wealth permitted an exaggerated debt that would eventually eat up those very rents.

During the entire *siglo d'oro*, Spain's public and private debts grew, even as its income and productive structure steadily declined. Interest payments on the debt soared. Both Braudel (1972, 694) and Carande (1967) have noted that patterns of borrowing moved in rhythm with access to American treasure and the rate of inflation—a natural development because the whole system of credits depended on the import of these metals from abroad as well as rising costs. A clear pattern emerges: treasure and debt generally rose in tandem, mutually reinforcing each other, until the end of the century. Once the high point marked by new silver discoveries in Mexico tapered off, their paths diverged: debt and inflation continued to rise sharply, while Spain's extraordinary revenues began an irregular sixty-year plunge.

During the end of its Golden Age, the Spanish government repeatedly declared bankruptcy at approximately twenty year intervals—in 1557, 1575, 1596, 1607, 1627, 1647, 1653, and 1680. Mining in the Americas eventually collapsed, and the precious metals ceased to flow, largely as a result of Spain's decimation of the subjugated Indian labor force. Spain itself was in crisis, the economic foundations of its power more fragile than before the boom. Budget deficits, inflation, rising taxation, food shortages, unemployment, and a sudden outbreak of the plague left the country on the verge of famine. Treasure had managed to hold the state together, but, as Elliot notes, "the price paid was a renunciation of any attempt to organize the Imperial finances on a rational basis and to plan a coherent economic programme for the various territories of the Empire" (1963, vol. 2, 197). The enormous expenditure of the state, the luxurious living of the aristocracy and the ruling class, and the widespread rentier mentality had reduced Spain to a state where people lived "outside the natural order," wrote Martín González de Cellorigo, a leading economist of the time, for "if Spain has no gold or silver coin, it is because she has some; and what makes her poor is her wealth."[11]

APPROACHING THE PROBLEM: SPANISH LESSONS FOR THE OIL-EXPORTING COUNTRIES

What lessons for analyzing oil-exporting countries can be derived from the Spanish case? The so-called bullion effect in Spain and the boom effect in the oil-exporting countries reveal a strikingly similar pattern. Spain and the oil countries received from the international system enormous windfalls that, for reasons of custom and law, accrued directly to the state. These new public revenues inflated regime goals and expectations as well as the jurisdiction of the state, primarily through spending. State expenditures had a multiplier effect. They stimulated rapid growth in aggregate demand and private initiative as well as in wages and prices, but they were also the catalyst for the Dutch Disease, even before windfall revenues began to plunge. The indicators were the same in both cases: budget deficits, overvalued currencies, soaring imports and subsidies, rising inflation, and foreign debt. The end result was also similar: a skewed economy, an incapacitated state, and a measurably increased dependence on commodity windfalls that could not be sustained.

Not surprisingly, governments in both cases increased public expenditures when suddenly blessed with enormous new revenues. What government wouldn't? What is puzzling, however, is their persistence in sustaining overspending in the face of powerful evidence calling for readjustments. For over a hundred years the Spanish monarchy failed to alter its development trajectory; centuries later oil exporters seemed destined for the same fate as they repeated in the 1980 boom many of the same decisions made in 1973, even though the ill effects from these earlier choices were already evident.

In both cases critical junctures presented opportunities for changing development models. The moments when crucial decisions needed to be made regarding the level and pattern of expenditures always followed periodic commodity peaks, such as the 1571 silver bonanza or the 1973 and 1980 oil booms. But decision-makers in these key moments generally sustained the development patterns of the past. The booms themselves cannot be held solely responsible for the failure of leaders to change course. As Schumpeter (1939, 231) has noted with regard to Spain, "Increase in the supply of monetary metals does not, any more than autonomous increases in the quantity of any other kind of money, produce any economically determined effects. It is obvious that these will be entirely contingent upon the *use* to which the new quantities are applied."

How can the choice of policymakers to sustain overspending be understood, especially when pragmatic economic rationality seemed to push for a readjustment? What accounts for the initial decision to overspend as well as subsequent decisions to persist in a particular development mode? The Spanish case points to two main answers.

First and most evident, access to exceptional treasure permits such choices to be made and then to persist over time by providing policymakers with an "easy" road. Spending becomes the norm for rulers because resources are available, at least initially, and because more difficult tasks like building administrative authority take time and provide few immediate awards. Indeed, spending becomes seen as *the* primary mechanism of "stateness," as money increasingly is substituted for authority. This is especially true when booms coincide with the initial stages of state building, which is the case in oil-exporting countries. This practice is allowed to continue because of the core role played by both gold and black gold in the international economy—a role that in turn produces a specific international environment. In the case of precious metals, the discoveries in the Americas, motivated by a genuine, critical European need to replace bullion, which had drained into the Near and Far East, altered the international system itself. Frantic demand for this lifeblood of trade created a set of specific institutions and models of development that arose around the discovery, mining, transport, and sale of gold and silver and that conditioned the eventual utilization of the bullion itself. In the case of petroleum, as we shall see, a similar phenomenon—an international oil "regime"—has defined the oil exporters' insertion into the international system, largely determined the rhythm of their booms and busts, and shaped the behavior of each individual state.

Neither of these minerals is unique in this respect. Indeed, bonanzas in other commodities, such as nitrates, guano, copper, wheat, and sugar, have produced rents for decision-makers elsewhere. Where both gold and oil differ, however, is in both the *magnitude* and the *duration* of their rents. In effect, both gold and oil provide decision-makers with the capacity to pay for their choices over a prolonged period without having to squeeze unduly their populations, at least initially. This fiscal capacity is repeatedly enhanced by the high creditworthiness of their key commodity, which permits spending practices to be extended through prolonged and repeated foreign borrowing. Access to lenders is guaranteed for longer than is the norm to these countries—thus postponing the day of reckoning.

But if the capacity to pay is necessary for understanding these choices, it is not sufficient. It alone cannot explain why structural readjustments are so difficult to achieve once it becomes evident that spending has its limits. Here a second explanation from the Spanish case is relevant: the covariance of weak states and mineral rents. The Spanish case reinforces the argument put forward in Chapter 1 that mineral rents transform the economic, social, and political structures of weak states in such a way that high barriers to change are created—both inside and outside the state. These barriers lock countries into the initial choice of a rentier development path. Possession of bullion or oil may offer easy and low-cost access to fantastic revenues, but only at the price of encouraging huge demands on resources, creating vested interests that then need to be satisfied, and killing off other potentially productive sectors of the economy. As a result, when revenues fall, the state's extraction costs rise dramatically because its authorities are incapable of going after new revenue sources. Such revenues simply are not there, or their extraction is not politically viable.

In the Spanish case, the structures and institutions in place prior to the discovery of precious metals were unable to counteract this tendency. Indeed, Spain's utilization of gold and silver was initially constrained by the very weakness of the state, the overly ambitious priorities of the monarchy, the rentier character of the nobility, and the peculiarly uneven development of its productive apparatus. In retrospect, such preexisting constraints to choice were reshaped in predictable directions. Massive rents flowing through the state encouraged the ambitions of kings, preempted the rise of a bourgeoisie, disrupted an adequate resolution of the agrarian question, and short-circuited capitalist development. Moreover, because high levels of external capital inflows coincided with the initial stages of state building, they permanently skewed the relationship between regulatory, extractive, and distributive state institutions. True, gold expanded the state's jurisdiction by creating a huge, financially autonomous distributive apparatus. But it also undermined the most essential authoritative function of the modern state, the power to develop a diversified fiscal base, and it led to the atrophy of all other sources of revenue.

The same transformations occur in oil-exporting countries. Here too dependence on mining rents alters economies, interests and institutional arrangements in a manner that ultimately overdetermines the decisions of policymakers in the midst of a bonanza. Chapter 3 demonstrates that black gold has had much the same impact as its predecessor, gold. As we shall see, when mineral-based commodity booms accrue directly to fragile states, an unfortunate relationship seems to exist between power and plenty: the state, so essential to the manner in which windfall revenues are utilized, may be rent asunder by the reality and fantasy of those very windfalls.

THREE

The Special Dilemma
of the Petro-State

Oil is not different from gold in one respect. When minerals are the key source of wealth for a state, these mining revenues alter the framework for decision-making. They affect not only the actual policy environment of officials but also other basic aspects of the state such as the autonomy of goal formation, the types of public institutions adopted, the prospects for building other extractive capabilities, and the locus of authority. The manner in which a state earns a living influences its own patterns of institutionalization. In petro-states, oil-provoked changes in state capacity are *the* "intervening variable"; they shape policy preferences and explain why the Dutch Disease and other disappointing political and economic outcomes are likely during a boom.

Understanding the capabilities of petro-states is no easy task, even if one borrows from a number of approaches formulated to explain state capacity. Interpretations differ about the appropriate starting point for such an analysis. Marxists and neo-Marxists emphasize the socioeconomic roots of state behavior, the function of the state as an arena of class struggle or an instrument of class rule, and the importance of class interests in influencing the choices of decision-makers (Marx and Engels 1979; Miliband 1969; Poulantzas 1973; Offe 1973b, 1974; Jessop 1977; Carnoy 1984). Statists conceive of states as coercive and administrative organizations that evolve over time in response to a perpetually changing interstate context, and they equate state capacity with autonomy and with successful goal achievement (Hintze 1975, Tilly 1975, Skocpol 1979). Organizational theorists understand the structure of the state and the behavior of officials to be uniquely proscribed by formal and informal norms, routines, and standard operating procedures, and they pay special attention to the development of administrative organizations (Weber [1921] 1968; March and Olsen 1976, 1984).

These different approaches yield different prognoses regarding the capabilities of oil-exporting states. Because both statists and neo-Marxists equate state capacity with the ability to act autonomously from social forces—that is, with a government's ability to achieve the goals it sets for itself—their approaches seem to predict especially high capacity levels for petro-states. In their view, "weak" states are characterized by their smaller jurisdiction, their tendency to be "captured" by various private interests, their fragmented or overly dispersed agencies, and their irrational behavior. They consider the "strongest" states—the ones most likely to act autonomously—to be those in which public jurisdiction over civil society is extensive, power and resources are highly concentrated in the executive, and the state resembles a rational and unitary actor.[1] Neo-liberal theorists would argue differently. For them this very size and influence over the private sector would place these states in a "low-capacity" category.

But a different definition of state capacity suggests a more nuanced analysis. If what matters is not only the size of the state and its internal distribution of power but also the coherence of the bureaucracy, the organizational forms adopted by both the public sector and private interests, and the predominant symbolic notions of the state itself, as Max Weber and organizational theorists suggest, then capacity cannot be theoretically equated with a government's ability to achieve the objectives it sets for itself at a given moment. A state could prove to be effective in implementing objectives that are determined through a highly ineffective decision-making process or that ultimately turn out to be irrational and even destructive to its own norms or institutions. Nor can capacity be reduced to a question of size or jurisdiction.[2]

Instead, state capacity has to be understood and judged in a larger sense as the sum total of a state's material ability to control, extract, and allocate resources as well as its symbolic or political ability to create, implement, and enforce collective decisions. Capacity is thus an aggregate, if imprecise, measure of the potential to raise revenues, provide services, exercise coercion, create consensus, and select and refine policies (Nettl 1968, Rose 1974).

When capacity is defined in this way, petro-states are at a disadvantage compared with many other states. State capacity of this sort necessarily develops slowly and unevenly, often in a particular sequence, and generally at great cost. States can build up remarkable capacities in some areas and remain seriously deficient in others. For example, they may become successful at externalizing power and establishing their jurisdiction over territory while remaining highly unsuccessful at institutionalizing authority. Or they may prove capable of institutionalizing authority without being able to achieve functionally separate bureaucracies that have some autonomy with respect to civil society (Schmitter, Coatsworth, Przeworski, n.d.).

In mining countries, dependence on a single commodity coincides with state formation, and this determines the shape of these different and often uneven capabilities. Thus, a sectoral analysis suggests that a reconnoitering of the terrain of oil states begin with the leading export sector, petroleum. Oil determines the patterns of acquisition of state capacities. It molds institutional development, and it affects patterns of taxation and administration, the ability to mobilize and direct resources, and the range of behaviors policymakers are likely to adopt. Other factors are also significant for determining "stateness." But the petro-state's technical and administrative resources, its symbolic content, its institutional separateness, and its own interests are most fundamentally shaped by its leading export activity. As we shall see, this process encourages similar behaviors by policymakers and private actors of all stripes and ultimately decreases the prospects for flexible and timely alterations to an oil-led development path.

This chapter seeks to explain state capacity in oil-exporting countries by illustrating how barriers to changing the development trajectory of oil exporters are created and sustained within the state itself. Drawing on insights from the Spanish case, it pays particular attention to how the framework for choice is altered as a result of dependence on oil revenues. It examines the contradictory international and domestic environments of petro-states, which produce a common set of problems for decision-makers in all these states. It then illuminates the political vicious cycle that favors one set of solutions over another by focusing on, first, the creation of interests that perpetuate oil-led development and, second, the ways in which the jurisdiction and authority of petro-states are skewed to do the same.

THE FEATURES OF EXTRACTIVE STATES

Dependence on minerals produces a bundle of characteristics that, when taken together, are unique to mining countries. With the exception of depletability, most of these characteristics are not given, as many economic theories postulate. They are the product of prior choices, made mostly outside these countries, about how mining industries should be organized. These "natural" characteristics are shared by all petro-states, but they are present in an especially exaggerated form; thus they can be considered a special subset of mining states.

First, mining states are economically dependent on a single resource. Oil exporters are differentiated from other mining states by the overwhelming acuteness of this dependence. For oil exporters in 1980, the average ratio of oil exports to total exports was far higher (96.3 percent for surplus oil exporters and 82.5 percent for other major oil exporters) than the equivalent average ratio for non-oil primary-commodity exporters (50.7 percent) Even those countries that are considered highly dependent on minerals, such as Zaire with its copper or Bolivia with its tin, do not reach the level of dependence of oil-exporting countries (International Monetary Fund, *International Financial Statistics,* and staff estimates; cited in Amuzegar 1983, 11). One result of this extreme dependence is often noted: petro-states are especially vulnerable to export-earning instability, which in turn has negative consequences for the rate of growth, levels of investment, and inflation (Glezakos 1973, 670–679; Soutar 1977; Nankani 1979, 47–51; Davis 1983).

Second, mining states depend on an industrial sector that is highly capital-intensive and that is an enclave. While capital-intensive, large-scale, and technologically complex industrialization is common in many developing countries, its magnitude is of a different order with petroleum. Petroleum and coal head the list of manufacturing industries ranked according to their degree of capital intensity (Lary 1968, cited in Nankani 1979, 29).

This extreme capital intensity has two key effects. Oil exporters historically have had unusually high levels of foreign ownership or control (or both) of their main resource because oil exploitation initially required capital and technology that they did not possess. At the same time, this industry is characterized by low employment generation and a skewed wage structure. Unlike comparable sectors in agricultural exporters, the oil sector employs only between 1 and 2 percent of the workforce. The small number of workers, the technical training they require, and the widespread nationalist sentiment against foreign control make it relatively easy for them to demand high wages through collective bargaining. Because their demands generally pose little threat to profit margins, concessions are eventually granted without the same degree of zero-sum strife that characterizes landlord/peasant relations. As the industry's wage scale surpasses that of other domestic sectors, it exerts an upward pull on the rest of the economy. The resulting wage followership produces a labor aristocracy, on the one hand, and underemployment among the unskilled, on the other. In effect, oil-led development results in a foreign-controlled, high-wage economy characterized by some strong unions and high unemployment (Nankani 1979, Lewis 1982).

Third, mining states rely on a primary commodity that is depletable. These states do not depend on agricultural cash crops like coffee or cotton, which can be replanted and reproduced year after year. Once minerals are processed and sold on the international market, stock is permanently and irreversibly depleted, which can be justified economically only by simultaneous investment that yields the highest possible rate of return. In effect, the tradeoff between extracting minerals and leaving them in the ground depends on both the expected rates of return on investment from oil revenues and projected oil prices (Jabarti 1977). Once again, this tradeoff is exaggerated in many oil-exporting states because of the relatively short time horizons they face before their reserves are depleted.

Fourth, mining countries and especially oil exporters are dependent on a resource capable of generating extraordinary rents. These rents are not "natural"; they are derived from the unusual organization of the world petroleum market (for example, monopoly rents), variability in the quality of fields or oil (for example, economic rents) and/or petroleum's special status as a strategic resource. Oil is the most important internationally traded commodity as measured by volume and monetary value (Danielsen 1982). The significance of its role leads to a relatively inelastic demand, which, when combined with the small number and large size of resource owners, the high entry costs into the industry, and the difficulties inherent in energy substitution, produces extraordinary rents with a distinctive character: they have almost nothing to do with the productive processes of the domestic economy (Hughes 1975, Davis 1983, Gelb 1986). In fact, there is no significant relationship between the level of oil production in an enclave and the performance of a local economy.

Finally, in developing countries mineral rents accrue directly to the state. By virtue of custom, laws that grant subsoil rights to the state, prior choices, and, eventually, nationalist ideology, export earnings from minerals are deposited into the national treasuries of developing countries. Though the amount of rent has depended on bargaining with foreign firms, these rents are not mediated through domestic private actors as they are in Anglo-Saxon countries. Therefore, all mineral states, including petro-states, are rentier and distributive states (Mahdavy 1970, Delacroix 1980, Katouzian 1981). Their economic power and ultimately their political authority rest on their dual capacity to extract rents externally from the global environment and subsequently to distribute these revenues internally.

These features have tremendous consequences for all mining states, but especially for petro-states. Their unique combination means that these states differ structurally from other states in the advanced industrialized and developing worlds, particularly agricultural or manufacturing exporters, whose products are not depletable or state-owned or as strategically important, as capital-intensive, or as foreign-dominated as petroleum. Petro-states also differ, albeit to a lesser extent, from tin, copper, and other mineral exporters, which share many of these properties but differ with regard to the magnitude and duration of their extraordinary rents.

Most important, the combination of these characteristics explains why oil-exporting states tend to bear a striking and broad resemblance to each other in state capacities and macroeconomic performance, despite differences in types of political regimes, cultures, geostrategic locations, and the like. Because the exploitation of petroleum has coincided with the process of modern state building, as we shall see in Chapters 4 and 9, these characteristics have been able to shape every oil state. Their combination produces similarities in the international and domestic environments within which petro-states must operate as well as in their abilities to address these problems. These commonalities eventually translate into similar packages of problems, similar ways of coping with these problems, and similar behaviors by officials in these countries. To understand this process, the manner in which these characteristics shape the decision-making environment for petro-states must first be examined.

MIXED BLESSINGS: THE CONTRADICTORY ENVIRONMENT OF THE PETRO-STATE

That opportunities for exceptional gain and loss arise from the possession of petroleum is unquestionable. In the twentieth century oil has replaced other important sources of fuel because, once it is found, the costs of extraction, distribution, and utilization are relatively low. Total world production has shown a steady rise, as has OPEC production since 1920 (Danielsen 1982, 16). Although prices were highly variable during certain periods, the nominal price of crude oil generally rose from the early 1930s to the 1970s, thus avoiding the wide swings that characterized the prices of other primary commodities.

These generally favorable production and price trends are no accident; they can be traced to petroleum's special features. Its critical strategic character obviously gives a constant boost to demand. At the same time, depletability exerts an upward pull on prices because it induces actors to create cartels or other cooperative arrangements to keep prices high. Only cooperation can prevent the twin dangers of early exhaustion and low prices.[3] If such cooperative arrangements are not made, prices fluctuate dramatically as market conditions move between more and less competition (Bobrow and Kudrle 1976, Osborne 1976, Sweeney 1977, Danielsen 1982).

The combination of oil's strategic value and its depletability provides the fundamental explanation for the unique international environment that conditions the behavior of petro-states and other industrial actors in the world petroleum markets. Once it is generally understood that cooperation produces especially high monopoly rents (which is a process of political learning), powerful pressures to form cartels contest traditional forms of competition. If cooperation is successful, prices subsequently rise, creating important opportunities for gain. But such opportunities are not permanent (Bobrow and Kudrle 1976, Osborne 1976). Ironically, cooperation that is too successful eventually promotes the entry of new actors into the market while simultaneously creating strong incentives for individual cartel members to "chisel" on either market shares or prices. The erosion of profits from this increased competition alters previously established agreements, undermines existing cartel arrangements, abruptly drives prices down, and makes imperative the establishment of new forms of cooperation.

This movement between competition and cooperation is evident in the formation, decline, and re-formation of the various energy "regimes" that have distinguished the history of the international oil industry.[4] Although these "regimes" have received extensive treatment elsewhere (Engler 1961, Adelman 1972, Schneider 1983), they warrant a brief description here because they shape the common prospects and the behaviors of officials in oil-exporting countries.

A few international oil companies dominated the market as well as the exporting states and managed cooperation quite well during the first regime, which was controlled by the "majors" (eventually known as Exxon, Mobil, Texaco, Socal, Royal Dutch Shell, and British Petroleum), from petroleum's discovery until the 1950s.[5] With the exception of a brief period in the 1930s, their oligopoly agreements to coordinate rates of production and share markets effectively reversed the downward price trend of oil and established a pattern of cooperation to keep prices up that endured until World War II. The absolute dominance of the oil companies over the exporting states characterized this regime and molded the development prospects of these states.

The market also stayed relatively orderly during the second oil regime, which existed from approximately 1954 to the early 1970s, but this stability masked critical changes in the industry: the gradual loss of control by the majors and the emergence of independent oil companies, whose entry into the world market in the postwar period was aided by the U.S. government. With this increased competition, oil-exporting countries were able to improve their bargaining positions vis-à-vis the companies, as was evident in the profit-sharing agreement initially won by the Venezuelans and later adopted by other exporters, as well as in the 1960 formation of OPEC, which successfully reversed the downward trend on prices.[6]

Price stability came to a dramatic end in the third oil regime after 1973, which was marked by the relative rise of the producer countries through OPEC as well as their inability to find stable forms of cooperation. Attempting to use OPEC as a price-setting cartel, they managed to reverse the downward trend of prices and, aided by unexpected political turmoil in the Middle East, to ratchet prices upward in several sharp movements, causing the booms of 1973 and 1980. But, as we shall see, because these countries so quickly developed enormous and inflexible demands for oil money domestically, they did not behave as "rational oligopolists" internationally by lowering prices to fend off new entrants into the market. Instead, their go-for-broke pricing strategy undermined their own hold on the market, created a high-risk environment, and contributed to the collapse of prices in the 1980s.[7]

In sum, all major exporting countries have faced the same external dilemma throughout their history. On the one hand, they have had to bargain hard, both individually and collectively, to emerge from the domination of the international companies that so profoundly affected their development paths. On the other hand, their gradual success paradoxically set the stage for sharp rises and falls in prices, a prolonged trough of lower prices, and an especially risky international environment. Similar contradictions permeate the domestic environments of petrostates. Oil has served as their engine of growth, but it simultaneously exerts a pernicious effect. In the tradition of staple theorists, Hirschman (1977, 73) has argued that the links a commodity generates with the rest of the economy can prove to be either especially beneficial or especially harmful to the development process.[8] Unfortunately, minerals are not likely to be among the lucky commodities that lead to new opportunities for productive economic activity. Mineral economies generate consumption and especially fiscal links, which Hirschman (1977) defines as the ability of the state to tap the income stream accruing from staples, but they do so at the expense of creating more productive linkages. Indeed, fiscal linkages actually block production linkages, especially when rents are high, because tapping the income stream provides the foreign exchange to buy abroad and removes incentives to produce at home. Ideally, development is based on staples that encourage the simultaneous presence of production, consumption, and fiscal links, but in minerals one type of link is found only at the expense of another.

Hirschman's "generalized linkage approach" has profound implications for analyzing oil-exporting countries. On the one hand, oil generates few backward and forward links. The capital intensity of oil technology means that its input requirements cannot be satisfied by domestic sources and must be imported, thereby providing little impetus for industrialization. The situation on the output side is no better. Unlike the export of coffee, for example, which fosters the need both for complicated transportation systems and for processing and packaging industries, oil is moved in pipelines, which cannot facilitate regional development, and, until recently, oil has been most often refined in the advanced industrialized countries (Nankani 1979, Corden and Neary 1982, Lewis 1982).

On the other hand, links on the income side fare little better. Consumption linkages are slow in forming and have a skewed effect. Although the high technical and capital requirements of the leading sector can potentially generate such linkages, better-paid oil workers are not employed in large enough numbers to create a significant internal market. When the circulation of petro-dollars eventually produces a domestic market, numerous studies show that the technological and wage dualism characteristic of mining renders this market highly inequitable and more prone than the market in non-mineral economies to a number of economic problems that hurt productivity (Baldwin 1966, Reynolds 1965). Thus the prospects for using petroleum as an engine of balanced growth are not favorable because it encourages neither a broad-based domestic market for consumer goods nor incentives for the local production of intermediate or capital goods.

Fiscal linkages, the "blessing" of oil countries, are supposed to offset this dismal picture. But their overwhelming presence, which is the chief advantage in petro-states, actually inhibits the development of agriculture or industry by encouraging overvalued exchange rates, which, in turn, promote a reliance on imports, services, and speculative activity rather than long-term investment (Timmer 1982, Roemer 1983). Thus, a modified version of the Dutch Disease, so important during a price hike, can also be observed during more normal periods: easy access to the high rents generated by petroleum creates a structural bias against agricultural and industrial activity, and the productive activity that does occur is highly subsidized.

Finally, as Hirschman (1958, 1977) notes, the unbalanced growth that results from the overwhelming presence of fiscal linkages is unlikely to be automatically self-correcting as long as these linkages predominate. Because decision-making in both the public and private sectors is responsive to special "push factors" that emanate from the product side of the economy, policymakers, recognizing these economic imperatives, are likely to make decisions that facilitate linkage-based activities. In oil exporters, where fiscal links dominate, these decisions flow from and revolve around a fiscal imperative—the levying of taxes on income streams in order subsequently to channel the proceeds elsewhere.

Thus, policymakers in oil countries face a common set of problems and strong incentives to pursue a common set of solutions. Domestically, because reliance on oil tends to discourage other forms of productive activity, they face a special imperative to diversify their economies by sowing the petroleum—that is, using oil revenues to encourage agriculture and industry—while simultaneously seeking mechanisms to alleviate the severe equity problems that plague mineral states. Internationally, they must find a way to levy taxes on their income stream to pay for this development without weakening international cooperation in a manner that might ultimately affect their monopoly rents. Their ability to accomplish their domestic goals depends on their special extractive capacity. Paradoxically, their ultimate ability to free themselves from petroleum depends on their capacity to create a new productive base that is not dependent on oil in the face of powerful push factors favoring resource-based industrialization. In Michael Shafer's words, "The sectoral characteristics of oil put a pot of gold at the end of the rainbow, but sow the road to it with mines" (personal communication, 1987).

Policymakers in other developing countries confront similar challenges of capital accumulation, diversification, and equity. But these problems assume a particular shape in oil states, where the expectations generated by petro-dollars are especially high, where development is markedly skewed by mineral dependence, and where the pressure on policymakers to meet their objectives before oil runs out is especially intense. In petro-states, the predominance of a peculiar set of oil-based linkages makes the combination of resource-based industrialization and ongoing reliance on petroleum seem to be the easiest and most available solution to these challenges. The extent to which policymakers might broaden these goals or choose other paths depends both on the strength of pressures from organized interests to go in a different direction and on the nature of state institutions. But these too are molded by petroleum.

ORGANIZED INTERESTS
AND THE POLITICS OF PETROLIZATION

Whether decision-makers can resist the push factors that stem from the exploitation of petroleum and succeed in sowing their natural resource rests on the presence (or absence) of organized classes and groups who will propel them in the direction of independence from oil. Specifically, they need organized interests who are programmatically tied to a diversified and equitable economic model that is progressively autonomous from petrodollars and who are influential enough to countermand the pull of petrolization. Instead, however, these states have oil-based social forces with strong vested interests in perpetuating oil-led development.

In fact, previous patterns of state expenditures actually create a client private sector, middle class, and labor force whose raison d'être is to sustain the existing model, even if they fight among themselves to have more of its benefits come their way. Thus, any decisions by officials to build an alternative fiscal base through taxation must be made in opposition to powerful countervailing social classes and groups that have grown accustomed to the advantages of a petroleum-led development model. Put another way, the export of oil fosters especially powerful organized groups with very real interests in maintaining this model.

The export of petroleum generates these social forces in several ways.

Because of the enormous capital and technological resources necessary to exploit minerals, foreign oil companies became the dominant internal actors in all oil exporters, especially during the first and second international regimes. In developing countries dependent on a manufacturing sector, a large number of small- or medium-sized firms can often make collective action difficult. But in petro-states the number of firms (few) involved in mining and oil activities and their size (large) enhance their ability to challenge the state (Olson 1965, Schmitter and Streeck 1981). They are able to subvert the political process by forming partnerships with local elites and other domestic allies (Evans 1979) or by relying on their home governments for support (Stork 1975, Schneider 1983). Their relative power vis-à-vis producing countries has diminished over time, especially during the third oil regime; nonetheless, the complexities of the international market, the continuing need for foreign investment and technology, and their links to other powerful actors mean that these companies still retain significant power even after nationalization.

Concomitantly, domestic bourgeoisies have less opportunity to develop on their own, and they remain notoriously weak. Given the opportunity, they quickly shift to production or consumption activities linked to petroleum, where the greatest profits can be made, or they become dependent on low-risk entrepreneurial strategies subsidized by petrodollars—a reality that further strengthens the role of the oil industry (Cardoso and Faletto 1969). Thus the dominant political actors in petroleum exporters have been foreigners and their domestic allies, who have an overriding interest in maintaining the centrality of oil. In the end, the high costs initially incurred by the companies to establish petroleum's dominance and the potential losses that might be suffered by domestic beneficiaries forced to reorient their activities are simply too great to overcome without a fight.

Whatever hopes remain for counteracting petrolization must be placed on the emergence of other organized interests, especially labor, which might counterbalance the enormous power of the oil companies and their allies by pushing for independence from petroleum. Although such interests have emerged historically, with important consequences, the characteristics of commodity-led development perversely affect labor's propensity to challenge the basic model of development. On the one hand, as Bergquist has pointed out (1986, 10–11), the dynamics of oil production encourage labor militancy. Owned by foreign capital, the petroleum enclave easily becomes the target of strong nationalist sentiment. Because workers are often isolated in communities where they eat, sleep, and work together, they are ripe for organization. The technical nature of their work and the specialized skills required mean that workers cannot be easily replaced; thus they possess more bargaining leverage than, say, coffee-bean pickers in a plantation economy. These factors create the prospect for a challenge to the oil-led model.

But, on the other hand, the powerful labor organizations that result from these unique configurations have a special interest in maintaining the dominance of the oil industry. Once again, the features of oil provide an explanation. Because state reformers are able to use the rents wrested from the oil companies to secure and maintain a compromise with organized labor, unions develop a vested interest in continued access to petrodollars. Better paid than their counterparts in other productive activities and thus forming a type of labor aristocracy, they tend to exercise political clout so as to protect their privileged position. The foreign oil companies eventually find it easier to make concessions regarding labor rights than to fight. Indeed, worried about their large-scale investments, they may actually seek a strong union to help avoid serious labor unrest (Shaffer 1980, Shafer 1994). The net effect is that the most powerful sectors of labor have a stake in the model of oil-led development. Although labor may push state officials for a new and more favorable distribution of oil revenues, it does so while respecting existing patterns of development rather than by raising challenges to the basic model.

Some organized interests do, however, promote equity and economic diversification. These are the code words for a broad distribution of oil rents that reflects the fact that they are the common property of the nation. But because the features of petroleum tend to discourage industry and agriculture, which are not directly dependent on petroleum revenues in some manner, such interests have a difficult time finding a well-articulated economic base that is separate from oil. Even if these interests exist prior to the initiation of petroleum-led development, they cannot compete successfully with powerful oil interests. They are either overwhelmed or coopted through employment creation, high protective barriers, or other forms of oil-based subsidies in non-oil sectors.

Because oil rents are captured by linking up with the state, the defining behavior of business, middle-class, and labor organizations in oil-producing countries is the search for political influence for economic gain. In sharp contrast, in agricultural or manufacturing exporters, the main resource is generally privately owned, revenues are more decentralized, and influence is often targeted at a number of centers. In oil

exporters, business, professional groups, and labor may initially compete for state access, but Tugwell (1975) has shown that cooperation
against the oil companies ultimately provides greater benefits to these
domestic actors by guaranteeing social peace. Where sectoral characteristics generate such strong organized interest groups and where substantial rents from outside can alleviate the zero-sum bargaining that characterizes other developing countries, it is ultimately mutually beneficial
for these groups to establish routinized relations with each other and
with the state that encourage predictable rules of governance and predictable distributions of power and resources.

That such cooperation is based on widespread political rent-seeking
behavior is its Achilles' heel, as is manifested in the predictable roles,
habits, and behaviors of organized interests, firms, and individuals.
Their share of oil rents depends on chasing after state patronage, high
tariff barriers, cheap imports, profitable contracts, and subsidies. These
goals are powerful incentives for them to form tight links with politicians and bureaucrats in order to offer favors for benefits received. Such
rent seeking, of course, is a classic formula for corruption, which in itself
raises new demands. It is also the antithesis of the efficient market mechanisms and productive economic decision-making necessary to create a
self-sustaining productive base separate from petroleum. This unfortunate rent-seeking dynamic between private interests and the state is self-
perpetuating, at least as long as oil rents continue to flow. Just as petroleum establishes distorted, inequitable, and self-reinforcing patterns in
the economy, it also produces a similar "political vicious cycle" in the
state (Krueger 1974). The wealth of the national treasury fuels the perception on the part of organized interests that exercising influence is the
only way to receive pecuniary rewards, and it undermines any public-
sector efforts to extract resources from civil society.

Meanwhile, the skewed development produced by petroleum fosters
the belief of state managers that market mechanisms do not function in
a manner compatible with socially approved goals. This belief leads to
a sometimes unhappy but seemingly stable marriage between entrepreneurs attempting to link up with the state and public officials seeking
to intervene further in the market. It also contributes to a rentier psy-
chology, which disproportionately admires and rewards those who can
"milk the cow" without effort rather than those engaged in less remu-
nerative but more productive activities.

In sum, the exploitation of oil eventually can encourage a type of oil-
based social contract among organized interests, but it does so at high

cost. The advantage of this arrangement lies in the prolonged periods of regime stability that oil exploitation can foster, regardless of the type of regime in place. Because oil revenues can mitigate the extreme polarization found in situations of scarcity by removing the violent zero-sum conflicts that often characterize agrarian societies, oil can produce a stable form of politics that regularizes relations among competing interests and perpetuates regimes in power. But this regime stability is based on a predatory relationship with the state and the perpetuation of oil dependence, which pressures from civil society are unlikely to change as long as oil revenues are continuous and relatively incremental. Restructuring of the development model, if and when it occurs, must be linked to a disruption in those revenues or to some special capacity of the state.

ASSESSING THE CAPACITY OF THE PETRO-STATE: THE UNFORTUNATE GAP BETWEEN JURISDICTION AND AUTHORITY

Whether states have the capacity to alter their development trajectories in the face of linkage factors and the demands of civil society depends ultimately on their own institutional development. Even if market forces set up common policy dilemmas for government officials while private interests seek to influence them in ways that perpetuate petrolization, policymakers conceivably could have both the will and the ability to resist these pressures. Indeed, reform-mongers once confidently argued that states were capable of altering the privileges and incentives inherent in existing structural arrangements by changing their development trajectories (Chenery et al. 1974, Hirschman 1971). In Fagen's words (1978, 193), many experts once believed the state could "spearhead a movement . . . that runs against the basic logic of classes and markets."

Not the petro-state. That the petro-state depends on revenues generated by a depletable commodity, that this commodity produces extraordinary rents, and that these rents are funneled through weak institutions virtually ensure that the public sector will lack the authority and corporate cohesiveness necessary to exercise effective capacity. The petro-state's fiscal dependence on oil revenues exacerbates an unfortunate institutional reality present in most developing countries: the wide gap between the extensive jurisdictional role of states on the one hand and their weak mechanisms of authority on the other. This gap between jurisdiction and authority ultimately works to the detriment of any state's ability to flexibly adjust to changing conditions, but it is greatly exaggerated in petro-states.

In developing countries in general, the origin of this gap can be traced to conquest and late development. The unusually large role of the state vis-à-vis civil society often began with colonialism. Colonizers faced the task of building some type of political superstructure, even if local social forces were weak and dispersed. Although the degree of state building by colonizers varied greatly from country to country and was often quite weak itself, it generally proceeded at a faster pace than the organization of local interests or socioeconomic development, producing an "overdeveloped" state, one whose boundaries and tasks expanded early and with unusual rapidly (Saul 1979, Alavi 1972).

Late development exacerbated the tendency toward intervention (Gerschenkron 1962). Even where colonialism did not formally exist, the dominance of foreign powers left behind weak and dependent bourgeoisies who could not lead the development process. Thus the state continued to extend its jurisdiction, a process that was exacerbated in the postcolonial period by factors that contributed to state expansion everywhere—industrialization, nationalist and etatist ideologies (Frank 1979, Cameron 1978), economic crisis (Wright 1978), rising demands for public goods and services (Lipset 1960), and bureaucratic proliferation (Weber [1921] 1946).

In petro-states and other mineral producers, however, intervention had an important additional impetus. The massive capital and organizational requirements associated with exploiting petroleum had the dual effect of further weakening the domestic bourgeoisie while simultaneously thrusting the state even further onto center stage. Because oil revenues poured into the state and not into private enterprise, each new discovery of reserves or price increase enhanced the role of the public sector. This rapid expansion of jurisdiction was accompanied by the intensive centralization of resources in the executive branch, where decisions about petroleum were made. As long as oil revenues continued to enter the national treasury and no conscious effort was made to reverse the process, intervention, centralization, and the concentration of power were virtually automatic.

Unfortunately, political authority did not develop at the same pace. Mere size has not equaled strength in oil exporters. To the contrary, as the state expanded, its institutional evolution proceeded far more slowly and unevenly. Rather than develop the corporate cohesiveness, bureaucratic coherence, symbolic notions of "stateness," and managerial abilities that underlie the capacity to direct decision-making productively, petro-states became weak giants that could be rendered ineffective by hundreds of rent-seeking Lilliputians.

This claim can best be understood by briefly contrasting the evolution of most developing states to that of European states. In the European experience, state building, defined here as "an attempt to design a centralized administrative system in order to 'penetrate' society to effect policies" (Dyson 1980, 58), arose primarily from the long and violent definition of national borders. The development of the modern state paralleled the growth of permanent standing armies because any state that wished to survive had to increase its extractive capacity to pay for professional armed forces. In effect, war generated an increased need for revenues that could be met only through taxation. But taxation often provoked violent opposition, which in turn required an administrative and coercive apparatus (Finer 1975). As Tilly (1975, 40) observes, the key to the success of political units' becoming national states was "whether the managers of the political units undertook activities which were expensive in goods and manpower, and built an apparatus which effectively drew the necessary resources from the local population and checked the population's efforts to resist that extraction of resources."

Colonialism or conquest initially blocked this process of primitive power accumulation in most developing countries and led to permanent distortions in the institutional development of petro-states. Colonizers drew the boundaries of developing states, thus saving them the trouble of having to define their own territories. But, in doing so, they inadvertently robbed these countries of the ability to successfully penetrate their own domains. By disrupting the tight circle connecting state making, military institutions, and the extraction of scarce resources from a reluctant population, colonial rule or conquest facilitated the establishment of sovereignty and the spread of jurisdiction but at the expense of the institutionalization of authority and the differentiation of control.

In petro-states, this disruption in the cycle of state building was especially acute because of an essential difference in their patterns of taxation once they became exporters. Conquerors and later local rulers did not expend the same efforts at building states in mining countries as they did in agricultural exporters. Intent on extracting rents from highly localized mineral enclaves rather than from agricultural areas spread throughout the country, foreigners needed merely to control specific mining and export sites. They did not need to subdue and appropriate the labor of an entire population nor penetrate inaccessible rural zones in order to control indigenous peoples.

Nor were they forced to collect taxes beyond the export sector, which might have helped them to develop more extensive extractive capacities. Instead, their earnings depended on a combination of coercion of and negotiations with local elites in the capital city and later on the concessions or royalties they were able to win. In Anderson's (1986) continuum between (nonmineral) countries like Tunisia, in which the colonial state had a monopoly of force and could formulate policies, and those like (oil-producing) Libya, which never acquired a state bureaucracy that could transfer resources internally, petro-states fell in the Libyan, and more unfortunate, category.

This poor history of state building was perpetuated in the postcolonial period. Given their access to easy revenues from petroleum, few rulers sought to supplement state income through substantial increases in domestic taxation. Instead, they yielded to the permanent temptation of avoiding unpopular domestic decisions by taxing foreign oil companies. The types of local administrative outlets that in other less-developed countries assured revenue flows and provided state penetration into the national territory were neglected. They were never developed in the first place, or if they had existed, they subsequently withered. Rulers became adept at statecraft in a different arena, however, eventually demonstrating unusual skill in monitoring, regulating, and promoting the oil industry at both national and international levels. But high stateness in this arena occurred at the long-term expense of their capacity to build extensive, penetrating, and coherent bureaucracies that could successfully formulate and implement policies.

This special fiscal situation of oil exporters is graphically illustrated through figures on comparative taxation. Oil countries generally had levels of taxation similar to their neighbors, but because they could rely on petrodollars, they never sought to tax their populations to the same extent. Non-oil taxes in producer countries historically remained extremely low by international standards. As Table 3 shows, they were only half the level of those in countries at comparable stages of development. Thus, for example, non-oil tax revenues were 7.6 percent of non-oil GDP in Venezuela, while the total tax revenues of other countries at comparable levels of GNP per capita were 18.2 percent of GDP. The non-oil tax revenues were similarly low in Nigeria, Iran, and Indonesia.

With the vital link between domestic taxation and state building severed—not merely for short periods, which could have been an

TABLE 3

COMPARATIVE TAX RATES OF OIL

AND NON-OIL PRODUCERS

Oil Exporters	GNP per Capita (U.S. dollars)	Non-Oil Tax Revenue as a % of Non-Oil GDP, Average for 1971–73
Indonesia	131	8.7
Iran	803	9.9
Nigeria	1,183	8.1
Venezuela	1,448	7.6
Algeria[a]	570	22.3

Range of GNP per Capita (U.S. dollars)	Average GNP per Capita (U.S. dollars)	Approx. Total Tax Revenue as a % of GDP, 1980
0–349	241	12.9
350–849	548	12.5
850–1,699	1,195	18.2
>1,700	3,392	22.7
All countries	1,330	17.8

SOURCES: Ratios for oil exporters: Amuzegar (1986, Table 13).
Ratios by GNP per capita: Tanzi (1987, Table 8–3).
[a] Because much of the means of production in Algeria is socialized, the ratio is anomalously high.

advantage, but for the state's entire modern history—the state's command of the mobile resources within its subject population, its ability to free resources embedded in traditional networks of obligation, and its capacity to apply such resources on a national scale were compromised. As a result petro-states generally lack the ability to establish functionally distinct public institutions with some autonomy from civil society. Because they never had to establish taxes as regularly required, compulsory levies on private interests to be used for public purposes, they were never forced to create a clear separation between public and private in state income. Nor were they ever forced to develop strong mechanisms of fiscal accountability toward their citizens.

The peculiar fiscal structure of petro-states had other profound effects on state capacity and on the behavior of officials. First, it delayed the development of a modern consciousness of "the state" and contributed to the perpetuation of traditional concepts of authority as the personal patrimony of rulers. Because oil revenues were distributed by the state, the key decisions regarding allocation or what Usher (1981) calls "assignment," were made through political decisions on public spending. In advanced industrialized countries and in other less-developed nations where the public sector was relatively less significant, prior agreements among contending groups about allocation were primarily the result of markets or social and religious norms that assigned the major part of income or other advantages in interaction with the state. But in oil exporters this task was completely politicized because it necessarily became the *sole* province of the state (and sometimes of a single individual!).

Second, by blurring the strict formal separation between political authority and private economic activity that is so characteristic of most advanced industrialized states, fiscal dependence on petrodollars institutionalized a permanent tendency toward rent seeking by state officials. Just as private interests had strong incentives to influence public authorities, politicians and bureaucrats quickly realized that they could expand their own domains, their budgets, and sometimes their own pocketbooks by favoring one group over another. This favoritism undermined efficiency, responsibility, caution, and accountability, and it left the state especially open to a variety of contradictory and often self-serving pressures from society.

Thus petro-states are the epitome of what Chalmers (1977) has called the "politicized state." In Europe, where the tradition of state building was stronger, perpetual warfare eventually created the imperative to tax and, consequently, a logical system of efficient public institutions to extract resources and direct them. Administrative institutionalization and executive competence became the bases for efficacious government. Accompanying this process, to varying degrees in each case, was an emphasis on the importance of depoliticization "so that the effectiveness of government would not be undermined by an overloading produced by the combination of increased political demands with cross-pressures of group interests" (Dyson 1980, 258).

Precisely the opposite process occurred in petro-states. Administrative institutionalization fell far behind the expansion of jurisdiction and the workings of pure politics, so that at every crisis, and to some extent for every decision, state actors were required to define the way in which the system would operate (Chalmers 1977, 35). In effect, instead of the guidance and constraints imposed by routinization and a respected state tradition, powerful incentives favored reliance on spending over statecraft and the exercise of influence outside established rules and procedures.

This, then, was the type of state that faced managing the abrupt ratcheting of prices after 1973. Molded by petroleum, it was especially susceptible to cyclical price changes and skewed development, permeable to foreign and domestic pressures, vulnerable to the intermingling of markets and authority, more politicized and less institutionalized than most other developing states. Although it controlled part of the world's most important strategic resource, the resulting revenues were the source of its weak state capacity. Petrodollars hid this institutional weakness, creating the tendency to spend to sustain political order. But in the process the state's ability to penetrate society in order to change actors' behavior, to develop and implement comprehensive, autonomously determined policies, and to place issues of purpose above the tug and pull of political pressures was sacrificed.

FACTORING IN THE BOOM: WHY CRISIS LIES AHEAD

We now return to the central question of this book: what is the impact of oil booms on oil-exporting countries? Given that petro-states are skewed by petrolized economies, permeated by interests vested in maintaining an oil-based model of accumulation, and institutionally too weak to resist further petrolization, can a crisis of wealth somehow shake them out of their oil-dependent development path? Can the abnormal experience of a massive boom somehow provide the capabilities for flexible adjustment that appear to be lacking during normal times? Economic crises generally provoke basic struggles over the rules of the game in politics, produce new solutions to these issues, and thus can become a watershed in a state's institutional development (Skowronek 1982), but nothing guarantees that these self-transformations will enhance state capacity. Just as crisis can bring about new and more responsive institutions, it can as easily encourage a type of public stasis in the midst of dynamism, or even a process of state decay, which is the outcome in petro-states.

The immediate result of an oil boom is what Serafy (1980) and Lewis (1982) have called the "absorption" problem. As we saw in Chapter 2, petro-states find themselves incapable of absorbing their surplus, even if they quickly generate new public-sector projects. But, facing the impending threat of massive inflation, worried about depletability, accustomed to seeing the state as the leader in development, and eager to put their new wealth to immediate use, oil governments rely on their standard operating procedures: they reach for large-scale, capital-intensive, long-gestation projects, or if such projects are already underway, they increase their scale and accelerate their completion dates. These projects epitomize a resource-based industrialization strategy; they emphasize processing and refining, petrochemicals, and steel. Not surprisingly, in the face of a powerful push to absorb petrodollars rapidly and a general relaxation of fiscal discipline, they are often wasteful and poorly conceived.

The boom not only provokes a grander, oil-led economic model but also simultaneously generates new demands for resources from both the state and civil society. Policymakers, once torn between their twin preoccupations with diversification and equity, now think that they can do both. The military demands modernized weapons and improved living conditions; capitalists seek credits and subsidies; the middle class calls for increased social spending, labor for higher wages, and the unemployed for the creation of jobs. As demands rise, unwieldy and inefficient bureaucracies, suddenly thrust into new roles, find themselves incapable of scaling down expansionist public-sector programs or warding off private-sector requests. Thus they ultimately contribute to growing budget and trade deficits and foreign debt. The boom effect is instantly at work.

At the same time, the influx of petrodollars hinders the search for independence from petroleum and for equity. Although seeming finally to provide funds for diversification, the monetary and resource movements provoked by a boom make sowing the petroleum more difficult. They create new obstacles to investment in agriculture and industry, encourage highly inefficient import-substituting industrialization, discourage the development of nontraditional exports, and promote a bloated service sector. And although improvements in income and employment generation become relatively easy in the short run, the boom exacerbates already great inequities. The powerful and wealthy benefit disproportionately from windfalls, and wage followership from the export sector helps to fortify an entrenched high-wage labor aristocracy as well as growing unemployment among those not able to find jobs in the modern sector (Lewis 1982).

Meanwhile, the problems of state capacity grow increasingly acute. The boom abruptly and automatically expands the jurisdiction of the state and concentrates power in the executive, while simultaneously encouraging the proliferation of new bureaucracies, the disorganization of old ones, and the general disarticulation of the administrative apparatus. Competing interests manipulate their access to the state to further their own goals, and they insist that the state respond first and foremost to their own concerns. As capacity diminishes and demands rise, the classic formula for a "demand gap" (Eisenstadt 1964) or "demand overload" (Crozier, Huntington, and Watanuki 1975) is set in place. Fearing instability, governments spend even more and become more dependent on revenues from petroleum to sustain themselves in power.

There are solutions for altering these unfortunate economic and political dynamics. Domestically, in order to control demand, exporters must "sterilize" their rapidly growing petroleum revenues by holding them outside the domestic economy. In other words, governments need to accumulate foreign reserves, match these with additional savings, and prevent petrodollars from becoming monetized inside their economies. This course of action would protect agriculture and industry from being disadvantaged by an appreciated exchange rate, reduce the problems of absorptive capacity, and mitigate against petrolization. Internationally, they must expand production to drop prices in order to fend off new entrants to the market, conservation efforts, or investments in alternative sources of energy. If they do not do so, prices will eventually collapse. Although other remedies might also help, only the combined strategy of withholding of petrodollars from the domestic environment—and introducing them later at a gradual pace—and protecting prices internationally can provide insulation from the outcomes described in Chapter 2.

But the prospects for following this strategy are dismal indeed. Booms not only exacerbate existing rent-seeking behavior but create such behavior where it did not already exist. Overnight, an oil boom relieves the "constant pie" orientation of governments accustomed to a stable, oil-based social contract. Distribution is not viewed as a zero-sum game involving winners and losers. The restraint inherent in more limited revenues, which gives governments a legitimate reason to resist the demands of a variety of constituencies or state agencies, is abruptly removed, both psychologically and in reality. Whatever the reasons proffered—diversification, employment creation, or the buying off of either opponents or supporters through some form of state largess—policymakers find it extremely difficult to resist demands, and they generate more themselves.

Their short time horizon exacerbates this tendency. Whether the state is democratic or authoritarian, the concern about political performance is universal and is measured in periods of months or, at most, several years. When combined with the virtual explosion of demands, the desire to spend quickly in order to purchase loyalty eventually endangers the prospects for international cooperation, as growing conflicts among exporting states over pricing policies and production quotas reflect their spiraling domestic political and economic needs. In the end, rational oligopoly and sterilization rapidly lose out to "petromania."

In sum, oil booms add another layer of overdetermination to the fate of petro-states. A boom increases demands for diversification and equity at the very moment that these goals become most difficult to achieve. It once again raises the assignment question, thereby further politicizing all decision-making just when planning, efficiency, and authoritative allocation are most necessary. It distorts and disorganizes the public sector by expanding jurisdiction and undermining authority precisely when the challenges facing the state require it to be the most cohesive. It creates the illusion that oil exporters have gained new autonomy, while actually making them more dependent on petrodollars. And, in the greatest of ironies, a boom lays the basis for a future bust. This is the petro-state's special dilemma.

Like Spain in the sixteenth century, petro-states find themselves locked into a particular development trajectory. To understand how and why this lock-in occurs, it is important to take a close look at one case. Thus we turn our attention to the first and oldest exporter among the OPEC countries, Venezuela. The choice of the country that Columbus called "little Venice" is not without historical irony. It is a curious paradox of our story that the borrowing of the Spanish Habsburgs, backed by gold and silver, financed the discovery and colonization of Venezuela. Obsessed with their search for the mythical town of El Dorado, Spanish conquistadors combed its jungles, mountains, and coasts, but to no avail. They could never find the city whose walls were said to be made of gold and whose streets were cobbled in silver brick.

But El Dorado did exist. In an unknowing presentiment of the future, the Spanish pinpointed the town's exact location in the province of Guayana, an area that subsequently yielded enormous deposits of petroleum as well as gold, diamonds, iron ore, and bauxite. Not far away, in water now filled with derricks instead of the Indian huts on stilts that so reminded Columbus of Venice, lay Lake Maracaibo, the source of some of Venezuela's richest oil deposits in the 1973 boom.

PART TWO

Democracy over a Barrel in Venezuela

You are actors in the great national transformation that is going to make Venezuela one of the great countries of the world. . . . A Great Venezuela because all Venezuelans can have work. A Great Venezuela because the future and the welfare of every member of our national society [are] being created. A Great Venezuela because we know how to utilize the instruments . . . of science and technology to transform our natural resources so that we may be incorporated—with our own personality and our own voice—into the concert of the great nations of the world.

President Carlos Andrés Pérez
September 11, 1974

And the sign on his cage said: "Beware, he is dreaming."

Nicolás Guillén, Guitarra

FOUR

The Making
of a Petro-State

For Venezuela, the oil boom year of 1973–1974 was the modern equivalent of the dream of El Dorado. Suddenly and unexpectedly, $10 billion flowed into the national treasury. Coinciding with this windfall was the landslide election of Acción Democrática's presidential candidate, Carlos Andrés Pérez. The oil boom provided financial resources of a magnitude never before seen in this small country of twelve million people, while the electoral sweep gave the new president the greatest popular mandate in the young democracy's history. His power apparently limitless, Pérez immediately embarked on the boldest and most ambitious development blueprint Latin America had ever seen. It seemed that nothing could stand in his way. "We are going to change the world!" he was said to frequently exclaim to his closest associates (interview, cabinet minister, February 1978).

Like those who sought El Dorado before him, Pérez based his plans on images of a possible future rather than on full comprehension of difficulties in the present. "I had a vision of *La Gran Venezuela*," he reminisced, "one that would be different from our country in the past. . . . It would be modern, industrial" (interview, March 1979). The first president since Rómulo Betancourt to have a *proyecto*—a grand overview of the political and economic changes necessary to accomplish the accelerated modernization of an oil-based country—he rapidly sought to utilize the revenues from petroleum to translate this vision into government policy. Everything seemed possible, nothing too difficult.

Yet Pérez immediately encountered obstacles that neither Venezuela's astounding new oil money nor his own popularity could overcome. His administration's decisions, the behavior of the citizens he governed, and even the vision he put forward would be shaped by past patterns of petrolization, skewed state formation, and uncertain regime consolidation—factors that proved to be too deeply rooted for even the most popular of presidents to overcome. This structuration of choice was generally not of his making; it was the product of hundreds of past decisions by his predecessors. But it was powerful enough to mold his own preferences, decision-making process, and policies.

Not surprisingly, when mulling over his record at the end of his first administration, the man who presided over his country's greatest oil boom and set the parameters of development for decades to come revealed his awareness of these limits: "I raised the hopes of our people and built confidence in our country, but there was too much that I could not do, that I, with all the oil money, could not change" (interview, Caracas, March 1979). Years later, not long before being forced from power during his second term, he was even more chastised. "A price spike is bad for everyone but worst for developing countries that have oil. It is a trap" (interview, Stanford University, 1991).

Not that the president lacked early warnings about the dangers of petro-development. Juan Pablo Pérez Alfonzo, the outspoken oil czar who became an early critic of the new administration, remembered, "He acted as if we had no cages, as if we could shed our poor history, as if we were somehow different from the rest of Latin America. Of course we *are* different. We look more like Saudi Arabia than Brazil. We are *Venezuela Saudita*" (interview, Caracas, November 1978). Such warnings had little impact at a time when Venezuela was literally drowning in money. But even presidents blessed by wealth, Pérez discovered, form their preferences and make their decisions within the framework of a state that encourages some options over others, awards some choices more than others, and blocks some actions temporarily or permanently.

This chapter examines the making of a petro-state in Venezuela. It is intended to lend historical specificity to the theoretical discussion just concluded by examining the process of state formation before the entry of the oil companies, the impact of the establishment of the oil enclave, and the transformation of the state between 1920 and World War II. In depicting Venezuela's uneven state capacity, it emphasizes, first, the absence of distinctive state interests or even of any centralized or impersonal apparatus of domination remotely resembling a modern state until very late; second, the manner in which the exploitation of petroleum expanded the state's jurisdiction, concentrated power in the executive, and undermined bureaucratic authority; and, third, the eventual emergence of a consensus for intervention based on the distribution of oil rents to subsidize non-oil activities.

However, a petro-state cannot be said to exist for these reasons alone. To the contrary, the consolidation of this state form is marked by a definitive shift in its institutional arrangements such that the selective mechanisms and overall incentives for policy become defined predominantly by petroleum, while state interests become separate from and sometimes even adversarial to foreign oil interests. The important markers of this process, as we shall see, are shifts in property rights and the structure of taxation.

The coincidence in timing of modern state formation and oil dependence is a critical historical fact in the Venezuelan case. No other event approaches in significance this historical sequence. From the moment the petroleum industry reached Venezuela, the demands of the production of oil for export shaped the institutions of the state, the evolution of the economy, the emergence of social classes, and the timing and direction of regime change. Indeed, every major development in the country after the introduction of the oil industry was conditioned by the meshing of a weak domestic political economy with the most powerful forces of the international economy.

Other, non-oil forces affecting state building throughout Latin America were not absent in Venezuela. But they were easily overwhelmed by petroleum, and the route through which the petro-state became centralized and interventionist is unique. Arturo Uslar Pietri, one of his country's foremost intellectuals, may sound like an economic determinist, but he scarcely overstated his case when he wrote (1972, 18, cited in Ewell 1984, 61):

> Petroleum is the fundamental and basic fact of the Venezuelan destiny. It presents to Venezuela today the most serious national problems that the nation has known in its history. It is like a minotaur of ancient myths, in the depths of his labyrinth, ravenous and threatening.
>
> The vital historical theme for today's Venezuela can be no other than the productive combat with the minotaur of petroleum.
>
> Everything else loses significance. Whether the Republic is centralist or federalist. Whether voters vote white or any other color. Whether they build aqueducts or not. . . Whether the workers earn five bolívares or fifteen bolívares. . . . All these issues lack meaning. . . .
>
> [Everything is] conditioned, determined, created by petroleum.

THE POOR LEGACY OF STATE BUILDING
FROM COLONIALISM TO *CAUDILLISMO*

Petro-states are built on what already exists. Had the oil companies encountered a developed state administration on their arrival, they would have met some form of bureaucratic resistance to the influence they wielded. But Venezuela, like many of its OPEC partners, could boast of no civil service, no independent central bank, and no impartial judiciary. Instead it suffered from a legacy of extreme administrative weakness that is remarkable even in the context of Latin America. Its history until World War I was replete with cycles of attempted centralization and breakdown; the resulting destruction and turmoil prevented the emergence of any structure resembling a modern state.

The weak legacy of state building predated the exploitation of petroleum. Indeed, when the oil companies descended on Lake Maracaibo in the early 1900s to exploit its vast petroleum deposits, the state had barely been formed. Scarcely populated and seemingly without resources, Venezuela had been marginal to the Spanish empire because it had little to offer the growing markets of Europe. Although the search for the mythical golden town of El Dorado generated an initial flurry of activity and helped to settle the western part of the country, the failure to discover quick and easy riches turned Spain's attention elsewhere. Nor were there many Indians to exploit for labor, although slave raids did occur from time to time. Geography, sea routes, and accidents of the location of early settlements exacerbated Venezuela's isolation. After the conquest of Mexico in 1521 and the discovery and conquest of Peru in the 1530s, Venezuela was virtually abandoned, attracting little attention from the Crown or from the royal court at Santo Domingo (Brito Figueroa 1966, Lombardi 1977).

Any state building that did occur ended with the Independence Wars against Spain and the decades of disorder that followed. The country that had stood on the sidelines during the heyday of the empire became the center of a continental civil war as Simón Bolívar's armies thrust Venezuela into the world spotlight—albeit at a considerable price. For over eleven years, this country bore the brunt of Latin America's struggle for independence. It lost close to 40 percent of its population, suffered enormous property damage, and saw almost all vestiges of its previous bureaucratic system destroyed (Lombardi 1966, 153–168). The duration of violence even after independence led to the dual disintegration of weak state institutions and traditional elites, which paved the way for still more decades of disorder.

Caudillismo, a set of political rules based entirely on force, was the expression of the fragility of the governing apparatus, and it left an enduring mark on state formation (Gilmore 1964). Because political, social, and administrative institutions were virtually nonexistent, self-organized militias and their leaders were the only possible bases of authority. They became the foundation of local and regional governments, with the strongest militia generally marching to Caracas to take control, at least momentarily, not so much of the central regime as of the central customs house, which represented the most important source of wealth in the country.

Characterized by the rule of a single strongman, *caudillismo* created a heritage of personalism and presidentialism that could never be totally eradicated. This ultrapresidentialism, which can be understood not merely as the result of attempts to strengthen the power of a particular individual but also as a response to the persistent need for a strong central authority, permanently stamped the country's political culture. Indeed, the networks formed by the president, the regional party bosses, and the professional army in Venezuela's democracy would bear a striking resemblance to the patterns established among presidents, regional chieftains, and local soldiers under *caudillo* rule.

Venezuela continued to fall behind most of the continent in state building as it entered the modern era. From the end of the Independence Wars until the installation of a military regime at the turn of the century, its history was dominated by struggles over centralism versus federalism and by fighting among *caudillos.* At the same time that the first oil drill was sunk in Titus, Pennsylvania, beginning the world's most powerful industry, the minimal state apparatus of Latin America's most important future oil producer unraveled once again in the Federal Wars (1858–1869). In this social revolution, more anarchic than the independence period, the white and privileged classes virtually disappeared, even though the latifundio structure of coffee production itself remained intact. Despite some steps toward establishing central authority over regional communities during the rule of Antonio Guzmán Blanco, war remained the central selective mechanism for access to office.[1] In all of Latin America, only Mexico experienced a similar degree of violence.

Weak social forces compounded this poor state legacy. A modern capitalist country did not exist at the turn of the century. In 1900, there were barely any urban social classes. Only six cities had a population of over twenty thousand people. The population of 2.4 million was over 85 percent rural, with over 2 million landless peasants working in latifundios (Fuenmayor 1975, 33). In a country divided between power-less landowners and a war-weary peasantry, and characterized by an extremely small internal market, almost no organized interests existed that could make demands on the state or contend with the oil compa-nies. The major export-import merchants, largely foreign, wielded the only significant power; they functioned as the nation's central bank, developed some infrastructure, and provided public credit.

The struggle for the centralization of state authority was finally won when a regional group, rather than a national dominant class, put an end to the deterioration of the public domain. The Grupo Táchira, composed of autocrats from the coffee-producing Andean region, began a full half century of political domination in 1899, when General Cipriano Castro seized Caracas, accompanied by a small band of sixty men, two of whom became the presidents who ruled Venezuela from 1908 to 1941. Castro's announcement of a government was greeted by renewed armed conflicts, the most extensive since the Independence Wars. These battles destroyed the prospect of building a viable administrative structure, but they suc-ceeded in centralizing power in Caracas once and for all—at the cost of economic disaster, political crisis, and loss of national sovereignty. Be-cause Castro was unable to pay back the foreign debts he had incurred, foreign powers blockaded Venezuela in December 1902 to force it to re-imburse its creditors. This historic blockade—which is best known inter-nationally for spawning the Roosevelt Corollary to the Monroe Doc-trine—led to Castro's overthrow by his own lieutenant, Juan Vicente Gómez, with the indispensable aid of the United States.[2]

The military ruler who would negotiate the terms of the oil industry's entry into Venezuela inherited a simple and underdeveloped administra-tive apparatus that relied on personal authority, capricious and infor-mal justice, and clientelistic forms of recruitment. The state's jurisdic-tion was extremely limited; it had virtually no capacity to extract, transfer, or distribute resources internally, and there were few demands on it to do so. A farmer who had never seen Caracas until he was forty-two, Gómez spent the next twenty-seven years bargaining with the world's most powerful capitalist enterprises and constructing the out-lines of a modern state. By his death in 1935, he had presided over the creation of structures that guaranteed the permanent consolidation of power in the central government and, most especially, in the presidency.

More than anything else, the need to secure the central government's victory over regional *caudillos* motivated Gómez's institutional innovations. Evidence for this motive can be found, first, in the creation of a professionalized national army and, second, in the consolidation of the control and accounting of all public revenues in the Ministry of Finance (Sullivan 1976).

Control over the military and the public treasury gave Gómez absolute power but little incentive to expand the jurisdiction of the state. Despite his strong support for financial reforms that granted the executive branch direct control over its revenues for the first time, Gómez was a strong proponent of maintaining a low profile of state activity. Running the country as if it were one of his farms, he jailed any opponents of his policies and instructed his finance minister to pay the interest on the foreign debt while balancing the budget by drastically cutting wages and public works. By the time revenues from the sale of petroleum began to enter state coffers, Venezuela's weak state had only the most essential administrative expenditures.

INTERNATIONAL OIL
AND THE SHAPING OF THE STATE

The coming of the international oil companies profoundly transformed the state's minimalist direction. For the oil companies, entering Venezuela was part of a global strategy to control and market petroleum and to punish hostile, revolutionary governments in Russia and Mexico by shifting production elsewhere.[3] But, for Gómez, oil was a means for consolidating power in the presidency, maintaining his own rule, and enriching himself and his friends. This mix of personal and regime concerns should not be confused with an autonomous bureaucratic logic or *raison d'état*. Gómez's state—characterized by the concentration of power in the hands of a corrupt president and the absence of the bureaucratic restraints that can arise from a developed administrative apparatus, an independent judiciary, or organized interests—never sought to be a match for the major oil companies. At the height of their global power and strong enough to punish governments that opposed them, the companies would have proved to be formidable opponents had Gómez chosen to challenge them. But, quickly seeing the advantages of forming links with foreign capital, he did not.

In place of the expression of autonomous state interests, foreign and domestic private interests meshed under the rubric of public authority.

McBeth's (1983) notion that this consolidation was accompanied by evidence of "statelike" behavior, such as efforts to extract the best possible returns or to supervise the industry, does not adequately take into account the degree of private influence over the public realm or the plunder involved.[4] The partnership between the oil companies and Gómez left little for the construction of an impersonal state bureaucracy or the development of the country, but it worked to the benefit of both parties: the companies achieved their central goal of capturing crude oil supplies; Gómez remained in power and managed to add to his considerable wealth.[5]

But if it was still premature to speak of autonomous state interests, Venezuela's new status as an oil exporter did bring important legal and administrative changes in the state. Realizing that competition among the companies for his favors increased his personal power and wealth, Gómez took advantage of the scramble for petroleum to augment the power of the executive. He established his authority to negotiate concessions with the companies without the intervention of Congress, and he created an Office of Mines in the Ministry of Development in 1909 to carry out his desires. Staffed by friends, relatives, and political cronies, the terms it put forward were the most attractive in the Americas.

From a long-range view, Gómez's petroleum laws, culminating in the Petroleum Law of 1922, were especially critical to reshaping the minimalist state. First, as Hausmann (1981) points out, they represented a fundamental shift of power from private property to the state and a qualitatively new definition of the state's jurisdiction. In the past, although Venezuela's many constitutions granted subsoil rights to the nation, in an extension of Spanish colonial law, in practice private landowners had possessed the right to obtain concessions on their holdings since 1885. If they wanted to sublet their land, they could charge royalties equal to up to one-third of the physical output of the concessions. Under this arrangement, landowners could develop a private relationship with oil companies, enter into contracts or symbiotic relationships of other sorts with them, and thereby become an alternative center of power.

It is one of the great ironies of history that foreign oil companies, the epitome of private enterprise, are largely responsible for the etatism characterizing Venezuelan development. The foreign companies fought against the existing system of private property rights because they believed it would reproduce some of the constraints on their activities already in evidence in the United States. Preferring to deal with one (weak) central authority, they engaged in a struggle, both legal and otherwise, to limit the authority of private landowners. Not surprisingly, Gómez sided with them.[6] In 1912, the attorney general and the Supreme Court ruled that any rights granted to private landowners by a previous code of mines were unconstitutional. From this moment on, only the state had the authority to deal directly with foreign companies, and the private sector was permanently relegated to a secondary role (Hausmann 1981, 98ff).

Second, the new laws reinforced the concentration of power in the executive, although with the loss of considerable sovereignty. Gómez's oligarchic alliance with foreign capital permitted him to reorganize existing administrative practices to achieve an unprecedented degree of presidentialism.[7] Gómez personally selected the governors of each state as well as legislators, the civil chiefs of districts, judges, and municipal councilmen. He also created a bureaucracy loyal to him by extending the clientelistic links of *caudillismo* throughout the public sector. In exchange for petrodollars to award his cronies, the majors virtually wrote their own ticket. Indeed, three U.S. oil companies and their lawyers drew up the final 1922 law (which they subsequently praised as the best law in Latin America!), awarding themselves low taxes and royalties, exemptions from import duties, less pressure to exploit their holdings rapidly, freedom from interference from the Congress, and a release from restrictions on the amount of land one company could hold.[8] From this point on, the companies dealt only with the executive branch, and ultrapresidentialism would persistently and damagingly endure.

Third, the new laws manifested a decisive shift in the origins of state monies and, consequently, in the importance of fiscal links as well as the definition of "stateness." This shift can be traced through changes in the tax structure. Traditionally customs revenues had dominated state finances, but by the fiscal year 1929–1930 internal revenues derived from oil activities finally surpassed customs revenues. In the fiscal year 1934–1935, these internal revenues rose to a high of 59.8 percent of total revenues, while customs dropped to 40.2 percent. As Kornblith and Quintana (1981, 147) note, this change captures the transformation of Venezuela from an agricultural exporter to a petroleum exporter. But it also marks a shift in the notion of the state to one that had the right and duty to capture rents from the national patrimony and utilize them as rulers saw fit.

Thus, from the beginning, the entry of the oil companies was associated with a pattern of state expansion and concentration of power that was qualitatively different from the minimalism and decentralization of the past. But increased jurisdiction was not accompanied by the creation of mechanisms to enhance state authority. On the contrary, these shifts encouraged predation, patronage, and the beginning of a consciousness on the part of rulers that petrodollars could be an instrument for maintaining regime stability. Indeed, petrodollars helped to shield Gómez from the types of strains that led to the downfall of authoritarian rulers elsewhere. The benefits from the petroleum law of 1922 permitted him to survive a major agricultural crisis and, soon after, lift the extraordinary war tax and other customs duties that had figured prominently in Castro's downfall. Thanks to petroleum, government revenues increased at an annual rate of 14.9 percent during the 1920–1929 period, almost tripling, and government expenditures also increased more than two and a half times, thus providing a welcome prop for dictatorial rule.[9]

"PETROLIZED" INTERESTS
AND THE CONSENSUS FOR STATE INTERVENTION

The exploitation of petroleum also built a strong and enduring political and social consensus for state intervention. By setting into motion the long-term structural transformation of the economy and society that I have called "petrolization," oil weakened non-oil interests and fostered the emergence of new social classes and groups whose fortunes were linked to the distribution of oil rents through state spending. Consequently, even former opponents of intervention became active proponents of an expansion of the state's jurisdiction. As they grew in force and their belief systems were fortified by statist ideologies from abroad, these vested interests eventually laid to rest all past notions of a minimalist or liberal state.

The transformation of older social forces and the creation of new oil-based interests began with the rapid, growing dependence on petroleum. In less than a decade, oil became the central pivot of the economy; between 1920 and 1925, oil's share of total exports leapt from 1.9 percent to 41.6 percent, and by 1935 it had reached 91.2 percent (Tugwell 1975, 182). By 1926, the value of oil exports and their derivatives had surpassed that of coffee and other agricultural commodities, and oil had become the country's most important export. By 1928, Venezuela was the largest exporter of oil in the world and the second largest producer following the United States (Vallenilla 1975, Tugwell 1975).

This shift to an oil economy had predictable Dutch Disease effects, delaying industrialization and exacerbating the decline of agriculture. Because an oil-mediated integration into the world market provided sufficient revenues for a continuous expansion of the country's low import capacity, incentives for other productive activities barely developed. The bias against productive links was further exacerbated by exchange-rate movements related to petroleum. Because oil caused the appreciation of the bolívar in relation to the dollar, it further encouraged imports and discouraged domestic activities. This delay was especially apparent during the Great Depression. While every other Latin American country faced large devaluations throughout the 1930s, the rapid recovery of the petroleum industry after 1932 meant that the bolívar appreciated 70 percent in that period.

The net effect was to shift production away from traditional activities and toward the development of an import and service sector, with fatal consequences for the country's weak agrarian elites and the maintenance of alternative sources of power. The already stagnant coffee industry declined dramatically, while the high import capacity for foodstuffs hurt the domestic market for other agricultural products. This development had an immediate impact on the structure of choice. Gómez's decision not to devalue the bolívar in 1934 following U.S. currency changes was logical because "his" state would lose precious revenues from the domestic bolívar payments of the oil companies; these revenues promised to be greater than those that could be gained from the reactivation of traditional exports (Baptista and Mommer 1987, 9–13). But the decision proved catastrophic for agrarian interests. Agricultural exports dropped in value from 129.7 million bolívares in 1928 to 43.3 million bolívares in 1944 (Aranda 1977, 109). Gómez's subsequent attempt to funnel petrodollars through the Banco Agrícola y Pecuario to support agriculture simply converted a formerly independent engine of economic development into an oil-subsidized activity and removed the landlord class's opportunity to be an autonomous political force. With the complete collapse of coffee and cacao exports during the Depression, Venezuelan agriculture and the prospects for non-oil elite interests died together: the sector's share of GDP sank from one-third in the mid-1920s to less than one-tenth by 1950, the smallest contribution in all of Latin America (Karlsson 1975, 24).

The decline of agriculture and the delay in industrialization, while destroying weak but traditional elites, also created a new dominant class with strong vested interests in the fate of the oil sector. As the attractiveness of rural investment declined, landowners sold their property to the oil companies in the "dance of the concessions," converting themselves into a rentier, commercial, and financial urban bourgeoisie dependent on petrodollars. This dependence took several forms. For those in the commerce or service sectors, the state's income from oil set in motion the demand for the types of activities they could deliver. Moreover, because the companies determined the value of petroleum exports, they controlled the amount of imports that could be bought from the foreign exchange realized through oil. As oil production grew, so did imports, which doubled in the short period between 1920 and 1929. For those involved in some form of production, their profits were predicated on either an exogenously determined internal demand or sufficient petrodollars to obtain inputs from the world economy.

Not surprisingly, contradictions and disagreements often arose among these domestic interests, especially with regard to exchange rates, tariff policies, and state intervention.[10] But where divisions of this sort became primary in other countries of Latin America, especially Argentina, in Venezuela they were overridden by the spread effects of oil rents. By the outbreak of World War II, commerce had become the principal non-oil activity of the country; the new, dominant commercial class also presided over a small manufacturing sector and internal market.[11]

The impact of agriculture's demise and of delayed industrialization was extensive at the mass level as well: the most important social phenomenon between 1920 and 1935 was the emergence of urban middle and (to a lesser extent) working classes who were vested both in the performance of the oil sector and in a potentially adversarial relationship with it. Faced with a loss of employment in their villages, rural laborers headed toward the lucrative jobs in the oil fields or employment in an urban public-works program (Donnelly 1975, 65–73). With the stagnation of agriculture and the pull of petroleum forcing peasants off the land, Venezuela experienced the fastest rate of urbanization in Latin America.[12] Petroleum workers became the first modern proletariat, but their potential militancy was always tempered by their small numbers (fewer than twenty-six thousand) (Petras 1978, 101). This was not the case with the middle classes, which experienced a rise in both propertied and salaried groups of artisans and white-collar workers in the private sector and in the state bureaucracy whose positions were financed by the circulation of petrodollars (Donnelly 1975, 61). The oil economy fostered an inverted pyramid of social classes, so different from the situation in most of Latin America: the generation and rapid circulation of petrodollars, the result of rent rather than real productive activities, meant that a largely nonproductive urban middle class preceded and outnumbered a slowly growing working class.

The aspirations of these urban *capas medias* dominated the political arena and became the source of the most significant demands for an interventionist and activist state. Gómez managed to contain these forces through a combination of state spending and coercion and cooptation; but his death from natural causes in 1935 unleashed an immediate outburst of long-suppressed demands aimed primarily at gaining additional benefits from the international oil companies. Dissatisfaction was expressed in a national petroleum workers' strike and in the formation of two nationalist political parties, the Partido Comunista and the Partido Democrática, the forerunner of Acción Democrática. In response, the country's first labor law was passed; petroleum workers were granted an eight-hour day; the right to strike was recognized; and equality of pay between nationals and foreigners was decreed (Godio 1980, Tennassee 1979).

These political stirrings, while unable to weather a new round of repression, marked a different consciousness about the purposes of the state. For the first time, it was seen to have a productive and social character that was in sharp contrast to the weak apparatus desired by the foreign companies and their domestic allies; it existed not merely to regulate social intercourse but also to correct the deficiencies of development through an equitable distribution of oil rents. This notion was codified in the new 1936 Constitution, which stated that the task of the state was "to promote production and establish the conditions of work . . . , keeping in view the social protection of the worker and the economic interests of the country" (Article 32).

Widespread consensus for a new jurisdictional role for the state, however, resulted only from the economic crisis provoked by World War II. Although the middle and working classes already looked with favor on increasing the state's production and distribution functions, the dominant commercial and financial class had stubbornly sustained its ideological predilection for a liberal state until domestic crisis convinced it otherwise. The temporary decrease in oil production, the decline of other exports, and the wartime disruption of markets in the developed countries—combined with growing middle-class demands for expenditures on health, education, and welfare —starkly revealed the dangers of relying exclusively on petroleum. As treasury reserves dwindled, the government accounts of E. López Contreras (1935–1941) and his appointed successor, I. Medina Angarita (1941–1945), showed deficits reaching as high as thirty-nine million bolívares between 1936 and 1942 (Salazar-Carrillo, 1976, 44; Aranda 1977, 118). These deficits translated into deep recession, shortages of goods, additional hardships for the population, rampant public dissatisfaction, and the threat of political instability.

This fiscal crisis produced a fundamental change in the ideology of the emergent commercial bourgeoisie and in prevailing notions of stateness. Prompted by the writings of Arturo Uslar Pietri, an influential intellectual, and of General Medina's Minister of Development, a young entrepreneur named Eugenio Mendoza,[13] conservative trade and financial figures began to turn away from their past liberal visions and publicly to support planning, protection, technification of the bureaucracy, new services such as social security, and an industrialization effort based on the country's abundant natural resources. "State intervention is necessary to guarantee Venezuela minimal economic normalcy," Uslar Pietri argued (1948, 189). Only the state could channel petrodollars to the private sector and provide the protection that would ultimately create an alternative productive economic base. Using words that would later become the slogan for democracy, he called for state subsidies to local manufacturing to "sow the petroleum" (quoted in Maza Zavala 1977, 515).

The notion of the minimalist state was buried once and for all at an important private-sector conference in 1944, the year of the founding of the umbrella business association Fedecámaras. Uslar Pietri argued that an interventionist state was the only real alternative for the future if Venezuela wanted to avoid depression, civil war, and socialism. Indirectly criticizing the importers and their oil-company allies, who opposed industrialization, he called for high tariffs to promote industry and legislation to protect the labor force. The country's leading bankers finally broke with the position of the major oil companies, who favored free trade and who well understood that state intervention was likely to be aimed at them in the future. Faced with the prospect of popular unrest, they had little choice. As González Gorrondona, one of their spokesman, remarked, "If the state abandons economic activity to the free play of private interests, as the liberals argue, this will lead to a systematic repetition of economic cycles, wars, and all types of other disturbances that bring anguish into our social life" (*La libertad económica y la intervención del estado* 1945, 109). In contrast, a new role for the state in productive life seemed a small price to pay.

Thus by World War II a strong consensus existed for an increase in the jurisdiction of the state. The prior absence of such demands—a situation necessarily imposed by the scarcity of state resources as well as by the lack of class formation—had been rendered obsolete by new state wealth and the appearance of modern social forces that clamored for transfers of oil money in their direction. But, despite the consensus that the state's primary role should be the extraction, administration, and distribution of oil rents, there were no concomitant demands to enhance its authoritative mechanisms, especially its ability to seek alternative revenue sources from its own population. Nor was there any attempt to pose and debate the criteria for transferring public resources into private property. Finally, there was absolute silence on the question of how using oil subsidies to encourage productivity in other areas could eventually lead to self-sustaining development. Venezuela was one step closer to a petro-state.

THE CONSOLIDATION OF THE PETRO-STATE

The Hydrocarbons Act of 1943—perhaps the most important piece of legislation in the history of Venezuela—ushered in the final stages in the consolidation of the petro-state. The expression of new demands for change in civil society, an emergent new capacity for innovative regulatory action in the public sector, and the development of state interests distinctive from those of the foreign companies that had so completely dominated Venezuela up to this point, the Hydrocarbons Act marked the second basic shift in the origin of state monies. Having already moved from dependence on revenues from agriculture to those from mining during Gómez's rule, the state now changed from taxes on customs and concessions to taxes based on income from mining. This shift institutionalized fiscal linkages as the dominant economic factor and had profound consequences for the manner in which state interests would be defined and pursued in the future.

The roots of the new income tax lay in the growing jurisdictional role and increasing complexity of the state, which in turn were a response to increased social mobilization. Both López Contreras and Medina Angarita extended the public sector into new social and productive activities, and they made some attempt to separate institutions from individuals in the process. As the tasks of the state became more complex, so did its own structure and its needs for revenues. The administrative apparatus of the central government was extended, and a number of new financial reforms, such as the creation of the Central Bank in 1939, were instituted (Kornblith and Maingon 1985, 36). The para-state (or what is known in Venezuela as the decentralized administration) was also developed. Following the example of Gómez, who had created the first decentralized state entities as a response to social conflict, both López Contreras and Medina Angarita created state enterprises and autonomous agencies from the confiscation of Gómez's property after his death. Although state enterprises remained subordinate to the central government, they grew more quickly, and the precedent of establishing state enterprises in response to rising demands was followed by nearly every subsequent administration (Bigler 1980).

The perpetual search for new revenues to fund these new state agencies led to the 1943 Hydrocarbons Act. Once again budget deficits were the immediate catalysts for government action, and the same fiscal crisis that had altered belief systems about the role of the state promoted institutional innovation. Even though state revenues from the sale of concessions and certain other taxes remained steady or even increased, total state revenues began to show a disturbing downward trend in 1940, just when demands increased. (See Table 4.) Because it was eco-

TABLE 4

ORDINARY FISCAL REVENUES, FISCAL YEARS 1929–1930
TO 1944–1945 (MILLIONS OF BOLIVARES)

	Customs Taxes	Other Taxes	Income Taxes	Total
1929–30	131.4	8.0	115.3	254.7
1930–31	94.8	5.4	105.0	205.2
1931–32	77.3	3.7	104.2	185.2
1932–33	67.0	3.2	101.7	171.9
1933–34	66.9	2.9	102.0	171.8
1934–35	73.3	3.3	106.4	183.0
1935–36	72.6	3.3	113.2	189.1
1936–37	119.5	6.6	127.5	253.6
1937–38	134.2	9.1	187.5	330.8
1938–39	145.5	8.7	186.6	340.8
1939–40	157.4	9.0	187.1	353.5
1940–41	118.0	7.3	220.4	345.7
1941–42	111.4	8.5	205.4	325.3
1942–43	88.1	5.9	202.8	296.8
1943–44	90.9	7.5	323.9	422.3
1944–45	120.0	7.13	480.4	614.1

SOURCE: Ministerio de Hacienda, *Cuenta general de rentas y gastos públicos,* various years.

nomically impossible to extract more revenues from the dying agricultural sector and politically unwise to tax the discontented and increasingly unruly urban social classes, the state was forced to turn to the only other viable source of new revenues—the oil companies.

The Hydrocarbons Law of 1943 was the first significant manifestation of distinctive state interests strong enough to confront the multinationals. For the first time a producing country instituted an income tax on the oil companies, a fiscal reform that was qualitatively different from the previous customs revenues or even the sale of concessions (Hausmann 1981). Arguing that revenues from concessions were no longer sufficient reimbursement for the exploitation of nonrenewable resources, President Medina established the "fifty-fifty" principle: companies should not be able to earn a greater net income from the extraction of oil than that which accrued to the state. In order to achieve this goal, the new taxes consisted of a complicated mix of royalties, an exploitation surface tax, and an exploration tax. Together, they brought an immediate increase in Venezuela's internal taxes that compensated for the loss in customs revenues and became the new main revenue source of the state (see Table 4).

The fifty-fifty agreement definitively altered the bargaining arrangements between countries and companies, leading to the second oil regime described in Chapter 3. Not surprisingly, the companies initially fought the new law, but they finally accepted it—with some generous sweeteners. Their continued clout was apparent in the design of the act. In secret negotiations with President Medina and his advisers, the majors defined the terms of the new petroleum code so that all previous concessions (which were about to expire) were converted into a uniform contract and extended for a full forty years beginning in 1943. The companies thus gained full legal rights to remain in Venezuela until 1983! To further placate the companies, the Medina administration granted huge new concessions in 1944 and 1945; more land was leased in these two years than in the previous thirty-five years combined (Hausmann 1981, 158). In effect, the state guaranteed the continued and expanded presence of foreign companies in exchange for the right to tax them.

Nonetheless, these sweeteners could not hide the overall ramifications of the new law. The 1943 Hydrocarbons Act created a new set of incentives governing state actions that would overdetermine the preferences and choices of *all* future governments by proving irresistible to state authorities, regardless of whether they were authoritarian or democratic. The new income tax institutionalized a process of fiscal extraction through bargaining between the companies and the state. Once concessions were replaced by this new form of taxation, the granting of access to land that had proved so beneficial to both parties gradually was substituted for a zero-sum negotiating game over relative shares of profits from the industry. Governments might be limited in their power by the perpetual threats of the companies to leave altogether, but they also had a ready mechanism to increase revenues in the future. In addition, they soon realized that their share of profits could be maximized if they encouraged other oil-exporting countries to drive similar tough bargains with the companies. The coincidence of interests that had characterized Gómez's rule was irrevocably broken.

The new law also institutionalized a fiscal structure that almost inevitably led to rentier behavior on the part of state authorities and private citizens. In place of augmenting domestic productive capacity, it established a permanent temptation to cut into the profits of foreign companies as a means of sustaining oil-subsidized activities while avoiding the taxation of domestic groups—a reality these groups understood. In the long run, it even created powerful incentives for state authorities to organize forms of cooperation among contending domestic social groups in order to enhance their bargaining power vis-à-vis the companies, who were especially vulnerable as nationalist targets. As Tugwell (1975) has documented so well, the very definition of state interests and the measure of state capacity eventually became identified with the successful pursuit of the extraction of oil rents and their domestic distribution to privileged social groups.

The institutionalization of these incentives is evident when Venezuela's tax structure is compared with that of neighboring Colombia (Table 5). The historically higher tax rates in Venezuela, which eventually (1977–1979) reached 20 percent of GNP (compared with 12.2 percent in Colombia in 1979–1981), are due to the exceptionally high corporate income tax on petroleum (14.1 percent in Venezuela compared with 1.6 percent in Colombia). All other taxes are significantly lower in Venezuela—most notably, individual income taxes, which are only approximately one-third of those in Colombia—a country not noted for its high rates of taxation. Simply put, petrodollars replaced and eventually eroded Venezuela's tax base.

The petro-state, Chapter 3 contended, is different from states in other developing countries. But the characteristics that have been discussed

TABLE 5

COLOMBIAN AND VENEZUELAN TAX REVENUES
AS PERCENT OF GROSS NATIONAL PRODUCT
AND PERCENT OF ALL TAX REVENUES

	% of GNP		% of Taxes	
	Colombia (1979–81)	Venezuela (1977–79)	Colombia (1979–81)	Venezuela (1977–79)
All taxes	12.2	20.0	100.0	100.0
Total income taxes	2.9	14.9	24.0	74.4
Individual taxes	1.3	0.8	11.0	4.1
Corporate taxes	1.6	14.1	12.8	70.3
Domestic indirect taxes	4.0	1.4	32.9	6.8
Foreign-trade taxes	2.3	2.0	18.8	9.8
Social security taxes	1.9	1.1	15.5	5.6
Wealth/property taxes	0.3	0.3	2.5	1.5
Other taxes	0.8	0.4	6.4	2.0

SOURCES: Tanzi (1987, 210–211, 214–215), McClure (1991).

thus far—the weak legacy of state building, the extreme centralization in the executive, the strong tendency toward expansionism, and the missed opportunity to build a capable administrative structure—can be found to varying degrees in virtually all of Venezuela's Latin American counterparts. Venezuela is unique, however, in the extent to which these features typify state development and the route through which they were acquired. Both can be explained by the central role of petroleum.

First, oil retarded the development of a distinctive state identity. True, this lack was initially due to particular historical factors unrelated to petroleum. But once the oil companies entered Venezuela, the state's capacity to externalize power was greatly constrained by them and by the U.S. government, which supported them. Together, they were able to effectively limit Venezuela's sovereignty by fashioning the international oil market and the conditions for domestic business in their favor, redesigning the country's property laws, keeping social forces weak, decisively influencing leaders, and, when necessary, helping to change actual rulers. The companies' persistent undermining of legalistic concepts that attributed distinctive roles and personalities to particular institutions rather than to individuals sustained a porous bureaucracy. In the process, the state's ability to institutionalize authority or differentiate control through the establishment of functionally distinct public institutions was compromised.

Second, oil exacerbated the already high degree of centralization of authority in the executive. Though centralization initially reflected the need to overcome the regional divisions that had historically wreaked havoc in the country, oil aggravated the form of presidentialism that could be found elsewhere in Latin America. Because petrodollars accrued to the central government, because the president had the power to appoint and remove all ministers, because the president was the final arbiter with the oil companies, and because no independent bureaucratic structure existed prior to petroleum, petrodollars became an essential tool for enhancing the political strength of the nation's ruler. This central element of politics—the undisputed authority of the chief executive in determining the final allocation of revenues—would remain unchanged and virtually unchallenged in the future, even under a democratic regime.

Third, the entry of the international oil companies expanded the jurisdiction of the Venezuelan state far beyond that of the private sector, thereby creating a permanent predominance of the public sector matched in Latin America only by socialist Cuba. The specific pattern of state expansion was tied directly to the petroleum industry. Because of the pressure of the multinationals, past conceptions of property rights were set aside and were replaced by new interpretations that granted subsoil ownership to the state. This result was by no means inevitable. Had the oil companies preferred to deal with numerous private entrepreneurs rather than one central authority, they could have insisted on a direct relationship with the private sector. The jurisdiction of the state in the economy and its role as the chief source of rents would then have looked quite different.

This is not to argue that the gap between jurisdiction and authority was due solely to petroleum. This critical oil-led dynamic was complemented by the other rationales for intervention found throughout Latin America at this time, especially power-seeking behavior on the part of leaders, pressure from below to use the state to assuage the demands of new social actors, and the popularity of statist ideologies in the postwar period. But the impetus provided by petroleum, when added to these more common factors, established the precedents for and the particular mode of state expansion that permanently characterized Venezuela. Eventually, intervention led to a more central role and a far bigger size for the state than for any other capitalist state in Latin America.

Finally, oil shaped the institutions that in turn structured the preferences and behavior of state authorities and private citizens. Because the origin of the state's revenues was an income tax on the companies, the incentive was overwhelming, first, to increase the companies' contribution to total taxes and, second, to rely on expenditures of oil revenues for resolving the social, economic, and political problems of oil-led development in one manner or another. These two activities, in turn, had a dual effect. On the one hand, the state became especially adept at international extraction, developing strong capabilities in its negotiations vis-à-vis foreign firms. On the other hand, as corporate taxes replaced other forms of domestic extraction, the state was robbed of the opportunity to benefit from the skills and talents that arise from the penetration of public authority to the far corners of a territory in search of revenues. In effect, the state missed a critical opportunity to build a capable national administrative structure while becoming fatally dependent on the substitution of statecraft for money.

Thus Venezuela entered its modern history as a petro-state, one whose capacity to create consensus and enforce collective decisions rested largely on the fate of the international oil market as well as on its ability to tax foreign firms and distribute its gains. The centralization of authority, the modernization of the central government apparatus, the appearance of a para-state, the establishment of a unified treasury and budgeting system, and the development of some form of income tax were signs of significant state building. Nonetheless, the state was increasingly being called on to play a larger role; but because domestic taxes and a civil service were virtually nonexistent, there was a striking lack of the juridical, complex, impersonal, and accountable bureaucracies necessary for managing its growing tasks.

This gap between jurisdiction and authority produced a hollow strength. The state could only give; it could not take. Rather than symbolize military conquest, national glory, cultural superiority, or territorial expansion, the Venezuelan state came to be viewed primarily as an enormous distributive apparatus, a huge milk cow that benefited those who were able to suckle at her teats. The historic cycle that followed—political rent-seeking behavior from all sides aimed especially at the executive, the continued centralization of authority and the expansion of the state's jurisdiction, the search for additional revenues through renewed oil dependence, petrolization, and the subsequent emergence of new demands on the state to redress growing imbalances—formed cages strong enough to define the actions of President Andrés Pérez several decades later.

FIVE

Oil and Regime Change

The Institutions of Pacted Democracy

Regime change is a critical juncture—a moment for dismantling or reinforcing cages. New regimes do not inherit a clean slate; they are grafted
onto preexisting state institutions. But they have some opportunity to
reshape these institutions, either by altering their characteristics or by
reinforcing existing political and economic practices and thus entrenching them more deeply. Surprisingly from the point of view of
democratic theory, the designers of Venezuela's democracy chose the
reinforcement path. Because democracy tends to disperse power
through the extension of citizenship rights, accountability, and the rule
of law, it might reasonably be expected to counteract patterns of extreme state centralization and intervention, fiscal dependence on petrodollars, rentier distribution of benefits, and the underdeveloped administrative authority that was the product of past state-building efforts.
But in Venezuela this was not the case.

Whether through conscious deliberation, unquestioning acceptance,
or lack of attention, elite actors fashioned a polity that fortified the
skewed patterns of the petro-state and, in turn, was fortified by them.
There was nothing inevitable about the creation of a mutually reinforcing pattern between the petro-state and Venezuela's democracy, although, as we shall see, powerful pulls explain the decisions of leaders
at the time. But once this reinforcement was set in motion, it exacerbated petrolization, became a major barrier to readjusting the development trajectory, and later shaped the strategic calculations of the Pérez
administration in unfortunate but predictable directions.

The explanation for this perverse cycle does not lie in the nature of democracy per se but rather in the symbiotic interaction between the overwhelming incentives created by the petro-state and the particular type of democracy established in Venezuela. Elsewhere I have labeled this *pacted* democracy.[1] Pacted democracies are established through elite bargains and compromises during the transition from authoritarian rule. They ensure their survival by selectively meeting demands while limiting the scope of representation in order to reassure traditional dominant classes that their vital interests will be respected. Because they usually promote regime practices that are simultaneously top-down, inclusive yet preemptive, and restrictive, they may bolster the patterns of the petro-state by establishing formal institutions and informal norms that limit contestation and by restricting the policy agenda and the autonomous organizational capacity of mass actors. The net effect may be an especially close fit between a type of circumscribed democracy and the uneven capacities of the petro-state.

Venezuela's *democracia pactada* reinforced the petro-state (and simultaneously sustained itself) in several ways. First, its development ideology strengthened the already powerful tendency to expand the state's jurisdiction vis-à-vis civil society, while its adoption of an explicitly presidentialist model exaggerated the concentration of power in the executive.

Second, its emphasis on containment through preemptive inclusion exacerbated clientelistic distribution, patronage, and political rent-seeking, in part by creating standard operating procedures based on excessive compromise and on conflict avoidance through the distribution of petrodollars. In the short run this practice nurtured regime stability, but in the long run it undermined the state's administrative and technical abilities by encouraging a complicated spoils system, perpetuating the extreme permeability of the public sphere, and awarding the predominance of politics over administration.

Finally, the deliberate restriction of the full workings of democracy produced rigid political institutions that benefited from the status quo and thus were not easily reformed or readjusted. In the most telling example, the two major political parties, Acción Democrática and CO-PEI, sought to keep the barriers to power especially high and to guard their role as the principal means of access to the state by sacrificing their programs and becoming machines for extracting rents from the public arena. Together these factors encouraged the persistence of a development trajectory fueled solely by the expenditure of petrodollars.

This chapter examines the transition and consolidation of Venezuelan democracy from 1946 to 1973. It is not intended to be a complete description of these years or an account of the three administrations that immediately preceded the oil boom. Instead, its purpose is to highlight the dynamic and mutually reinforcing interplay between the petro-state and pacted democracy, which set the parameters for and defined the preferences that shaped the responses of policymakers in the 1973 oil boom. Because the manner in which the democratic regime reinforced both the institutions of the petro-state and the perpetuation of oil dependence was established in the critical years from 1958 to 1960, the chapter pays particular attention to the emergence of the foundational pacts of 1958 as well as the policy consensus, institutions, and norms they engendered.

PETROLEUM AND POLITICAL PACTS
IN THE TRANSITION TO DEMOCRACY

Petroleum was the single most important factor in shaping the structural conditions for the breakdown of military rule, the subsequent creation of a reformist political space, and the maintenance of a *democracia pactada* in Venezuela—even if it cannot explain the specific timing, shape, or direction of regime change.[2] Three oil-led changes described in the previous chapter augured especially well for the emergence of some type of reformist rule in Venezuela: the creation of an independent class of urban dwellers whose livelihood was removed from the land, the predominance of the middle class over a small working class, and the gradual elimination of what Moore (1966, 422) calls "the peasant question" through the transformation of the landlord class into an urban commercial elite.

When a group of young military officers, influenced by democratic ideologies during their service in World War II, led a coup against Gómez's successor, General Medina Angarita, these structural changes provided the basis for the formation of reformist parties, which subsequently encouraged the officers to opt for an electoral regime. That few other viable options existed was due mostly to petroleum-related changes. The decline of the landlord class with the demise of agricultural exports had removed any incentive to form conservative, peasant-based parties or repressive agrarian rule, and oil eased the virulence of landlord-peasant disputes that wracked other Latin American countries by providing a permanent "exit" from the land for both elites and masses (Karl 1987). At the same time, the relative weakness and small size of the urban proletariat made successful revolution unlikely.

Acción Democrática (AD), the young, middle-class party the military installed in power, governed for three crisis-filled years (referred to as the *trienio)* before being overthrown by the armed forces in 1948. During its short rule, this embryonic government gave the first indications of how democracy might fortify the petro-state.[3] First, AD laid the programmatic basis for an increase in the state's jurisdiction. A reformist party intent on uniting the peasants in declining agrarian sectors with the newly militant oil workers as well as the emerging middle and industrial classes in Caracas, it embraced the ideology of sowing the petroleum through protected industrialization to cement an alliance between competing social forces.[4] This multiclass program required an interventionist state, a commitment reflected in the Constitution of 1947. Thus the *trienio* government rapidly extended the state's role by almost doubling the number of state enterprises and institutes (creating ten in 1946 alone) and founding the Corporación Venezolano de Fomento (CVF), the first important public-sector enterprise designed to channel oil revenues directly into the process of private capital accumulation.[5]

Second, AD embraced a model of resource-based industrialization, which extended and deepened oil-led development and which set the parameters for economic policy for decades to come. In 1947, the government negotiated the entrance of U.S. Steel to the Guayana region and gave it claim to Cerro Bolívar, the most important iron ore discovery of modern times. Aided by U.S. advisers, who were awed by the immense power of the Caroní River, state managers devised a major electrification plan and proposed a feasibility study for a state-run steel industry that would draw on the iron ore as well as the massive hydroelectric power. In the first juridical expression of the state's new role as direct producer, Article 73 of the 1947 Constitution granted the state the right to reserve specific industries for itself and to plan and rationalize production.

Third, AD used the state to create loyal but highly subsidized organized interests who were tied to and supportive of a resource-based economic model and an interventionist state. Taking advantage of its brief rule to organize labor and peasant associations under the domination of the party and therefore to preempt their capacity for autonomous action, it established the nation's first labor federation, the Confederation of Venezuelan Workers (CTV), and formed the Peasant Federation. In a mere three years, the number of legal unions rose from

252 to 1,014, and over 100 collective agreements were signed. The number of peasant syndicates leapt from 53 to 515 (Powell 1971, 79). The party won immediate benefits from its strategy. Because unions led by its militants received government favors (including access to credits, public-works projects, and water and sewage systems) and union leaders rapidly advanced in the party hierarchy, mass organizations became a "captured" clientele and a loyal electoral base (Boesch 1972, Fagan 1974). As a result, political parties had to be responsive to the demands of these sectors, and the loyalties of unions also had to be continuously purchased with petrodollars.

The *trienio* government accomplished all these goals through the expansion of public spending, and therein lay its essential weakness. Predictably, it sought first to distribute oil rents to cement its political support; when these became scarce and opposition to the new democratic regime grew, it initiated new battles over shares of oil rents with the foreign companies. Quick to understand the novel possibilities offered by the 1943 Hydrocarbons Act, Pérez Alfonzo, then Minister of Development, tightened the fifty-fifty agreement, limited the awarding of concessions, formed a national petroleum company, and encouraged the organization of the Petroleum Workers Federation. When the companies (also predictably) retaliated by threatening to move their operations to the Middle East, Pérez Alfonzo encouraged Saudi Arabia, Kuwait, and Iraq to adopt the fifty-fifty agreement—the first example of cooperation among producer countries (Kubbah 1974, 7).[6]

But this move against the oil companies proved costly. It turned the U.S. government against the regime and helped to cement an antidemocratic alliance of the companies, economic elites frightened by the rapid organizing of workers, church officials opposed to secularization, other political parties alarmed by the hegemony of AD, and the army. Although total government revenues in 1948 grew to six times their 1942 level, they arrived too late to support the party's efforts to remain in power, and AD was overthrown by the armed forces.

The military rule of Pérez Jiménez (1948–1957), which replaced the *trienio,* is a striking example of the politically unsettling effects of oil booms. A major oil boom, which seemed at the time to promise to sustain authoritarian rule, proved instead to be the backdrop to regime change. As a result of soaring demand for petroleum in the postwar period, the Iranian crisis of 1954, and the closing of the Suez Canal, Venezuela experienced a phenomenal bonanza. Between 1950 and 1957, Venezuela accumulated more foreign exchange than any other nation in the world except West Germany (which was enjoying the fruits of the Marshall Plan). Crude exports expanded 7.4 percent per annum, while the sale of petroleum products increased 14 percent per annum throughout the decade. Daily production registered an enormous jump from 1.498 million barrels to 2.779 million barrels (Hanson 1977, 64). Treasury reserves tripled, permitting high levels of public expenditures and the parallel expansion of aggregate demand. As the market grew and domestic production became profitable for the first time, manufacturing grew 313 percent, and the average rate of investment was a staggering 28.3 percent (Salazar-Carrillo 1976, 101, 117; Araujo 1969).

The enormous amount of money circulating in the economy might have supported authoritarianism for a longer period despite the social changes traced in the previous chapter had Pérez Jiménez been able to manage the boom. But, in the midst of plenty, he curtailed social expenditures and stopped subsidies that AD had granted to industry as a whole. Instead, he spent money on his own favorite projects; construction contracts awarded by the state became the primary source of illegal enrichment in the country, leading to permanent industrial problems.[7] In contrast to the results of AD's reformist policies, between 1950 and 1957 labor's share of the national income dropped from 52.4 percent to 49.8 percent (Aranda 1977, 174). Income-distribution figures for the final year of the dictatorship show that 88 percent of all Venezuelans received about one-half of the national income, while a mere 12 percent accounted for the other half (Araujo 1969, 78). At the same time, Pérez Jiménez's financial policies brought the economy to the point of total collapse.

But overspending in the wake of the boom was not enough by itself to provoke a regime change. In 1957 Pérez Jiménez's announced intention to remain in power indefinitely catalyzed opposition to his rule. When outlawed political parties, led by AD, moved into open protest, they were joined by economic elites critical of the mismanagement of the economy and the slashing of industrial credits. Pérez Jiménez attempted to paper over his overspending and corruption by selling new concessions to the oil companies despite the provisions of the 1943 Hydrocarbons Act, but this attempt simply fueled controversy. By January 1958 the Catholic Church, his own armed forces, and even former cronies in the Cámara de Construcción had joined the opposition.[8] On January 23, with the entire city of Caracas mobilized and demonstrations taking place around the country, Pérez Jiménez agreed to leave the country. Four days later, in the midst of riots and a death toll climbing over 250, a military junta announced that Venezuela would be democratic (Stambouli 1979, Karl 1986).

The need to secure this fragile alliance for democracy shaped the actions of the AD leader, Rómulo Betancourt, and the other designers of the new polity.[9] Their recognition that the army, the oil companies, and traditional dominant interests were still strong enough to unravel democracy produced what noted Venezuelan scholar Juan Carlos Rey (1986) has called their "obsessive preoccupation" with appeasement. This preoccupation was formally and informally institutionalized through a series of negotiated compromises in which all major contending forces agreed to forego their capacity to harm each other by extending guarantees not to threaten each other's vital interests. The type of democracy that eventually emerged—inclusive, preemptive, and restrictive—made the prospect of challenging petrolization dubious at best.

The desire to appease all interests through the liberal use of petrodollars and to avoid hard political choices regardless of the economic consequences is exemplified by the first actions taken during the acute crisis following the fall of Pérez Jiménez. On the advice of the foremost political and economic supporters of democracy, the new provisional government announced a *Plan de Emergencia* consisting of, first, an agreement to pay the outstanding debts of the military government despite the illegality of most of its contracts, and, second, a massive public-works campaign and high wage subsidies intended to defuse popular discontent. The combination of these welfare policies and the payment of a whopping $1.4 billion to bankers and industrialists to ensure their support for the new regime resulted in "a huge dole given on terms that had never been equaled in any other country" (Alexander 1964, 59; Hanson 1977).

Pacts were the mechanisms of containment, and they established the policy style of giving something to everyone and the postponement of difficult choices that subsequently characterized the young democracy. New institutional arrangements were established through several interlocking, elite-negotiated accords formulated in 1958 and refined during the first years of the Betancourt administration. The Pact of Punto Fijo, the Declaración de Principios y Programa Mínimo de Gobierno, and the Avenimiento Obrero-Patronal, signed prior to the country's first elections by all contending presidential candidates, bound all signatories to the same basic political and economic program and established specific parameters of action, regardless of the electoral outcome.[10] Together, they guaranteed that oil-led development would continue to be pursued through some form of representative democracy.

A more complete discussion of these pacts is available elsewhere (Karl 1986). Our interest here is in the specific arrangements that fortified the petro-state while so circumscribing democracy that a fundamental alteration in the oil-dependent development trajectory became increasingly unlikely. The Pact of Punto Fijo reaffirmed the central role of parties, but it laid the basis for the political allocation of state offices and placed strong limits on the range of debate. It guaranteed that all parties would maintain a "prolonged political truce" and share power in a manner commensurate with the voting results. Regardless of who won the elections, each party was guaranteed some access to state jobs and contracts, a partitioning of the ministries, and a complicated spoils system that would ensure the political survival of all signatories. In effect, administrative coherence was sacrificed to political stability.

Debate over the direction of economic policy and the interventionist role of the state was constrained by the Minimum Program of Government. All parties agreed to support oil-led development, broad state jurisdiction in matters of production and social welfare, and high protection for and subsidies to local industry. To reassure the oil companies, the Minimum Program ruled out the expropriation or the socialization of property; although it proposed agrarian reform, it promised that changes in land tenure would be based on the principle of compensation. The first AD government would later establish policy guidelines based on increased participation in revenues from oil and a firm "no-concessions" rule. Earlier promises to nationalize the petroleum industry were quietly shelved (Herrera Campíns 1978).

The Pact of Punto Fijo and the Minimum Program were complemented by basic agreements between workers and employers and between organized interests and parties. Following the (expensive) guidelines of the *Plan de Emergencia,* capitalists and organized labor pledged, in the Worker-Employer Accord, "harmonious collaboration" through the establishment of commissions with equal labor and capital representation. They also agreed to widespread social spending; new legislation regarding health, education, and social security; and strict adherence to collective bargains and the Labor Law. In order to further minimize conflict, the leaders of the political parties created a unified labor confederation based on the proportional representation of all parties (McCoy 1986). These actions gave labor a strong stake in capturing subsidies from petroleum and the organizational clout to do so. AD and the other political parties received a quid pro quo: control over both the state and petrodollars.

Taken together, the Minimum Program of Government, the Worker-Employer Accord, and the Pact of Punto Fijo thus represented a classic exchange: a party system that for the first time offered the potential for channeling competing demands and alternating power in return for removing fundamental development issues from the political agenda and tightly constraining choice before elections were ever held. This changed what could have become potential issues of national debate into established regime parameters by removing them from contestation. This depoliticization of broad economic questions was guaranteed to continue as long as the basic compromise represented by these pacts bound all parties. Although their signatories would struggle over issues not included in the Minimum Program and although the boundaries between different realms would be hotly disputed, these fundamental understandings would not be contested until the 1973 boom.

Not that *pactismo* went unchallenged. In order to bring along reluctant constituents, reassure fearful elites, and placate the United States, AD founder Betancourt excluded the Communist Party from these institutional arrangements, abandoned the mobilizational tactics of the past, aggressively purged leaders of peasant and labor federations who insisted on deeper reform or organizational autonomy, and ceased all efforts to create new party constituencies from previously unorganized groups. His decision to remove any hint of socialist development was bitterly resented by young *adecos* who had risked their lives in a clandestine struggle while Betancourt was living in exile. In April 1960, the entire youth branch of AD left the party in protest over the expulsion of their leaders, formed the Movimiento de Izquierda Revolucionaria (MIR), and launched the largest guerrilla movement in Latin America to that date.[11]

The importance of the subsequent defeat of this guerrilla movement—a defeat led by Betancourt's Minister of the Interior, Carlos Andrés Pérez—for the institutionalization of pacted democracy cannot be overemphasized. As Levine (1978, 98) writes, "More than any other single factor, the development of a leftist strategy of insurrection in the early 1960s consolidated democracy by unifying center and right around AD in response to a common threat." But the high price of this victory was measured in more than the loss of thousands of lives. Although Betancourt's preoccupation with appeasing conservative forces permitted him to finish his term and pass the presidential reins to others, it also resulted in the permanent demobilization of mass organizations, the freezing of political institutions, and the persistent addiction to oil rents.

CONSTRUCTING COMPLICITY:
PACTED DEMOCRACY AND OIL-BASED DEVELOPMENT

The pacts of 1958 led to the institutionalization of a democracy with a dual, even contradictory, character. On the one hand, representation was ensured by the holding of regular and fair elections in which all citizens could participate, a formal juridical framework safeguarding democratic rights and the rule of law, and important acts of statecraft by the new regime's first president, Betancourt. On the other, representation was restricted by *pactismo*. Petroleum rents underlay this new system of reconciling competing interests by turning all organized interests into subsidized clientele and thus permitting them to avoid the zero-sum economic games that have proved so detrimental to democracy in the rest of Latin America.

These were not temporary characteristics designed solely for overcoming the uncertainty of the transition. To the contrary, the regime norms and practices that were institutionalized had the permanent effect of privileging the political parties, their organized constituencies, and those capitalist interests that had the potential capacity to undo the democracy. These practices could not easily be eliminated once the regime was stabilized, and they created over time a new political community whose members squabbled but supported each other in the maintenance of the status quo.

This political community rested first and foremost on consensus about an interventionist state and oil-led development. Not only did oil play the central role as the engine of the economy, but this statist economic model was constructed in such a way as to offer substantial subsidies and benefits to all politically significant social groups, including state officials, without simultaneously laying the basis for competitive economic development independent of petroleum. Pushed by linkage factors, state-led industrialization continued to center on steel, aluminum, hydroelectric projects, and petrochemicals—all placed under the auspices of the Corporación Venezolana de Guayana (CVG), a holding company (presided over by a general of the armed forces) with broad authority to plan the economic development of the region formed by the confluence of the Orinoco and Caroní rivers. But though the CVG performed better than other state enterprises, easy access to petrodollars removed pressures to make these new industries competitive, and they generally proved to be a drain on public resources years after they should have been producing profits.[12]

Sustaining the long-term support of the capitalist class through subsidized and protectionist import-substitution industrialization and low taxation was another pillar of this new political community. Influenced by the doctrine of the Economic Commission of Latin America (ECLA), all democratic administrations committed themselves to the same broad outlines of an import-substitution industrial policy. To some extent, this industrial pattern was typical of Latin America: it concentrated first on consumer goods and building materials, then shaded gradually into producing complex consumer durables and steel, engineering, and chemical products (Díaz-Alejandro 1965, 495–509).

But because Venezuelan industry was financed by petroleum revenues, it had certain distinctive features that did not bode well for self-sustaining development. Characterized by an unusual system of protection, the result of a reciprocal trade agreement that had been established to facilitate oil exports to the United States and that prohibited tariffs, protection was based on import licensing rather than the ad valorem tariffs used throughout the rest of the continent. The advantages of the system for the private sector were extensive; Naím (1993, 41) has observed that protection reached as high as 940 percent! This system of protection was complemented by tax exemptions and investment incentives across a wide range of activities, which made up to 100 percent of income earned tax free (McClure 1991, 18).

This form of import licensing also had substantial advantages for state officials because it granted enormous discretionary power to them. Quotas were awarded on an individual basis, and no firm could survive without protection. Although formal criteria existed for the awarding of licenses, they were in fact handed out through personal or political contacts. This system encouraged influence trafficking and created extensive, though often hidden, links between powerful family-based economic groups and state managers. Public officials also distributed long-term credits at subsidized interest rates because banking laws prohibited commercial banks from giving credits for more than a two-year duration. From 1958 until the oil boom, the CVF alone awarded close to a billion dollars in long-term, low-interest credits to industry, which was 45.5 percent of its total financing (Corporación Venezolana de Fomento

1976, 12). Finally, by selectively restricting imports or using price controls, the government could raise or lower the domestic price of any product on the market. This capability made entire industrial sectors dependent on favorable treatment from officials in the Ministry of Development.

Benefits accrued disproportionately to the economically most powerful groups, either foreign or domestic, who were best able to influence state officials, exaggerating strong tendencies toward foreign penetration and oligopoly. Foreign capital was attracted by especially hefty profit rates, which were estimated at three times those of the United States (Nolf 1978, 88); by 1971, Venezuela had the largest gross accumulated foreign investment of any Third World country, 86 percent of which was concentrated in the petroleum sector (Mayobre 1970).

This strong foreign presence was closely linked to the domination of industry by many of the same family groups that had prospered under Pérez Jiménez and some newcomers. Although all democratic governments promised to break up oligopoly ownership, concentration grew substantially. The pattern of awarding import licenses, tariffs, and credits effectively barred new entrants into a sector, limiting the number of firms receiving protection and thereby contributing to the maintenance of economic concentration. Large firms had clear advantages: their access to public officials was easy, and they controlled or strongly influenced private banks, which permitted them to regulate the flow of credits to smaller enterprises and to eliminate potential competitors.[13] By 1975, a mere 8.9 percent of all industrial establishments accounted for 76.8 percent of total capital in manufacturing, 75 percent of production value, and 58.6 percent of employment (Ministerio de Fomento 1977). Such concentrated economic power was in place when the first oil boom occurred and would prove especially difficult to ignore.

Subsidizing the private sector to encourage industrialization also brought some benefits to the working class, thus incorporating politically privileged unions into this network. Manufacturing created 343,700 jobs between 1961 and 1974, jumping from 18.7 to 23 percent of total employment. It soon became apparent, however, that the capital-intensive and anti-agrarian bias of the model was incapable of generating enough jobs to offset the country's serious equity problem (Hassan 1975)—a problem augmented by government policy. Low customs duties on machinery and equipment, tax exemptions for fixed investment, subsidized loans to industry, the maintenance of an overvalued exchange rate, and other policies designed to please the private sector substantially contributed to lowering the price of capital and sustaining these structural biases.

Thus social spending, subsidized by petrodollars, became the key mechanism for delivering jobs and services to the middle and lower classes (preempting more radical demands for redistribution) and for fostering patronage. This policy is evident in the dramatic shift in public expenditure patterns following the demise of authoritarian rule. As Kornblith and Maingon (1985, 205) demonstrate, social spending, which includes expenditures for health, education, water and sanitation, housing, recreation, and labor relations, grew substantially, from a paltry 5.3 percent of total spending under Gómez to 11.4 percent under Pérez Jiménez. But it leapt to an average of 28.1 percent of total spending in the democratic period from 1958 to 1973; between 1969 and 1973, the years immediately prior to the boom, it was 31.4 percent of total spending! [14]

The development of patronage networks can be easily seen in the noticeable increase in current expenditures compared with capital expenditures, which rose to an all-time high of 69.5 percent in 1972 (Kornblith and Maingon 1985, 209). Much of this increase is attributable to expenditures for personnel, the time-honored means of sustaining clientelist loyalties. According to the Ministry of Finance, personnel expenditures grew from 22.7 percent of total central-government payments in the transition year of 1958–1959 to 33.7 percent a mere two years later, a level they subsequently sustained (Kornblith and Maingon 1985, 211).

In essence, Venezuela's democracy (like most others) was based on a pattern of public policies and state expenditures aimed at winning the political support of every major organized class or social group. What differentiated this democracy from its counterparts was its prolonged "positive sum game," which was due to its fiscal reliance on petrodollars—an often plentiful, sometimes erratic, and always vulnerable revenue source. This reliance on oil money placed an especially high premium on gaining access to the state. Pact making, electoral outcomes, and the exercise of influence were the bases for the assignment of shares among contending forces, and political authority, not markets or custom, decided allocations. Thus the institutionalization of privilege depended primarily on the rules and mechanisms regulating access to power and modes of decision-making. In Venezuela, these rules first established and then reproduced the entitlements of parties, organized labor, and the capitalist class, entrenching these interests in a new status quo and deepening dependence on petroleum.

CONSOLIDATING COMPLICITY:
INSTITUTIONALIZING ACCESS TO THE PETRO-STATE

Assessing how the privileges of various constituencies have been institutionalized in order to illustrate how pacted democracy ultimately perpetuated an inefficient and uncompetitive development model is not an easy task. Several observers of decision-making in Venezuela (Gil Yepes 1978, Blank 1984) have remarked on the divided, even contradictory, character of the policy process and have assessed its functioning through a complicated mix of interest-group, elite, and pluralist theories. Drawing on this work as well as on a scanty, yet growing, body of policy studies (Tugwell 1975, Martz and Meyers 1977, Naím and Piñango 1984), I find it useful to conceptualize Venezuela's democratic rule as what Schmitter (1988) calls "partial regimes": the various institutionalized parts that, when linked together, constitute a regime. Each partial regime in Venezuela—the constitutional order, the set of party and electoral rules and practices, and the concerted representation of organized interests—structures the competition and alignment of contending groups, regulates the interactions among them, encourages the ascendancy of some over others, and perpetuates the patterns of the petro-state.

The constitutional order designed during the transition to democracy established the formal distribution of activities among state agencies, empowered specific institutions rather than others, and bound future generations to rules that proved difficult to amend. In this respect, the most striking aspect of the 1961 Constitution was its reaffirmation of state intervention and extreme presidentialism. Believing that only the state could distribute the fruits of the nation's patrimony and that democratic forces needed a mediator who could rise above the kinds of partisan conflicts that had destroyed the *trienio,* the constitution validated the tradition of highly centralized power and made the president the supreme political arbiter. It gave the office of the president control over the nation's defense, monetary system, all tax and tariff policy, exploitation of subsoil rights, management of foreign affairs, and a variety of other powers; it granted authority to name all cabinet ministers, state governors, and officials of state enterprises. The president was also empowered to declare a state of emergency and to receive special powers to govern by decree.

The absence of effective controls over the presidency during the entire five-year term by any of the other partial regimes is especially notable. Although a no-reelection clause guaranteed a lapse of ten years between any individual's presidential terms in order to prevent *continuismo*, even this rule had its drawbacks. When combined with norms designed to free the president from party discipline after election, it removed an important mechanism that might permit electorates to pressure for compliance to party programs. Because the president could not be held responsible for performance by being denied reelection, the president was less subject to the pulls of party and voters. But the president was also more open to the influence of interest groups that permeated the state. In sum, with the noted exception of times when the opposition party held a congressional majority, almost no mechanisms of accountability existed for the presidency.

The weakness of Congress reinforced these ultracentralized patterns of authority. Congressional committees were virtually impotent, with few financial or human resources at their disposal, which made it difficult to initiate legislation or even to adequately criticize laws originating in the executive. Not surprisingly, the volume of legislation passed by the Congress was small: it approved an average of only 27.9 laws per year from 1959 to 1982, which compares unfavorably to the Argentinean Chamber of Deputies (300) and the Brazilian Federal Senate (827) and favorably only to the Cuban People's Assembly (27) (Coppedge 1993, 105). Even its power over the budget was circumscribed because a significant share of public spending (the majority after 1973) took place through state enterprises or other financial networks that were not subject to congressional oversight. Indeed, Congress became politically significant only when the opposition party was in control and could block some presidential initiatives.

The rules and norms of the party-based electoral system did not counteract these centralizing tendencies, but instead encouraged them. True, the democratic regime was based on national political parties, whose access to power was obtained through universal suffrage by secret ballot and who could be held accountable through regularized elections. A strong independent body, the Consejo Supremo Electoral, oversaw the integrity of these elections, and voting was designed to be especially easy. Elections provided an important degree of representation for the sectors that formed the mass base of the parties, especially in election years, when the parties took special care to gear their performance and program to the electorate.

But entry into the political process was severely circumscribed by what Coppedge (1993) has called "partyarchy." So powerful were the

parties that AD and COPEI could constrain nominations, voting, legislative action, and freedom of organization to a greater degree than parties in any other democracy. In AD, for example, only the twenty to
thirty members of the National Executive Committee (CEN) had the
right to choose all party candidates for the Senate and Chamber of Deputies and for state legislative assemblies. Tight party discipline reinforced control over militants; AD members supported the party 100
percent, or they were expelled. Because political supremacy resided with
the president, the government party generally limited itself to supporting the administration's plans and projects (which were worked up in
consultation with the party's central committee), even renouncing certain responsibilities of oversight and criticism that devolved upon it
(Rey 1986, 40).

This consensus between the government and its party and within
parties, however, was always fragile. Because parties were the road to
state patronage and control of petrodollars, powerful incentives existed
to form highly personalistic factions linked to different leaders, especially in the year prior to candidate selection and elections. Factionalism
was not based on ideology; these types of differences had been erased
through party purges during the guerrilla war. Instead, as Coppedge
(1993) demonstrates, they were naked power struggles that defied electoral rationale since they damaged party support but had a clear power
raison d'être.[15] Factionalism most often afflicted parties when they governed—that is, when they had goods to distribute; and it divided parties
between those on the president's team and those united around potential presidential candidates.

This top-down yet divided organization of the parties encouraged
rent-seeking behavior and clientelistic forms of participation, while discouraging the formation of a competent bureaucracy. Careful studies of
Venezuelan clientelism by Ray (1969) and Powell (1971) and of public
administration (Stewart 1977, 215–234) demonstrate how this worked.
Local leaders made local needs known to national party heads, who
then passed requests to top party leaders, the relevant minister, or the
president. The response was filtered through the ministry back to the
local agency. Individuals or organizations had virtually no hope of being heard unless they utilized party networks and followed party guidelines. The procedure encouraged favor seekers to find some way to go
to the top of the decision-making apparatus because lower-level bureaucrats would often refuse to take any action without the approval of the
president or a minister.

The dominance of political criteria, a direct outgrowth of the partitioning of the state by the Pact of Punto Fijo and of the subsequent rise of factionalism, often prevented the attainment of high technical standards within the bureaucracy. Although standards based on achievement carried some weight in the selection of state personnel, merit generally took a back seat to political affiliation, factional allegiances, and personal relationships. Such partisan manipulation of the bureaucracy was considered a legitimate "political overhead cost" by party leaders intent on conflict avoidance. But it mitigated the possibility of establishing a viable civil service, and turnover in personnel after each election occurred at all levels of the hierarchy as party factions sought to maximize their opportunities for patronage. In this context, political and administrative manipulation was more highly rewarded than the efficient performance of business.

Broad political competition among parties might have provided a helpful corrective to these centralizing and rentier tendencies, but such competition was constrained in two crucial ways. First, while voters could protest a party's lack of responsiveness by changing their partisan preferences, meaningful options for this form of "exit" were limited by the predominance of two status quo parties whose own contestation was restrained by the political style of compromise initiated by the Pact of Punto Fijo. Second, the barriers to entry for new political parties, while not strict in the legal-formal sense, were formidable in reality. The growing professionalization of parties as electoral machines and the extraordinary cost of political campaigns in a petro-state required phenomenal financial resources, which could not easily be raised by parties not associated with business or those that had not previously occupied the seats of power.

Rules of access to the state were less fixed and more easily contested (perhaps because the financial stakes were so high) in the practices governing the representation of organized interests. Under authoritarian rule, business had generally exercised influence and gained access to the state through informal personal ties to the executive branch, in part because no formal channels existed. Despite the introduction of numerous new access points, this pattern continued after 1958 because the extensive power granted the executive to award import licenses, exonerations, credits, and subsidies on a case-by-case basis created enormous incentives for influence trafficking aimed at the top. Survey data (Bond 1975, 143–145) reveal, first, that contacts based on personal ties were considered the most effective means for receiving favors and, second, that high government officials, especially ministers, were the preferred targets. Because presidents were seen as supreme arbiters and because the personal reputation for probity of the earliest leaders was so strong, chief executives were considered to be above the fray—a perception that gradually eroded in tandem with the increase of petrodollars.

The new aspect of interest representation in the democratic regime, however, was the establishment of a semicorporatist network of commissions and organizations. Patterns of access to the state that had been hinted at during the *trienio* were gradually institutionalized, especially in the state-enterprise sector. For the first time, specific private associations had formal public status. The democratic regime granted legal status in decision-making to those private and minority interests who had supported the transition from authoritarian rule, especially business through its umbrella association, Fedecámaras, but also labor through the CTV and some professional groups.[16]

This growing mix of consultative bodies and commissions was especially important for capitalists. Historically unable to build representation through a party of the right, unpopular with the leadership of AD (which they considered the "party of their servants"), and constrained by the size and wealth of the petro-state in their ability to influence parties through financial means, capitalists gained for the first time a direct mechanism for influencing policy as an organized class (Combellas 1973, Bond 1975, Gil Yepes 1978). Such representation was exceedingly welcome because it maximized their capacity to put forward their interests effectively: corporatist commissions operated in closed administrative settings, which were removed from public opinion and not particularly subject to partisan debate; these settings encouraged an administrative style that relied heavily on technical solutions, where capitalists had an advantage.[17] Furthermore, state recognition of Fedecámaras encouraged capitalists to reach policy consensus among themselves, thereby fostering the class unity that always proved essential to the attainment of any important capitalist objective.

To a lesser extent, this semicorporatist regime also granted a privileged position to labor. The state recognized the CTV, the unified labor confederation, as the legitimate bargaining unit for the working class and helped it to become one of the wealthiest labor federations in the world by providing over half of its financing. But though the CTV was often given equal and occasionally majority representation on various commissions and boards, its ability to represent labor as a sector was constrained. Unlike Fedecámaras, the unions did not have enough properly trained technicians or equal access to information about the economy, thus they tended to wait for AD to take a formal position on any public policy.

The decision by the parties to create a unified labor confederation based on proportional representation had the advantage of promoting unity by preventing parallel unions in the same industry, but it discouraged the responsiveness normally nurtured by competition, and it limited the possibility of autonomous action on the part of the unions themselves. Furthermore, because the Labor Code discriminated against workers in small enterprises by establishing a minimum membership of twenty for a plant union, hundreds of thousands of workers in artisan shops, services, and commerce were not represented by the CTV and were unable to influence its decisions or benefit from them. Unlike Fedecámaras, which sought to express the aggregate preferences of an entire class, the CTV remained the province of only a portion of the working class, and nonunionized workers (about 56 percent of the labor force) had no representation at all.

This mix of constitutional arrangements, party relations, and rules governing interest representation both reflected and reinforced the patterns of the petro-state. Each of these partial regimes had a conservative bias, which made substantive change of the development trajectory difficult at best. But there were still important differences in degree among them, and they tended to grant different levels of access to different groups. Not surprisingly, then, the boundaries of each partial regime, especially those dividing the spheres of party and semicorporatist networks, became the object of intense struggles. As we shall see in Chapter 7, one of the most prominent and persistent conflicts was between capitalists and the political parties over the lucrative state-enterprise system.

Despite conflicts over relative shares, the overriding ethos was one of excessive compromise, even complicity. The combination of expanding oil rents and the rules and practices that evolved directly from the pacts of 1958 encouraged a form of cooperation among existing organized groups even as they discouraged the entry of other new actors. Together, they sustained an elite consensus and systematically insulated policymaking from substantive debate or unbridled contestation. Venezuela's democratic rules served as "selective mechanisms" that organized elites into new political communities based on petrolization while perpetuating the exclusion and disorganization of subordinate classes and groups.[18] This function was reinforced by fiscal dependence on petrodollars. Because the sum total of state expenditures (and therefore the net benefits that might accrue to competing individual interests) could be increased through coalition building that strengthened the government vis-à-vis the oil companies, cooperation was beneficial. Indeed, the actual sum of gains depended on the cooperative strategies that actors adopted (Rey 1986, 26). Just as Chapter 3 argued, oil revenues could and did transform struggles among domestic actors over shares into coordinated strategies to extract more taxes from the oil companies.

Evidence of this complicity was plentiful: it could be seen in the formal coalitions between AD and COPEI that lasted until 1968; the elaborate spoils system based on doling out public employment, agencies, and monies to political parties; the rotation of personnel among private enterprise, the ministries, and the state enterprises; the extensive private networks, influence trafficking, and financial links among the parties and large, family-based economic groups;[19] and even the surprisingly peaceful labor relations (which were especially important in the early years of the democracy).[20]

This complicity both arose from and depended on the petro-state. Only because the Hydrocarbons Act of 1943 institutionalized access to revenues from an external, not a domestic, source could the state assuage competing interests and reconcile heterogeneous demands through public spending without having to make definitive choices, hurt any significant interests, or raise taxes at home. For pact makers, oil created a politician's dream—a positive-sum game that permitted a democracy without losers. Complicity sustained the basic premises of political life: the obsession with avoiding the conflicts inherent in any attempt to establish priorities, and the consequent pursuit of multiple, even conflicting, goals to please multiple constituencies. For the petro-state, *pactismo* simply widened the gap between jurisdiction and authority even further.

SHAPING THE CONJUNCTURE OF THE BOOM

When the 1973 oil boom loomed, Venezuela's pacted democracy had lasted fifteen years. In that time it had acquired some routinized policy practices and a record that exemplified the "mixed blessings" of petroleum dependence. This record would define the immediate conjuncture of the boom, while the standard operating procedures shaped the response to a crisis of wealth.

The policy rules governing the behavior of decision-makers were a direct outgrowth of the petro-state and the pacted democracy grafted onto it. First, all democratic administrations, regardless of party, followed a paramount rule of maximizing gains from the oil companies. The state, though administratively weak and politicized elsewhere, became exceptionally capable in this highly localized arena. In 1957 the government retained only 52 percent of oil profits and was paid $968 million by the oil companies. By 1970, as a result of efforts by the state, the government retained 78 percent of the profits and was paid $1.4 billion (Tugwell 1975, 150). Venezuelans repeatedly took the lead among producer countries in designing innovative ways to maximize profits. Having earlier set standards with the fifty-fifty agreement, Pérez Alfonzo was to first to break this accord by announcing that government royalties would be treated as a cost to be taken out of profits and could no longer be deducted from the companies' income taxes. The revenue increase from this new arrangement was the largest in the history of world oil. Venezuela, as noted earlier, also became the catalyst for the formation of OPEC, which also helped to increase its earnings.

Second, all policymakers sought to sow the petroleum and expand the state by creating state-directed, resource-based industrialization and simultaneously fostering import substitution in the private sector. Fueled by state spending, the average rate of growth of industry was 7.1 percent per annum, the most rapid growth on the continent. Employment in manufacturing doubled in the first decade of democracy, and by 1973 the sector employed 15 percent of the active population and generated 17 percent of the global product (Nolf 1978, 27–30). The expansion of commerce, services, and finance was even more rapid.

Third, all policymakers followed an "appeasement" rule: they sought to simultaneously satisfy all politically relevant social actors. The results were evident both in the achievement of fifteen years of democracy as well as in the notable positive changes in the distribution of income. When compared with data from the prior, authoritarian period (1957), statistics from 1970 demonstrate a decline in the shares of the country's richest 5 percent (from 25 to 22 percent), the growth of the middle class (with shares up from 56.1 percent to 58 percent), and a small relative improvement in the position of the bottom half of society (with shares up from 18.9 to 20 percent) (Chossudovsky 1977a, 227). The uniqueness of this pattern can be best understood by comparison with other Latin American countries. In Venezuela, the median income of the richest 5 percent of the population ranked lower than that of Brazil, Argentina, Colombia, or Mexico, while the average income of the next 15 percent was by far the highest (Chossudovsky 1977a, 223).

But however impressive the results of these policy rules might seem when compared with Venezuela's past, citizen discontent was high in 1973, especially among those unorganized constituencies not represented through *pactismo*. The causes were evident. Parties were overly centralized and out of reach; representation was inadequate; and accountability was nonexistent except during election periods. The state was inefficient and riddled with favoritism. The economy was severely unbalanced and skewed toward wealthier consumers,[21] highly concentrated, and characterized by the highest import coefficient, lowest productivity, and lowest utilization of industrial capacity on the continent (CORDIPLAN, *Encuesta industrial*. 1973, vol. 1, 9). Equity statistics were dismal. A quarter of the population was unemployed or underemployed, while almost half lacked sewage systems and running water. The average income of the poorest 20 percent was lower than that in Colombia, Argentina, Mexico, or Brazil. In comparison with fifty-five other middle-income countries ranked by the World Bank, although Venezuela ranked a fifth in per capita GDP, it was seventeenth in life expectancy, twenty-second in infant mortality (falling below Mexico, which had a per capita income one-third lower), and fortieth in levels of caloric intake (where it fell behind Paraguay, prerevolutionary Nicaragua, Brazil, and Cameroon).[22]

Uneasiness about the future was pervasive. By the early 1970s, signs were readily visible that trouble was on the horizon: growth had slowed considerably, the rate of investment had dropped, and strains on the balance of payments began to manifest themselves in deficits in the current account beginning as early as 1968. Efforts to sow the petroleum notwithstanding, oil still provided 90 percent of export earnings, 65 percent of government income, and 20 percent of GDP (Nolf 1978, 8). But the petroleum industry itself was in a dangerous decline. Because the companies had quietly stopped all exploration and investment, anticipating a planned reversion to national control in 1983, Venezuela, which in 1950 had been the world's second largest producer with 14.4 percent of world production, had dropped to fifth place and accounted for only 4.4 percent by 1975 (Banco Central de Venezuela, *Informe económico,* 1977, 87). Limits to oil-led development loomed on the horizon.

For average citizens, disquiet was reflected in the party system, which showed worrisome signs of fragmentation as voters deserted the two leading parties. Minor parties, which received 3.2 percent of the presidential vote and 8 percent of the congressional vote in 1947, were receiving 40 percent and 46.4 percent, respectively, by 1968 (Consejo Supremo Electoral 1968). This fragmentation was accompanied by the rise of antisystem parties and so-called electoral phenomena: loose organizations that coalesced around the candidacy of one well-known individual. Survey data of the period reveal a growing cynicism about the performance of politicians. For example, Martz and Baloyra (1978) found that although Venezuelans thought highly of the capacity of public officials, less than 20 percent of their respondents evaluated their actual practice in either a positive or very positive fashion. Two-thirds of their respondents viewed politicians in very negative terms, with 81.1 percent claiming that "Venezuelan politicians always lie." The loss of support for parties was greatest among the lower classes, where patronage was least effective.

For policymakers, this uneasiness manifested itself in a pervasive fear that the oil model and consequently Venezuela's treasured stability might be coming to an end. Readjustment meant finding an alternative fiscal basis for the state, but doing so was bound to entail conflict. Despite warnings as early as 1959 that a tax system should be developed to replace petrodollars in anticipation of the dwindling of oil revenues (Shoup 1959), democratic governments had firmly avoided domestic taxation. Why should they tax when, as one IMF adviser observed, "a change of a few dollars in the international price of petroleum would have a much more marked effect on government revenue than a difficult and costly improvement in administrative techniques for [collecting] internal taxes!" (cited in McClure 1991, 56). Vividly recalling that AD's one effort to cover a shortfall in oil revenues by raising taxes, in 1966, had plunged the country into its gravest crisis to date, they were bound to try any other option first. But as a "post-oil" Venezuela seemed to hang over decision-makers like a sword of Damocles, other options were not readily apparent. Little wonder then that the 1973 elections were filled with dire predictions of economic trouble ahead and "the last chance" for Venezuelan democracy.

Venezuela, the poet Thomas Lander once wrote, is a "nation of accomplices." The interaction of the petro-state with pacted democracy turned his prose into reality, as oil helped to create diverse new interests and then underwrote a particular mode of reconciling them. On the one hand, this interaction had beneficial regime effects because it helped to construct and stabilize a new democracy in a country with virtually no previous democratic experience. Regime consolidation rested on a fortunate combination of statecraft and petrodollars: the state's capacity to grant extensive favors and contracts to capitalists while charging the lowest taxes on the continent, permitting some of the highest profits, and supporting a mode of collective bargaining that resulted in the highest wages and food subsidies in Latin America.

On the other hand, this same interaction was pernicious. It postponed having to confront petroleum dependence, reinforced an oil-based trajectory, erected new barriers to change, and further politicized the public sector. In one sense, Venezuela was not different from other populist and distributive regimes that sought to avoid making necessary adjustments by practicing the politics of *deferenda* (Hirschman 1979)— that is, spending lavishly and leaving hard decisions to their successors. But the combination of the petro-state and political pacts definitively set Venezuela apart. Together, they created prolonged incentives for policymakers to avoid conflicts by spending indiscriminately. Meanwhile, their interaction blocked the improvement of state capacity in the critical realm of directing development; it placed a greater premium on the ability of private interests to penetrate and "capture" portions of the state for their own benefit than on the long-term institutionalization of administrative capacity or executive competence.

There was nothing inevitable about this particular interaction between state and regime. At numerous points, the demise of authoritarian rule could have taken a different form: the transition could have occurred through less restricted reform or possibly even revolution; the consolidation could have been characterized by other bargains, a different mix of partial regimes, or more decentralized patterns of decision-making. The designers of democracy could have insisted on parliamentarism rather than presidentialism, continued their early efforts to build an impartial civil service and pass a tax reform, or made agriculture rather than industry the crux of their development model.

Nonetheless, such choices would have been unlikely in the oil-defined Venezuela of the 1960s. Instead, regime norms and practices were institutionalized that reinforced centralization over decentralization, states over markets, preemption over autonomous reaction, restrictiveness over contestation, the purchase of elite support over the autonomous organization of the masses, networks of complicity over broadly debated policies, politicization over administration, and appeasement over hard choices. These practices would define policy behavior in the 1973 boom.

SIX

The Instant Impact of a Bonanza

"Democracia con Energía" proved to be an especially apt campaign slogan for Carlos Andrés Pérez, Acción Democrática's (AD) presidential candidate in the 1973 elections. Tough, disciplined, and hard-working, Pérez had a vigorous dynamism and audacity unmatched by other Venezuelan politicians. His campaign—brilliantly orchestrated by foreign advisers—captured these qualities in countless programmed walks through the cities and villages of the country. His television image was especially effective: moving at a half-run, Pérez swept through the streets of Venezuela, shaking hands, greeting local party functionaries, visiting plazas and radio stations, and leaping mud puddles in the unpaved barrios.[1] Striding across Venezuela, he literally walked his way into the presidency.

But "Democracy with Energy" captured far more than Pérez's vigorous personal style. At the same time that the future president was combing the towns of Venezuela for votes, international oil prices began to soar. In 1973, democracy was indeed linked to energy, but in a manner that even the most astute campaign advisers were unable to foresee. In a mere five years, the Pérez administration would receive more fiscal revenues than did all the other Venezuelan governments since 1917 *combined.* (See Table 6.) Originating in changes in the international oil market, overwhelming, and completely unexpected, the quadrupling of oil prices became the basic underlying factor in the restructuring of political and economic relations that occurred in Venezuela after 1973.

TABLE 6
FISCAL REVENUES OF VENEZUELAN GOVERNMENTS,
1917–1978 (MILLIONS OF BOLIVARES)

Government	Total Income	Average/Year
Gen. J. V. Gómez (1917–35)	476	25
Gen. E. López Contreras (1936–40)	471	94
Gen. I. Medina Angarita (1941–45)	971	194
Acción Democrática (1946–48)	2,337	779
Gen. M. Pérez Jiménez/junta (1949–52)	4,963	1,241
Gen. M. Pérez Jiménez (1953–57)	9,615	1,923
Government junta (1958)	2,713	2,713
Rómulo Betancourt (1959–63)	16,285	3,257
Raúl Leoni (1964–68)	25,573	5,114
Rafael Caldera (1968–73)	36,952	7,390
Subtotal [a]	100,356	
Carlos Andrés Pérez (1974–78) [b]	148,640	29,728
Total Revenues	228,758	45,752

SOURCES: Banco Central de Venezuela (1987b and 1979).
[a] Because inflation was negligible in Venezuela until the early 1970s, revenues are given in current terms until the 1974–1978 period.
[b] Constant 1973 prices.

How these petrodollars would be used depended largely on the "cages" of the past—that is, the economic linkages encouraged by oil-led development, the petro-state with its dynamic of expansion and concentration of power, and pacted democracy with its policy style based on distribution and appeasement. These factors shaped the preferences and behavior of the new president. Together with the specific conjuncture of 1973—the boom, the huge electoral victory of AD, and the widespread belief among policymakers that some reorientation was imperative before oil ran out—these factors generated a strong sense of opportunity for transforming Venezuela and a highly contradictory program of action that could only perpetuate oil-led development.

The following several chapters on Venezuela shift the level of analysis from the broader parameters of states, regimes, and economic models to the level of government decision-making. Above all, they demonstrate the ramifications of how choice has been structured in this oil-exporting country. When the oil boom collided with preexisting institutions and practices, it exacerbated (and even overwhelmed) incentives for "more of the same"—only faster and bigger. But "more of the same, only faster and bigger" accelerated and deepened negative tendencies already present in the polity and economy, while creating new ones. The boom expanded the state's jurisdiction and weakened its already fragile authority; at the same time that the boom loaded new roles and responsibilities onto the state, it undermined any efficacy that had been achieved previously as well as the legitimacy of pacted democracy. Though not understood at the time, the response to the 1973 boom set in motion the gradual destabilization of the polity, which exploded with disastrous consequences almost two decades later, in 1992.

To policymakers in 1973, the oil boom evoked a sense of politics without limits—a once-in-a-lifetime opportunity to restructure the economy and polity. The combination of the oil bonanza and Pérez's massive electoral victory fostered the notion that the government had the political and economic resources to accomplish anything it wanted. Like the Spanish kings centuries before, the government saw aspirations transformed and perceptions altered regarding the feasibility of, and the optimal time horizon for, reaching its goals. Government officials believed that they had an immense opportunity to move the country onto a different development trajectory. As $800 million poured into the treasury each month, the aim of constructing *La Gran Venezuela* replaced a more modest attempt at political and economic reorientation.

With hindsight, the deceptiveness of politics without limits was visible as early as 1974. However welcome Venezuela's new policy setting may have seemed to decision-makers at the time, it left little room for real choice. The boom immediately generated contradictory dynamics. On the one hand, it altered the existing policy agenda by creating an economic imperative to attend to the management problems inherent in a financial bonanza of this magnitude. This imperative required the rapid "repressing" of the circulation of petrodollars, if only to avoid rampant inflation. On the other hand, the boom swelled the aspirations of policymakers, raised expectations, and instantly exacerbated the rent-seeking behavior of actors accustomed to the distributive habits of the past. This cycle made the curtailment of spending highly unlikely.

Instead, the reality of an expanded pie created new "assignment" battles over the allocation of shares between the public and private sectors and between capital and labor; given a policy-setting style based on excessive compromise, these battles created additional new incentives to increase government spending.

True to Venezuela's institutional arrangements, conflicts over the extent and direction of spending were both aimed at and resolved in the office of the presidency. Thus the immediate response to the boom rested primarily with Pérez and his state managers. His decision was predictable: the choice between sterilizing petrodollars for the future use of another politician or building *La Gran Venezuela* on his watch while meeting the clamoring demands of his constituents was virtually no choice at all.

This chapter demonstrates how and why Venezuela's policymakers resolved the tension between sterilizing petrodollars and distributing them. The actions of policymakers in the first six months following the boom are especially significant. They strongly reinforced the existing development trajectory and fixed in place new constraints that determined the rent-seeking behavior of every successive government as well as organized interests. They also provide a clear example of the political and institutional underpinnings of economic phenomena like the Dutch Disease by illustrating the political rationale behind the "irrational" leap in spending and the loss of economic control that took place, not only in Venezuela but also in other oil-exporting countries. Finally, by demonstrating how competing demands arise and their origin within the state, the chapter contradicts the assumption that mass pressures from below explain the rise in expenditures in oil-exporting nations. In Venezuela, as we shall see, elites in both the state and the private sector created a spending explosion—and they did so without strikes, demonstrations, or even effective political-party input.

CHANGING THE PARAMETERS OF STATE POWER

The quadrupling of world petroleum prices in 1973–1974 was without precedent in Venezuelan history. Although the country had experienced other bonanzas with the establishment of the oil enclave, the implementation of the fifty-fifty agreement, and the closing of the Suez Canal, this boom—compressed into several years rather than a decade, and of overwhelming magnitude—was more dramatic than those of the past. Between 1972 and 1975, the average realized price per barrel of

Venezuelan oil jumped from $2.10 to $10.90, an increase of 419 percent! The fiscal income per barrel of exported oil rose from $1.65 to $9.68 in the same period, an increase of 587 percent. International reserves leapt from $1.7 billion to $8.9 billion (Banco Central de Venezuela 1978b).

That the boom instantly transformed the institutional setting for decision-making is indisputable. Its impact on the domestic economy was far-reaching. Between 1972 and 1975 the country's fiscal income more than tripled. By 1976, the per capita fiscal income of Venezuela equaled that of West Germany and was double that of Italy. New revenues brought a 250 percent increase in expenditures in their wake. Because the absolute level of fiscal spending is the single most important indicator affecting the internal economy, this increase had an immediate expansionary effect. Monetary liquidity rose 241 percent from 1972 to 1975, and GDP, aggregate demand, consumer expenditures, and capital formation almost doubled over a mere three years (Table 7).

Overnight all the dimensions of the public sector changed—a reality best appreciated through comparative data. The fiscal income of Venezuela reached close to 40 percent of GDP, which was four times the percentage in Brazil, more than four times the percentage in Mexico, and almost twice the percentage in socialist Yugoslavia in 1976 (Sánchez and Zubillaga 1977, 17). The rapid expansion of the Venezuelan state is also graphically shown through combined central-government financial investment and capital transfers as a percentage of GDP. This measure makes evident the extraordinary new weight of the Venezuelan state in the economy (17.2 percent in 1974), especially when Venezuela is compared with the next largest state, Brazil (3.6 percent), with Mex-

TABLE 7

CHANGES IN THE DIMENSION OF THE ECONOMY,
1972–1975 (MILLIONS OF BOLIVARES)

	1972	1973	1974	1975
Fiscal income	12,546	16,432	42,834	41,001
Internal expenditures	12,618	14,006	24,333	31,491
Liquidity	17,205	21,284	28,047	41,406
GDP	60,608	72,482	111,331	116,351
Aggregate demand	58,303	65,211	83,086	104,976
Consumer expenditures	40,597	43,935	56,391	70,492
Capital formation	15,783	18,616	20,984	30,598

SOURCE: García Araujo (1979).

ico (1.8 percent), or with itself before the boom (3.7 percent) (World Bank, internal memo, 1976).

But the oil boom was not the only factor that changed the institutional setting for decision-making. The December 1973 landslide victory of Pérez altered the distribution of power within the state at the same time. Reversing the historic decline of AD, Pérez captured a resounding 48.7 percent of the vote, rivaling Betancourt's vote in his historic sweep in the 1958 elections.[2] The scope of the AD victory was unprecedented: it swept the legislature, gaining 28 of the 49 seats in the Senate and 102 of the 203 seats in the Chamber of Deputies. It also won control of every state government except Zulia's.

Pérez's stunning electoral triumph effectively smashed past patterns of interaction between the executive and the Congress by removing the necessity to form interparty or intraparty alliances to obtain working majorities in the Congress. Prior to 1973, every president had been forced to seek compromises with Congress. Although Congress was historically weak, its relative strength in each successive administration was determined by coalition building and by whether the majority party was also the president's party (Kelley 1977, 40). This created a more active legislature, provided some checks on the executive, and led to an eventual agreement between COPEI and AD to minimize the tensions between the president and Congress. But the wide margin of Pérez's victory meant that neither coalitional constraints nor minority status in Congress could restrain presidential power; thus, virtually all political limitations on the office of the presidency were removed. Since AD maintained a majority in both houses, opposition parties could not influence Pérez by offering or withholding support for specific policies. Furthermore, because all of AD's members were constrained by party discipline, individual dissidents were bound to vote the official line. Given the structure of the state and its regime rules, only the regular holding of elections, the no-reelection clause in the Constitution, the influence wielded by the government party over its new leader, and Pérez's own character could act as checks on executive hegemony. With the exception of constitutional constraints, which would not become effective for five years, these other checks never became operative.

The exuberant personality of the man who won the 1973 elections was certainly no brake on presidentialism. At first glance, the new president matched the profile of a typical Old Guard *adeco*—one who put his party above other concerns.[3] But Pérez's political career was exceptional.[4] A generation younger than other members of the party Old

Guard, he was never a member of their inner club. As the protégé and personal secretary of Betancourt, his relationship to other party members was complex; his personal fortunes ebbed and flowed with the influence of Betancourt, who publicly proclaimed him "the son I never had."[5] Ironically, Pérez's political future was assured with AD's defeat by COPEI in the 1968 elections. Working tirelessly to rebuild the demoralized and splintered organization, he became secretary general and, once party president Gonzalo Barrios had renounced any intention of running for office, the party's candidate for president. He accepted the position while maintaining his wariness of many of the party Old Guard.

Pérez's strong personality reinforced party factionalism. Although distancing him from party professionals and weakening his ties of obligation to them, it also helped him build his own network of loyalties. Confident because he received far more votes than the polls had predicted, he no longer considered himself a protégé. His charisma was legendary. He spoke of his dream of *La Gran Venezuela* and saw the petrodollar boom as a providential sign—one that bid him to propel his country out of underdevelopment and into the twentieth century. His frequent use of Bolivarian symbols enhanced the view that he was *the* leader capable of seizing the opportunity facing his country. Within a few months he had managed to link his future electoral success to the ultimate achievement of economic independence, development, social justice, and democracy.

The president's desire to limit one faction's influence on the administration surfaced quickly in the aftermath of the elections. The Pérez team, convinced that the AD victory was due almost entirely to the charisma of the candidate, believed the president could legitimately appoint cabinet members from outside the party. After minimal consultation with the Old Guard, Pérez filled only ten of the eighteen cabinet positions with party members; the other eight were awarded to independents personally loyal to the president, including Gumersindo Rodríguez, the controversial new Minister of Planning.[6] The selection of the cabinet precipitated one of the many bitter disagreements between the Pérez administration and members of the party that were to characterize the next five years.

The composition of the cabinet was the first indication that Pérez would choose the route of highly personalistic rule over party government, and this choice had immediate policy consequences. The creation of a small inner circle of "president's men" narrowed the already slim scope of critical evaluation and debate in the formulation of policy, and it contributed to the concentration of power in the executive. The strong personality of the president and the backing of his closest associates presented a formidable front to those who might disagree with him in the cabinet. Criticism was not encouraged. Thus, the presidency, now more centralized than ever, also grew increasingly removed from competing ideas.

Thus, even before Pérez began to formulate or implement his plans, the policy setting had changed substantially. The oil boom expanded fiscal resources, the dimensions of the economy, and the boundaries of the public sector. The election results altered the balance between the executive and the Congress in favor of the president and contributed to the weakening of ties between the president and his party. Pérez's aggressive and messianic personal style, his access to enormous financial resources, and his extraordinary popularity all contributed to the concentration of power. Yet the dangers of this situation were far from visible in 1974. Many citizens and much of the press viewed Pérez's success as the nation's success and his hopes as the nation's hopes. As an editorial in *El Nacional* (March 11, 1974, D1), a leading newspaper in Caracas, proclaimed: "Today in Venezuela, CAP [Pérez] is the image of the man on the move.... In Venezuela, to move means to make something a reality, to make it count, to make it known, make it happen. 'Ese hombre sí camina!' [This man *moves!*] And, yes, it is possible to move at his side, opening the pathway to *La Gran Venezuela.*"

BUILDING *LA GRAN VENEZUELA*

The oil boom transformed the scope and scale of Pérez's agenda. Backed by his ministers, the president immediately decided to embark on a vast and bold development plan, the most important single decision of his administration. He reminisced (interview, 1979):

> The decision to build a modern industrialized economy was mine. There were others who wanted to move more slowly. But we had to take advantage of this moment given to us, pull Venezuela out of her underdevelopment, and propel her into the twentieth century. There was no real decision to make. This had to be done—and quickly. We couldn't lose time. We even began without a plan because we had already decided what we were going to do.

What was new about the model was its huge scale and its emphasis on accelerated development; otherwise it was an extension of the resource-based development plans of the past. To Pérez, the need for urgency and scale stemmed from a variety of factors: the new financial power of the state; the pressing need to address the problems of growth, diversification, and equity stemming from petrolization; the removal of controls over the executive branch; his own overwhelming popularity; and the persistent fear that oil was running out soon. An opportunity of this sort was unlikely to present itself again. Although Pérez's vision of development would not be specified until it was incorporated into the Fifth National Plan two years later, the word was out: the government was going to build fast and big.

The plan to construct *La Gran Venezuela* had two basic elements: fighting poverty by expanding demand through a combination of price controls, income increases, employment creation, and social services, and diversifying the country's export structure while deepening import substitution. The core of this model, derived from the linkages already fostered by petroleum, lay in the expansion and nationalization of basic industry, especially petrochemicals, aluminum, and steel. Growing directly from the development strategies of the past, this model assumed that Venezuela should concentrate on industries for processing domestic mineral resources as well as highly energy-intensive industries in order to take advantage of its plentiful electricity and fuel, abundant mineral wealth, and favorable geographic location in relation to the U.S. market (CORDIPLAN 1976). By 1976, of the total public investment of 118.2 billion bolívares foreseen in the Fifth Plan, close to 60 percent was intended to be spent in mining and petroleum, electricity, and manufacturing. Despite the fact that these same strategies for public investment in capital-intensive and large-scale industry had not resolved unemployment and equity problems in the past, planners believed that plentiful petrodollars meant that they would succeed.

The cornerstone of the industrialization drive was the soon-to-be-nationalized oil industry. Facing only twenty years of proven reserves, seven to ten years of easily accessible light crude, and no major new discoveries since the oil companies stopped looking in 1958, Venezuela threatened to be the first OPEC country to face a day of reckoning. Because of the neglect of the companies as they prepared for nationalization, production capacity had declined dramatically, although every proven method of secondary recovery had been used to coax oil from reluctant wells.

Long-term hope lay in the Orinoco Oil Belt, the world's largest accumulation of nonconventional oil, which was conservatively estimated at 1.8 trillion barrels. But before this deposit could be exploited, billions of dollars would have to be invested in technology that could strip the heavy crude of its high sulfur and metal content. In order to begin to develop this "sleeping giant," General Alfonzo Ravard, president of Petróleos de Venezuela (PETROVEN), estimated that investments in petroleum would have to increase from a planned 1.2 billion bolívares in 1976 to a whopping 7 billion bolívares by 1980 (interview, 1978). Thus the first use of petrodollars would be to guarantee the life of the industry for the future.

Steel was the second priority. Despite the fact that Venezuela's first large steel mill had scarcely become productive after twenty years, the Fifth Plan eventually called for a sharp increase from the current capacity of 1.2 million tons to 9.8 million tons produced in two new plants: SIDOR Plan IV and ZULIA. The next largest program was the expansion of the Guri Dam to exploit Venezuela's huge hydroelectric reserves; this program was aimed at quadrupling capacity. Spurred by discoveries of a large bauxite deposit, aluminum was added to petrochemicals as another priority. Smaller investment programs were eventually drawn up for nickel, cement, pulp and paper, the assembly of small aircraft, and other industrial activities.

Pérez's strategy grew directly from past development efforts in that it continued to emphasize resource-based development at the expense of agriculture and other priorities. But, thanks to the oil boom, it differed in several important respects. First, it stressed an accelerated transformation of the economy—that is, it sought to compress twenty years of industrialization into a mere five or ten. Second, it was extremely ambitious. In gross public and private fixed investment, what eventually became the Fifth National Plan was double the size of the Fourth Plan. This *gigantismo* was specifically encouraged by the executive branch. State planners were frequently told that the projects they had designed were too modest and were encouraged to "think big."[7] Large capital-intensive projects were favored over everything else. Thus, whereas Rafael Caldera's Fourth National Plan had targeted 35.4 percent of public investment for education, housing, health, urbanization, and government services, the Fifth Plan cut this percentage to 19.9.[8]

Finally, the development strategy marked a conscious effort to expand the jurisdiction of the petro-state by challenging the boundaries between public and private enterprise that had been established during the transition to democracy. When the Fifth Plan was unveiled in 1976, it called for an increase in the public share of gross fixed investment of 53.2 percent, an impressive jump from the 1970–1974 average of 32 percent (CORDIPLAN 1976, 3). Public investment was aimed most exclusively at the basic industries, but it would also enter manufacturing sectors that had previously been dominated by private capital (CORDIPLAN 1976, 45). Private capital was limited to no more than 20 percent ownership in the production of basic materials; it could own up to 40 percent of enterprises manufacturing secondary-stage products.[9] These rules reaffirmed and strengthened the state's role in controlling the decisive stages of the production process and the orientation of the economy as a whole. They also created an important new source of economic and political power for the government.

What is perhaps most striking about the development strategy announced in the wake of the boom is the total lack of debate surrounding it. Because it deviated so little from past patterns, it seemed the logical and natural step to take. There were virtually no discussions over the optimal scale or speed of the model, nor were alternative strategies for investing the oil bonanza ever advanced. No one made the case for developing agriculture as the country's top priority; no one insisted on taking seriously the obvious inflationary dangers of moving rapidly; no one questioned whether Venezuela had the labor skills to expand resource-based industrialization at the planned pace; no one challenged the notion that the state could effectively be everywhere at once. Given the consensus for state-led industrialization that had been forged during the transition to democracy and the tradition of ultra-presidentialism, which was heightened by Pérez's overwhelming popularity, the president's proposals were accepted without question. Only Pérez Alfonzo warned that oil prices might not continue to rise in the future and argued that Venezuela should drastically cut oil production until it could productively absorb the revenues from the boom. But his was a lonely voice of opposition.

THE SPECIAL POWERS ACT

The oil boom shaped more than the economic aspirations of the new government; it also had an immediate impact on Venezuela's political arrangements by creating a crisis situation that ultimately undermined the *pactismo* of the past. When Pérez was sworn in on March 12, 1974, euphoria was replaced by a sense of emergency. With so much money entering the treasury every month, the fear of inflation quickly supplanted all other concerns. Opinion polls indicated that inflation was the number one issue in the public mind (*El Nacional*, March 3, 1974, D4). Although the rising cost of living had not yet reached 5 percent per annum—a remarkably low statistic by Latin American standards at the time—Venezuelans were accustomed to a 1–2 percent inflation rate, and they wanted to return to that standard (Banco Central de Venezuela 1979, 291). The boom brought menacing indications to the contrary. In one of his first public pronouncements, the new Minister of Finance, Hector Hurtado, warned that if action were not taken immediately, the extra oil income "could become a block of ice that would end up melting on us" (quoted in Fuad 1974, 8).

With Hurtado's warning in mind, Pérez set to work at a frenetic pace. In the first 100 days of his presidency alone, he announced an avalanche of decrees, resolutions, and draft laws—issued at the rate of nearly two a day. He immediately declared a ninety-day price freeze on all goods and services. This was an emergency measure, his government claimed, implemented in order to slow down the rising cost of living. Predictably, the price freeze was applauded by the trade unions and the political parties, and opposed, albeit weakly, by Fedecámaras. This attempt to regulate the cost of living was followed by a host of other measures aimed at winning popular support, including the formation of a commission to study the nationalization of petroleum. These early actions, announced with great fanfare, added to the president's fund of political and economic resources. By April, reputed to have the support of over 75 percent of the population, he was undoubtedly the most popular leader in Venezuela's contemporary history.[10]

A mere forty-eight days after taking office, the president drew on his fund of popularity. Invoking the precedent of Betancourt's actions during the outbreak of guerrilla war, he went before Congress on April 29, 1974, to request "extraordinary executive authority" to enable him to confront the challenges of the oil boom. Specifically, Pérez asked for the authority to implement a package of important economic and financial measures including a reform of the income-tax system, a complete reorganization of public financial institutions, and an across-the-board wage and salary hike. Like each president before him, he wanted to raise the taxes of the foreign oil companies, but, unlike his predecessors, he called for the nationalization of the foreign-owned iron ore industry and the formation of a commission to study the nationalization of petroleum. A drastic package of this sort, he claimed as he stood before Congress, required drastic action: he asked the legislature to grant him special powers (Pérez 1974).

The president's public rationale for the Special Powers Act was based on the crisis provoked by the oil boom. Venezuela faced major political and economic dislocations that would affect the living standards of workers, peasants, and the middle class (Pérez 1974). "The government," Pérez claimed, "cannot develop its plans efficiently through normal channels. . . . The complexity of the problems, the need to make daily decisions on a variety of matters, the urgency in their execution . . . make the ways of ordinary legislation inconvenient."[11] In effect, the boom had created demands for the acceleration of policymaking and new channels of decision-making.

The private rationale may have been somewhat different. To the president's chief aides, the request for special powers was based on an ambitious vision. According to one cabinet member (interview, 1978):

> We had this new conception of development, a plan to pull Venezuela into the twentieth century, and we had a state that resembled the old schemes and conceptions. We didn't have time to talk about every idea, every decree. We had to get that state moving, . . . build a new one, get around limitations. We wanted the Special Powers [Act] because we had plans to carry out quickly .

Privately, several cabinet members cited Pérez's personal impatience with the delays inherent in observing administrative norms as the chief motivation for the Special Powers Act. One top presidential adviser explained (interview, 1978):

> You know the president's style. He wanted action, speed, plans, ideas. He fired out orders and wanted to see results. We kept preparing laws, *proyectos de leyes,* and decrees, but he would get impatient. He was frustrated with having to go to Congress for everything. He wanted a modern style of administration with technicians carrying out the plans. The Special Powers Act gave him what he wanted. We all thought it was a good idea .

For some, there was yet another rationale. One minister, describing his own motivations rather than those of Pérez, questioned the desirability and utility of the democratic system for a developing country (interview, 1978):

> Frankly, I don't believe that the democratic system is the only way—or even the best way—out of underdevelopment. In fact, I would say that we may do better with another type of system. But my interpretation of the Special Powers Act is that it allowed us to get around the slowness and the restrictions. Congress is just a restriction here. The president needed decree power . . . so that he could preserve democracy in the end.

The Special Powers Act, in their view, would allow the President to carry out his goals, whatever they might be, as rapidly as possible.

Not surprisingly, Pérez's request sparked an immediate uproar in Congress. Because his proposed bill granted executive authority to intervene in almost every area of the nation's economic and financial life without restraint, the opposition, led by COPEI, immediately raised cries of usurpation. Initial controversy centered around the legality of the proposal, but Pérez was easily able to demonstrate that the 1961 Constitution permitted the executive "to dictate extraordinary measures in economic and financial matters when required by the public interest and when the Executive has received authorization through a special law" (Article 190, Section 8).

The congressional struggle over the Special Powers Act, however, evoked issues of democratization far more fundamental than the interpretation of a particular law. At stake was the indispensable equilibrium between the executive and the congress, on the one hand, and between the dominant political parties, on the other—an equilibrium that had been designed through *pactismo*. COPEI insisted that the president's desire for power, not the international crisis, lay at the root of his request; external events were merely a justification for an unwarranted measure.[12] To the opposition, the viability of democracy was at stake. If the president could not plan the country's development in conjunction with Congress, especially one dominated by his own party, then he was in effect claiming that efficiency was not compatible with democracy.

The real controversy was over the future of *pactismo*. From the opposition's point of view, the Special Powers Act was a violation of the practices initiated in 1958 and a bid for hegemony on the part of AD Fernández explained:

> This is the only institutional tribunal that the opposition currently has in the country. If these powers are awarded as they are envisioned in this law, we might as well talk about the flora and fauna of South Africa here instead of the important problems which affect the life and development of the country. It isn't conceivable that a democratic party can put forward a formula by which it removes the only institutional tribunal that the opposition has to formulate its opinions and ideas. This is indispensable to the political balance which exists between the government and the opposition, an equilibrium which will surely be compromised if the law presented by the National Executive is approved (Fernández 1974).

But on May 31, 1974, an AD-dominated Congress overrode the objections of COPEI and awarded President Pérez "extraordinary executive authority." Only COPEI and the Movimiento Electoral del Pueblo (MEP) voted against the law. In a surprising move, congressional representatives from the far right and from the major parties of the left—the Movimiento al Socialismo (MAS), the MIR, and the Communist Party—supported the president's proposal.

The Special Powers Act was a decisive turning point in Venezuelan politics. First, it altered norms of *pactismo* and replaced them with a precedent for power grabs. Rather than making a conciliatory gesture toward the Christian Democrats after their defeat at the polls, Pérez had used his victory to increase their isolation and feelings of impotence. COPEI was forced into the only remaining viable political role— a vehement and increasingly radical opposition. From this moment until democracy foundered in 1992, relations between the parties would never return to their former level. Second, and more significant for policymaking in the short run, the Special Powers Act weakened AD's control over its own government. Because Pérez no longer had to consult Congress, his government was also freed from the formal necessity of consulting its own party.[13]

By changing the relationship between the two major parties, and between the government and its party, the Special Powers Act broke the trust that had regulated conflict in the past and replaced it with an enduring atmosphere of confrontation. The founders of democracy, Betancourt and Caldera, made repeated efforts to soften tensions between the parties by holding strategic "summits" in the years ahead, but to no avail. Unlimited financial resources had laid the basis for unlimited executive authority, at least temporarily, and they provided a rationale for permanently altering the party system. Whatever the intention, the results were apparent. In the words of one astute observer, "Pérez obtained what Napoleon Bonaparte won on the 18th Brumaire—and in passing he got the *adecos* off his back" (*El Nacional*, June 12, 1974, D1).

ECONOMIC POLICY UNDER EXECUTIVE DECREE

From May 31, 1974, to June 1, 1975, President Pérez ruled Venezuela by decree. He appeared to have total authority to carry out the dual goals of containing the revenues from the oil boom and improving the lot of the poor through the implementation of a new development model. But if "politics without limits" created the impression within the administration that anything was possible, the reality proved different. Shortly after taking the initiative to liberally spread petrodollars to his electoral constituency, the president was forced to meet the growing demands of an entrenched capitalist class accustomed to being appeased through subsidies. Plans to retain control over government spending went rapidly out the window, and the cost of Venezuela's development strategy began to shoot up as rent-seeking interests clamored for more.

However, some efforts to "repress" oil revenues were made through two mechanisms. First, Pérez ordered a reduction in the level of oil production from its average of 3.4 million barrels per day in 1973 to 3.0 in 1974, and, eventually, 2.3 in 1975; similarly, oil exports dropped from an average of 2.1 million barrels per day in 1973 to 1.8 million in 1974 and to 1.5 million in 1975 (Banco Central de Venezuela, *Informe económico*, 1975, A-175). Even though this reduction went against rational cartel behavior for defending the price of petroleum because it helped maintain the price at its overly inflated level, it did lower the revenues entering the country. More important, it protected the ailing oil industry because it slowed the process of depreciation of equipment and inventories, which was strained to the limit by the companies' disinvestment policies.

Second, the government established the Fondo de Inversiónes de Venezuela (FIV), an innovative financial institution whose chief purpose was to prevent the petrodollars from entering the domestic economy. The fund maintained the value of Venezuela's earnings through investments in the exterior until they could be gradually and profitably introduced into the country. The FIV also took on the role of financing international cooperation with other developing countries that had been hurt by the oil-price increase, primarily by funneling aid to Central America and the Caribbean. Originally intended to receive half the total income from petroleum through the entire five-year period of the administration, the FIV was initially established with assets of $3.23 billion (Hurtado 1974).

The government then sought a wide-ranging tax reform to compensate for "repressed" petrodollars and to lay a diversified fiscal base for the future. The brainchild of Finance Minister Hurtado, the proposals that were initially floated encompassed sweeping changes in the income-tax law, increases in customs and levies and the inheritance tax, and a business and property tax. The idea was that ultimately taxes would "replace" petrodollars in the national budget.

But from the beginning this plan to sterilize petrodollars was in trouble. The very whisper of tax increases in the midst of the most massive boom in history set up howls of protest, even from within the government. Furthermore, the establishment of the FIV damaged prospects for maintaining fiscal control. Because Pérez insisted on ensuring the FIV's ability to function in the exterior, its income was not subject to the budgetary oversight traditionally exercised by the finance ministry and the Congress. Thus FIV's income would not be distributed through normal budgetary channels and would instead fall under the direct supervision of the president.[14] The finance ministry, one of the most highly respected state entities, therefore lost oversight over enormous sums of public monies as well as its overview of total government expenditures. Only the president could now force the FIV to play its required role of repressing petrodollars.

But Pérez, turning his attention to the promises of his electoral campaign, showed no signs of thrift. Convinced that the way to fight poverty was to overcome the impasse in Venezuela's process of import-substitution industrialization, he adopted a series of costly measures aimed at broadening the market by bolstering the purchasing power of the masses. He decreed the first legal minimum wage in Venezuela's history—fifteen bolívares ($3.50) per day for all but domestic workers—which raised the general wages of nonunion workers between one-third and one-half over their previous level.[15] The minimum wage was immediately followed by a nationwide across-the-board pay increase, which ranged from 5 to 25 percent for employees earning less than five thousand bolívares per month. Salary and wage hikes applied to all employees in the public sector, the private sector, and the armed forces.[16]

Pérez also began to create jobs by decree, especially inside the state. In a mere five years, the number of white-collar fixed-position employees working for the national government almost doubled, jumping from 153,971 to over 300,000.[17] In order to circumvent new restrictions against partisan stacking of the state bureaucracy established in the Ley de Carrera Administrativa of 1970, Pérez issued Decree 211, which permitted the administration to increase the number of nonclassified public employees as well as the number of positions of *confianza,* or political appointments. By drastically augmenting the number of employees excluded from the Civil Service Law, the president obtained almost unlimited authority to fire people as well as to create positions for his supporters.[18] The growth of the state bureaucracy and the higher wages granted by the general wage and salary increase were reflected in the expenditures for personnel in the budget, a figure that almost tripled between 1973 and 1979 (Banco Central de Venezuela 1979, 85).

The culmination of Pérez's costly populist decrees was the Law against Unjustified Dismissals, which hit the business community like a bomb and created the first sustained opposition to his policies.[19] An outgrowth of the administration's fears that employees in private industry would lose their jobs as a result of mandatory wage increases, it protected employees against dismissal by making the process of firing both difficult and costly for the employer.[20] Threatening in an especially effective public-relations campaign that this law was an attack on free enterprise that would provoke disinvestment and capital flight (Fedecámaras 1974, 319–340), Fedecámaras accused the government of interfering with the prerogatives of private management. Businessmen decried the new government's frenetic policy style and its *decretomania,* which had already turned a favorable investment climate into a highly uncertain atmosphere.[21] Fedecámaras demanded that the government clarify its intentions toward business and threatened to provoke a recession in the midst of plenty if the concerns of capitalists were not assuaged.

Surprised by the vehemence of the private sector's response, the government initially refused to meet its demands, but soon disillusioned barrio dwellers, nonunionized workers, and others in the popular sector added their complaints to those of business. The president's actions had raised the purchasing power of all Venezuelans, but this increase had occurred without planning. Because the productive structure could not respond quickly enough and imports were not readily available, by September serious shortages of basic items such as black beans and eggs plagued the market. As prices soared, capital began to flee the country, and investment slackened well below normal postelection levels. Pérez's popularity began to plunge. According to one private polling agency, his approval rating dropped from 75 to 30 percent between March and August.[22]

In this context, the president took the classic path of appeasement and spread petrodollar wealth to his strongest critics. On September 5, 1974, in a major policy address, Pérez announced a number of new measures that represented a distinct shift away from the populist objectives of the past six months and toward the satisfaction of the private sector (Pérez 1974, 509). Rather than emphasize demand creation, the administration stated that it would henceforth make growth and productivity its central priority by providing huge subsidies to capitalists. Instead of raising their taxes, Pérez granted new widespread exemptions to stimulate growth, including tax deductions of up to 20 percent for investments (*Gaceta oficial extraordinaria,* no. 1.681, September 2, 1974, Decree 330), a modification of the General Banking Law to facilitate business lending (Decree 343), and tax exemptions to the construction industry for a period of ten years (*Gaceta oficial extraordinaria,* no. 30.491, September 4, 1974, Decree 346). Similar important exemptions were given to agriculture, ranching, fishing, and forestry (Decree 276), as well as to tourism (Decree 377), export industries (Decree 378), electricity and transport (Decree 379). The most significant part of the new economic package was the immediate activation of two new credit funds to finance industry and agriculture. These funds, which would each be given one billion dollars over a five-year period, provided low-cost and long-term loans to business, which complemented the $3.2 billion set aside for both state and private industry in the FIV.

The planned net transfer of resources to the private sector was enormous. When combined with the previously established CORPOINDUS-TRIA for small- and medium-sized industry, the soon to be created Urban Development Fund for the construction industry (Hurtado 1974), and the newly reinforced CVF, Venezuelan Industrial Bank, and regional development corporations, it reached an unprecedented level. Although exact figures are not available, the enormity of the state's direct transfers to the private sector can be appreciated best through a comparison of the performances of one agency. In its entire thirty-year history (1946–1975), the CVF—the state's most important credit agency for the private sector—had transferred $2.3 billion in credit to the private sector (Corporación Venezolana de Fomento 1976, 3). In a mere five years, the industrial and agrarian credit funds alone were slated to provide half that amount, and net transfers from all other public development agencies would far surpass it.

The new funds to promote industry and agriculture provided a substantial boost to the banking sector as well. In order to avoid setting up a national financial network to administer credits, the Pérez administration decided to use already existing state and private institutions, which, in its view, would facilitate the awarding of credits. Although the new institutions would make use of state financial agencies, they would also rely heavily on private banks, thereby subsidizing them as well. Given the increase in money flows through these institutions, the earnings of the banks rose precipitously.[23]

Finally, to further assuage the private sector, Pérez announced the Law for the Protection of the Consumer to replace his former system of price controls and made known his intention to shelve a proposed antimonopoly law. Specific subsidies were promised in the production of foods such as corn, wheat, beans, sugar, and milk, but only those items judged indispensable for a basic diet, and defined as such in the law, would be strictly regulated. Many other items would be freed entirely from controls or only partially regulated. Because the law regulated items product by product, it strengthened the discretionary power of the government, but, by removing many products from regulation altogether, it pleased the private sector. Most significantly, the new law was adopted after a high level of consultation between the administration and business. Although entrepreneurs would have no say in the actual decision to set prices, they would be able to have significant input into the drafting of future regulations—the first representation of business in price-control legislation since 1946.[24]

The private sector was elated over the president's shift of emphasis in economic policy. Although it was unable to change the Law against Unjustified Dismissals, it won a substantial share of the petrodollar surplus and gained a new level of representation in economic policymaking. In the weeks following Pérez's September 5 speech, newspapers were filled with declarations of renewed confidence in and support for the administration, and Fedecámaras expressed full support for Pérez, proclaiming its "profound satisfaction" over the new measures *(El Nacional,* September 14, 1974, D1).

But the net effect of moving between its own populist and expansionist impulses and the demands of organized capitalists was predictable: government spending soared out of control precisely when repressing petrodollars was the only means of avoiding Dutch Disease and other adverse consequences. During the year of the Special Powers Act alone, government expenditures almost tripled (CORDIPLAN 1979b, 18). Permitting state expenditures to rise massively, abruptly, without a plan, and with no clear relationship to productivity was the single most important (non)decision of the government. An action that could never be reversed, it immediately changed the dimensions of the domestic economy, set off a "boom effect" that could not be contained, and accustomed some Venezuelans to a standard of living that could not be sustained.

To foreigners observing Pérez's economic policies, the government's actions seemed irrational. How could planners, worried about the dangers of inflation and the prospects of oil running out shortly, have set off a spending spree unprecedented in Venezuela history? But what appears to be a profoundly contradictory, expensive, and self-defeating policy from the outside was rational to Venezuelan policymakers both determined and apparently possessing the means to diversify the economy while assuaging entrenched interests who might threaten "the last chance for democracy." True, government planners did not take into account the huge rise in demands on state revenues that soon came from Venezuelan capitalists, nor did they expect the proliferation of rent-seeking demands that shall become evident in the next chapter. But even so, in the heady days of the boom, there appeared to be enough for all organized interests. From these policymakers' perspective, to act otherwise would have been politically difficult. In the context of plenty, there was simply insufficient motivation to do otherwise.

The rise in public spending set in motion during the first year of the boom was the catalyst for a series of negative effects on the economy, the government, the regime, and the state. At the government level, politics without limits produced a "paradox of popularity" (Quick 1980). Because the president appeared to have total power and, for a short time total support, programs went unchallenged and mechanisms of accountability did not function. In its first critical year of government, the administration was never forced to set priorities, define programs, or produce concrete proposals. Given the wide range of needs in this underdeveloped country, any idea could be justified in terms of some goal. Lacking the benefit of adversaries who could force clarification, the president and his advisers were free to adopt multiple, ambiguous, overly ambitious, and often contradictory objectives without constraints.[25] For them, everything could be a priority. Yet, if everything is a priority, there are in fact no priorities at all.

But everything was not a priority. The changes *not* made in the year of decree power—the roads not taken—are eloquent testimony to how difficult it can be to go against the structural grain. Despite the government's initial proposal of a wide-ranging tax reform that would extract significant state revenues from domestic economic activity for the first time, it never used its decree powers to implement a redistributive income tax. An antimonopoly law designed to break up the private sector's oligopolistic structure quietly disappeared. Most important, although the Pérez administration created the FIV with the intention of preventing petrodollars from entering the domestic economy, the FIV never received fully half of the oil revenues as mandated, and it received no new petrodollars at all after 1975.

At the regime level, deconsolidation set in at the very moment when the oil-price increase thrust new tensions and responsibilities onto the political system. The boom—in itself an unusual crisis of wealth—gave rise to an unusual political response. Petrodollars resurrected populism, a frequent Latin American response to crisis, and undermined *pactismo*. Populism—the prominence of a single personality over a party, the confusion between the aims of a leader and the aims of a nation, the appeal to traditionally subordinate social classes and groups, and the exercise of arbitrary rule—increasingly came to challenge the institutions of pacted democracy. Such a challenge was easy in a country with a long *caudillo* tradition. Even AD, the principal founder of democracy, acquiesced in the expansion of presidential power, the weakening of Congress, and the embittering of party relations without ever seriously questioning the need for the Special Powers Act. Yet with the exception of the creation of the FIV, virtually every other measure could have been submitted to and passed by the AD-dominated Congress without generating the dislocations caused by these extraordinary measures.

At the state level, the types of policies adopted in this period changed the institutional setting for policymaking by disrupting traditional forms of public-sector organization and exacerbating the gap between jurisdiction and authority. Two examples mentioned in this chapter stand out especially: the decision to create the FIV outside all preexisting financial controls and the decision to change the Civil Service Code to permit a radical increase in political appointees just when the state needed to be most efficient. Carrying out these policies in the climate of uncertainty created by *decretomania* only heightened the sense of disruption, lack of accountability, and loss of control, at the very moment when effective administrative performance was especially critical.

Other barriers to success would become obvious down the road, as it became apparent that the development strategy of the Pérez administration was based on a set of dubious assumptions. Foremost among them was the belief that all difficulties could be overcome, that bigger and faster meant better, and that labor, equipment, and know-how could be imported from outside. The plan anticipated a continuous rise in oil revenues to cover the vast expenditures being initiated, despite the fact that high prices had already attracted the entry of Mexican and North Sea oil into the market. The plan rested on the belief that a consumption binge could be avoided, that the existing industrial infrastructure could support a rapid expansion of demand, that agriculture was less important than industry, that corruption could be curtailed, and that inflation could be contained. It assumed that state ownership and control necessarily meant a progressive redistribution of the benefits of modernization. Finally, it presupposed the existence of sufficient institutional and managerial capacity in the state to administer newly gained wealth with the criteria of scarcity. Each of these assumptions would prove to be false.

SEVEN

The Politics of Rent Seeking

Had Venezuela possessed a relatively coherent bureaucracy, a functioning civil service, routinized tasks, and standard operating procedures, its public institutions should have been able to place some barriers to halt the contradictory demands and gigantic programs put forward in the first year of the Pérez administration. But such actions should not be expected from a petro-state. Instead, the state, already characterized by weak authority structures and high levels of politicization, was thrown into turmoil by the deluge of petrodollars. The rapid proliferation of new state agencies with ill-defined jurisdictions simply compounded the problem. But even without this additional confusion, the components of the petro-state had never been designed to rein in executive power. To the contrary, as we have seen, they had been explicitly structured to promote centralization, rent seeking, and obedience to presidential authority—and this is precisely what they continued to do.

One of the great ironies of petro-states is that administrative reform, so often put forward to correct inefficiency, instead can become a mechanism for the further deterioration of state capacity. The reason is evident: because the petro-state is the center of accumulation, reform has the potential for setting up different filtering processes for organized interests—a new set of "selective mechanisms," in Offe's (1973, 1974) terms, which can insulate policymakers from certain interests and tie them even more closely to others. Thus when Venezuela's president announced a broad administrative reform to complement his ambitious development plans, the understanding began to dawn that the administration's notion of *reforma del estado*, which encompassed reforms of the state-enterprise system, the planning apparatus, and the rules of access to decision-making, actually meant a remaking of the state—that is, a whole new design for economic policymaking that differed from the basic pacts of the past.

Changing the rules of the game in the midst of a boom added to the chaos and lack of economic control. Because these reforms would govern access to the state, which ultimately meant access to the petrodollar bonanza flowing into the public coffer, proposing them stimulated the rent-seeking behavior so ingrained in Venezuelan economic and political life. On the one hand, capitalists, both as a class and as individual entrepreneurs, sought to shape the reforms so as to facilitate most easily their exploitation of the public sector. On the other hand, state officials attempted to further concentrate authority as well as rentier opportunities in their own hands by orchestrating the entire public sector as well as business-government relations through the office of the president. The end result was the formation of a new clique composed of certain private interests and high-level public officials which aimed at capturing, if not pilfering, public revenues. In effect, the nature of administrative reform turned the petro-state into the subject and object of predation.

Challenging the existing rules of the game by throwing into question previously established boundaries and norms had economic and political costs. Although some of the proposals described in this chapter were never implemented, the attempt to remake the petro-state in the name of technocratic efficiency further politicized the accumulation process, disorganized public agencies, exacerbated the gap between the formal jurisdiction and actual capacity of the state, and marked the end of *pactismo*. The demise of party collaboration was most evident in the sharp rise in factionalism, both within and among parties, and in the unmistakable deterioration in economic policymaking that occurred during these years. The oil boom did not create the dynamics of rent seeking, state disorganization, and regime decay, but it exacerbated this cycle acutely.

This chapter traces the cycle of rent seeking and political deterioration that set in during Pérez's first government and became a permanent feature of the regime. These events are important for two reasons. First, they set in motion the pattern of political behavior that formed the backdrop of the democratic crisis of 1992. The blatant awarding of rent seeking and the failure to sanction corruption at the highest levels undermined the legitimacy of pacted democracy and its capacity to set any coherent economic policy. Indeed, the moral decay and economic mismanagement that provoked two coup attempts years later have their origins in this period. Second, these events show how attempts at institutional reform can reinforce a perverse development trajectory and how, in turn, this trajectory can shape political institutions so that the states designed to exploit petroleum themselves become the object of plunder.

THE EMERGENCE OF STATE REFORM

Reforming the state, though by no means a new idea in Venezuela, was given fresh salience by the oil boom.[1] The boom, combined with Pérez's statist predilections, brought about an astounding growth of state enterprises and other administrative entities.[2] Many of these enterprises were huge, especially Petróleos de Venezuela (PETROVEN), which after nationalization became the ninth largest oil company and the sixteenth largest industrial firm in the world (Randall 1987, 46). They played key roles in petroleum, mining, electricity and water, industrial finance, educational and research services. Statistics illustrate their importance. By 1976, state-owned mining and petroleum firms provided a full 85 percent of total central-government revenues, and by the late 1970s state enterprises accounted for 85.9 percent of all public-sector investment (Bigler 1980, 39, 40).

The malfunctioning of these enterprises was notorious. Studies criticized the lack of clear objectives, technocratic expertise, and coordination in planning, as well as the unsuccessful implementation and evaluation of projects; and they emphasized the organizational irrationality of the state that resulted from its rapid, chaotic, and unplanned growth.[3] This irrationality—when coupled with a general lack of juridical guidelines, delays in administrative procedures, and the partisan appointment of public employees regardless of their qualifications—contributed to the disorder and improvisation rampant in the state even before the oil boom. Few controls over the spending of public monies and the absence of virtually any bureaucratic accountability fostered low-level corruption and mismanagement. The resulting waste was truly impressive. In 1973 prior to the oil boom, the Ministry of Finance reported that accumulated losses from the leading state enterprises had reached a full one-third of the national budget (El Universal, December 16, 1974, D1).

This situation could not continue. The decline of the oil industry and especially its impending nationalization meant that petrodollars could no longer be relied on to paper over this inefficiency. In the past, the assured flow of oil revenues to state managers had left them little incentive to maximize the efficiency of state enterprises. Thus it is not surprising that they had an abysmally low capacity for self-financing—only 7.2 percent in 1973—and relied instead on direct subsides from the central government (25.4 percent) and local and foreign borrowing (67.4 percent) (Banco Central de Venezuela, *Informe económico,* 1976, A-248).

But the nationalization signified that Venezuela's troubled oil industry—faced with rapidly declining reserves of light crude, spiraling domestic demand for oil, declining capacity because of the long moratorium on investment by the foreign companies, and soaring costs of new technology to exploit its reserves of heavy oil—had to marshal its own rents.[4] Oil experts warned that it could hardly be expected to subsidize the rest of the state indefinitely. As Finance Minister Hector Hurtado (interview, 1978) explained, "We are no longer taxing the multinationals to pay for our losses; we are taxing ourselves."

More immediately, the nationalization of petroleum and, to a lesser extent, iron ore threatened the "pockets" of administrative efficiency that had been carefully crafted to protect the state's extractive capacity, and this threat enhanced the urgency of administrative reform. Fears that the notorious disorder and inefficiency of the public sector would eventually "contaminate" the country's most important industries were repeatedly expressed, especially as it became evident how sharply the two nationalizations transformed the balance between the public and private sectors. This change is captured through figures for the national product and investment. Before the two nationalizations, the public sector's share of GDP never reached 15 percent, as Table 8 shows, but immediately after them this figure leapt to an impressive 42.9 percent.[5] Immediately before the boom, the private sector accounted for close to 68 percent of investment, virtually double that of the public sector, but the Fifth National Plan intended to reverse that relationship by 1977, raising the public sector's participation to 61 percent while dropping that of the private sector to 39 percent (*Gaceta oficial extraordinaria,* 1979, II-6, II-7).

Such important changes in policy domains necessarily disrupted the existing boundaries between the state and domestic and foreign capital, which had been so carefully drawn during the transition to democracy, and new boundaries had to be quickly renegotiated by state managers. Behind the curtain of a purely technocratic administrative reform,

TABLE 8

PARTICIPATION OF PUBLIC AND PRIVATE SECTORS IN GROSS
DOMESTIC PRODUCT, 1970–1978

	1970–72	1973–75	1976	1977	1978
A. Total GDP (millions of current bolívares)	57.433	106.732	132.496	152.796	170.323
B. Public-sector GDP (millions of current bolívares)	8.278	14.592	56.920	62.121	64.086
Participation of public sector (B/A) (%)	14.6	13.7	42.9	40.7	37.6
Participation of private sector (%)	85.4	86.3	57.2	59.3	62.4

SOURCES: Banco Central de Venezuela, *Informe económico,* 1974, 1977, 1978.

policymakers grappled with key questions. Who would run the newly
nationalized industry? Who would determine the balance between
growth and equity? What would be the industry's relationship to foreign and domestic capital, the executive branch, the rest of the bureaucracy, and the party-controlled legislature?

Such basic questions were not confined to the oil industry alone. As
Mauricio García Araujo (1975, 13), a noted economist, pointed out:

> Today in Venezuela we have fifty-six corporate boards that as a group man-
> ages 19.298 million bolívares a year and that delegates the power of deci-
> sion-making to its president. . . . This generation of Venezuelans is witness
> to the rise of a very special new oligarchy—. . . fifty-six people generally
> designated by political or party criteria—who decide how to spend, how to
> employ, how to invest, and how to administer 19.298 million bolívares a
> year, each year. The economic power that is accumulating in this bureau-
> cratic oligarchy . . . has no parallel in the rest of the economy.

The Pérez administration's proposals for state reform, if adopted,
would determine the prospects for improving the state's ability to direct
development. They would establish who could designate this "new oligarchy," what qualities the directors of state corporations would be expected to possess, and who would set the priorities and goals of the
decentralized state administration. These were not simply technical
questions. Instead, fundamental issues like the balance between growth
and equity, the future role for foreign capital, and the relative power of
organized interests in economic decision-making were at stake.

RENTIER REFORM IN THE STATE-ENTERPRISE SYSTEM, PLANNING, AND *CONCERTACIÓN*

The Pérez administration announced the first part of its broadly conceived reform—an ambitious project to reorganize the state-enterprise system—in December 1974. The reform clearly differed from all past efforts to address the problem of state enterprises, especially the recent broad initiative by President Caldera's administrative expert, Alan Randolph Brewer-Carías. Brewer-Carías had proposed strengthening the oversight functions of democratic institutions, especially the ministries and the Congress.[6] The reforms proposed by Pedro Tinoco, director of Pérez's newly formed Commission for the Integral Reform of Public Administration (CRIAP), had the opposite logic. They sought to increase the power of the executive and the private sector while circumventing political parties and other democratic institutions. This proposal reflected Tinoco's own predilections. A former supporter of Pérez Jiménez's dictatorial rule and the 1973 presidential candidate of the conservative Movimiento Desarrollista, he had campaigned on a platform of building an "efficacious state" (Tinoco 1973). Tinoco's party posited that party rule impeded economic growth, that income distribution should not be the concern of governments, that greater centralization produced more efficiency, and that "the current regime of representative democracy based on political parties" should be replaced (Andrade Arcaya n.d., 47; Mimob 1973, 47).

The attempt to create a new policy arena dominated by a partnership between the private sector and the executive marked the culmination in a decade-long quest by Venezuelan capitalists to institutionalize what is misleadingly called "democratic planning" in Venezuela (Blank 1969, 1973). Since the installation of a democratic regime, private-sector leaders had sought to incorporate businessmen directly into decision-making at the agenda-setting stage and to confine economic policymaking to closed administrative settings removed from public scrutiny. Although initially opposed to corporatist arrangements, they had come to see these commissions as an appropriate mechanism for coping with a highly interventionist state and had unsuccessfully encouraged them in the past. Despite AD's protests that Pérez should not link himself to a man with Tinoco's dubious democratic credentials, both Pérez and Tinoco believed that the oil boom had created a new opportunity for an explicit partnership between capital and the state, thus reopening this quest.[7]

Loosely based on a "presidentialist model" borrowed from Italy and

Spain, the CRIAP proposals centralized the control of the state-enterprise system in the executive branch.[8] They called for the formation of eleven new holding companies organized by sector; each would be responsible for designating the directorates of the operating companies, managing finances, planning technological development, negotiating participation in mixed enterprises, and approving investments and operating budgets in its sector.[9]

One huge entity, the National Council of Sectoral Corporations, would oversee all the sectoral corporations, and it would be responsible for the entire system of state enterprises. Its members, appointed by the president, were to be the heads of the eleven sectoral corporations, plus five other "persons of exceptional qualifications and experience in the management of enterprises," which was widely understood as a code for leading businessmen. Final control—including control over appointments, salaries, and bonuses for management—would lie with a committee of the full Council, which would be composed of its president and the five representatives of the private sector. Any existing external controls that might hinder rapid decision-making—for example, auditing by the comptroller general—would be eliminated.

This centralization of the state-enterprise system was to be accompanied by a reorganization of the planning apparatus (which was headed by Minister Gumersindo Rodríguez).[10] This reorganization was aimed at strengthening the authority of the executive and had two basic objectives. First, it would extend under CORDIPLAN's authority the existing network of commissions and councils that linked business and organized labor to the state. Second, it would upgrade CORDIPLAN under Rodríguez's direction and strengthen its ties to the presidency. As part of this package, the draft law of 1974 proposed the creation of a Technical General Secretariat to the Presidency, a type of superministry whose chief (Rodríguez) would exercise complete authority, subject only to the direction of the president, over a wide range of activities including the formulation of a long-term development strategy, the national five-year plan, the annual plan and the annual budget, the national system of coordination between the public and private sectors, the elaboration of all laws of an economic character, and the negotiation of bilateral technical-cooperation agreements with other countries.

This proposed reform involved a major shift of power from the Ministry of Finance, the most technically qualified and routinized ministry, to planning, and it was linked to Pérez's reform of the Central Bank, which moved the Central Bank's oversight responsibilities from the Finance Ministry to the presidency (*El Nacional,* July 7, 1974, D1; *El Nacional,* October 2, 1974, D1). Under the proposed arrangements, the Finance Ministry's core agencies, the Central Offices of Personnel, Statistics, and the Budget, would be placed under the control of the new planning agency. Because the Finance Minister's authority was derived largely from establishing the revenue budget (which by law limited the total size of the budget) and to a lesser extent the expenditure budget—both tasks of the Office of the Budget—the proposed plan would make CORDIPLAN and not the Ministry of Finance the prime target for influence seekers. With the National Office of Concertation also located there, this superministry, presided over by Pérez's (and Tinoco's) closest-collaborator, would become the most important agency after the presidency itself for seeking influence and favors.

The final element in the administrative reform was the expansion of Venezuela's system of *concertación,* or public-private commissions. Having been granted the right to form advisory commissions through the Special Powers Act, Pérez needed no new laws to create a complicated network of both permanent and ad hoc representative bodies, which he directed. The most important one, the Tripartite Commission, included, for example, officials from Fedecámaras, the CTV, and the government, and was presided over by the president; it discussed unemployment, relations between capital and labor, and a broad range of macroeconomic policy issues.[11] Commissions of this sort essentially contracted out public policymaking power to the country's most powerful organized private interests to a degree and in a formalized manner not previously seen. "I created and implemented a new form of decision-making," President Pérez boasted (interview, March 1979), and in fact the number of commissions during his administration far surpassed that of his predecessors (*El Nacional,* May 22, 1974, D2). The president contended that these commissions were an invaluable mechanism for building elite consensus.

REASSIGNING PETRODOLLARS:
RENT SEEKING AND THE DEMISE OF *PACTISMO*

But no consensus resulted from these reforms. To the contrary, because the proposals potentially affected the distribution of power and benefits to particularistic interests, they set off a new battle over assignment—that is, over the allocation of petrodollars and the boundaries between public agencies and private groups. The stakes were high. The ability of any individual or economic group to link up to the state meant the difference between normal economic gains and spectacular profits. With the boom, a single commission on a credit or contract could make a millionaire out of the fortunate middleman who could steer the state to favor a client.[12] In this climate, massive government contracts were awarded outside of regular procurement procedures; large sums of money passed through state agencies without controls; millions of dollars worth of loans were granted without regulation. Previously existing forms of illegality were exacerbated: for example, the juggling of bank accounts, the padding of budgets and expense accounts, the awarding of contracts without a public bidding process, the private purchase of properties with public monies, the diversion of budgetary funds for purposes other than their allocation, the awarding of commissions on loans and contracts, the issuance of large loans without sufficient security.

The reform proposals, when combined with rule by decree, threw normal institutional responsibilities and roles into doubt. In the ensuing confusion, the president was the only fixed participant in the process for making important decisions, and his office became the focus for private lobbying. In a classic pattern described by Marx and Weber, individual businessmen utilized the increased autonomy of the office of the chief executive in order to make the state an instrument of their private interests.[13] Pérez, in turn, was able to weave together a highly personalized system of economic and political alliances—a network that traded economic favors for political support. Although this *amiguismo* was a normal practice in Venezuela, the network around Pérez was a break from the past in two respects: for the first time, these trade-offs gave the appearance of involving the very highest levels of government, which had not previously been tainted by charges of rent seeking, and they took place outside the regularized parameters of party-directed machine politics.

The economic clique close to the Pérez administration, popularly known as the "Twelve Apostles," was composed of wealthy second-level entrepreneurs who rose to prominence through their contacts with several high officials, most notably Rodríguez, Diego Arria, Tinoco, and Pérez himself.[14] Their access was the result of past political support.[15] Although the exact nature of their interactions cannot be traced, the names of these businessmen consistently appear and reappear in the most important contracts awarded by the state from 1974 to 1978, including those for the Guri Dam, the Zulia steel mill, the construction of Parque Central, and Cementos Caribe.

Two important projects in the cement and petrochemicals industries, Cementos Caribe and Pentacom, best illustrate the new *amiguismo* that marked boom politics. In 1974, in the wake of a construction boom and a new demand for cement, Venezuela's two largest cement manufacturers, the Mendoza group and the Delfino group, sought state credits to expand their capacity; the Mendoza group was turned down despite its longstanding ties to AD. Instead, on the advice of Minister Rodríguez and Governor Arria, huge credits were awarded to a new plant called Cementos Caribe, whose board of directors included Tinoco and other friends of the president (*El Nacional*, December 5, 1975, C4). Overnight, another large economic group was created in the cement sector to rival the dominance of the Mendoza group, even though Cementos Caribe had failed to win financing or support from the Venezuelan Development Corporation, the agency normally responsible for these bids. News of the company's spectacular subsidies and credits began to leak out, and word spread that it had put up little capital of its own.[16] The head of the FIV resigned after refusing to award credits to the new group, but his replacement promptly approved generous subsidies despite the fact that Cementos Caribe had not even submitted a project evaluation (*El Nacional*, December 5, 1974, C5).

Cementos Caribe and other controversial projects challenged the traditional rules of the game and the distribution of petrodollars, especially the virtually automatic favoritism granted to the country's largest economic groups. But more contentious still was Pentacom (short for Pentacomplejo Petroquímica), a contract that challenged the boundaries between the public and private sectors in the petrochemicals industry. Unlike Cementos Caribe, it involved contracting to private interests the control of a state-owned enterprise central to the successful implementation of state-led industrialization. Pentacom itself was a consulting company established to promote new petrochemical companies with state participation and to offer management services to the resulting enterprises; its leading shareholders were several of the best-known Apostles. It proposed the formation of a mixed enterprise with the Venezuelan Petrochemicals Institute and the FIV to carry out feasibility studies and to develop a coherent program of action, after which time Pentacom itself, a solely privately owned firm, would assume the entire management of the petrochemicals industry.

To its proponents, Pentacom had the potential to rescue the petrochemicals industry, the major white elephant among the state enterprises.[17] But to its opponents, including AD's two most prestigious figures, Betancourt and Gonzalo Barrios, it was an attack against the domination of the state from rentier capitalists who had no technology, capital, or management ability to offer in its place. Instead, Pentacom included figures who had been involved in past scandals in the petro-chemical sector.[18] All the political parties viewed Pentacom as an attempt to circumvent their influence and as an example of corruption. The Pentacom scandal produced continually contradictory statements by high government officials, the leaking of secret documents, endless emergency meetings, and a bitter struggle over personnel. To Pérez, the presence of the Apostles represented his attempt to democratize capital by breaking down the hegemony of the traditional large economic groups. In his view, the Pentacom group was the crux of a new, emergent bourgeoisie that could break up the oligarchical structure of ownership.[19]

The struggle over Pentacom and the Apostles provoked the most bitter political exchanges of the Pérez administration, pushing COPEI into a harsh and denunciatory stance far removed from the *pactismo* of the past and a faction of AD, led by Betancourt, into open opposition to its own government.[20] In essence, corruption turned the irritant of poor partisan relations into a running sore. Not that corruption was new. But during the first three administrations it had been relatively restricted, leaving broad policy arenas relatively untouched. Public tolerance for pork-barreling was based on a widespread faith in the personal integrity of Venezuela's political leaders. Although occasionally a minister would be caught in open influence trafficking for personal economic advantage, the moral stature of the country's presidents was unquestioned, and party figures took great pride in the fact that the behavior of former Presidents Betancourt, Leoni, and Caldera stood in sharp contrast to that of a Gómez or a Pérez Jiménez.

The president's links to the Apostles belied the public's trust, and the parties' vehement opposition was a startling departure from past political behavior. COPEI claimed that some capitalists were being unfairly favored by the government through the awarding of huge state contracts and credits without appropriate bidding. It charged that "a new oligarchy is being created in the country under the umbrella of fiscal prosperity [that] aspires to reinforce the popularity and the political power of the government and its party" (*El Nacional,* December 6, 1974, D1). AD presented a strong public facade of unity with the president, challenged COPEI to publish specific names and contracts, and, in an implicit threat, noted that favoritism had existed during the Caldera administration as well.[21] But fearing that charges and countercharges between the parties could prove extremely dangerous, AD suggested a formal accord on corruption—an offer that fell on deaf ears. Instead, when José Vicente Rangel, an independent congressman representing the MAS, enumerated specific charges against the Apostles, COPEI quickly joined him in calling for an investigation of charges that the government was using large contracts and credits to pay back contributors to Pérez's 1973 campaign (*Semana*, no. 344, December 12–18, 1974, 11).

The debate against corruption reached crisis proportions with an astonishing and poorly timed suggestion by *adeco* congressional leader David Morales Bello, a close supporter of President Pérez, to set aside a constitutional provision against reelection of the president. The suggestion, interpreted as the first step toward a 1978 candidacy for Pérez, proved to be a bombshell. AD immediately rushed to quash any attempt to change the constitution, but in the tense political environment created by Cementos Caribe and Pentacom, it took more than the assurances of party leaders to lay to rest the fears of the opposition parties. Carlos Canache Mata, the general secretary of AD, was forced to announce to Congress that the president himself did not want the constitutional provision set aside.

The debate in the Chamber of Deputies over the role of the Apostles, in which the names of industrialists and financiers linked to the highest levels of government were repeatedly mentioned, broke the silent complicity of the past. It deeply exacerbated tensions between the parties, the executive branch, and the legislature, and between AD and its government. By April 1975, relations had grown so acrimonious that the parties were charging each other and the Pérez government with threatening the future of democracy. As the debate dragged on, AD found itself in the unheard-of position of publicly denouncing the friends of its president (by charging they had also received substantial favors from the previous COPEI government) and giving confidential details of how such favoritism worked.[22] AD's attack was happily joined by the left, who centered its attention on Tinoco, the designer of administrative reform. Tinoco, it was pointed out, had concentrated enormous political and economic influence in his person through the CRIAP commission, Pentacom, Cementos Caribe, a refinery in Costa Rica, and participation in the drafting of the Special Powers Act, the law nationalizing iron ore, and the banking laws. Most important, he served simultaneously as the president of Banco Latino, an important privately owned bank, and head of the legislative section of the Permanent Commission on Finance in the Chamber of Deputies—a clear conflict of interest. Public outcry was so great that it effectively killed Pentacom as well as the reform of the state—at least as it had been formally advanced. President Pérez was forced to publicly support the principle that basic industry should remain in the hands of the state (Presidencia de la República 1975–1978, vol. 1, 131). To save face, AD adopted the position toward the administrative reform proposals that was put forward by the comptroller general: the CRIAP reorganization, by attempting an all-encompassing reform in the midst of the boom, could actually paralyze the productive functions of the state (*El Nacional*, August 19, 1975, D1). Internal party memos were more specific: they criticized the circumvention of the party, the lack of auditing and controls, and the extreme centralization. But most important the party strongly condemned as "absolutely unacceptable" the plan to place the newly nationalized oil industry under the authority of the soon-to-be-formed National Council of State Enterprises, which in turn would be governed by businessmen appointed by the president. As AD leader Luis Esteban Rey wrote, "The so-called Tinoco Plan is the most ambitious and intelligent strategy of . . . Venezuelan capitalism (or sectors of capitalism) to assume control of the economic apparatus of the state, beginning with nothing less than the petroleum industry. . . . This is not acceptable" (*El Universal*, November 3, 1975).[23]

The virulence of the opposition effectively killed the proposed reform of the state. But what occurred instead was the worst possible development—an attempt to adopt the CRIAP proposals in modified form without party sanction. When AD stalwarts insisted on maintaining ministerial rather than direct presidential supervision over the state enterprises, Pérez circumvented them by creating the new position of Minister for the Promotion, Organization, and Supervision of Basic Industry, the virtual equivalent of a super holding company to oversee the huge industrial projects in mining, steel, energy, petrochemicals, and metallurgy. He then appointed Carmelo Lauría, his close associate and the rising star of Fedecámaras, to the post.

But the viability of the new ministry was questionable from the start. Administrators in the CVG and PETROVEN, the two most important holding companies in basic industry, as well as officials in the Ministry of Finance, saw Lauría as a distinct threat to their institutional autonomy. Serious jurisdictional disputes broke out with them, with the Minister of Mines, and with the heads of the Offices of Statistics and Personnel, who had formerly reported to only the Finance Minister. Although Lauría was careful not to overlap the jurisdiction of or to come into conflict with Rodríguez, who remained a presidential favorite, within a year he had replaced the Planning Minister as Pérez's chief economic adviser with new tasks and a new title, Minister of the Secretariat of the President.

Thus, a reform of the state that was to be based on legal, institutionalized roles and rules for increased efficiency was replaced by greater patrimonialism, centralization, corruption and bureaucratic infighting, and by an astonishing level of disorganization. Personal relations with the president defined the organization and lines of authority in the public sector; but because these relationships often shifted, so did these institutional realities. At the same time, relations among the parties and between the government and AD had been badly damaged. In an unprecedented public warning to the president, Gonzalo Barrios demarcated the limits of presidentialism by cautioning that "Acción Democrática does not bow to anyone, not even its own government" (*El Universal*, June 4, 1975, D1). If the government were to present projects in Congress that the party considered inappropriate, he said, they would be rejected—a startling political notion from a party ruled by strict democratic centralist discipline. Pentacom was the first project to be rejected; there could be others. In Barrios's words: "I don't believe that President Pérez would take any unjustified initiative, but if by some curious phenomenon he would do so, we can envision a case in which AD—either convinced by the opposition or on its own—would not approve these measures. This could *occur*" (*Resúmen*, July 6, 1975, 6, emphasis in original).

UNCONTROLLED SPENDING
AND THE TURN TO FOREIGN BORROWING

The deteriorating relationship within and between parties and the rise in corruption could not fail to affect the most important economic decisions of the Pérez government. Factionalism and disagreements among the parties distorted the policy agenda, diverted government leaders from their responsibility for managing the economy, and drove expenditures up as the president tried to placate interests and preempt opposition. Key decisions that should have been marked by consensus became conflicts, badly needed reforms were set aside, and important policies were substantially modified—not by normal or even partisan bargaining but by factional disputes. Deep divisions in AD pitted Pérez's cabinet members against each other. These dynamics were evident in the majority of significant economic decisions from 1975 to 1978, especially decisions to nationalize petroleum, promulgate the Fifth National Plan, and use foreign borrowing as a substitute for taxation.

The nationalization of petroleum, perhaps the single most important act of the government and one that should have rallied widespread support, revealed the growing partisan divisions in Venezuela. Although the nationalization itself, accomplished on January 1, 1976, was widely praised for its professionalism, it nonetheless evoked strong discontent in political actors and deepened dissension among the parties.[24] To some extent, this result was not surprising. Several political parties and the oil-industry employees presented competing nationalization bills to Congress in an effort to both influence and gain credit for this historic event. Regardless of their differences, these bills revealed the widespread sentiment for accelerating nationalization—sentiment that still could not be molded into consensus in the bitter political climate of the time.

The Pérez administration initially made more efforts to build consensus for the nationalization of petroleum than for any other issue. Abandoning his normal reliance on narrow, concerted accords with Fedecámaras and the CTV, Pérez established the Presidential Commission on Reversion, the most broad-based task force in his government, which included representatives from all political parties, a number of professional associations, the private sector, the army, the universities, and the key economic ministries. This task "requires the unity of will of all Venezuelans," he exhorted commission members during their swearing-in ceremony on May 16, 1974. "It is not simply a matter of government decision-making" (Presidencia de la República 1975–1978, vol. 1, 144). On October 17, 1974, the Reversion Commission presented the president with a draft bill that had the support of virtually every organized social force with the important exception of Fedecámaras.[25]

But Pérez soon bypassed the carefully constructed draft law of the Reversion Commission and submitted his own bill to Congress. Backed by both factions of AD and drafted by Oil Minister Valentín Hernández and CVG President General Alfonzo Ravard, it contained a controversial new clause (Article Five) that permitted foreign capital to participate in the newly nationalized industry and that implied the multinationals might eventually return as part owners through a mixed-enterprise arrangement. In the bitter political atmosphere, the addition of this article destroyed any prospect for a new agreement. When the vote was taken in Congress, the nationalization of petroleum—perhaps the single most important law in Venezuela's recent history—was ratified by AD with the support of only a small *perezjimenista* party. In the final vote on August 22, 1975, COPEI, MAS, MIR, URD, the Partido Comunista Venezolana (PCV), and all the other political parties opposed the bill. Later COPEI boycotted the nationalization ceremony.[26]

Factional divisions in AD also shaped the Fifth National Plan and the fatal decision to embark on a huge program of foreign borrowing. When Minister Rodríguez submitted a disastrous preliminary draft of a national plan a full two years late, the party Old Guard issued a bitingly critical report that both criticized the emphasis on basic industry to the detriment of developing an equitable development model and argued that the Fifth Plan stood in open contradiction to La Acción del Gobierno, the party program elaborated for Pérez's 1973 campaign (*El Nacional,* January 28, 1976, C4). Most important, AD criticized the proposed method of financing the Fifth National Plan.

Because it had quickly become clear that the financing needed to complete steel, aluminum, hydroelectric, and other huge projects would soon outrun oil revenues, the Pérez government decided to initiate a major program of foreign borrowing.

The government's reasoning for seeking international credits was strongly supported by foreign banks eager to recycle petrodollars abroad. International credits were seen as desirable because Venezuela, backed by its oil as collateral, could get favorable terms during the recession that plagued the industrialized countries. While the country made use of these credits, oil left in the ground rather than sold would continue to appreciate in value, thereby providing enhanced future revenues. Thus the advantages of the oil boom could be extended through this bid to gain cheap capital for the creation of new assets. Again, Pérez emphasized the need for speed. "We don't know when our country will have another opportunity to . . . make Venezuela a developed country by the year 2000," Pérez argued (*El Nacional,* February 4, 1976, D1).

But party leaders, though favoring some borrowing, believed that the amount of debt sought by the government (sixty-three billion bolívares, or $14.734 billion) was excessive. Influenced by Acting Finance Minister Iván Pulido Mora's devastating objections, they pointed out that the Central Bank, Venezuela's most respected financial institution, had objected to an earlier proposal for borrowing that was only 60 percent of the current request. Pulido Mora argued that a successful debt strategy had to be linked to a concrete development plan, and individual projects had to be broken down by their annual investment requirements and percentage of debt needed. None of these projections existed. The government had made no studies of the effects of borrowing on prices, employment, liquidity, or the balance of payments, and it had not determined the amount of oil exports and sales expected in the coming years to discover whether the country could afford to borrow. Finally, Pulido Mora noted, the new thesis about the advantages of borrowing simply could not be reconciled with the previous policy of "repressing" financial resources to avoid inflation. After resigning in protest over debt policy, Pulido Mora (correctly) showed that expected revenues from borrowing would probably be less than future debt service (*El Nacional,* May 2, 1976, D9).[27]

The simultaneous revelation of the disastrous condition of the Fifth Plan and the government's decision to seek massive new revenues abroad led to a wave of criticism from all sectors and, eventually, some initial brake on the government's borrowing spree. Through internal AD negotiations the gigantic Fifth Plan was cut down, with planned investment levels dropping from 230 billion bolívares to a still whopping 120 billion bolívares. The debt request, although still extremely high, was also scaled back by almost half (*El Nacional,* March 21, 1976, D1). In the long run, however, this compromise proved to be problematic. While promising to cut back the financing for its development projects, the government simultaneously committed itself to more social programs without agreeing to scale down its plans for basic industry, thereby continuing to lay down the basis for more spending and a future fiscal crisis.

Perhaps most damaging in the long run, foreign borrowing replaced efforts aimed at implementing a wide-ranging tax reform. Once borrowing was approved, it undercut the rationale for raising taxes by making it impossible to convince Venezuelans that the state needed additional revenues. Indeed, state officials saw borrowing as a substitute for a tax increase. When the Central Bank published a technical report on the president's debt request, as required by the Constitution, it specifically declared that the large projects of the Fifth Plan could be financed through the combination of income generated by oil, the state enterprises, and debt alone *"if the alternative of financing the activities of the public sector through greater internal taxation is postponed for now"* (emphasis added, *El Nacional,* May 12, 1976, A1). This carefully worded statement masked the intense internal struggle between Pérez supporters and *betancourtistas* in the Finance Ministry and the Central Bank over the tradeoff between tax reform and debt. With Pérez insisting on the debt policy, tax reform was put on the back burner.[28]

So great were the tensions within and among the parties over economic policy in late 1976 that COPEI called for the formal censure of three economic ministers for the first time in the history of the young democracy, believing that it might get the support of a faction of AD But AD's battles remained internal affairs. Rather than vote against the president's men, the Old Guard sought to limit his power in the party in the future by not permitting him to choose his own successor. Thus, a full two years before the presidential elections, the struggle between *betancourtistas* and *carlosandresistas* over economic policy was converted into a fight over the selection of AD's next candidate. Occupying the full-time energies of many party and public officials, the disputatious precampaign inside AD distracted attention from the business of government during the entire second half of the administration.

Between 1976 and 1978, as economic problems began to appear on the horizon, *adecos* fought over personalities rather than policies. After an especially grueling struggle over the candidate for the 1978 presidential election, Luis Piñerúa Ordaz was chosen over Pérez's choice, Jaime Lusinchi. Piñerúa was widely perceived as being the antithesis of Pérez. Praised by Betancourt for his "obsessive practice of administrative honesty" (*El Nacional*, September 14, 1976, D1), he stood for returning to the traditional heritage of AD and a renewal of *pactismo* with COPEI.[29] His campaign slogan, later used in the presidential campaign, was *correcto*, a word that carried the connotation of incorruptibility, especially in the management of money. Lusinchi, meanwhile, had consciously linked himself to the president's vision of *La Gran Venezuela*.[30]

The precampaign foreshadowed the repudiation of Pérez's economic policies in the 1978 elections. Divisions within AD were so intense that Betancourt and Pérez, fearful of a split that could decimate the party, repeatedly had to intervene to maintain unity. The precampaign was eloquent testimony to how divisive the performance of the Pérez government had become inside the party and, with 41 percent of AD's 1.3 million party militants abstaining from voting, to how disenchanted party members felt. In the general campaign Piñerúa's attempt to disassociate himself from the government turned him into what COPEI candidate Luis Herrera Campíns called "my best ally because each time he speaks against administrative corruption, he undermines the government of President Pérez" (*El Nacional*, October 19, 1977, D1). Piñerúa then sought to link himself to the government, but either position was damaging in a campaign where the high cost of living, the deterioration in services, and the government's overall record had become the key issues.

The central figure in the 1978 presidential campaign was a man not running for office: Carlos Andrés Pérez. Although Venezuelan law prohibited him from participating in the electoral campaign, Pérez claimed that no law prevented him from crisscrossing the country to inform people about the government's successes. Praising the steel, aluminum, and electricity projects of the Guayana region, he boasted of reducing unemployment, defended his debt policy as a necessary step for building *La Gran Venezuela,* and ignored charges of corruption. But even as his charisma helped him outshine the other candidates, his slogans—"I live better today" *("Hoy vivo mejor")* and "Step by step, the government's program is being accomplished" *("Paso a paso se cumple la acción del gobierno")*—paled besides the devastating message of COPEI: "Where has the money gone?"

Most important, even as he campaigned, for the first time in Venezuela's democratic history the president himself stood under an ever-darkening cloud of corruption charges. Rumors of Pérez's involvement in the disappearance of millions of dollars during the purchase of the presidential airplane and a refrigerator ship were rampant. Shortly before the elections, a leading Caracas lawyer investigating a fraudulent real estate deal involving some of Pérez's closest associates was killed in a death-squad action ordered by the head of the federal police, a presidential appointee *(Daily Journal,* April 20, 1979). As the level of sordid stories about presidential involvement in corruption mounted, the president's credibility and that of his party plunged. After leaving office, Pérez himself was forced to stand trial in the Congress—escaping by a mere one vote the condemnation that would have denied him the right to run for reelection and prevented his subsequent comeback.

To its stunned surprise, AD lost both the presidency and its congressional majority in the 1978 elections for the first time in its history. COPEI's Herrera Campíns received 46.3 percent of the vote compared with Piñerúa's 43.3 percent. The congressional vote was evenly split at close to 40 percent each. The principal party of the system, AD had been defeated once before, in 1968, but this defeat had been blamed on the its third division. The 1978 elections, the party's first out and out defeat, were soon compounded by the results of the 1979 municipal elections, in which AD's share of the vote dropped sharply to 30 percent, the worst defeat of its entire history. In some traditional *adeco* areas, the "party of the people" almost disappeared altogether.

Political observers blamed the scope of the AD defeat on the president, and indeed both elections had been turned into a plebiscite on the record of the government. According to Datos, a polling agency, Venezuelans were most concerned about the high cost of living, the failure of public services, and the scarcity of foodstuffs and other supplies, which stemmed directly from the rapid overexpansion of the economy; all these issues were linked to Pérez's economic policy (Naím 1981). Foreign electoral consultants concurred that the overriding issue in both the presidential and the municipal elections was the economic performance of Pérez's government; AD's loss was a "punishment vote," according to David Garth, who served as COPEI's campaign consultant (personal communication, June 1979).[31] "People were not happy about how he managed the boom." Nonetheless, a mere ten years later, as Venezuelans reeled from the consequences of the oil bust, they would look back on the Pérez years as a better time and eventually return him to power.

The 1973 oil boom and the policies following in its wake mark a watershed in Venezuelan democracy. Bonanzas change institutions one way or another. The Pérez administration sought to consciously take charge of this process by designing a reform aimed at bifurcating state functions into separate political/administrative and entrepreneurial areas. In theory, these systems were to have different forms of governance. The political/administrative state, presided over by the ever-weaker ministries, would perpetuate the ideologies and social programs of the political parties, as well as express the formal division of power among the branches of the government. The entrepreneurial state, presided over by advisory councils and directors of public holding companies reporting directly to the executive branch, would assume responsibility for basic production by applying technocratic criteria to decision-making and ensuring the insulation of decision-making from party politics.

On closer examination, the reforms were not quite so schematically neat. They promised to increase the influence of some capitalists inside the state, especially the associates of the president, at the expense of traditional economic interests, political parties, and the congressional and ministerial arenas they controlled. The reformers also hinted that industrial sectors reserved for the state could become privatized—a significant change in the standard operating procedures of Venezuela's democracy. As the president of the Public Administration Commission, Enrique Azpurua Ayala, observed in a letter to Tinoco (December 16, 1974), "To hand over to a group of businessmen the direct control of state resources represented by the state enterprises breaks the social equilibrium, . . . placing the management of a fundamental part of our revenues into the hands of only one national sector."Though carried out in the name of economic efficiency, an attempt of this sort was bound to intensify politicization and encourage rent seeking in an institutional setting where the state had the power to distribute raw materials, grant tariff exemptions and subsidies, finance private firms, set price controls, and decide who might enter an industry. The difference with past practices in Venezuela's democratic history was in the enormity of the sums involved and in the extent to which these efforts reached directly into the executive branch. Rentier behavior at this level had the potential eventually to pervade all state functions and finally to destroy the social fabric of Venezuela—a reality that the founders of Venezuelan democracy understood. Speaking prophetically and with more vehemence than he had at any time since his own presidency, Betancourt denounced illegal enrichment through the awarding of government contracts and warned, "If AD is not implacable toward those—militants or not—who commit crimes against the public treasury, we will not only lose the next elections, but we will lose our national prestige as well" (*El Nacional*, December 2, 1974, D1).

But despite numerous rhetorical denunciations by all the parties, no strong bills were adopted against *presupuestíveros* (literally, "budget eaters") or other exploiters of public resources, and not a single important government official or entrepreneur was punished for corruption during the Pérez years. Despite substantial evidence of presidential wrongdoing, Pérez himself escaped sanction. Indeed, if it had not been for the deteriorating relations between the parties of status, knowledge of the extent of corrupt activities would have remained confined to top political circles, where it might have had less effect. Instead, the damaging combination of party conflicts and subsequent governmental inaction helped to create a dangerous climate of corruption that slowly undermined the legitimacy of democratic rule.[32] "In Venezuela," Barrios was quoted as saying, "people rob because there is no reason not to."

Corruption and party polarization fed into each other in a vicious cycle, qualitatively changing the tone of political debate in Venezuela's democracy. Rather than discussing the appropriateness of an oil-based model or patterns of distribution, parties were involved in struggles over the allocation of petrodollars, party control, and personalities—symptoms, in Michels's (1949) view, of political exhaustion. To a great extent, this absence of fundamental debate can be explained away by the consensus over oil-led development forged in the democratic transition and by the enthusiasm for *La Gran Venezuela* that sprung from this consensus. But partisan struggles over corruption helped to guarantee that, in general, substantive discussion about the path of development or the wisdom of a borrowing strategy would be replaced by a whole new level of political cannibalism.

This vicious cycle created new stakes in rent seeking even as it undermined state capacity and pacted democracy. As the long-term stabilizing benefits of *pactismo* were quickly forgotten, militants in the government party quickly understood that they had a short-term interest in maintaining a highly partisan climate because, given the innumerable opportunities for gain, they could only stand to lose by any interparty or even intraparty accord that shared jobs in the bureaucracy, contracts, or other types of favors. Thus, pressure from below was exerted on the leadership of the parties in favor of an aggressive stance toward political rivals, which damned efforts to contain the patronage system.

Conversely, this rent seeking exacerbated political polarization both within and among parties because competent people were denied administrative positions on the basis of their political loyalties. Given these incentives, it is little wonder that Ellner's (1984–1985, 38–66) study of interparty agreement and rivalry in Venezuela, which compares the period 1967–1971 with 1976–1980, finds an appreciable increase in "the continuous questioning of the motives of political rivals, accusations of violations of the rules of the political game, and constant warnings regarding the gravity of the political situation" during the 1976–1980 interval.[33]

This intense polarization and rent seeking virtually assured that the administrative reform of the state would have perverse results. Instead of strengthening the corporate cohesiveness of the state, it led to the further distortion and disorganization of public agencies. By throwing the established bureaucratic rules into flux, these proposals expanded the prospects for exerting influence outside previous channels. This distortion was especially evident in the undermining of the office of comptroller general (the only state agency dedicated to monitoring performance and accountability),[34] the weakening of the Central Bank and Finance Ministry, and the deliberate creation of numerous new bureaucracies that duplicated the functions of previously existing yet less pliable ones. Duplication, in turn, led to new rivalries and widespread confusion over tasks at double the cost to the state. The CRIAP itself was a symbol of this policy of circumventing institutions not currently in favor; its role replicated that of the Commission on Public Administration.

In turn, the proliferation of new rules, proposals, and agencies severely hampered state performance. The mere announcement of grand schemes to rationalize state organization was enough to throw existing lines of authority into disarray. This disorganization had especially severe consequences for fiscal control. The Ministry of Finance and the Central Bank cautiously sought to modify the president's *gigantismo*, and, as a result, their autonomy was compromised just when their fiscal management was most needed. The Office of the Budget became the site of constant warfare between the Finance Ministry and an upgraded CORDIPLAN.[35] Tax reform was once again delayed; and the watered-down bill that was finally adopted in 1978 after Hurtado's resignation bore scant resemblance to the sweeping proposals of November 1975. The original program of "repressing" oil revenues through the FIV was replaced by a borrowing spree. "The most important weapon of a finance minister when faced with multiple budget requests is to be able to say '*no hay*' ('there is no money')," Hurtado noted (interview, October 1978), "but how could I say '*no hay*' with all of this money around? And how could I say '*no hay*' when any petitioner could go ask someone else?" In this context, the oversight of Venezuela's finances became next to impossible, and the persistence of a perverse development trajectory more than probable.

EIGHT

From Boom to Bust

The Crisis of Venezuelan Democracy

"God is Venezuelan," *Caraqueños* often proudly claimed when re-counting how frequently timely bonuses from petroleum seemed to re-solve potential political and economic problems. A second huge oil shock in 1980—the result of the revolution in Iran (1978–1979) and the subsequent war with Iraq (1981)—seemed to bear out their belief. The limits of the first boom had barely become apparent when this sec-ond boom produced an initial doubling of the per barrel price of petro-leum, from $12.70 in 1978 to $28.67 in 1980, then a continued upward climb to a high of $33.47 in 1982 (Table A-1). Just as the 1973 boom had supposedly granted a "last chance for democracy," the 1980 price hike seemed providential for overcoming the economic dislocations and political dissatisfactions brought about by the earlier bonanza.

But this hope too proved to be an illusion. Instead, the second boom, even more than its predecessor, led to a leap in state expenditures that delayed necessary adjustments, exacerbated state disorganization, fos-tered even greater rent seeking, and laid the basis for the acute economic problems and regime crisis that wrack Venezuela today. The second boom quickly turned to bust as oil prices started downward in 1983, and then plunged dramatically from $27.99 to $13.08 a barrel between 1985 and 1986. Relieved only by a quick rise during the Iran-Iraq War in 1990, prices showed no real prospect of recovering to the previous high level (Table A-1).

The decline in oil prices was the most visible expression of a major new challenge confronting Venezuela: the demise of the rentier model of accumulation that had been the basis of its economic prosperity and political stability for thirty years. Two oil booms did more than change Venezuela; they also altered the structure of the international oil market in a manner detrimental to the OPEC countries. Concerted efforts by the advanced industrialized countries to diminish their dependence on OPEC oil, the development of alternative energy supplies, the flooding of the market with crude oil newly discovered in the North Sea and Mexico, and the inability of OPEC to function as a fully effective cartel in order to stabilize a new international oil regime set in motion the rapid downward price spiral. Prices threatened to remain relatively low for some time.

In effect, the ability of producers to increase total rents by raising prices rather than volume finally reached its limits. This limit was openly acknowledged in mid-1985, when Saudi Arabia took the lead in making sharp price reductions that subsequently reduced rent per barrel by half and definitively put an end to Venezuela's traditional rent-maximizing oil policy (Espinasa 1985). Between 1979 and 1985, OPEC was forced to cut production by half (Espinasa and Mommer 1991). The consequences of lower rents were dramatic: between 1980 and 1988, the value of Venezuela's oil exports plunged 51.8 percent in real terms (Table A-13).

But if the economic challenges confronting Venezuela had grown, the capacity of both state and regime to cope with them had deteriorated. To make matters worse, even though the basis of Venezuela's economy had radically changed, expectations had not. Because the traditional policies of rent extraction from the international system had been successful for more than five decades and because Venezuela had recently benefited from two major booms, neither the government nor its citizens could believe that the future would not simply be an extrapolation of past trends (Baptista and Mommer 1987). Thus even when oil prices and government income plunged, government behavior did not change: public expenditures and investment outlays did not go down—and in some years they even increased! Rentier behavior in both the public and private sectors, the continued need to assuage various political constituencies, widespread corruption, and the lock-in caused by giant investment projects already underway meant that government spending patterns did not adapt to the cycles of the oil market (Gelb 1988). Instead, in a pattern reminiscent of that in Spain in the sixteenth century, public spending stayed high and foreign debt replaced mineral rents as the preferred mechanism for smoothing over budget deficits, institutional disarray, and political tensions.

Events in the 1980s and the early 1990s, which this chapter examines, demonstrate the playing out of the patterns of oil-led development in Venezuela. Faced with the demise of the rentier economic model, the institutions of the petro-state and pacted democracy strongly conspired to shape and to encourage the short-term preferences of governments to avoid necessary adjustment, even at the expense of future economic productivity and political stability. Most striking in the period covering the administrations of COPEI's Luis Herrera Campíns (1979–1983) and AD's Jaime Lusinchi (1984–1988) are the persistent efforts of governments, regardless of party affiliation, to appease immediate interests and postpone the profound policy changes that sooner or later had to be made. Although throughout the 1980s distortions of all kinds were accumulating at a alarming rate, the response to this deteriorating situation was, at best, partial reforms, half measures, and perpetual debt renegotiations. At worst, it was a notable increase in corruption, politicization, and rent-seeking behavior on the part of those who seemed to understand that "the dance of the millions" was coming to an end.

The avoidance of painful economic adjustments by elected governments is not surprising; at first glance this behavior merely places Venezuela in the same category as many other countries. But the leeway granted to this oil producer by international finance to continue untenable fiscal patterns far beyond any economically or politically justifiable point is distinctive. Rather than begin a gradual adjustment to a new reality, for an entire decade Venezuelan governments were able to rely on foreign borrowing to sustain unusually high public expenditures— the glue that cemented together parties and capital, labor, and the state, despite increasingly bitter conflicts. Thus public spending could continue even when there was nothing left to spend! Again reminiscent of the Spanish case, when adjustment finally came, it was more painful and more disruptive than it had to be. In a twist of fate, the consequences of this *deferenda* were brought sharply home during the second presidency of Pérez, who, amidst riots and coup attempts, was forced from power in May 1993, the victim of the expectations raised by his own past grandiose vision.

THE FISCAL CRISIS OF THE VENEZUELAN STATE

The backdrop to the crisis of contemporary Venezuela is its necessity to make a transition from a rentier to a postrentier economy. This imperative became most evident because of the fiscal crisis of the state. Although governments had long been accustomed to paying for increasing public expenditures by using petroleum to extract additional revenues internationally, this ability had become significantly curbed because of the uncontrolled growth of public spending that began in 1974 and because of new constraints on the revenue side of the equation.

Nowhere is Venezuela's addiction to petrodollars more apparent than in the huge growth in public expenditures. Once the budget was allowed almost to triple in the first boom (1973–1974)—the antithesis of sterilization—there was no turning back. During the second boom (1979–1981), government expenditures doubled again (Table 9). As the frenzy of spending expanded throughout the bureaucracy, initial budgetary requests became insufficient. In some cases, agencies were asked to revise their budgets upward so that the government could spend more money more quickly. In order to escape oversight, state agencies relied increasingly on additional credits, which had the advantage of being removed from congressional scrutiny (see Table 10). A testament to lack of planning, these credits reached an astonishing 192 percent of the initial budget for 1974 and averaged 31 percent of the initial budgets during the next four years. This pattern did not change when presidential power shifted from AD to COPEI, despite Herrera Campíns's pledge not to repeat the mistakes of the past. During the second boom, between 1979 and 1981, they averaged 25.3 percent. Additional credits were especially useful for covering government overspending immediately prior to and following presidential elections. In 1989, for example, they represented a whopping 88 percent of the initial budget (Table 10).

The huge increase in current expenditures is another important indicator of the inchoate nature of state spending (Table 9). Although current expenses declined substantially as a percentage of total government spending during the Pérez years—falling from 67.1 percent of total expenditures in 1973 to 53.6 percent in 1978—by 1992 they were more than fifty times total government spending in 1972. Largely a response to the imperatives of political patronage, they tended to increase sharply in preelectoral periods. That Venezuela was living beyond its means is apparent in one startling statistic: in some years the combination of current expenditures and debt service alone surpassed the annual value

TABLE 9

CENTRAL-GOVERNMENT EXPENDITURES, INVESTMENT,
AND DEBT, 1970–1992 (MILLIONS OF BOLIVARES)

	Total Expenditures	Current Expenditures	Investment	Public Debt
1970	10,295	7,159	2,959	177
1971	11,915	8,057	3,141	717
1972	12,842	8,924	3,489	429
1973	15,042	10,087	4,485	470
1974	40,059	15,368	24,103	588
1975	40,370	19,339	20,676	355
1976	39,468	21,250	17,615	603
1977	52,041	25,638	24,256	2,147
1978	49,905	26,745	20,956	2,564
1979	47,569	32,157	10,945	4,467
1980	68,551	41,209	21,987	5,955
1981	92,182	54,616	32,753	4,813
1982	88,942	54,440	27,438	7,064
1983	80,134	54,042	20,399	5,693
1984	99,706	68,797	19,461	11,448
1985	110,545	73,750	24,380	10,920
1986	117,658	72,224	32,212	13,222
1987	173,232	112,401	38,771	22,060
1988	212,794	161,894	30,596	20,304
1989	308,667	260,317	22,586	25,764
1990 [a]	565,509	439,263	60,090	66,156
1991 [a]	734,152	537,913	105,400	90,839
1992 [a]	887,178	665,014	132,890	89,274

SOURCES:

1970–1978, 1981–1990: Banco Central de Venezuela, *Informe económico,* annual issues, section III ("Finanzas Públicas"), table "Clasificación Económica del Gasto Pagado del Gobierno Central."

1979–1980: Oficina Central de Estadística e Informática (1985).

1990–1991: Oficina Central de Estadística e Informática (1993).

[a] Preliminary figures.

of petroleum exports—a pattern that became a permanent feature in the 1980s (Table 11).

This extravagance left virtually no money for the huge investment projects begun under the Fifth National Plan, even though, because of large sunken costs, these projects could not simply be abandoned. The initial costs of these projects, already inflated, were subsequently increased by poor planning. Officials had seriously overestimated the capacity of basic industry to absorb massive expenditures productively

TABLE 10

UTILIZATION OF ADDITIONAL CREDITS IN THE
BUDGET, 1970–1989 (MILLIONS OF BOLIVARES)

	Initial Budget	Additional Credits
1970	9,886	475
1971	10,988	1,800
1972	13,412	187
1973	13,858	1,036
1974	14,549	27,957
1975	41,396	4,356
1976	33,041	1,837
1977	35,634	19,461
1978	44,293	9,328
1979	46,341	8,265
1980	56,686	18,605
1981	75,744	19,239
1982	86,943	7,723
1983	76,382	3,059
1984	77,041	28,341
1985[a]	102,844	14,831
1986[a]	122,283	4,619
1987[a]	158,020	26,447
1988[a]	185,122	10,053
1989[a]	182,101	159,594

SOURCES:

1970–1977: Controlaría General de la República de Venezuela (1978).
1978–1980: Banco Central de Venezuela, *Informe económico,* annual issues,
section V ("Sector Público"), table "Gestion Presupuestaria."
1981–1989: Banco Central de Venezuela, *Informe económico,* annual issues,
section III ("Finanzas Públicas"), table "Gasto Acordado del Gobierno Central."
[a] Preliminary figures.

without creating bottlenecks in other sectors, and they had made inadequate provisions for crucial investments in infrastructure expansion.
The resultant chaos in the ports, airports, and internal transport system
was legendary and led to incalculable waste. The government also had
not provided for inevitable cost overruns and had scarcely budgeted for
certain huge projects, such as the Zulia coal and steel plants. So great
were government miscalculations that one early study by economists
Robert Bottome and Carl Prunhuber (1980) estimated the cost increase
at 54 percent.

Even more serious, government planners never calculated the full
cost of completing the huge projects of the Fifth Plan. Because planners

TABLE 11

COMPARISON OF PETROLEUM EXPORTS WITH CURRENT
EXPENDITURES INCLUDING DEBT SERVICE, 1970–1993
(MILLIONS OF U.S. DOLLARS)

	A Current Expenditures	B Debt Service	Subtotal (A+B)	Value of Petroleum Exports	Petroleum Exports as % of Subtotal
1970	2,210	121	2,331	2,371	102
1971	2,496	173	2,669	2,882	108
1972	2,893	267	3,160	2,857	90
1973	3,308	389	3,697	4,328	117
1974	5,330	586	5,916	10,548	178
1975	6,422	594	7,016	8,324	119
1976	7,625	454	8,079	8,763	108
1977	9,838	916	10,754	9,110	85
1978	10,794	976	11,770	8,740	74
1979	10,437	3,107	13,544	13,633	101
1980	13,002	6,037	19,039	17,562	92
1981	19,680	5,695	25,375	18,609	73
1982	19,683	5,935	25,618	15,633	61
1983	17,087	4,644	21,731	13,857	64
1984	11,766	4,726	16,492	14,824	90
1985	12,609	4,304	16,913	12,956	77
1986	13,015	5,103	18,118	7,178	40
1987	12,065	4,872	16,937	9,054	53
1988	16,247	5,552	21,799	8,158	37
1989	9,431	3,831	13,262	10,001	75
1990	10,874	4,990	15,864	13,953	88
1991	12,725	3,321	16,046	12,302	77
1992	12,058	3,331	15,389	11,208	73
1993	11,176	3,945	15,121	10,565	70

SOURCES: 1970–1989 figures for current expenditures and value of petroleum exports calculated from International Monetary Fund (1993, lines 70a.*d*, 82, and wf); 1990–1993 figures from International Monetary Fund (1996, lines 70a.*d*, 82, and rf). Debt service 1970s figures from World Bank (1988); 1980–1984 figures from World Bank (1989); 1985–1987 figures from World Bank (1993); 1988–1993 figures from World Bank (1996).

NOTES: Breaks in series occur in source for expenditures (1983, 1987) and oil exports (1987); 1993 figures are preliminary in source.

operated on five-year cycles, estimates were based on disbursements through 1980 only, even though several of the projects were planned to extend through 1985 and some extended beyond that date. Thus the problem of financing troubled and half-finished megaprojects like the expansion of the Guri Dam and the construction of the Caracas metro fell to subsequent administrations, which would have little choice but to complete them. The cost to these administrations was huge, especially as these megaprojects continued to produce losses. In the single year of 1984, for example, the steel company SIDOR reported a net loss of 1.9 billion bolívares, mostly because of payments on debt for the construction of its new plant (Hellinger, 1991).

As pressure on expenditures grew and policymakers continued to spend as if there were no long-term constraints on revenues, the reality was quite different. By the 1980s the capacity of the petroleum industry to produce the enormous rents of the past had changed significantly, in part because of the long-term changes in the international oil market mentioned earlier. As a direct result of the 1973 oil-price leap and the subsequent search for less costly alternatives, oil's contribution to the world's primary-energy mix dropped from its peak of near 50 percent in the early 1970s to about 40 percent by 1988 (Linden 1988, 251). In addition, OPEC's and hence Venezuela's ability to control prices declined as its contribution to the world oil supply dropped from 82 percent in 1973 to only 60 percent in 1990.[1]

As a result, with the exception of a brief surge caused by the interruption of supply during the Iraq crisis in 1990, by 1994 oil prices were approximately one-half their 1980 level (see Table A-1). Oil revenues still remained the largest single component of government revenues, despite the fact that falling prices diminished their importance in the budget. But, as we have seen, the growing gap between the value of oil exports and state expenditures meant that petrodollars alone could no longer sustain the government's spending addiction, as Figure 1 dramatically illustrates.

Traditionally policymakers reacted to a gap between oil revenues and government expenditures simply by opening the oil spigot—that is, by increasing the taxes on the oil companies or by raising international prices. But "turning the tap" in this fashion now was ruled out—first by the changes in the oil market, then by the 1976 nationalization, which put Venezuela in the position of raising taxes on itself. Instead, in order to remain competitive with both non-OPEC oil and other sources of energy, the logic of the market dictated that future increases in oil rents would have to be relatively small and would more likely have to occur through an increase in volume rather than price. This requirement placed a new premium on the productivity rather than the rentier nature of the oil industry and gave a whole new meaning to "sowing the petroleum."

The new emphasis on productivity further curtailed revenues avail-

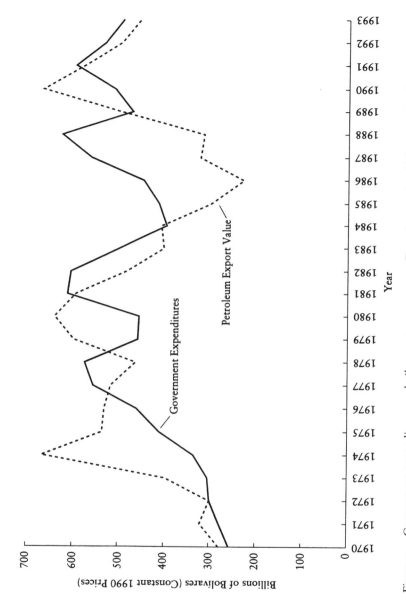

Figure 1. Government expenditures and oil exports, 1970–1993. From International Monetary Fund (1995).

able to the state because the petroleum industry, long the golden goose of development, itself became one more claimant for petrodollars. Decades of neglect by the foreign petroleum companies had created an urgent need for large infusions of capital that could not be delayed if the industry was to stay competitive (Coronel 1983, 276). Petróleos de Venezuela (PETROVEN) faced the immediate and expensive tasks of searching for highly valued but scarce light oil, improving secondary recovery, exploring the continental shelf, implementing tough new environmental standards for its gasoline, and ultimately developing the huge belt of heavy oil in the Orinoco. State revenues from petroleum were also adversely affected by rising production costs and domestic consumption rates. One barrel of oil, which cost $1.80 to produce in 1976, cost over $3 per barrel in 1979, and the cost reached $6 by the late 1980s (interview with PETROVEN official, 1991)—a sum that included the cost of sophisticated technology services and marketing arrangements with the multinationals.

PETROVEN's new investment plan was costly. With the country's oil fields suffering a potential decline in output of 22 percent per annum, more than $2 billion per year had to be invested simply to maintain crude output at its present level. Investments in refining improvements to meet the provisions of the U.S. Clean Air Act alone were expected to exceed an additional $3.6 billion (*Financial Times*, December 4, 1992, 14). The company's investment plan through 1996 estimated expenditures at a full $32 billion (*LAWR*, June 6, 1991, 3). In a sudden reversal of the 1976 nationalization policy that was to become highly controversial, planners sought congressional approval to permit vital foreign capital to reenter the industry.[2] As investments in oil soared from $325 million in 1976 to over $5 billion per annum by 1985, huge sums were absorbed into the industry that formerly had been available for other purposes (Baptista and Mommer, 1987, 100). As PETROVEN President Gustavo Roosen summed up the situation, "The most limited resource that our petroleum industry has today is money" (*Financial Times*, December 4, 1992, 14).

With the oil industry requiring ever-increasing investments to maintain productivity, the logical alternative to raising state revenues through petroleum was domestic taxation. But, as we saw in Chapters 4 and 6, oil revenues undercut efforts to establish a domestic tax base. More than any other South American country, Venezuela lacked a historically honed capacity to extract revenues from its own population. Opposition to establishing such a tax system was especially great from organized business interests who distrusted the efficacy of the state and mistakenly believed that petrodollars could adequately provide for their needs. Ever since the tax crisis of 1966, even minor government efforts at raising taxes had been easily pushed aside.

The results of this rentier phenomenon, seen earlier in the contrast between Venezuelan and Colombian tax structures (Chapter 4), are also evident when the structure of Venezuelan taxation in the late 1970s is compared with that of most other countries Table 12). In dramatic contrast to the other countries in the Western Hemisphere, which received an average of 14.75 percent of their tax revenues from corporate income taxes, or to all developing countries, which averaged 16.53 percent, a full 70.3 percent of Venezuela's taxes were derived from corporate income taxes (essentially from the oil industry). This arrangement permitted Venezuelans to pay strikingly less individual income tax, domestic tax on goods and services, and tax on imports than the majority of citizens in the Americas, where, for example, the percentage of taxes raised from domestic taxes on goods and services alone was five times higher. Equally as remarkable, Venezuela's percentage of tax revenues raised from individual income taxes was less than half that of other developing countries.

But petroleum revenues, which freed Venezuelans from normal tax burdens for their entire modern history, also served as the excuse for

TABLE 12

STRUCTURE OF TAXATION IN VENEZUELA, DEVELOPING
COUNTRIES, AND THE WESTERN HEMISPHERE
(PERCENT OF TOTAL TAXES)

	GNP per Capita[a]	Corporate Taxes	Individual Taxes	Domestic Taxes on Goods and Services	Import Duties
Venezuela 1977–79	4,220	70.30	4.07	6.75	9.78
Western Hemisphere	1,841	14.75	7.53	31.03	18.77
Developing Countries[b]	1,330	16.53	10.25	27.93	24.98

SOURCE: Tanzi (1987, Tables 8-2, 8-A2).
[a] 1981 U.S. dollars.
[b] Sample of eighty-six primarily developing countries with per capita incomes ranging from $100 to about $6,000.

repeated postponements of the tax issue and eroded an alternative tax base. In addition, there were no real sanctions for the nonpayment of taxes, and plentiful petrodollars created an environment in which responsible taxpayers were ridiculed. Even President Lusinchi stated, "In Venezuela only the stupid pay taxes" (*LAWR,* July 30, 1994, 4). In this environment, it was not surprising that the petro-state failed to develop a trained cadre who could design tax systems, encourage systematic research on taxation, and strengthen the capacity for collection. Thus it was especially ill-prepared to take the types of measures that might alleviate the most acute fiscal crisis in its history (McClure 1991, 27–30).

If raising new revenues from petroleum was economically impossible because of changes in the market, altering the tax situation seemed politically impossible. The deeply ingrained belief that Venezuela was rich—the result of fifty years of growing revenues and two massive booms—would have undermined efforts to demonstrate the contrary, had such efforts even been made. But few politicians would risk the consequences of calling for higher taxes, which, at best, would subject them to unpopularity and, at worst, to powerful citizen demands for accountability for their squandering of petrodollars. With increased revenues from either oil or domestic taxation virtually ruled out, governments turned to what appeared to be the easiest solution: foreign borrowing.

THE RISE IN FOREIGN DEBT: 1975–1989

External borrowing, which originated as part of a strategy to finance the large-scale industrial projects of the Fifth Plan, rapidly became the chief mechanism for coping with fiscal crisis. As early as 1977, when current-account deficits first appeared, debt rapidly soared beyond the maximum of $7.25 billion authorized by Congress in 1975. By the final year of Pérez's first term, official long-term foreign debt had surpassed $8.56 billion. In the Herrera Campíns administration this figure rose precipitously to $23.69 billion in 1983, and in 1986 it reached a high of almost $33 billion under President Lusinchi, making Venezuela the third largest debtor in Latin America (Table A-9).

This growth of debt is especially striking when compared with that of Brazil or many other leading debtors because of the context in which it occurred. In effect, debt increased by a factor of more than thirty in the midst of two massive booms (Table A-9), rising from 8.76 percent of GNP in 1970 to 49.07 percent in 1988 and to 53 percent in 1994

(Table A-14). Total debt service rose from $267 million in 1972, prior to the booms, to a peak of $5.1 billion in 1988 (Table A-10), and the ratio of debt service to exports soared in that same period from 7.81 percent to 40.1 percent (Table A-11). Thus, by the end of the 1980s, for every dollar earned on a barrel of oil, Venezuela was paying almost $0.40 back to foreign banks!

But these official figures, high as they are, seriously underestimate the extent of total borrowing. The Pérez government and those that followed, upon finding the financial resources from the boom and official debt insufficient, made wide use of so-called floating debt—obligations incurred by state enterprises and autonomous agencies that did not have to be recorded in official debt totals or be approved by Congress. Because a loophole in existing legislation permitted public enterprises to seek foreign credits without any oversight or regulation as long as the borrowing was short-term, floating debt was an easy way to paper over problems of economic mismanagement.

The figures on floating debt are dramatic testimony to mismanagement, corruption, and administrative chaos. Without auditing or controls, this form of borrowing spiraled wildly. In 1977–1978, for example, total government spending rose nearly 50 percent immediately prior to elections, and this increase was financed through floating debt. The disarray in public finance caused by the misuse of floating debt was so great that the incoming president, Herrera Campíns, had to establish a special commission solely to discover the amount of unregistered debt. According to figures later announced, an estimated 43.5 billion bolívares (approximately $10 billion) in additional government spending had been financed via floating debt—a figure the COPEI government would continue to augment substantially. Most of this total was not reflected in any official budgetary statistics. Once the floating debt was added to the official debt statistics, Venezuela's indebtedness was nearly double the sum approved by Congress.[3]

Because floating debt was short-term, it was especially costly. Eager to avoid accountability in Congress, officials failed to take full advantage of Venezuela's strong international reserves to borrow systematically at long-term, lower interest rates. As a result, in 1982 the country's borrowing profile was unusually tilted toward short-term, high-interest credits (59.7 percent) compared with the Latin American average of 47 percent (Bank for International Settlements 1982). The high cost of Venezuela's debt is perhaps most graphically suggested through a comparison with Brazil, the leading less-developed debtor country in the world in the mid-1980s. By 1978 Venezuela's debt had become 17.1 percent of its GNP; by 1986, it had risen to a whopping 50.5 percent and then dropped to 41.1 percent in 1988. These figures are substantially higher than those of Brazil (15.6, 31.9, and 26.3 percent, respectively), although Venezuela's strong reserves somewhat offset the gravity of this picture.[4]

The use of foreign borrowing to substitute for the declining ability of petrodollars to cover the state's expenditures could not last. If petroleum revenues once (mistakenly) appeared to be free, similar illusions about debt were quickly dispelled by the banks. The calculations behind the original plan to substitute cheap foreign credits for exhaustible oil wealth did not take into account the impending decline of oil prices, the rapid rise in interest rates, the maturity structure of Venezuela's debt, the limited absorption capacity of the economy, and the dangers of perpetuating Venezuela's addiction to easily obtained dollars. Nor did these calculations anticipate the especially uneven bargaining power of Third World governments and of international banks, which, unlike the oil companies, did not have fixed assets that required an ongoing presence and whose willingness to lend money anywhere in Latin America plunged after the 1982 Mexican debt crisis.

By the early 1980s, the debt that once had been sought for development purposes had become a considerable burden (Table A-10), reaching a stunning 69.7 percent of GNP in 1989 (Table A-14). As the decade proceeded, bankers' demands for adjustment began to grow increasingly insistent, although they were initially willing to postpone an International Monetary Fund (IMF) structural-adjustment plan because of Venezuela's strong petrodollar reserves. Plagued by repeated foreign-exchange crises and persistent episodes of capital flight ranging from $30 billion to $80 billion (Naím 1992, 6), by 1989 Venezuela faced an ultimatum from the banks: either implement an IMF austerity plan or, for the first time since oil had been exported a half a century earlier, receive no more money.

THE POLITICS OF POSTPONEMENT: 1979–1989

The Herrera Campíns (1979–1983) and Lusinchi (1984–1988) administrations, which followed Pérez, tried to ensure that whatever costs had to be borne in the transition to a postrentier economy would not fall on their watch. To offset the looming threat of intervention by the IMF, officials dipped into reserves, carried out a number of financial manipulations to improve their external balance of payments, sacrificed the stability of the currency, and spent almost half the state's oil earnings on the interest and principal of its loans. In the process, even the autonomy of PETROVEN, a sacrosanct institution, was compromised by their efforts. Their attempts to sustain public spending as a mechanism of appeasement and to avoid adjustment can be traced through repeated refinancing discussions, which took place every single year between 1982 and 1989.[5] But the results can be seen most easily in the profound economic and political crisis that confronted the second Pérez administration.

The situation of COPEI's Herrera Campíns was especially difficult because his was the first government to face the consequences of negative economic growth and inflation after the initial reprieve of the 1980 boom. In addition, unlike Pérez before him and Lusinchi afterward, he confronted persistent opposition from the AD-dominated CTV as well as from a divided legislature that his party did not control (Table 13).[6]

TABLE 13
CUMULATIVE VOTES OF THE TWO MAJOR
PARTIES FOR THE PRESIDENCY AND
LEGISLATURE, 1958–1988 (PERCENTAGE)

	Presidency		Legislature	
1958	Betancourt	49.18	A.D.	49.45
	Caldera[a]	16.21	COPEI	15.20
1963	Leoni	32.81	A.D.	32.77
	Caldera	20.18	COPEI	20.86
1968[b]	Caldera	29.13	COPEI	30.94
	Barrios	28.24	A.D.	32.90
1973	Pérez	48.70	A.D.	44.44
	Fernández	36.70	COPEI	30.24
1978[b]	Herrera	46.65	COPEI	39.81
	Pinerua	43.31	A.D.	39.68
1983	Lusinchi	56.72	A.D.	49.95
	Caldera	34.54	COPEI	28.71
1988	Pérez	52.91	A.D.	43.2
	Fernández	40.42	COPEI	31.12

SOURCE: Consejo Supremo Electoral (1988).
[a] Caldera actually placed third in this election behind independent candidate Wolfgang Larrazabal, who received 34.61 percent of the vote.
[b] COPEI won the presidency but did not win absolute control over the legislature.

To cope with these pressures, he pushed government spending to new heights despite his repeated promises to rein in expenditures, and he resorted to new foreign borrowing, even though he had bitterly criticized his predecessor for having passed on a "mortgaged nation." Confrontations among the parties over economic policy had the salutary effect of putting some brakes on the government's tendency to spend, as AD demanded a sharp reduction in foreign borrowing, rejected a number of new expansionary state projects, and blocked COPEI's efforts to increase the 1981 budget from $16.3 billion to $21.3 billion. But interparty fighting also encouraged COPEI repeatedly to circumvent the AD-dominated Congress by resorting to costly short-term borrowing and dipping into the reserves of the Banco de Trabajadores.

The sharp drop in oil prices beginning in 1982 forced an abrupt devaluation of the bolívar and plunged the country into its worst recession in the postwar period, which sent the Herrera government scrambling for new revenues. In desperation, it turned to the one state enterprise that had remained relatively uncontaminated by politicization, PETROVEN. PETROVEN's reserve fund was taken over for general budgetary purposes in 1982, forcing the oil company to turn to world capital markets to finance its own expensive investment projects. The government was able to improve Venezuela's image with foreign banks merely by moving $5 billion from the company's funds to the Central Bank. Occurring when the company's director, General Alfonzo Ravard, was out of the country, the government's actions struck a blow at PETROVEN's hallowed financial autonomy, a cornerstone of the oil-led development model (*LAWR*, October 1, 1982, 3).

But maiming the proverbial goose that laid the golden eggs was obviously no permanent solution; thus financing the deficit was the central preoccupation of the final two years of the COPEI government (Mayobre 1985). The results were some cuts in government spending, a renewal of fierce in-fighting within the government and among the parties, and the implementation of a complicated three-tiered system of exchange controls aimed at protecting the country's scarce foreign reserves. The new foreign-exchange agency, known by its acronym, RECADI, actually compounded economic problems while becoming a breeding ground for a level of corruption that dwarfed past practices. Indeed, the controls eventually exemplified the epitome of political rent-seeking behavior; using political influence to maneuver for the largest possible quota of foreign exchange at the lowest available exchange rate became the most important economic objective of private interests in the 1980s. But beyond this single (and highly ineffective) decision to limit access to foreign exchange, no other policy measures were implemented.

Repeated efforts to seek additional foreign credits were aimed at masking the extent of economic decline, but to no avail. In September 1982, the comptroller general announced that the national debt had reached "dangerous proportions"; he received a public rebuke from the president for his dire warning. Government recordkeeping and control over public firms and private debts were so poor that the two could not even agree on the actual debt, with the comptroller general claiming a figure of $54 billion and Herrera Campíns claiming $29 billion (*LAWR*, September 17, 1982, 2).

This confusion influenced the terms of new loans, which continued to worsen as open fighting broke out between the new Finance Minister and the head of the Central Bank. By 1983, with the economic crisis spiraling out of control (capital flight caused international reserves to fall by $254 million in one week alone!), foreign banks insisted that Venezuela get IMF approval for its economic plans just as Brazil, Mexico, and Argentina had done. Though indignantly rejecting this suggestion, Venezuela's Finance Minister finally admitted that its external obligations were to great for the country and announced Venezuela's intention to seek for the first time unconditional loans from the IMF.

The highly politicized issue of IMF conditionality, opposed by both AD and COPEI, permeated all political and especially electoral debate between 1983 and 1988. Herrera Campíns completed his administration by managing to put off IMF negotiations until after the December 1983 elections. Meanwhile, economic policy remained virtually at a standstill while the president's economic ministers fought among themselves (*LAWR*, August 5, 1983, 2). Though his decision to break off talks with the IMF was popular at home, it angered creditor banks, pushed AD candidate Lusinchi to declare his opposition to bargaining with the IMF, and raised the cost of debt rescheduling when it eventually came to pass.

Nor did the decision bring payoffs to COPEI in the 1983 elections, as it had hoped. Stricken by the most serious economic difficulties of the democratic period, Venezuelans strongly repudiated COPEI, even though its candidate, former President Rafael Caldera, remained popular. Instead, they handed 56.72 percent of the vote to Lusinchi, the highest percentage ever won by any president, as well as full control over the legislature to AD (see Table 13). This election returned the country to the ultracentralization that had characterized the Pérez administration, and it permitted Lusinchi to request and win the same special powers for managing the economy that Pérez had received. But changing parties and giving the president extraordinary authority seemed to make little difference in a state that had become thoroughly permeated by rent-seeking behavior. Torn by party factionalism as well as by divisions between those state agencies and private organizations favoring austerity measures (the Central Bank, the Ministry of Development, and Fedecámaras) and those advocating higher public expenditures (the Ministry of Planning and the labor unions), the Lusinchi government faced opposition even from AD's traditionally most loyal ranks. Measures adopted in February 1984, which contained some of the policy prescriptions advocated by the IMF, provoked the open opposition of the CTV and ultimately encouraged the rise of independent, radicalized new unions in Ciudad Guayana and elsewhere (Davis and Coleman 1989, 255). Meanwhile, despite Lusinchi's (short-lived) popularity in the polls, corruption flourished at the highest levels.

Postponement could not remove the realities imposed by Venezuela's burgeoning debt service. Between 1984 and 1988, the government's basic strategy was to try to refinance its debt directly with the foreign banks by adopting an economic adjustment plan that would meet most of the demands of the IMF without incurring the political costs of a formal IMF agreement (Bigler and Tugwell 1986, Alvarez de Stella 1988). In its continuing negotiations with its creditors, Venezuela pledged to unify the exchange rate by 1986, restore the financial autonomy of PETROVEN, ease import controls and free prices by 1986, reduce government spending, and maintain its distance from Latin American efforts to form some type of debtors' cartel (*LAWR,* July 6, 1984, 2). These promises were never kept despite the fact that Lusinchi, like Pérez before him, had been granted the right to rule the country by decree precisely so that he could resolve the debt crisis. Instead, debt agreements were repeatedly postponed by the Lusinchi government until it left office;[7] and government spending, especially unproductive current expenditures, rose to new heights during the electoral year of 1988 (Table 11).

STRUCTURAL ADJUSTMENT
AND THE CRISIS OF VENEZUELAN DEMOCRACY

As elections loomed in 1988, the AD administration discovered that it had no more room to maneuver in its efforts to avoid IMF conditionality. The banks were finally unwilling to consider any new renegotiations without the IMF, and they refused to grant any new credits to Venezuela. Yet agreeing to IMF conditionality was politically impossible in an electoral period—even with debt payments eating up more than half of oil revenues. Instead, the government publicly took a tough (and domestically popular) stand by declaring that, as a result of falling oil prices, Venezuela would not be able to make a $2.5 billion debt payment due in November. Privately, however, even as both presidential candidates campaigned on pledges to reactivate the economy without bringing in the IMF, the government agreed to negotiations as soon as the elections were over.

Despite the gravity of its economic situation, the AD government initiated a major expansion in public spending, with desired results; the 1988 election-year economy grew by almost 5 percent. As crisis loomed, many Venezuelans were thus lulled into the false sense that their immediate future would look better, and they returned to power for an unprecedented second term the candidate they most associated with prosperity, Pérez.[8] Notwithstanding his large margin of victory in the presidential elections, Pérez lacked a 50 percent congressional majority and a unified party, and any thoughts of governing by decree were therefore ruled out (see Table 13). Instead, the new president would have to bargain, almost on a case-by-case basis, for virtually every policy initiative.

The cost of the brief 1988 respite, when combined with a decade of postponed adjustment, was enormous. As Pérez assumed office in 1989 amidst promises of sustained recovery and expectations of prosperity, the economy collapsed. Price controls and artificially repressed inflation, somehow held in check during the elections, produced a burgeoning black market, rationing, and the most severe shortages in Venezuelan history. Foreign reserves plunged by half, and the current-account deficit reached a whopping $5.8 billion (Table A-6). The budget deficit, which had stood at 3 percent of GDP in 1985, shot up to 9 percent of GDP. As real wages plunged, real per capita income barely equaled what it had been in 1973. By 1989, the number of households living below the poverty line had increased tenfold since 1981 (Naím 1993, 8–14).

With no money and no congressional majority, the structure of decision-making for the president at this moment could hardly have differed more from that of 1973–1974. Not surprisingly, Pérez's policies changed as well.[9] Democracy's greatest spender grew thrifty, its most enthusiastic statist became a privatizer, its ardent nationalist encouraged the influx of foreign capital, its consummate centralizer dispersed power. Completely hemmed in by the country's desperate fiscal situation, Pérez embraced neoliberal economic reforms. Immediately following the elections, he entered into direct negotiations with the IMF, and in February 1989, with virtually no warning to the public, which associated him with the booming economy of the past, he abruptly announced a package of painful market-oriented reforms.

What became known inside his government as *el gran viraje* (the great turnaround) and on the streets as *el paquetazo* (literally, being hit by a package) represented a 180-degree shift in economic policy. In exchange for desperately needed new loans, the government agreed to the following measures: the elimination of nontariff barriers covering 94 percent of local manufactures, the reduction of tariffs from their average of 35 percent to a 1990 target of 10 percent, an increase in internal interest rates of up to 30 percent, the reduction of the fiscal deficit to no more than 4 percent of GDP, and the elimination of the scandal-ridden foreign-exchange agency, RECADI, with its system of preferential exchange rates. Disregarding his electoral debt to labor, Pérez also lifted price controls on all but eighteen basic food items, cut subsidies for public services (including a 50 percent increase in utility prices and a 30 percent rise in transport fares), increased the domestic price of petroleum (with the first price hike to be 100 percent), and froze employment in the public sector (Kornblith 1989, Naím 1993).

El paquetazo, together with other measures, brought an abrupt dismantling of the three economic pillars that had thus far underwritten democracy: state intervention, the subsidization of organized private interests, and sustained increases in social spending. The sudden announcement of this economic shock plan, the antithesis of economic policy for the past thirty years and a far cry from electoral promises, triggered an explosion of violence. Precipitated by IMF-mandated increases in bus fares, massive riots spread throughout Caracas and into other cities on February 27, 1989, leaving an official toll of 350 dead (and an unofficial toll of 1,000). Just two weeks after taking office, Pérez was forced to declare a state of emergency, suspend civil liberties, and call out over ten thousand troops to conduct sweeps through neighborhoods where tens of thousands were arrested. As the United States, the IMF, and more than fifty creditor banks rushed in with emergency bridge loans, the president tried to defuse the crisis by calling it an understandable social response to austerity (Kornblith 1989). Still, he pledged to sustain the adjustment program. Despite the riots, the 1989 budget was reduced 10 percent in real terms.

The immediate impact of *el paquetazo* was dramatic. The 1989 economy shrank by almost 10 percent, and unemployment rose from 7 to 10 percent in one year. Real salaries declined 11 percent, bringing the decade decline to an astonishing 45 percent (Naím 1993). As the inflation rate climbed to an unprecedented 93.8 percent, government and military officials persistently disavowed rumors of a coup, and the president and his defense minister were forced to declare repeatedly that democracy was stable (*El Nacional,* March 6, 1989, D1). But without petrodollars to smooth over the protests, these assurances rang hollow. After the February riots, the CTV convoked an extraordinary National Congress, only the second in its history, which called for an unprecedented one-day national strike on May 18 against the government it had helped to elect. The business community complained about the lack of protection and about the slow pace of privatization. Opposition was perhaps strongest from the ranks of the president's own party, where militants accused the government of failing to establish an adequate social "safety net" for the poor and successfully wrested control of AD from the Pérez faction (*LAWR,* June 20, 1991, 4).[10]

By early 1992, President Pérez was under strong pressures at home to modify his economic policies and to resign, and he was simultaneously being pushed by the IMF to enter a second and more severe phase of structural adjustment. There was irony in his situation. The harsh measures of the past several years showed some important signs of engendering economic success. In 1991 Venezuela had one of the fastest growing economies in the world; it expanded 10.4 percent after a 1990 growth of over 7 percent. Private industry gave indications of revitalization from the stagnation of the 1980s, capital flight was reversed, and foreign investment flowed into the country as international reserves almost doubled (Naím 1993, 62–70).

But the political impact of the *paquetazo* was devastating. Widespread riots and strikes from 1989 to 1992 were painful testimony to the diminishing capacity of the democratic regime to implement its economic program and to manage conflict without the lubricant of petrodollars.[11] Because the costs of austerity were distributed unevenly and because efforts to improve social welfare were hindered by chaotic institutions, Pérez's popularity plunged;[12] opinion polls showed AD in a poor third place for the first time in its history, overtaken not only by its chief rival COPEI but also by the left (*LAWR,* August 9, 1990, 3).

The party's lack of popularity was exacerbated by constant corruption scandals and, after 1989, by almost daily announcements of court proceedings against prominent personalities, of which charges against the once-popular President Lusinchi, his former Ministers of Finance, and his mistress were the most damaging.[13] Disenchantment with both major parties was reflected in inordinately high rates of abstention in internal party elections (a full 80 percent of those entitled to vote in AD's internal elections abstained) and in local government elections (almost 60 percent abstained). More disturbing still, evidence of regime deterioration lay in the rising numbers of Venezuelans who claimed that violence was justified in changing the system (*Political Impact*, May 22, 1992).

The full extent of Venezuela's political decay was brought home on February 4, 1992, when young military officers attempted to overthrow Latin America's second oldest democracy. Calling for corruption trials, the reversal of Pérez's neoliberal policies, the establishment of an emergency program to combat poverty, the formation of a new constituent assembly, and the defense of national sovereignty, the leader of the rebels, Lt. Col. Hugo Chávez Frías, became an instant folk hero despite the failure of his efforts (*LAWR*, February 20, 1992, 4). Although Pérez and the international banking community unconvincingly denied that the coup attempt was a direct result of the government's austerity measures or rampant corruption and focused instead on dissatisfactions in the military, the economic team of the cabinet was jettisoned and *el paquetazo* was quickly modified.[14] Pushed by public opinion polls revealing that 81 percent of Venezuelans had lost confidence in the president and 57 percent said they would "change the government immediately" (*Zeta*, February 13–24, 1992, 66), politicians unsuccessfully demanded that the presidential mandate be shortened, a new constituent assembly be called, and a government of "national reconciliation" be formed (*El Diario de Caracas*, April 30, 1992). Meanwhile, as constant demonstrations against the government grew, several generals publicly urged members of the armed forces to "fight to ensure democratic institutions."[15]

Implementing a coherent economic policy in the midst of political chaos proved impossible. As it became increasingly clear that the government would experience a new budgetary shortfall because of declining oil prices, increased social spending, and high debt service, Pérez was forced to announce a second harsh austerity package to stave off hyperinflation and a fiscal disaster. Aimed at coping with the collapse in the tax-supplying capacity of the oil industry (which had an estimated deficit of more than $3 billion for 1992 with a projection of double that figure for 1993), the August 1992 package took a series of unprecedented and politically explosive steps to wean Venezuela from oil dependence: firing large numbers of public employees and freezing the salaries of others, banning the purchase of new military equipment, slashing the payroll and operating budget of PETROVEN, and placing shares of the state-owned petrochemical industry, once the object of an intense fight against privatization, on the world market.

Most important in the long run, the government announced plans to raise personal income taxes while simultaneously establishing a general sales tax as well as a tax on capital assets. If implemented, this plan would have constituted a radical transformation of the fiscal basis of the petro-state. "There is absolutely no other way out," Pérez announced to a stunned population (*International Herald Tribune*, August 25, 1992).

But because of the demise of *pactismo* the president had absolutely no support. Opposition legislators, skeptical of the government's proposals and virulently against Pérez's remaining in office, threatened a complete policy stalemate. COPEI, having previously decided to reject a rapprochement with AD that was widely portrayed as a return to the Pact of Punto Fijo, joined repeated calls for the president's resignation. Warning that they would block the 1993 budget unless Pérez left office, legislators (including many from AD) also indignantly rejected hints that the government might favor resumption of foreign investment in financially strapped PETROVEN. In effect, their actions made it impossible for Pérez to achieve day-to-day control of the government.

This situation exploded dramatically on November 27, 1992, when members of the Venezuelan military once again tried to unseat President Pérez. Compared with the previous coup attempt, this second uprising took far longer to suppress, involved larger numbers of troops and civilian allies, included members of the high command for the first time, and took a far heavier toll in lives (with estimates ranging from 170 to 500). It was fueled by new charges of corruption, this time directly against President Pérez and his mistress as well as several military leaders.[16] Although mayoral and gubernatorial elections did take place in a show of normalcy only a week later, approximately half the electorate abstained from participation, and the greatest advance was made by Causa-R, a radical, labor-based party completely outside the pacted arrangements of the past.

Badly rattled by the results of the elections, both AD and COPEI experienced new splits, in part over the fate of the president. This was finally resolved on May 20, 1993, when the Supreme Court moved to indict Pérez on charges of embezzling $17 million in government funds, which paved the way for his removal from office. With the Senate ratification of this ruling, Pérez lost his presidential immunity and was immediately suspended from office, leaving Venezuela in the most severe crisis of its modern history.

Venezuela, as argued earlier, may be the "best case" for handling oil booms well, yet its record in this respect is unambiguous. Two massive booms over two decades produced economic deterioration, severe state disorganization, and regime decay. Even a chastened Pérez could now see the dangers of bonanza development. "This is phony money that we're making," he commented about the unexpected windfall that fell briefly to his government following Iraq's 1990 invasion of Kuwait. "Whatever it can buy today, it may bring us damage and dangers tomorrow" (*Time*, November 12, 1990).

But this political learning was late in coming. Venezuela entered the 1990s, a decade of heightened international competition, with institutions and ingrained behaviors especially resistant to reform. In the manner of a petro-state, rent seeking had become the central organizing principle of its political and economic life, and the ossified political institutions in existence operated primarily to perpetuate an entrenched spoils system. Both state agencies and political parties had given up their programmatic roles to become machines for extracting rents from the public arena. Their subsequent loss of legitimacy when rents diminished is striking: in a 1992 poll only 2 percent of the population deemed existing political parties "reliable," compared with 40 percent attributing this characteristic to the armed forces (*El Diario de Caracas*, April 30, 1992, 8). Thus it is not surprising that Caldera, known widely as "the last honest president," was elected president for a second term in 1993, but only after he had publicly repudiated COPEI, the party he founded.

In this rentier setting, austerity was the main catalyst for reform. The drying up of oil rents was the essential backdrop for efforts to transform pacted democracy. Innovations aimed at breaking its preemptive and circumscribed character included the direct elections of state governors and mayors and the introduction of some aspects of nominal voting into the selection of municipal councils. When combined with the introduction of primaries and other attempts to democratize party structures, these reforms began to diminish the concentration of power in the presidency, granted new importance to local government, increased competition among the parties, and opened new space for opposition parties (Coppedge 19939, Shugat 1989). But they also contributed to a climate of growing uncertainty in the midst of economic crisis—one that relied on unpredictable political alliances for some degree of short-term security rather than the stability once offered by the party system.

Stop-and-go economic reforms accompanied these uncertain political changes. As external pressures from the banks for structural adjustment, temporarily relaxed during the interim government that followed Perez's departure, grew after 1993, the harsh reality of Venezuela's fiscal crisis convinced even President Caldera, the strongest opponent of Perez's *paquetazo,* to implement many of its provisions. Nonetheless, the depth of the crisis seemed beyond the grasp of his government, which argued that putting a brake on corruption was sufficient to alleviate the crisis. Lacking government and opposition leaders accustomed to dealing with a shrinking pie or willing to explain the long-term nature of the crisis, few citizens understood that the years of living beyond Venezuela's means were over. Just as Spaniards had once waited for the next ship of gold from the New World to rescue them, Venezuelans seemed to believe that another boom in black gold was just around the corner.

PART THREE

The Impact of Oil Booms on Oil-Exporting Countries

"All in all, I wish we had discovered water."

*Sheik Yamani, Oil Minister of Saudi Arabia,
citing a colleague in an interview with the
author, Caracas, 1979*

NINE

Petro-States
in Comparative Perspective

Venezuela and Spain are not the only countries where mineral rents have translated into economic deterioration, state disorganization, and regime decay—and where structural adjustments proved especially difficult to make. Algeria, Nigeria, Iran, and, to a lesser extent, Indonesia share this same development pattern. These oil-exporting countries also share the especially tight intertwining of power and plenty that occurs when the state owns the central source of accumulation. As in socialist countries, the dynamic relationship between economic development and institutional change is particularly close, and political fortunes are inextricably tied to economic ones.

Lack of time, space, and data does not permit an in-depth treatment of the manner in which frameworks for decision-making were historically constructed and altered by petroleum in these countries.[1] Yet even a brief examination of their development trajectories lends support to my contention that countries dependent on the same leading sector share properties of "stateness," despite the fact that their actual institutional arrangements may be quite different in most other respects. Indeed, when petro-states are examined in comparative perspective, they reveal a strikingly similar structuration of choice, which penetrates all levels of political domination—their states, their regimes, and their governments—and which can be traced back to the shared origin of their states' revenues.

This chapter probes the relationship between structure and agency in oil-exporting countries through the use of comparative analysis. It first examines the similarities and variations in outcomes in Venezuela, Nigeria, Algeria, Iran, and Indonesia. It then concentrates on highlighting the reasons for Indonesian "exceptionalism." Next it contrasts the experience of one developed oil country, Norway, with that of developing oil countries. Finally, it explores the applicability of arguments developed in Part I of this book for understanding outcomes, paying special attention to the relative impact of varying degrees of "stateness."

Through these comparisons, the chapter seeks answers for some remaining questions. Can the concept of the petro-state be fruitfully extended to other capital-deficient oil-exporting countries? What explains variations in performance, most especially the unusual ability of Indonesia to escape thus far from the high level of economic and political turmoil that has plagued other oil states? Finally, what difference does it make when booms occur in the context of the high state capacity and democratic polities characteristic of advanced industrial societies—for example, Norway?

To forecast my main findings, the chapter contends that, first, the notion of the petro-state is indeed useful for understanding the experiences of other oil exporters and, second, differences in both state and regime are important for explaining broad variations in economic and political performance. But properties of stateness are most significant. Rentier states, a category that includes petro-states and extends beyond them, suffer from diminished state capacity. When states do not have to depend on domestic taxation to finance development, governments are not forced to formulate their goals and objectives under the scrutiny of citizens who pay the bills. At the same time they are permitted to distribute funds among sectors and regions on an ad hoc basis. Excessive centralization, remoteness from local conditions, and lack of accountability stem from this financial independence. As we shall see in Chapter 10, any regime grafted onto this structure, whether authoritarian or democratic, is likely to be considerably arbitrary, irrational, and volatile when making economic policy—the antithesis of the environment necessary to confront a boom successfully.

COMPARING OUTCOMES: IRAN, NIGERIA, ALGERIA, AND INDONESIA

Other capital-deficient oil exporters bear a marked resemblance to Venezuela in their response to booms. Chapter 2 already demonstrated how the governments of Iran, Nigeria, Algeria, and Indonesia substantially increased public spending as state revenues shot up in tandem with the rise in the price of oil (Tables A-1 and A-2) and how most chose to make speedy use of their oil rents to perpetuate their resource-based development model. They also chose to borrow heavily to finance this development plan (Table A-9). High public expenditures eventually produced Dutch Disease, and the relative size of the oil exporters' initially small agricultural and manufacturing sectors fell as their economies were skewed toward nontradeables rather than tradeables (Table A-12). These economies came to be characterized by inflation, continuous fiscal deficits, and balance-of-payments problems (Tables A-6, A-7, A-8). Eventually, their overvalued currencies led to the stagnation of non-oil exports, while the shrinkage in their GNPs—measured even in current prices (Table A-15)—adversely affected the domestically oriented ore industries, which had been the crux of most of their resource-based industrialization plans. Thus plans for "sowing the petroleum" remained stymied.

But within this common overall framework were significant variations in performance. Public-expenditure priorities differed. Algeria and Indonesia, for example, emphasized the development of natural gas, and Algeria showed the strongest bias toward heavy industry. Venezuela and Nigeria concentrated on metals, most notably steel and aluminum, and both spent heavily on education. Iran had unusually high expenditures on defense. Exporters differed in the sectoral mix of their investments, the types of enterprises they favored, and their macroeconomic policies. According to Auty's (1989) study of eight oil exporters, those countries that emphasized the development of natural gas over ores, relied on joint ventures rather than wholly owned state enterprises, and had more timely exchange-rate corrections generally outperformed their counterparts.[2]

Economically, one petro-state, Indonesia, fared considerably better than the others—an outcome that can be traced to government choices during the boom years. Not only did it fall into Auty's "best case" category, but it had better control over its expenditures; pursued a development strategy more balanced among physical infrastructure, education, agricultural development, and capital-intensive industry; directed a higher proportion of spending toward rural areas; and accrued less foreign debt. Table 14 illustrates the differences between Indonesia and other capital-deficient countries. Its "great leap forward" into a higher level of government expenditures following the 1973 boom was considerably less than that of its counterparts (row A). The decline of its GNP

TABLE 14

VARIATIONS IN MACROECONOMIC PERFORMANCE

	Indonesia	Iran	Nigeria	Venezuela	Algeria
A. Estimated growth/ government expenditures 1974–75, %	19.8	35.9	29.9	38.5	n.a.
B. Ratio of 1980 to 1986 GNP	.96	.88	.46	.81	1.51
C. Percent change in ratio of tradeables to non-tradeables (1965–82)	−61.8	−1.6	−59.3[a]	−6.9	−5.7
D. Increase in ratio of total external debt to GDP, 1975–80 as % of 1975 ratio	−26.6	n.a.	87.7	265.2	41.5
E. Incremental capital/ output ratio (ICOR)	5.2	n.a.	39.2	8.5	n.a.

SOURCES:
  A. See Table A-3.
  B. All figures except Iran are taken from Table A-15. Iran is taken from International Monetary
     Fund (1988b).
  C. See Table A-12.
  D. Calculated from Table A-14.
  E. Calculated by Auty (1989, 357).
[a] Change in ratio 1965–1987.

was relatively slight when compared with that of Nigeria, Venezuela, or Iran (B).[3] Indonesia's Dutch Disease indicator was less than that in the other countries (C), and its debt burden during the first boom, when other countries borrowed heavily, actually dropped (D). Although it did not make efficient use of its capital, which would be indicated by an ICOR ratio of 3 or under, it was more efficient than other oil exporters (E).

This record is confirmed by studies carried out by country experts. Arndt (1984, 136) notes that Indonesian "national management coped with the disruptions [from both oil booms] better than might have been expected." Pinto (1987), in comparing Indonesia with Nigeria, concludes that important differences in fiscal and exchange-rate policies as well as borrowing and agricultural strategies explain Indonesia's relative success. Auty (1989, 358) reaches a similar determination. Although he emphasizes the disappointing results of the exporters as a group, he concludes that Indonesia's performance was "superior (and significantly so) to the average for all eight countries."

When political outcomes are examined, a similar pattern emerges, as might be expected given the indistinct boundary between the economy and polity that is a characteristic of petro-states. Even before oil prices plummeted in 1982, none of the individuals or political parties, whether authoritarian or democratic, that managed the 1973 boom, except Suharto, were able to remain in power. Venezuela, Iran, Nigeria, and Algeria shared a common pattern of regime change or acute regime crisis, even though the direction of the change, its timing, and its extent differed. One country (Iran) had an Islamic social revolution, which involved a change of state as well as regime. One (Nigeria) played out the combination of ethnic, religious, and economic tensions by making a transition to democracy in 1979, reverting to authoritarian rule in 1983, beginning an uncertain (and frequently interrupted) transition once again between 1986 and 1991, then suffering a military coup in 1993. Two countries (Algeria and Venezuela) were confronted with severe regime crises in 1992, marked by high levels of social violence beginning in the late 1980s. Algeria was also threatened by a possible change of state through revolution or civil war following the surprising electoral showing of Islamic fundamentalists, the subsequent cancellation of elections, the assassination of its president, Mohammed Boudiaf, and the vacillation between military and civilian rule. Only Suharto, having already enjoyed power for twenty-five years, managed to stay in office, relatively unchallenged, for a sixth five-year term.

Table 15 ranks these political outcomes according to the degree of change exhibited by 1992. Norway has been added for purposes of comparison later. Actual alterations in regime type (Iran and Nigeria) are ranked above threatened changes (Algeria and Venezuela), and

TABLE 15
POLITICAL INSTABILITY OF PETRO-STATES, 1974–1992

Rank	Change of Government	Change of Regime	Change of State
1. Iran	+	+	+
2. Nigeria	+	+	−
3. Algeria	+	Threatened	Threatened
4. Venezuela	+	Threatened	−
5. Indonesia	−	−	−
6. Norway	+	−	−

changes in the state are measured by a fundamental shift in the fiscal structure or institutions of violence (or both). Changes in government are not considered a manifestation of instability in political democracies, where alternation in power is a characteristic of the system. Thus Iran, which has experienced a change in regime and state, Islamic revolution, and war, has the greatest level of instability, closely followed by Nigeria. Indonesia and Norway have been most stable although the former has incipient signs of instability.

A purely structurally determinist analysis—that is, one that attributes little or no significance to human agency—would contend that these outcomes are the result of factors beyond the control of policymakers, most especially the size of the windfall. An analysis of this sort would claim that the magnitude of exogenous events—for example, the booms of 1973 and 1980—determines endogenous change. There is some support for this position. Table 16, which examines the size of the oil windfall of capital-deficient exporters as well as their level of instability, indicates some relationship between the sudden increase in state revenues and political upheaval, and it lends credence to the argument that the greater the magnitude of external change, the more likely the presence of domestic difficulties. Yet neither measure in Table 16 explains any case except Iran well.

This is not surprising. As Chapter 3 argued, windfalls in themselves, regardless of how they are measured, are not a satisfactory predictor of political outcomes. Because these revenues have no economic impact

TABLE 16
WINDFALLS AND POLITICAL INSTABILITY

Country	Windfall as % of Nonmining GDP (Rank)	Windfall per Capita[a] (Rank)	Rank Based on Political Instability
Iran	36.7 (1)	2,057 (1)	1
Algeria	27.1 (2)	353 (5)	3
Nigeria	22.8 (3)	437 (4)	2
Indonesia	15.9 (4)	148 (6)	5
Venezuela	10.8 (5)	1,918 (2)	4
Norway[b]	5.5 (6)	700 (3)	6

SOURCES: Figures for windfall as percentage of nonmining GDP from Gelb (1986), except Norway, which is from International Monetary Fund (1988b). Figures for windfall per capita calculated from International Monetary Fund (1990) and Table A-13.
[a] Increase in real oil-export earnings 1970–1974/1974 population.
[b] Boom year is taken as 1976.

unless they are spent domestically and because their subsequent economic effects are so closely tied to political outcomes, a better indicator of eventual political performance is the magnitude of the boom effect—that is, the increase in spending that takes place immediately after the rise in prices. Where boom effects are high, political instability is always present. Where they are medium or low, polities remain more stable. As Table 17 demonstrates, Venezuela, Iran, Nigeria, and Algeria belong in the high-effect category; Indonesia and Norway are in the medium-low category.

These findings are even more suggestive if the two democracies, Venezuela and Norway, are temporarily excluded from the sample. Without these two cases, countries in which the sudden jump in state spending was highest tended to experience the highest and most rapid instability. Regimes in both Iran and Nigeria toppled at the first sign of economic disruption from this spending at the end of the 1970s. In Indonesia, where the increase in spending was smaller and less abrupt, the regime managed to preserve its viability longer under potentially disruptive conditions. (This evidence would be considerably stronger if the sample were larger and if actual statistics were available for Nigeria and Algeria.) In Venezuela and Norway, the levels of spending would seem to predict higher and faster levels of instability than either has experienced thus far. To anticipate the argument I will make in Chapter 10, in these cases regime type and, especially, certain advantages of democracy over authoritarian rule mitigate the anticipated level of instability.

TABLE 17
BOOM EFFECT AND POLITICAL INSTABILITY

Rank Based on Boom Effect	Boom Effect[a]	Rank Based on Instability
1. Venezuela	High (686)	4
2. Iran	High (286)	1
3. Nigeria	High (n.a.)[b]	2
4. Algeria	High (n.a.)[b]	3
5. Norway	Medium (102)	6
6. Indonesia	Low (0.5)	5

SOURCES: Calculated from Table A-3 and International Monetary Fund (1990).
[a] Percent increase in the average rate of growth of government expenditures in 1974–1975 over the pre-boom 1971–1973 average. Figures for Norway are for 1976–1977 over 1973–1975.
[b] Existing evidence suggests that Nigeria's initial spending leap was in the range of Iran's (Pinto 1987, Olayiwola 1987, Struthers 1990), while Algeria's was somewhat lower (Raffinot and Jacquemot 1977, Rabhi 1979).

The strong relationship between the boom effect and political instability suggested in Table 17 is testimony once again to the enormous significance of the initial decisions made by policymakers in the wake of the 1973 boom, and it bears out the importance of policy choices at critical junctures. The logic of this relationship was already developed in Chapter 3 and illustrated by the Venezuelan case, where a high boom effect provoked the rapid expansion of the state's jurisdiction, an increase in rent-seeking behavior, economic deterioration, and a concomitant decline in the regime's capacity to handle multiple economic and political challenges. Indonesia's economic decision to permit smaller and more gradual increases affected in a positive manner not only the economic health of the country but also its political stability.

Still, the puzzle remains. What explains differences in the magnitude of boom effects? Why are some governments able to put up at least some resistance to the temptation to overspend? If Indonesia is a petrostate (and it certainly fits the definition developed in Chapter 3), why and how did it manage to contain its excessive spending better than its counterparts did? If this case is to be the exception that proves the rule rather than the negation of the argument of this book, Indonesia's distinctive policy choice cannot be the result simply of better leadership, farsighted decision-making, or historical accident—even though all these factors may play a role. Nor can it be accounted for solely by a smaller opportunity to spend since windfall sizes (Table 16) do not correlate especially with the magnitude of spending (Table 17). Nor can these outcomes be explained by a simple tautology: the countries that overspent were already unstable, and their overspending, which brought about further instability, was merely a reflection of this reality. Certainly countries like Algeria and Venezuela did not have indicators of instability any higher than those in Indonesia.

Instead, if this argument is correct, Indonesia should have exhibited some significant differences historically in the nature of its economic and institutional development so that by the time of the 1973 boom its degree of "petro-stateness" was distinct from that of its capital-deficient counterparts. This difference in development would make it less locked in to an oil-led trajectory and more flexible in its responses. Concomitantly, Iran, Nigeria, and Algeria should more closely resemble the trajectory illustrated by Venezuela. A closer look at these five countries shows that this is indeed the case.

THE COMMON EXPERIENCE
OF VENEZUELA, IRAN, NIGERIA, AND ALGERIA

The case of Venezuela suggests that at least three critical junctures shape patterns of decision-making that can be generalized to other oil-exporting developing countries prior to the 1973 price hike: the entry of international oil companies into weak states; the imposition of income taxes on companies as a prime source of the state's fiscal revenues; and regime changes that either reinforce or counteract reliance on oil rents. These critical junctures are path-dependent—that is, they are initially set off by the entry of the oil companies. They either occur in a distinct sequence, as they did in Venezuela, or overlap, as we shall see. But regardless of their timing or sequencing, they accompany one another. The institutional legacy of these events shapes a common decision calculus for policymakers in petro-states and also helps to explain variations in their responses to the boom.

In Iran, Algeria, Nigeria, and Indonesia, the dynamic interplay between their shared mode of economic growth and their institutional development began with the arrival of the multinational oil companies into their territory. As in Venezuela and sixteenth-century Spain, most important in every instance is the critical coincidence of mineral exploitation and the early stages of modern state formation. None of these countries possessed administrative structures capable of creatively resisting the process of petrolization. Instead, their states were easily penetrated by foreigners. Executive power became linked to the fate of the oil industry, and states centralized while expanding their jurisdiction in an oil-propelled dynamic.

As oil became the leading export sector in each of these countries, state frameworks for decision-making were quickly molded to facilitate the perpetuation of oil-led development, primarily through their adoption of the central institutional feature of the petro-state, its fiscal dependence on petrodollars. In Nigeria, Algeria, and Indonesia this dependence was a relatively recent phenomenon, while in Venezuela and Iran it occurred after World War I (Table 18). Without exception, diffusion (often through OPEC) accounted for the fact that newer producers adopted the same tax arrangements developed originally by Venezuela and described in Chapter 4;[4] and their states were quickly characterized by the same fundamental economic policy pattern: maximizing the external extraction of rents for subsequent domestic distribution through public spending according to a political logic.

TABLE 18
FUEL/MINERAL EXPORTS AS A PERCENTAGE OF
MERCHANDISE EXPORTS, 1960–1987

	1960	1965	1977	1982	1987
Venezuela	74	97	97	97	91
Iran	88	87	99	n.a.	n.a.
Nigeria	8	32	93	96[b]	91
Algeria[a]	12	58	97	99	98
Indonesia[a]	33	33	71	85	54
Norway[a]	22	21	32	60	51

SOURCES: World Bank, *World Development Report,* 1979, 1980, 1984, 1985, 1989.
[a] Figures include significant exports of ores or natural gas.
[b] For 1981.

The reshaping of these states is especially visible in comparative data illustrating the structure of taxation and other oil-derived revenues. Table 19 shows how oil exporters came to resemble each other in their surprisingly high rate of income taxes, of which corporate taxes (including taxes paid by the oil industry) make up the majority, and their lower than average taxes on goods and services. This pattern is especially striking when these countries are compared with the non-oil developing countries in Table 19. For the older exporters (Venezuela and Iran), these changes occurred prior to the 1973 boom, which simply exacerbated them. For those countries whose industries came on-stream primarily in the 1970s (Indonesia and Nigeria), the institutional shift to a petro-state happened during the boom. The case of Nigeria is especially dramatic in this respect. By 1975 Iran, Indonesia, Nigeria, and Venezuela averaged a mere 4.6 percent of total state revenues from goods and services, compared with 30.9 percent in non-oil developing countries.

Table 20 makes the same point. It graphically illustrates how distinctive the structure of taxation in oil countries is when compared with taxation in other developing countries with approximately the same GNP per capita. Non-oil taxes are significantly lower and corporate taxes higher. While Nigeria, for example, received approximately the same percentage of its GDP in total taxes as its non-oil counterparts, Nigeria's taxes were derived almost entirely from the oil industry—14.71 percent compared with the relatively minor (3.25 percent) corporate contribution in other developing countries.

Furthermore, as we saw in Venezuela, this reshaping was self-reinforcing. As oil money flowed into state coffers on an ever-increasing basis, it became politically more and more difficult to raise domestic

TABLE 19

TAXES AS A PERCENTAGE OF THE TOTAL REVENUE OF THE
CENTRAL GOVERNMENT, 1972–1985

	Total Income (1)	Individual Taxes (1.1)	Corporate Taxes (1.2)	Taxes on Goods and Services (5)	Nontax Revenue (V)
Indonesia					
1972	45.5	4.1	35.9	22.7	10.6
1975	66.0	2.8	58.2	12.8	8.4
1985	66.1	3.3	61.7	16.1	12.7
Iran[a]					
1972	7.2	1.1	5.9	4.9	68.7
1975	7.7	0.6	7.0	2.4	80.6
1985	13.4	1.2	12.1	8.0	54.4
Nigeria[b]					
1972	42.7	0.0	42.7	26.1	13.6
1975	72.0	0.2	71.9	1.3	12.1
1985	50.5	0.1	50.4	6.6	53.1
Venezuela					
1972	53.1	3.7	48.4	6.6	25.8
1975	60.7	1.9	57.7	2.7	26.1
1985	61.6	3.0	48.9	4.8	14.7
Non-oil developing countries					
1972	20.9	n.a.	n.a.	27.9	15.4
1975	22.4	n.a.	n.a.	30.9	14.7
1985	19.5	n.a.	n.a.	34.0	17.9
Norway					
1972	11.9	10.3	1.6	44.8	6.0
1975	11.7	9.8	1.9	41.4	7.0
1985	24.6	7.7	16.9	39.1	14.3

SOURCE: International Monetary Fund (1978, 1984, 1988a). Non-oil statistics in International Monetary Fund (1988b).
NOTES: Figures for Algeria are unavailable. Numbers in parentheses refer to IMF categories in Table A country tables. Rows do not add to 100 because selected categories are given.
[a] Oil income accrues to the central government primarily as nontax revenue from public enterprises and is listed on that line.
[b] Oil revenues are listed under corporate tax and under nontax revenue.

taxes. Thus none of these petro-states took full advantage of the fiscal respite provided by the boom to set in place strong non-oil tax systems capable of raising revenues for the post-boom period. Gelb (1986, 61) notes that trade taxes did rise as a result of the rapid increase in imports during the boom period, but even this rise was compensated for in most cases by a cut in the taxes levied on domestic goods and services (Table

TABLE 20

STRUCTURE OF TAXATION IN COMPARATIVE PERSPECTIVE, SELECTED OIL EXPORTERS
(PERCENTAGE OF GROSS NATIONAL PRODUCT)

	GNP per Capita (U.S. dollars)	Total Taxes	Total Income Taxes	Individual Taxes	Corporate Taxes	Domestic Taxes	Taxes on Foreign Trade
Indonesia (1980–82)	530	20.85	16.94	0.39	15.59	2.22	1.25
Countries with average GNP per capita of 350–849	548	12.50	5.50	2.15	2.97	4.14	6.62
Nigeria (1976–78)	870	18.89	14.72	0.01	14.71	0.60	3.56
Countries with average GNP per capita of 850–1,699	1,195	18.16	5.75	2.15	3.25	4.73	5.31
Venezuela (1977–79)	4,220	20.0	14.89	0.81	14.08	1.35	1.95
Countries with average GNP per capita of 1,700	3,392	22.75	8.08	2.35	5.00	6.30	3.19

SOURCE: Tanzi (1987, Tables 8-1, 8-2, 8-3, 8-4).

19). Gelb demonstrates that, on average, non-oil taxes remained fairly steady as a proportion of nonmining income during the first boom, then declined slightly in the second. Thus, even after two booms, the fiscal basis of these states, the central expression of oil dependence, remained relatively unchanged.

A close look at the experience of these other oil exporters illustrates the utility of the petro-state category in a more nuanced manner. Iran most closely resembles Venezuela in the sequencing of its critical events and the longevity of its petro-state. Oil emerged as a factor at the turn of the century, at about the same time that the companies were arriving in Caracas, and prior to the growth and centralization of a state administrative apparatus. Petroleum development rapidly destroyed the remnants of the traditional absolutist state it encountered, which had been founded on the notion of state-communal property, and, as in Venezuela, oil-led development introduced legal notions of private property for the first time (Bashiriyeh 1984, 7–28). The waves of intervention by the British, Russians, and Turks that followed the discovery of black gold ensured that there was no central government at all by the end of World War I; separatist movements managed to control the various provinces (Katouzian 1981, 108–110, 244–253). Oil revenues were used mainly to supplement the private incomes of regional authorities and were not even incorporated into the general budget.

Petrodollars subsequently shaped modern state and regime formation as thoroughly as they had in Venezuela. Just as American companies sought to buffer a dictator's position in Caracas, British multinationals were instrumental in supporting Reza Shah's rise to power in 1921 and for much the same reasons. They encouraged the new ruler's efforts to build a modern army, which could enforce government control over the entire country and thus provide them with one reliable bargaining partner instead of many. Oil money was tied directly to the process of centralization; by the early 1930s, direct and indirect revenues from petroleum were the largest single source of income for the government (Katouzian 1981, 255–273). As in Venezuela, the companies simultaneously insisted on agreements that "turned Persia into a private mandate for Great Britain" (Fesharaki 1976, 11–16). After the Allied invasion during World War II almost destroyed the Pahlavi regime, it was reestablished with the backing of the United States and the oil companies (Halliday 1979, 20–31). From this point, the key pillars of the regime were the army and other domestic beneficiaries of petroleum and foreigners.

The fate of the Pahlavi regime, state building, and the oil industry were inextricably intertwined. From 1954, when the United States intervened directly to stop the nationalization of petroleum and to once again prop up the dynasty, to the downfall of secular authoritarian rule in 1979, oil revenues financed a rentier, interventionist, centralized, and highly coercive but administratively weak state under the absolute authority of the shah (Katouzian 1981, 108–110). As in Venezuela, oil-led development reshaped social classes in a manner that perpetuated petrolization by decreasing the power of the landlords in the countryside, encouraging a highly protected commercial and industrial elite, and provoking massive urban migration (Looney 1982, 41–58). In the process, the agricultural sector suffered a severe decline, and oil-led development reigned supreme.[5]

After Venezuela negotiated its well-known fifty-fifty agreement, Iran adopted similar tax arrangements, which produced a sizeable revenue not linked to the productivity of the indigenous economy. This development had expected effects. State efficacy was sacrificed in tandem with the shah's increasing reliance on the political distribution of these rents to foster attempts at Western-style capitalism and to placate the regime's narrow support base (Kadhim 1983, 10). As in Venezuela, state interests became identified with the extraction of maximum revenues from the international companies rather than domestic taxation. Instead of providing fiscal support for the state and therefore being able to demand some accountability from it, the professional and business classes and even the bureaucracy became the clientele of the state, dependent on it for their income and privilege (Katouzian 1981, 244–253). Kadhim (1983, 10) remarks that this financial independence imprinted an irrational "cabalistic, even personalistic touch on the whole planning process" because ultimately all decisions had to conform to the shah's constantly shifting desires.

Iran's response to 1973, "a spending spree such as it had never experienced," was simply an extension of past regime behavior (Moghtader 1980, 256). Unlike Pérez in Venezuela, the shah never even considered the possibility of sterilizing petroleum wealth. Instead, sharing Pérez's grandiose vision of development, he sought to modernize through investments in heavy industry, encouraged a consumer boom to keep the commercial and educated classes quiet, actively destroyed politically uncontrollable traditional forms of nomadic agriculture and religious life, built up the military, formed his own political parties, and created a police state to quash opposition to his rule (Katouzian 1981, Saikal 1980).

But years of institutional decay took their toll. When oil revenues remained flat after 1975, the economic problems presented in Chapter 1 soon appeared, and the shah's government proved incapable of adjusting. State agencies, ridden by factionalism and confusion, simply ignored instructions to observe "the utmost care and economy," and they badly distorted their budget figures to give the impression that orders were being followed (Graham 1978, 93). Regime structures proved no more durable. As Katouzian (1981, 255ff) notes, "Without oil revenue, the attempt to sustain Iranian despotism would not have succeeded. Oil was *the* independent variable of the whole socio-economic fabric." Because the regime lacked an alternative basis for authority, the scarcity of petrodollars had predictable consequences for political stability. At the first sign of economic difficulty, Iran's oil-based regime dramatically came apart (Looney 1982, Nasri 1983).

This same pattern of oil dependence and institutional alteration is also evident in Nigeria, Algeria, and Indonesia, with one important difference. Their petro-states were much newer than Iran's or Venezuela's, and their transformations occurred in a more compressed and less distinctly sequenced period. The change in Nigeria's and Algeria's export profile took place in the 1960s, as Table 18 illustrates, and Indonesia's was even later. This difference had important ramifications for the velocity of institutional change. On the one hand, these countries missed the "robber baron" years, and they were able to benefit from the bargains with the oil companies previously struck by the older producers, especially through their membership in OPEC. Thus they tended to increase participation in oil rents and control over their industries relatively quickly. On the other hand, as previously noted, their contact with oil countries and companies led to the rapid diffusion of oil-based taxation and its unfortunate patterns of stateness.

Algeria illustrates some interesting variations from the previous cases in this context. As in Venezuela and Iran, the birth of its independent state coincided with the exploitation of oil by foreign, mainly French, companies.[6] But this historic coincidence took place during the eight years of revolution from 1954 to 1962. Huge fixed assets made the companies unwilling to abandon Algeria despite the independence struggle, and nationalist leaders were quick to encourage them to stay. But because oil constituted only 12 percent of merchandise exports in 1960 (Table 18), when bargaining began in earnest between the French companies and the new revolutionary regime, Algeria's main preoccupation was to recover from the war rather than to extract maximum tax benefits from the companies. Because of the great destruction wrought by the French and the precipitous decline of commercial agricultural output with the departure of most European farmers, the new regime sought substantial French development assistance over a five-year period in exchange for Algeria's retreat from the demand for a 51 percent tax, which was won by all other exporting countries (Horne 1977).

This arrangement had implications for patterns of modern state building. Although Algerian tax data are not available, oil taxes appear to have remained relatively low prior to the boom. Algeria maintained the unusually high taxes on domestic goods and services instituted by the French, which sustained some notions of accountability. Furthermore, the legitimacy accorded to those who had led the independence movement against France meant that rulers had a base of authority separate from petroleum revenues, which initially helped them weather economic downturns.

Still, Algeria is undoubtedly a petro-state. Oil provided an increasingly important economic base for the newly independent state, and by 1965 petroleum accounted for almost 60 percent of merchandise exports (Table 18). These revenues helped to unify a new state whose administrative apparatus was deeply divided, incoherent, and without clear lines of authority. But, with at least four sets of elites vying for power, seven military organizations seeking to form the core of state administration, and the exodus of Europeans crippling the former colonial apparatus, bureaucracies were too weak, politically divided, and riddled with patronage to limit or channel these revenues effectively (Nelson 1979, 206–213). Instead, as elsewhere, factionalism encouraged a rapidly growing dependence on oil (Quandt 1969, 278–279). Production and taxes on the companies climbed steadily during the 1960s, and by the mid-1970s oil earnings accounted for the majority of government revenues.

The priorities of the new revolutionary regime, influenced by the statist ideologies of both France and the socialist world, strongly reinforced the economic "biases" of oil-led development. As in other oil-exporting countries, government development plans prior to the boom stressed heavy industry, but in Algeria this emphasis was not the result merely of linkage effects from petroleum. Socialist planning also heavily emphasized industrialization over agriculture, capital accumulation over consumption, and the production of capital goods over consumer goods (Raffinot and Jacquemot 1977, 138). The 1973 boom simply permitted Algeria's resource-based industrialization to go faster, further, and deeper than it did elsewhere.[7] Socialist beliefs also reinforced the jurisdictional expansion of the petro-state. Burgeoning state enterprises sought to increase their budgets as a sign of political importance, but this practice soon became a source of rigidity that held the regime captive to its initial development priorities. In the process, Algeria became the largest borrower in the Arab world.

These rigidities were exacerbated by the same patterns of rent-seeking behavior inside the state that we have seen in other cases. The private sector, denied the opportunity for unlimited activity by socialist ideology and state expansion, systematically infiltrated the administrative apparatus for its own benefit. Simultaneously, state officials gave preferential treatment to friends and relatives, and administrative action was determined largely by ties of obligation (Etienne 1977). As economic problems appeared, divisions over policy provoked a broad development debate inside the regime with critics calling for a reordering of priorities to favor agriculture, light industry, and consumption (Grimaud 1976, 73). These policy differences heightened party factionalism and disputes over patron-client networks, impeding state efficacy in a pattern reminiscent of Venezuela's. They also helped to create a policy stalemate (Cubertafond 1981, 152).

So locked into resource-based development, oil-based patronage, and divided policy was the regime that it could not coherently manage the public sector. Nor could it adjust to a new strategy. As in Venezuela and Iran, economic problems appeared as early as 1976, especially in agriculture, and by 1977 rising prices and shortages had led to the first social unrest since the war of independence. Unlike the situation in Iran, the coherence and legitimacy stemming from Algeria's revolutionary legacy permitted the regime to weather these difficulties. Yet, despite these warning signs, subsequent budgets showed only a relatively small shift toward new priorities, and heavy industrial development remained the basis of long-term strategy. This policy exacerbated the decline in agriculture caused by both the war and petroleum exploitation (Table A-12), and farm output virtually collapsed, leaving the country especially dependent on food imports purchased with petrodollars (Balta 1981, 114–115). These imports increased at an average rate of more than 30 percent per year until oil prices plunged in 1986 (Entelis 1986, 132).

The petroleum bust, which cut Algeria's purchasing power in half between 1986 and 1988, was the catalyst for massive rioting over food shortages in 1988 and sharp questioning of the "people's" regime. Like Venezuela and Iran, Algeria entered a spiral of economic deterioration, state disorganization, and regime decay. It sought to democratize political structures as a mechanism for increasing legitimacy and accountability. But by the 1990s, with inflation increasing (Table A-8), Islamic fundamentalism on the rise (primarily as a reaction to economic hardship), its new president assassinated, and a possible transition to democracy aborted, Algeria's economy had ground to a halt, and its polity was threatened with the total collapse of order (Amair 1992, Mortimer 1993).

Nigeria, even more than Algeria, illustrates just how quickly a petrostate can be made; in this respect it too differs somewhat from the older petro-states. Foreign companies exploited oil discoveries relatively late, and the first exports virtually coincided with independence in 1960 (Olayiwola 1987, 79). As in Venezuela and Iran, a weak new state was unable to direct or to stem the process of petrolization. Unlike the situation in Algeria, there was virtually no basis for establishing regime legitimacy or state authority. To the contrary, the legacy of the British—who united formerly autonomous ethnic groups into one territory and then pursued a divide-and-rule strategy—ensured that Nigeria would experience especially great difficulty in establishing political institutions capable of winning the allegiance of all Nigerians, much less confronting the strongest bulwarks of capitalism. Thus there was virtually no resistance as petroleum became the dominant sector of the economy. Oil exports, which were only 8 percent of total exports at the time of independence, soared to 93 percent by 1977 (Table 18).

Petroleum exploitation changed the Nigerian state in a manner that would make the stability of any regime grafted onto it even more acutely dependent on fluctuations in prices than other petro-states were, regardless of whether prices rose or fell. As a result of the impact of oil, the civil war in Biafra, and other factors, the public sector shared the same dynamic of expansion, centralization, and growing involvement in direct production that marked all oil exporters. But in Nigeria expanded jurisdiction took place in the context of unresolved ethnic and religious differences that were localized in different regions. The combination of the creation of new states in 1967 and 1975 as a means of assuaging regional tensions and the growth of the federal budget from petrodollars made the competing (and often hostile) local governments increasingly dependent on transfers from a vastly enlarged federal pool (Watts and Lubeck 1983, 108). By the early 1970s, the central government, especially the executive, became the focus of not only class but also a variety of ethnic and religious demands. Not surprisingly, the distribution of petrodollars became the main mechanism for cementing loyalties and sustaining social peace in a fragile and divided system (Watts 1987, Diamond 1990).

In this context, fluctuations in oil prices, whether up or down, were especially perilous. As in all oil exporters, changing the size of the pool again raised the problem of assignment and threw into question all past class and sectoral arrangements. But in Nigeria, in contrast to these other cases, the increasing pool also opened the dangerous political issue of the distribution of previously agreed-on shares to regionally based ethnic groups. Frank (1984) has seen the relative decentralization of Nigeria (when compared with the ultracentralized Iranian state under the shah) as an advantage for regime stability. However, this decentralization was in fact based on a volatile combination of expensively won loyalties, conflicting identities, and highly uncertain revenues—a formula that virtually guaranteed instability. Repeated intense fights over budgetary allocations to state governments, frequent new arrangements regarding their number and relative power, and constant alterations in electoral rules and rulers were the recurrent manifestations of this problem (Diamond 1990). Between 1970 and 1985, Nigeria was governed by five military administrations and one civilian government, and almost all these changes in rulers closely matched shifts in the price of petroleum.

With virtually no administratively capable state or authoritative regime arrangements in place to resist the temptation of rent seeking, perpetual overspending and later overborrowing were more than probable; they were almost inevitable. In 1973, this temptation was compounded by the enormously expensive task of reconstruction following Nigeria's thirty-month civil war. Faced with an army that had grown powerful in the war, ethnic groups calling for the creation of more states, the politically sensitive issue of conducting a national population census that would determine the size of competing communities, and crying social needs, the government embarked on a huge national plan aimed at achieving rapid industrialization, the highest possible growth rate, and indigenization.

This plan—like almost any economic plan that could have been devised—had little chance to succeed. Costly swings between military and civilian rule added to the inchoate nature of the state and the expense of governance. In a vicious cycle, as regime instability encouraged an increased reliance on petrodollars to purchase loyalties and fuel patronage, petrodollars fostered an acute form of political rent seeking. Because instability was so high, regime maintenance (of whatever sort) had a surprisingly short horizon, which exacerbated the predatory character of the petro-state. In Nigeria, the widespread corruption that marked Venezuela, Iran, and to a lesser (or perhaps more hidden) extent Algeria reached epidemic proportions. It became the most visible expression of how the state was targeted and rendered dysfunctional by "pirate capitalists" (Schatz 1984), politicians, and other rent seekers, who were especially venal because they believed they had little time to benefit from their links to the state (Frank 1984, Falola and Ihonvbere 1985, Diamond 1990).

Soaring state expenditures set off a process of petrolization that may be one of the worst cases of Dutch Disease on record. It badly affected the rural sector and other productive areas of the economy. Farming declined: the proportion of labor in agriculture dropped from 71 percent in 1960 to 54 percent in 1980 (Olayiwola 1987, 138), and the annual production of major cash crops fell dramatically. Nigeria shifted from being an agricultural exporter to being a major importer of food.[8] As oil prices dropped throughout the 1980s, the resulting economic chaos discredited military leaders and eventually encouraged coup-prone Nigeria to seek a transition once again from military to civilian rule; but by 1993, in another manifestation of political decay, elections were postponed indefinitely, and unstable military rule was the order of the day (Adejumabi and Momoh 1995). Thus Nigeria too, like Venezuela, Algeria, and Iran, lived out the prophecy of the petro-state.

EXPLAINING THE INDONESIAN "EXCEPTION"

Indonesia shares similarities with these four "old" and "new" petro-states. But we have already seen how thus far it has escaped the severe economic deterioration and consequent regime instability of its counterparts. Possessing one of the world's oldest oil industries, it exhibits the especially tight intertwining of an oil-based economy, the state, and the regime characteristic of other petro-states. But, unlike the situation in these other states, neither modern state building nor regime formation completely coincided with oil's domination of the economy. Thus petroleum could not mold institutions during this first critical conjuncture to the same extent as elsewhere, which had a long-term impact on state capacity and the structuration of choice.

Unlike the wartime experiences of Nigeria and Algeria, where the petroleum industry was only briefly affected, Indonesia's oil exploitation was severely disrupted by Dutch scorched-earth measures, the Japanese occupation, and bombardments by the Allied forces in World War II. Thus even though the newly independent state was itself quite weak from the accumulated effects of three centuries of Dutch colonialism, Indonesia had a "breathing space" in the beginning of its modern state formation that was denied other oil exporters. Crude output grew at a relatively low (for oil exporters of the time) annual rate of about 8 percent between 1950 and 1966, exploration was at a standstill, and oil taxes remained less than 1 percent of GDP until 1968 (Arndt 1984, 137; Gillis 1983, 237).

This disruption of the oil industry continued until the end of the 1960s because of the Sukarno government's escalating nationalism. Eventually Shell withdrew from Indonesia altogether. Not until the new Suharto regime adopted an unusually favorable foreign-investment law in 1967 were American and Japanese companies willing to negotiate large concessions and production-sharing arrangements. Thus, until 1968 only approximately 10 percent of state revenues came from corporate taxes on petroleum, and oil made up little more than a third of exports (Table 18). After that date, Indonesia finally began to show signs of growing petroleum dependence; production between 1968 and 1973 rose at an average annual rate of 17 percent, and expenditures for exploration leapt from $38 million in 1968 to $807 million in 1974 (Arndt 1984, 138). Still, dependence never reached the level of that of the other exporters.

The interruption in Indonesia's oil history meant that the Suharto regime was defined less by its relatively modest reliance on petrodollars than by the devastating economic legacy of the Sukarno period. As a result, sustaining the combination of favorable tariffs on trade, foreign borrowing, and especially high foreign aid from Western countries eager to combat the threat of communism initially outweighed any concern with extracting the maximal amount of income from the companies. Putting top priority on reversing economic setbacks (as well as physically annihilating up to a half million Sukarno supporters), the regime adopted two unique state features in reaction to its predecessor. These changes subsequently shaped its spending behavior in a distinctive manner.

First, the Suharto regime strengthened state capacity by literally borrowing expertise from elsewhere. Suharto granted unusual prominence to an internationally oriented economic team who became the functional equivalent of an autonomous civil service and whose long tenure provided a continuity in economic policy that has rarely been matched. In addition to encouraging a strong outward orientation in state agencies, these technocrats held on to two principles "with particular tenacity": the avoidance of any quantitative controls on exchange rates and the "balanced-budget rule" (Gillis 1983, 13–16). Both had particularly significant implications for the flexibility of Indonesia's oil-exporting state.

To avoid exchange controls Indonesia devalued its currency regularly in 1966, 1971, 1981, and 1983, thus avoiding some of the overvaluation associated with petroleum and escaping the greater trauma stemming from postponement that plagued its counterparts. In effect, it carried out the type of gradual adjustment that had eluded the other oil exporters. Meanwhile, the balanced-budget rule, adopted to contain the large deficits of the Sukarno years, had two results. On the expenditure side, austerity reigned—the antithesis of petro-state patterns. On the revenue side, domestic taxes increased nineteenfold, so that the share of taxes in the 1969 GDP nearly doubled, to 9 percent, and only 1.7 percent of these taxes came from oil (Gillis 1983, 18).[9] These policies set Indonesia apart, and they induced a diversified tax base and a measure of fiscal discipline that was absent in other petro-states (Pinto 1987, 429) (Table 19).

Second, the regime adopted agriculture, and especially rice self-sufficiency, as a principal objective, thus counteracting much of the bias of oil-led development (Mears 1984).[10] In stark contrast to the policies of the other four capital-deficient exporters, rice self-sufficiency was a major, if not the central, development goal in every five-year plan of the Suharto regime. This preoccupation with the expansion of rice production led to heavy government subsidies for fertilizer use and the restoration and expansion of irrigation networks in Java. As a result, rice production grew by 4.2 percent per year between 1968 and 1978, the oil boom notwithstanding, and Indonesia avoided the serious deterioration of the agricultural sector that plagued other petro-states (Pinto 1987, 432).

Thus, by the time the 1973 oil boom occurred, Indonesia was in a development trajectory somewhat different from that of the other oil exporters, which augured better for managing the boom and hence for political stability. Its degree of "petro-stateness," as measured by export as well as fiscal dependence on petroleum, was significantly less than that of the other developing oil countries (see Tables 18 and 19). Rather than being totally permeated by rent seeking and institutional rigidity, its policy patterns were based on fiscal austerity and domestic taxation as well as monetary flexibility.

Whether these patterns would have held throughout the overwhelming temptation of two booms is uncertain. In 1973 Suharto initially behaved much like other governments as Indonesia's foreign-exchange earnings doubled for two years in a row. His first reaction was to revise the 1974–1975 budget upward, double the salaries of civil servants, increase subsidies to provincial governments, and greatly expand social-welfare programs (Arndt 1984, 141). But government largess slowed abruptly in late 1974 as a result of a "fortunate" misfortune of major proportions in Pertamina, its oil industry. This historical accident reinforced Indonesia's differences from the other exporters and meant that caution eventually overruled the politics of plenty.

Pertamina, like other national oil industries, was somewhat autonomous from the rest of the state apparatus. Under the corrupt direction of General Ibnu Sutowo, it had used more than $1 billion in oil revenues due to the government to cover its excessive short-term borrowing. When digging into government revenues proved insufficient to cover its debts and international creditors insisted that the government assume responsibility for the Pertamina fiasco, the euphoria evoked by the boom immediately vanished. Instead, by 1975, as the spending of other petro-states continued to shoot up, Pertamina's debts had reached a whopping one-third of GDP, and the country's credit standing had been badly damaged. As the Suharto government sought frantically to repair its image by repaying its external debts, international reserves failed to rise from 1974 to 1976 even though exports increased by 41 percent (Gillis 1983, 62).

The Pertamina crisis effectively did what governments elsewhere had failed to accomplish: it sterilized a good share of Indonesia's petrodollar windfalls.[11] Indeed, as Arndt (1984, 67) remarked, it proved to be "a blessing in disguise" because there could hardly have been a more antiinflationary use of the oil windfall than to repay foreign debt. Thus, as spending rose relatively slowly until 1978 (Table A-3), inflation, which reached a peak of 40 percent in 1974, actually dropped thereafter—a reversal of the trend in other oil exporters. The ripple effect of Pertamina was also felt elsewhere. Unable to borrow extensively until it could restore its rating with the banks, Indonesia was the only petro-state that did not take advantage of low interest rates and high oil prices between

1974 and 1980 to borrow heavily to finance its development. Instead, its ratio of total external debt to GNP actually dropped between 1975 and 1980, contrary to the tendency of most other exporters (Table A-14).

Still, the Pertamina crisis, however well-timed, is not in itself a sufficient explanation for Indonesian exceptionalism. A powerful example of rent seeking, it cannot explain the unusual flexibility of state agencies and government officials compared with those in other capital-deficient countries. The explanation is rooted instead in the different path taken earlier—a path delineated by powerful interests vested in agriculture, not petroleum, and the ability of state agencies to enforce budgetary restrictions.

This different path yielded different outcomes. Unlike Iran's inability to even recognize a problem, Venezuela and Nigeria's costly exchange-rate controls and postponement of adjustment, or Algeria's incapacity to shift away from heavy industry, the Indonesian government was able to recognize problems promptly and define workable solutions. It had early and gradual devaluations of its currency and managed to protect its non-oil exports.[12] While huge investments in steel threatened to produce white elephants of awesome proportions in Venezuela and Nigeria,[13] the Suharto government canceled or postponed a number of dubious large projects planned by technocrats at the first hint that oil prices might drop (Auty 1989, 369). Indonesia avoided severe disruption of the agricultural economy, and it was able to keep its food imports per capita relatively steady between 1976 and 1982 (Pinto 1987, 434). Perhaps most indicative of its unusual capacity, while Venezuela and Nigeria sought to avoid antagonizing their private sectors over domestic taxation, Indonesia alone took advantage of the fiscal respite provided by oil-price increases to enact a significant tax reform prior to the sharp plunge in oil prices in 1986.

Yet these differences between Indonesia and the other exporters, important as they are, should not be overstated. Indonesia is a variation on the theme of the petro-state. Although it has thus far survived the booms and busts of the 1970s and 1980s better than the other countries here, it shows familiar and disturbing signs: oil dependence has grown considerably (Table 18), and so has rent-seeking behavior inside the state, especially by the children of Suharto (*New York Times,* November 11, 1990, A3). This rent seeking has permeated the bureaucracy and weakened the ethic of tight fiscal management. Meanwhile, the army, which has benefited handsomely from the regime, has become increasingly sensitive to the widespread anger over the rapacious business activities of the president's family and some of his closest associ-ates, and it is uneasy about the problem of succession (*New York Times*, November 11, 1990, A3). The lesson from other oil exporters is clear in this respect: should acute economic problems be added to this situation, political decay could quickly turn into regime crisis, and Indonesia would look surprisingly like the other petro-states (Booth 1992).

Above all, Venezuela, Iran, Nigeria, Algeria, and Indonesia share a path-dependent trajectory that began when the exploitation of petro-leum altered their economies and states. This trajectory strongly en-courages using petrodollars to replace other fiscal revenues, expanding the jurisdiction of the state, adopting resource-based industrialization, and increasing public spending significantly. At the same time, it erodes the authoritative mechanisms of the state by establishing incentives for rampant rent seeking. In each case, these choices have moved these five countries further along the road of petrolization, while simultaneously creating vested interests in perpetuating the process. At present, with world oil supply plentiful and prices relatively low, weak states that were initially unable to place clear limits on their rentier activities must learn to do so if they are to make the transition to competitive econo-mies. But such adjustments are especially difficult in an institutional context where standard operating procedures are based on spending and where oil-based interests defend their protected status.

THE IMPORTANCE OF STATENESS:
THE CASE OF NORWAY

How different these development trajectories might have looked had the exploitation of petroleum not coincided with modern state forma-tion—that is, had they been managed by a highly institutionalized appa-ratus and strongly entrenched routines! Norway provides an interesting comparison with the five oil exporters examined above for precisely this reason. The fact that its economic and institutional development diverged substantially from that of Venezuela, Iran, Nigeria, Algeria, and Indonesia prior to becoming an oil exporter provides an opportu-nity to demonstrate the advantages of a more highly institutionalized and less politicized administrative structure for handling bonanzas.

To a surprising extent, the experience of Norway after the 1962 dis-covery of North Sea oil resembles the pattern of boom behavior we have already seen. It thus confirms the powerful pressures delineated in Chapter 3 to shift economies into higher (but only temporarily higher) public and private consumption growth in the wake of a boom. Although Norway's windfall in 1976, when net exports started to flow, was considerably smaller than that in other countries (Table 16), and although it had the added advantage of being able to plan its response because its newfound wealth was the result of a discovery and not a sudden price increase, the initial reaction of policymakers was the same as government revenues from petroleum exports shot up—from 1.5 billion kroner in 1970 to 14.5 billion in 1975—public expenditures in 1976 rose 17.1 percent over the previous year, then continued to grow more slowly until 1979 (Table A-3).

Expectations rose in tandem with spending. The Labor Party, which had ruled almost continuously for fifty years, saw the acquisition of petrodollars as an opportunity to achieve its three main goals of full employment, greater equality through redistribution, and expansion of the welfare state. It increased spending on social services, pensions, and public employment (Galenson 1986, 13). It also granted huge subsidies to agriculture (*New York Times,* April 20, 1978, D13) and industry (especially shipping, fisheries, and manufacturing), and real wages rose by about 25 percent from 1974 to 1977 (El Mallakh, Noreng, and Poulson 1984, 88).

The combined effect of these policies was a huge expansion of the public sector and a boom in consumption. The extent of this increase is best captured by Eliasson's (1983) comparison of public consumption in Norway with that of Sweden, which was also in full expansion, and the countries of the OECD between 1972 and 1983 (Figure 2). Like its other oil-exporting counterparts, Norway was in a spending spree that left other European countries far behind.

Norway's boom effect created predictable problems. Inflation rose sharply in 1975, well above the pre-boom 1970s average of about 7 percent, then continued to increase more slowly (Table A-8). The current-account deficit became the highest of any OECD country except the United States, and external debt was the highest ever in any OECD country. Symptoms of Dutch Disease appeared, as agriculture declined from 6 to 4 percent of GDP and manufacturing from 20 to 15 percent between 1977 and 1982 (Table A-12). The exploitation of offshore oil resulted in a marked deterioration in Norway's competitive position as its labor costs became among the highest in the world and as the relative average value of manufacturing exports fell steadily (Noreng 1980, 58; Lind and MacKay 1980, 23).

These economic problems translated into political change as the elec-

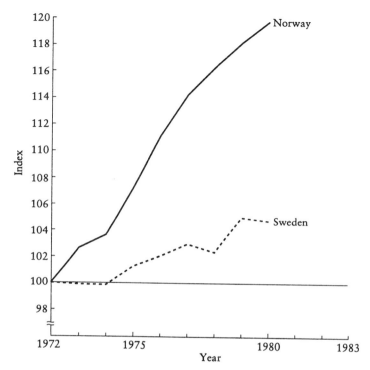

Figure 2.   Public consumption: Norway, Sweden, and
OECD, 1972–1983; index: 100 = OECD. From Eliasson
(1983).

torate began to abandon the Labor Party for the Conservative Party; by
1981 the Conservatives became the dominant force in the country, end-
ing a half century of Labor domination. Unable to cope with the daunt-
ing task of reorienting a country whose industrial decline was only
barely masked by the rise in oil's contribution to total exports to a high
of 60 percent in 1982 (Table 18), Conservatives saw their domination
end in 1986, as oil prices plunged . Although a weakened Labor Party
managed to return to power, Norwegian politics were characterized by
unpredictable alliances for the first time in its modern history.

   But, as familiar as this story seems, it is in fact quite different. Norway's economic crisis was much less severe than that facing the developing oil-exporting countries. Although the government changed, Norway experienced no regime crisis, and it was able to protect some of its
traditional exports—for example, cement, aluminum, pulp, and paper

(Galenson 1986, 2–5). Unlike all other exporters, it established substantial control over petroleum policy on the basis of consensus, protected against the worst excesses of petrolization, and permitted voluntary and relatively rapid adjustment. In effect, its highly institutionalized state structures provided a type of "creative resistance" to the overwhelming impact of the bonanza that was simply unavailable to the developing countries.

The contrast to other exporters from the point of departure—that is, from the discovery of oil on the North Sea shelf—is telling. The structures that "received" Norway's boom could hardly have been more different from those of the developing countries. Oil companies, especially eager to exploit resources outside of OPEC's dominion, did not encounter a poor country, a weak state, undeveloped social forces, or a predatory, authoritarian ruler. Instead, Norway in the 1960s was already one of the world's wealthiest, most equitable, and most democratic countries. The most thinly populated country in Europe was characterized by relative cultural homogeneity, relatively low levels of urbanization, and a diversified economy based primarily on agriculture, forestry, fishing, shipping, and manufacturing. Unemployment was close to nil, growth had been steady for two decades, and poverty was virtually eliminated by a welfare state supported by a diversified tax base (Table 19).

The state in Norway was, in Olsen's (1983, 122) words, "a typical civil servants' state," which came remarkably close to what Weber labeled an ideal bureaucracy operating under rational legal authority. Its strong roots could be traced back to at least 1680, and its legal status was enshrined in the first independent constitution of 1814. In the absence of competing political and socioeconomic elites, this long continuity firmly established the irremovability of civil servants, their professional qualities, their career paths, and their unity. After the 1840s, state officialdom became more heterogeneous, more specialized, more expert, and more open to those groups most affected by public policies. By the 1970s, when oil was discovered, civil servants were considerably entrenched in a long bureaucratic tradition, and they formed the core of a lean, autonomous, and highly efficient public-sector apparatus.[14]

Several features of this civil-service state were especially notable. First, recruitment was solely by merit; thus civil servants were the best educated of all major elite groups and among the most prestigious. Because they were an elite group, they realistically perceived their opportunities as better inside the state than in the private sector.[15] Second, civil servants were unusually insulated from and impervious to influence peddling. Advancement depended on nominations from the top civil servants, and outsiders rarely could sway these choices. Although bureaucrats were more engaged in political parties, interest organizations, and other public activities than the population at large, strong norms made arbitrary intervention by political leaders or organized interests illegitimate. To the contrary, actions of this sort were likely to be strongly criticized in the parliament and the mass media. Third, corruption was simply nonexistent. Since the eighteenth century, strong mechanisms of accountability, including ombudspeople, special courts, and public access to documents, and even stronger norms ruled out such behavior (Elder, Thomas, and Arter 1982, 138ff).[16] Fourth, the behavior of civil servants was predictably cautious and incrementalist and was based on expertise and strong organizational routines.[17] In sum, this "civil-service state" was the complete antithesis of Venezuela and the other politicized states examined previously.

This unusually high degree of stateness was complemented by Norway's open and participatory democracy. Its regime, though well known for the predominance of a single party, was characterized by an unusual combination of high participation and stability, as well as an orderly system of "corporate pluralism," in which associations of workers, employers, farmers, and fishermen bargained with each other and with the state over development priorities. Although the combination of party and corporate representation might seem to have resembled Venezuela's pacted regime, in Norway these actors had carefully defined jurisdictions and prerogatives, just as civil servants acted within highly institutionalized networks of organized interests. The resulting balance of forces moderated pressures toward politicization and also prevented Weber's "dictatorship of the bureaucrats." In this exceptionally favorable environment, the prevailing policy style emphasized caution in the face of change, respect for standard operating procedures, segmentation according to issue area, consensus building, and egalitarianism (Elder, Thomas, and Arter 1982, Olsen 1983).

The discovery of huge oil and gas fields occurred in this context. In marked contrast to the situation in all other oil-exporting countries, multinational companies were forced to bargain with the representatives of a highly developed state bureaucracy who felt no strong need for a qualitatively new revenue base. Organizing a framework for controlling the oil industry required a high degree of sophistication in planning and administration, which Norway, unlike other oil exporters, possessed in abundance. Thus, as the companies negotiated with the state, they came up against top civil servants whose lack of knowledge about petroleum matters was counterbalanced by their expertise, prudence, and incorruptibility. In contrast to their counterparts in the developing countries, they were in no rush to start oil production, which was initially viewed as adding marginally to an already healthy growth rate, and they could not be pushed to proceed until they were institutionally ready (Noreng 1980, 43).

The comprehensive oil arrangements that resulted in the early 1970s after significant public debate were far from the original agreements acquiesced to by Venezuela's Gómez or Iran's Reza Shah a half century earlier, and they contained features that other oil exporters in the developing world had spent decades to achieve—at the cost of fabulous amounts of lost rents. Aimed at securing a fair domestic share of the revenues while guaranteeing the technology and expertise necessary to undertake exploration, they established the predominant role of the state through a reorganized Ministry of Industry and a new state oil company (Statoil), an explicit role for private and foreign companies under state supervision, and a system of corporate taxation of the oil firms (Noreng 1980, 37–44). In developing these guidelines, Norway benefited from OPEC's considerable experience as well as from its own experience and standard operating procedures.

In sharp contrast to the 1975 Venezuelan state reform, which attempted to cope with similar issues of jurisdictional boundaries and institutional reorganization, Olsen (1988, 23) emphasizes how oil issues were interpreted and dealt with in the light of previously established bureaucratic routines. Although oil policy was a new issue with an apparent lack of guiding rules, the state followed several experience-based standard operating procedures. For example, the state's struggles with international companies over the ownership of Norway's waterfalls in the early twentieth century provided a frame of reference for its concession policies. In another example, because the Maritime Directorate (normally responsible for safety on floating rigs) did not have experience with oil rigs, it treated them as "a somewhat peculiar ship" and hence knew how to handle them. "Important decisions thus appeared obvious, natural and reasonable" (Olsen 1988, 23). Norway was thus able to extend its bureaucratic norms to new areas, avoid an unwieldy duplication of functions, and escape the damaging politicization that accompanied the establishment of new public-private arenas elsewhere.[18]

The contrast with Venezuela, Iran, Nigeria, Algeria, and Indonesia is also evident in Norway's superior capacity to control the impact of petroleum on its existing institutions. This ability was due not only to the professionalism of the civil service but also to the existence of non-oil-based "vested" interests who were able to present their concerns in a democratic context. Debate over the appropriate rate of development, which took place in other oil countries only after the adverse consequences of the boom were clear or never took place at all, occurred well before oil revenues became significant to the Norwegian economy. Most organized economic and political forces professed some hostility to this potential threat to the Norwegian way of life (even as they welcomed its benefits), with the fishing industry, environmental groups, and farmers the most consistent opponents of oil-led development (Lind and MacKay 1980, 141–142). Only oil-related industries and some businessmen, trade unionists, and Western allies pressured for faster exploitation.

These concerns were quickly channeled back to the civil service through parliament and the cabinet, thus reinforcing the state's own "go-slow" bias (Stinchcombe and Heimer 1985, 94). This combination of widespread social concern and bureaucratic expertise ultimately led to a 1974 parliamentary recommendation to adopt a restrictive approach to oil based on caution, state control, moderation, and long-term planning (Noreng 1980, 28). The eventual compromise over oil policy meant that Norway's boom effect was significantly less than it could have been (Table 17). The Norwegian government itself, unlike its counterparts, was able to put a brake on its initial expenditure imprudence.

Norway also stands in marked contrast to the other oil exporters in its ability to ward off the insidious rentier behavior that accompanied booms elsewhere. Its governments could thus retain the historically acquired flexibility that permitted them to limit lock-in and to engage in timely (rather than postponed) adjustments. Oil revenues were not dissipated through corruption and white-elephant projects (Lind and MacKay 1980, 45). Although they were utilized to increase government borrowing very rapidly, more than half of external debt was used to develop the petroleum sector (Galenson 1986, 54), and once the dangers of overborrowing were apparent, even Statoil was no longer permitted to seek credits in its own name (*Financial Times*, May 11, 1982, 30). Unlike the other exporters, Norway virtually halted borrowing as a part of voluntary contraction efforts between 1978 and 1981. By 1983, when other oil exporters were sinking into a dangerous debt cycle, Norway's foreign debt had been largely paid (El Mallakh, Noreng, and Poulson 1984, 134).

Perhaps most indicative of its different behavior, the Norwegian government sought to protect the state's non-oil fiscal capacity. As corporate revenues from petroleum shot up, it resisted the strong temptation to permit oil revenues to replace its normal revenue base by lowering taxes. Unlike all other exporters, it managed to sustain its domestic tax base, although it did suffer some erosion (Table 19). Taxes remained progressive, and they contributed to another unique outcome: petroleum revenues, which produced wider income disparities in most other exporters, contributed to a more equal distribution of income here (Galenson 1986). Rather than replace non-oil taxation, Norway put much of its recent bonuses into a "petroleum fund," set up to store wealth for the time next century when its oil starts to run out. Taken together, these factors cushioned the adjustment necessary in the face of oscillating oil prices and generally protected Norwegians from the tremendous swings that citizens in other exporting countries experienced.

The cases presented in this chapter yield two significant and somewhat contradictory lessons. On the one hand, strong preexisting institutions in both state and regime make a significant difference both for managing the entry of the petroleum industry and for handling subsequent booms. In Norway, where state capacity is high, such institutions counteracted the temptation to accelerate development, defused potentially divisive political issues through the use of routine procedures, developed clear policy alternatives, corrected mistaken policy decisions, and controlled the spread of rent-seeking behavior. The contrast with all other exporters, where oil exploitation seemed to transform state institutions and practices virtually overnight, is especially striking in this respect. Even in comparison with Indonesia, where the boom effect was also relatively low and where policymakers demonstrated their ability to resist some of the temptations of oil addiction, Norway had constraints against spending far more firmly institutionalized. It did not depend on "borrowed" state capacity from international advisers, a "fortunate" misfortune that produced the sterilization of rents, or the arbitrary decisions of one-man rule.

On the other hand, all these cases, but especially Norway, are powerful testaments to the "overwhelmingness" of booms. Even a stable democracy that faced no immediate need to purchase the loyalty of its citizens and that was blessed with a diversified economy and developed state was initially incapable of resisting the tremendous incentives to spend more than it should. As a result, Norway too experienced great dependence on oil revenues, which grew to almost 20 percent of all fiscal revenues, as well as manifestations of Dutch Disease, which continued to be related to the way oil revenues were previously spent in expanded public consumption (Galenson 1986). Faced with such tremendous pressures, the weak political institutions of colonized or semi-colonized countries could hardly have failed to be remolded. Indeed policymakers in the developing oil exporters, believing they could not afford to wait to overcome the legacies of underdevelopment, actively encouraged the reshaping of their public sectors and regimes by exploiting their petroleum as fast as possible. In the process they weakened even their most efficient institutions.

Once again the contrast with Norway is telling. "Professors and so-called experts from other countries give us advice to speed up oil production," Norway's prime minister once remarked. "We don't want it. The point is to be sensible and careful" (*New York Times,* September 28, 1975, 1). His words point to more than a different attitude or set of preferences; they underline different power relations and a different structure of choice. From the relative points of departure of the oil exporters examined here, only Norway had both the luxury and the state capacity to resist petroleum's recasting of its institutions. To the contrary, its institutions managed to turn petroleum into "just another raw material" (Olsen 1988, 24).

TEN

Commodities, Booms, and States Revisited

"The revenue of the state *is* the state," Edmund Burke remarked in *Reflections on the Revolution in France,* and his words are emphatically confirmed by the experience of oil exporters. The origin of a state's revenues reveals the links among modes of economic development, the transformation of political institutions, the shaping of preferences, and, ultimately, the capacity of states to design or alter their development trajectories. The experiences of mining states, both sixteenth-century Spain and contemporary oil exporters, demonstrate how frameworks for decision-making are transformed to systematically favor one path over another, and they poignantly illustrate how difficult the process of reorientation can be.

Most striking in the comparisons of oil exporters is the similar political behavior exhibited across historical time, geographic regions, regime types, religions, and cultures regardless of the diverse intentions expressed by policymakers. When petroleum exploitation is introduced into weak institutions, the transformations it triggers fundamentally alter the decision calculus of public officials. In each case examined here, incentives were quickly created that encouraged the use of state power to extract maximum resources internationally and to redistribute them domestically. The rules of assignment were based on political rent seeking rather than economic efficiency, and these rules became the standard operating procedures of the state. So relentless were these structural pulls that they persistently overwhelmed even the best intentions to "sow the petroleum," resulting instead in economic deterioration and political decay.

This concluding chapter takes a final look at the relationship between structure and agency in petro-states. After reexamining how commodities, booms, and states combine to produce a narrow range of choice, it investigates several remaining questions. First, is oil-led development, which is so central to the remaking of states, "neutral" with regard to regime—that is, is its impact the same regardless of type of polity? More specifically, can democracy or authoritarian rule better counteract the ill effects from the petrolization of the economy, state, and society, or does regime type not matter in this respect? Second, is oil, in Hirschman's (1977) words, a villain or a hero? Finally, what theoretical and policy implications stem from an analysis that links leading commodities not only to economic and social change, as other scholars have done (especially Cardoso and Faletto 1969), but also to state formation and state capacity? What light might the study of oil exporters shed on such crucial debates as the role of the state in economic development or the relative utility of structural versus choice-based approaches to understanding developing countries?

STRUCTURING CHOICE
IN OIL-EXPORTING COUNTRIES

Contemporary developing oil exporters are similar to sixteenth-century Spain in the manner in which both long- and short-term commodity booms transformed their institutional structures "in a spectacular manner." [1] Mining booms encouraged a rentier development model, created powerful interests vested in the perpetuation of this model, and reshaped public agencies so that they became wedded to the model. These transformations occurred rapidly at all levels of political domination—the state, the regime, and the government—and they took firm hold when mining revenues replaced other income as the state's primary fiscal base. As the ambitions and goals of public officials and private interests quickly expanded to meet and then exceed these revenues, a permanent and overwhelming incentive to substitute reliance on public expenditures for other forms of statecraft was institutionalized.

All these cases exemplify the decision-making that results from the interaction of commodities, booms, and weak states. In Spain, the Habsburgs quickly spent American treasure, then resorted to foreign borrowing, which, in turn, was guaranteed by this treasure. The monarchy became so overextended that it eagerly awaited the arrival of new booty from Mexico and Peru solely to maintain itself—the origin of the phrase "when the ship comes in." In the oil exporters, rentier states overspent and then also turned to borrowing, which first supplemented and then supplanted petrodollars. The pattern was the same: debt and extraordinary revenues rose together in a mutually reinforcing relationship, then their paths diverged, with debt rising and mining revenues falling. States next embarked on a desperate (and eventually useless) search for new revenues to pay back the debt, with Spanish conquerors exploiting Indian workers to the breaking point, and policymakers in oil countries raiding the coffers of their own newly nationalized oil industries.

The difficulties such states face in altering their development trajectories are enormous. Because mining involves high sunken costs and high rents, influential interests have a strong stake in the existing arrangements. In Spain, nobles and clergy, often made wealthy through the largess of the state, lived off rents and encouraged the efforts of the Crown to keep them flowing. In the oil exporters, foreign oil companies, rentier capitalists, state-based political elites, and organized labor benefited from and defended the status quo, even as they fought among themselves to alter the distribution of shares. From the public coffers, oil revenues produced private goods for both individuals and organizations. Whether these goods took the form of enormous profits, overemployment, unusual amounts of leisure, excessive salaries, astonishingly high protective barriers, bloated contracts, or outright corruption, these hugely unproductive factors raised the social cost of government. Not surprisingly, they were ferociously defended by their beneficiaries for as long as possible, even when economic and political rationality clearly illuminated the folly of such persistence.

Less well understood is the fact that mining states in developing countries also encounter high barriers to change raised by their own institutions. Because power and plenty are so closely linked and because alternative sources of authority tend to be weak, "state interests" are uniquely identified with perpetuating the state's traditional fiscal base by advancing the existing development model and fostering social interests that will support state policy. Petro-states are not just the product of the struggle of classes and organizations; they play a singular role in actually creating their own clients. Budget-maximizing bureaucracies' subsequent attempts to increase their own organizational rents and those of their clients at the expense of others have a self-perpetuating dynamic: the greater the budget, the more clients, and vice versa. Paradoxically, this relationship especially holds during periods of prolonged plenty or sudden price spikes—that is, just when alternative futures might be most easily envisioned and financed.

Most notable in the Spanish and developing-country cases presented here is the "overdetermination" that seems to define their realities. Once these countries embarked on their development trajectories, perpetuation of these trajectories became the easiest and most logical choice. Thus, despite the fact that booms made policymakers believe in "politics without limits," these cases illustrate a surprisingly narrow space for agency because of the interaction between mineral development and preexisting institutions. Political struggle in the critical conjuncture of the booms was only over the domestic distribution of rents. It was never over the broader issue of whether, when, and at what rate they should be permitted to overwhelm the economy and state or what alternative development models might be appropriate.

But this structural interpretation still leaves a number of questions unanswered. Economic deterioration and political decay were not inevitable in either Spain or contemporary oil exporters. Discrete choices by actors and agencies permitted mining revenues to enter the domestic economy and determined their immediate (if not ultimate) use. Alternatively, these funds could have been successfully "sterilized" abroad and more gradually and productively invested internally. At issue, then, is the extent to which decisions are overdetermined in oil states.

Because we have explored the Venezuelan case in the greatest detail, its reexamination is especially useful in addressing this question. In the story told in Part II, several fundamental policy choices stand out: first, the decision by Juan Vicente Gómez, dictator during the entry of the oil companies, to remove petroleum from national private ownership and place it in the state; second, the decision of the Medina Angarita government to levy an income tax on the foreign oil companies that became the fiscal basis of the state; third, the decision of Rómulo Betancourt and others to design a type of pacted democracy that depended on oil rents and thus reinforced petrolization; and, fourth, the decision of Carlos Andrés Pérez to create *La Gran Venezuela* in an accelerated, distributive, and capital-intensive fashion.

In each case there were conceivable alternatives, even though they were rarely if ever considered, and each choice proved critically determinative of the ones that followed. The *estatización* of petroleum provided the central impetus for the expansion and centralization of the state and the erosion of non-oil-based authority. The income tax established a pattern for policymaking based on the extraction of rents from the companies and their internal distribution to politically relevant actors. Pacted democracy exacerbated these earlier dynamics by establishing a set of standard operating procedures based on further statism, presidentialism, and an unusual combination of preemption and inclusion. Finally, the choice of an accelerated, resource-based development strategy in the wake of the boom further locked Venezuela into its addiction to extraordinary mineral rents.

These decisions made a significant difference, yet they do not contradict the argument that the range of choice is especially constrained in petro-states. To the contrary, they demonstrate that there was never an equal probability that other choices would be made in their place; that each decision was related to and grew from the previous one; and that, except during uncertain moments of regime change, the range of choice narrowed from one decision to another as Venezuela moved further into its oil-led trajectory. In other words, these decisions lend powerful support to notions of path dependence and structured contingency.

A review of these decisions demonstrates the reasons for these conclusions. Gómez could have decided to leave the exploitation of petroleum and the bargaining with foreign companies in private hands, but Chapter 4 pointed out the improbability of his taking this route. Not only would he have failed to take advantage of an exceptional opportunity to enrich the state (and himself)—an act hard to imagine in such a highly personalistic, authoritarian regime—but he also would have had to go against the overwhelming power of the foreign companies who (ironically) protested vigorously against having to bargain with numerous private actors, pushed for state control over the industry, and repeatedly threatened to abandon Venezuela for the Middle East if government cooperation was not forthcoming. Once Gómez tied state revenues and the political fate of rulers so closely to the rents from oil, it was only a matter of time until the extraction of these rents was regularized through a tax on the companies.

Making changes in this new fiscal framework was an unattractive option for policymakers of any stripe. An income tax on the companies removed the incentive for extracting resources internally, which, in turn, facilitated the state's task of forging social alliances and, as Chapter 5 demonstrated, subsequently made pacted democracy easier to install and sustain. Though the transition to and consolidation of this type of democracy depended on statecraft and took a number of unpredictable turns unrelated to economic development, its core features of extreme centralization in the public realm, concentration of power in the executive, and revenue transfers to a variety of private interests through the state were already in place prior to democratization.

Finally, as Chapter 6 showed, the preemptive distribution of rents across all politically relevant organized groups, combined with the economic linkages fostered by petroleum and the extraordinary availability of revenues, determined the direction, level, and rate of spending in the boom years. They also encouraged the transformation of programmatic political parties into rentier machines, the extraordinary increase in influence seeking, and the decay of democracy—the central lessons of Chapters 7 and 8. These decisions were not inevitable, but in each case policymakers saw one road as being clearly preferred, and each of these roads took Venezuela farther along its perverse development trajectory.

Data from the other oil exporters reinforce the argument that petro-states share a similar path-dependent history and structuration of choice. Indeed, the normal stuff of politics—changes in regimes and the particularities of governments, parties, or leaders—pales in explanatory power beside the decision calculus created by this framework. Where states characterized by overwhelming incentives for rent seeking are put in place, institutions at the deepest level of political domination will shape whatever regime type or government is grafted onto them. The evidence is powerful: as Chapter 9 illustrated, the exploitation of petroleum produced a similarity in property rights, tax structures, vested interests, economic models, and thus frameworks for decision-making across different governments and regime types, ranging from personalistic authoritarianism (Venezuela, Iran, and Indonesia) to military rule (Nigeria), socialist authoritarianism (Algeria), and democracy (Venezuela, Nigeria). Only Indonesia was able to deviate from this pattern in key ways, largely because its oil-led trajectory was dramatically interrupted and an alternative fiscal basis could be built. This evidence suggests that the strong emphasis placed by political scientists on regime types and regime change needs to be tempered with more and better historically based analyses of the state formation and state capacity upon which the performance of these regimes rest.

FACTORING IN REGIME TYPE: THE ADVANTAGES OF DEMOCRACY FOR WEATHERING ECONOMIC CRISIS

Yet even if variations in regime type and the idiosyncrasies of government agents are relegated to a secondary level of explanation in petro-states, they still matter a great deal. Indeed, these variations may be the key factor in determining which regimes survive a boom-bust cycle and which do not. They also set the parameters for the strategies and expenditure patterns pursued to ensure the survival of rulers; thus they determine who benefits the most and gains the least from petroleum-led development.

To some extent, the exploitation of petroleum appears to be regime neutral under normal circumstances—that is, when oil revenues are gradually and incrementally on the rise, as they were for almost 120 years prior to 1974. Under these circumstances, petrodollars play an important role in underwriting all regimes in power, regardless of type, by providing a slowly expanding economic base. This was the case in Venezuela prior to 1973 (with the brief exception of the 1956–1957 boom, which destabilized Pérez Jiménez), Iran under the Pahlavis, Algeria after independence, and Indonesia under Suharto. Especially in Venezuela, scholars have attributed this unusual regime stability to a number of special factors intrinsic to the (democratic) polity (Martz 1966; Levine 1978, 1985), while failing to note that it operated across regime type during the Gómez dictatorship as well as across regions when solid international oil regimes were in place to moderate prices. In this respect, Venezuela's thirty-five years of stable democracy despite the presence of dictatorships throughout South America is no more unusual than Gómez's durability during the 1930s, when other regimes were tumbling throughout the rest of Latin America.

In other words, the experience of oil exporters illustrates how a gradually expanding pie helps any type of regime survive, a corollary to recent econometric evidence that fails to uncover any clear regime effect on economic growth (Przeworski et al. 1996, 40). The finding that democracies can survive in poorer countries if they generate economic growth with a moderate rate of inflation—and are even more likely to survive where income inequality is declining over time—is probably not specific to a particular regime type. It undoubtedly extends to authoritarian rule as well, as the East Asian development experiences indicate.

But variations in regime type do have a visible impact in exporters when oil revenues fluctuate widely, as they began to do in the early 1970s (Figure 3). The cases examined here permit the investigation of two broad rival hypotheses. On the one hand, authoritarian regimes weather boom-bust cycles and other forms of economic crisis better than democracies. Democracies, this argument contends, require more consultation and debate; as a result, they move too slowly and are

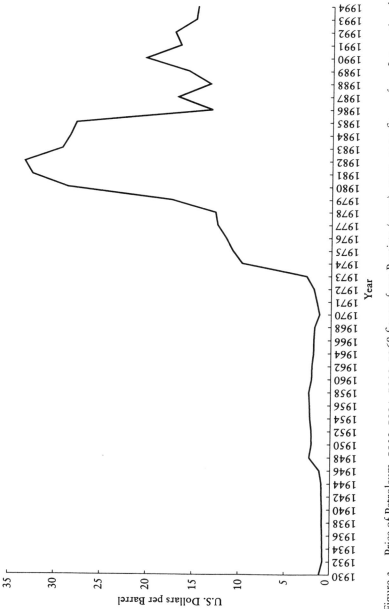

Figure 3. Price of Petroleum, 1930–1994. 1930–1968 figures from Baptista (1991); 1970–1994 figures from International Monetary Fund (1988b, 1993, 1995).

bound to be inefficient. Moreover, the regularity of elections, especially in presidentialist regimes, ensures systematic and opportunistic manipulation of the political business cycle in an effort to control public opinion. Furthermore, because elected governments are beholden to and are held accountable by their differing constituencies, their policies are necessarily contradictory; they cannot have the continuity of policymaking found in some autocracies. These were precisely the arguments used by President Pérez to gain special executive powers in 1974.

On the other hand, proponents of the opposite hypothesis contend that democracies are more capable of surviving economic crises of either boom or bust. The extensive consultation and debate required in democracies ensure better policy formulation and more compliance in policy implementation, while the open and uncertain competition among contending groups forces governments to define and defend their goals in a relatively transparent setting. Even more significant, elections allow the population to hold leaders accountable and to change them in an orderly and predictable manner, thus providing an escape valve for growing tensions. Finally, the notion of democracy as an abstract principle of government with its links to equality and participation provides it with alternative sources of legitimacy that do not rely solely on economic performance. The case of Norway is notable here.

Venezuela, where three major booms occurred in the postwar period under two distinct regime types, provides an especially useful temporal comparison for examining these hypotheses. When the response of autocrat Pérez Jiménez to the boom of 1956–1957 is compared with that of Pérez in 1973, some arresting differences surface. Although in both cases policymakers behaved in a similar fashion (expanding state expenditures and state power abruptly while concentrating power in their own hands) with similar results (rent seeking, economic deterioration, and political decay), and although regime type made little difference in the rate of expenditure increase or the need for showcase projects, it did affect the choice of development model, the patterns of assignment in the wake of a boom, and the availability of alternative sources of legitimacy and regime duration.

Pérez Jiménez's rule depended on military force and economic success for its survival. Not surprisingly, he paid high "protection rents" to the armed forces and police but remained unconcerned about competing demands for industrialization and for social welfare from various organized interests and social classes. Thus, he had extremely narrow support, which quickly disappeared as oil rents dropped. In democratic

Venezuela, on the contrary, the transition in 1958 institutionalized a qualitatively different and broader-based pattern of spending; democratic rulers, unlike their predecessors, repeatedly responded to the claims of a large constituency by distributing subsidies, transfer payments, and programs to benefit the middle and working classes as well as the elites. When rents began to dry up, this more inclusive policy, combined with the possibility of rotating power to a different party, helped to sustain democratic rule.

The contrast between these two cases lends support to the contention that democratic regimes have distinct advantages for surviving economic crisis, even though this type of regime cannot avoid the effects of a boom-bust cycle. Regular elections provide the opportunity for peacefully rejecting unwelcome incumbents, while freedom of association promises more just and equitable arrangements in the future. Together, these characteristics may motivate citizens to support their regime even as they reject their government.

In 1958, because no routinized channels of influence existed, no mechanisms for succession were established, and no inspiring ideologies operated, the only way to alter the policies of Pérez Jiménez was to overthrow him. But when Venezuelans wanted to protest the policies followed by their democracy, they could substitute one government for another at election time, which they repeatedly did. Even when it became evident that pacted democracy inhibited broad debate and responsiveness, removed some of the most important checks on the decisions of leaders, fostered corruption, and erased the differences between parties, the legitimacy accorded to democracy as a form of rule (rather than to the political parties themselves) remained exceptionally high. In May 1992, with two former presidents charged with corruption, political parties discredited, and an interim democratic coalition ruling an uneasy country, only 8 percent of Venezuelans polled favored a military government over a democratic regime (Myers 1992, 23).

Further evidence of democracy's superiority in defusing economic crisis is evident through the reexamination of Table 17 in Chapter 9. This table demonstrates that countries with high initial spending leaps, or boom effects, experience political instability, and it correctly predicts high levels of instability for Iran, Nigeria, and Algeria. But it also shows that Venezuela should have experienced even more instability given that its boom effect was so much greater than that of the other oil exporters. Pressures toward regime change were certainly present when grave economic problems first surfaced, but military unrest quickly abated when

Pérez was removed from power through a constitutional process. While a counterfactual argument of this sort is not reliable in itself, it does illustrate that rotation in power, rule of law, and civilian control over the military have important stabilizing effects during extraordinarily destabilizing times.

Evidence from the other capital-deficient oil exporters lends additional, although still inadequate, weight. Norway clearly demonstrates the advantages of broad representation, rotation of power, widespread debate, and accountability for handling a crisis of wealth, but we have no example of democratic performance to examine among the developing countries. Clearly, however, personalistic authoritarian regimes collapsed rather easily under boom-bust conditions, with Suharto's regime being a notable exception. The robustness of his rule once oil prices became volatile, however, is due primarily to a different degree of "petro-stateness" and the revenue sterilization resulting from the Pertamina crisis rather than to specific characteristics of authoritarian rule. Should economic policy become less successful or a succession crisis arise, which is a virtual certainty under one-man rule, any form of personalistic rule is unlikely to survive. Nigeria sheds no light on this question because it is so torn by especially weak stateness, ethnic and religious rivalries, and rent seeking that it has been unable to stabilize any type of regime, democratic or authoritarian.

Even if the evidence is not conclusive from these other countries, in three of the five cases in this study (Algeria, Nigeria, and Venezuela), more democracy is explicitly seen as one solution to the multitude of problems that have arisen during the boom-bust cycle. In Algeria, where the revolutionary heritage, support for secularism, and some defined rules of succession helped to sustain alternative mechanisms of authority through the early 1990s, greater democracy is seen as the only real alternative to a further descent into civil war. In Nigeria, the military is the chief obstacle to a transition to a new regime type. In Venezuela, the central demand of citizens is for a transition from one type of democracy to another—one that is less restrictive, more inclusive, and more competitive. The cherished notion of *pactismo,* once synonymous with complicity among parties and organized interests, is now explicitly seen as a short-term stabilizing device to cope with political crisis rather than a long-term set of accords that could freeze restrictive new institutional arrangements in place. Even in Indonesia, where authoritarian rule has received the least challenge, pressure for democratization is linked to a growing critique of political rent seeking.

Nonetheless, the observation that democracies may be able to weather economic crisis or resolve at least some of the current problems of petro-states better than autocracies must be treated with caution. Democratization may have unpredictable consequences in the context of the rapid deterioration of the quality of life, especially in countries torn by deep ethnic or religious differences. Because it creates the potential for the emergence of new forces, alliances, and understandings, its immediate impact in Algeria, Nigeria, or Indonesia may be to raise the level of fragmentation, immobility, and uncertainty rather than to tackle the challenges confronting the petro-state.

Furthermore, ultimate success in avoiding extreme outcomes in a boom-bust cycle may depend more on the type of democracy or on the type of authoritarian rule than on the broad differences between the two. Where regimes are based on the indistinct boundary between public finances and the private funds of ruling groups, as in highly personalistic rule, there is no brake on rent seeking by the state short of the demise of the regime itself, and these regimes are most vulnerable. Where regimes are less predatory—meaning that some of the social surplus is used for the citizenry as a whole and not merely for the incumbents and their friends—it is reasonable to assume, first, that the pattern of assignment will be more broad-based and equitable and, second, that these regimes will have alternative bases of legitimacy that help them survive the ups and downs of a boom-bust cycle. Such regimes can be either democratic or authoritarian.

OIL: BLACK GOLD OR THE DEVIL'S EXCREMENT?

Booms have an adverse impact in oil-exporting developing countries, as we have seen, but how should the long-term impact of petroleum be judged? A complete answer would compare the overall political and economic performance of a group of oil countries with the performance of a comparable set of non-oil countries over a prolonged period of time. Yet even if a study of this sort were to be carried out, the assessment of petroleum exploitation as a development "good" will never be easy for two reasons. First, full information is not available, especially over a sufficient span of time. Because reliable income-distribution statistics are generally not obtainable in these countries, for example, it is difficult to trace accurately how oil benefits some groups disproportionately.

Second, weighing the relative gains versus losses from petroleum in some value-neutral manner is well nigh impossible. Is oil's role as an occasional buffer for regime stability more valuable than, say, its adverse effects on gains in productivity? Are political collective goods worth the economic costs to individuals that they might entail? These are the types of issues that have preoccupied scholars for centuries, and their resolution will not be readily found in a comparison of oil versus non-oil countries.

Comparing the record of Venezuelan economic development with development in the rest of Latin America gives some idea of the tradeoffs involved. Petroleum placed Venezuela in a most enviable position in several respects. Between 1920 and 1976, it had the highest per capita income on the continent; in 1976, for example, per capita GDP was $1,344 compared with $898 for all of Latin America. Its rate of growth over this same period was exceptionally high (2.6 percent) when compared with that of other Latin American countries (1.7 percent) or even that of the advanced industrialized countries (2.1 percent). This growth rate enabled it to satisfy the needs of organized groups much faster than would have been possible under "non-oil" conditions (Baptista 1984, Table 2). In the twenty years between 1960 and 1980, which included two booms, Venezuelans enjoyed almost double the resources for investment, a significantly faster growth in salaries, a longer life expectancy, lower infant mortality, and more education than their Latin American neighbors—and they did so without paying close to comparable taxes (Baptista 1984, 26, Table 3). These economic outcomes underwrote political stability.

But by the 1980s this extraordinary record was finished. Uneven growth rates were coupled with a sharp descent in labor's share of income and extreme income inequities for the rest of the population. Rapid industrialization was accompanied by Dutch Disease and a decline in productivity.[2] Although inflation had been even lower than that in most industrialized countries because petrodollars had supported an unusually stable currency (per annum inflation rates were a mere 1.7 percent between 1953 and 1973) (Rodríguez 1985, 7), it climbed above 80 percent in 1989. Furthermore, the propensity to import was higher than in any other Latin American country. Even in the midst of a grave economic crisis between 1986 and 1988, imports remained far higher than the Latin American average.[3]

High social costs were the most damaging legacy of Venezuela's oil-led economic model. In this respect it resembled the rest of Latin America, where significant portions of the population were also marginalized as both producers and consumers during the "lost decade" of the 1980s. But Venezuela's fall was faster and farther in the wake of two enormous booms. By 1996 it was one of only nineteen countries in the world where per capita income had dropped below the 1960 level; Venezuela shared this unfortunate status with countries like Haiti, Nicaragua, Liberia, Ghana, and Rwanda (*New York Times,* July 15, 1996, A3). This shift in fortune was rapid and dramatic. The World Bank reports that in 1989 the poverty level was 53 percent, up from 32 percent in 1982, while a full 22 percent of all households did not have enough income to cover the minimum daily food requirements, up from 10 percent in 1982 (World Bank 1991, cited in Naím 1993, 6). The gravity of this situation is apparent in the projections of Venezuelan economist Bernard Mommer (1990, 59–61), who estimated that it would take well past the year 2000 to return to the levels of production and income per inhabitant reached in 1977.

Most striking in the comparison of Venezuela with the rest of Latin America is the illusory nature of its development. Although Venezuela's growth in GNP, employment and capital stock was higher than the rest of the continent or even the industrialized world, its productivity was significantly lower, especially during the boom years of 1974–1978, and it declined throughout the 1980s.[4] For a twenty-year period, productivity was little more than half the Latin American average (Baptista 1984, Table 5). More troubling still was the decline in both the average annual growth rate of non-oil capital stock (from 9.4 percent in 1920–1943 to 0.5 percent in 1986–1990) and the average annual growth rate of non-oil GDP (from 5.6 percent in 1920–1943 and a high of 9.4 percent in 1943–1958 to 0.5 percent in 1986–1990), further testimony to the failure to use petrodollars as the basis for a healthy, diversified economy (Espinasa and Mommer 1991, 19).

These statistics paint a disturbing picture: rather than creating a self-sustaining development model potentially independent of petroleum, Venezuela was living on a false economy, borrowed money, and borrowed time. Because state structures were formed precisely to perpetuate this model, Venezuela's readjustment to a productive nonrentier economy promised to be among the most difficult in Latin America.

This brief comparison underscores the difficulty of assessing the ultimate impact of oil or any other commodity. The question is not whether oil is a blessing or a curse, but rather what specific type of political and economic-development trajectory it encourages and whom it benefits.

A particular commodity in itself is not a development plus or minus;

its ultimate effect depends on how it interacts with preexisting institutions to create new ones. Thus democratic Chile eventually managed to build a relatively efficacious bureaucracy and ingrained rule of law even though it was dependent on mineral production. And Hirschman (1977, 95), upon reviewing the impact on development of various paired commodities, could remark, "In Cuba sugarcane is the villain and tobacco the hero, in Colombia tobacco is the bad guy while coffee is the good guy." The difference is located in the preexisting institutional framework within which commodities are inserted and the manner in which this framework is subsequently reshaped.

LESSONS FROM THE PARADOX OF PLENTY

Why countries exhibit different patterns of accumulation and distribution over the course of their development is one of the essential questions of political economy. Uncovering and interpreting distinctive patterns of development depend on exposing the complex interaction between economic growth and institutional change. Economies shape political institutions and are in turn shaped by them. The fiscal link between economies and polities is by no means the only explanation for the differing capacity of states, but it is a fundamental one. Based in part on the origin of their revenues, as we have seen, states gain the ability to regulate the use of authority and power, and they provide actors with resources, legitimacy, perceptions, standard operating procedures, identities, symbolic meanings, and norms of acceptable behavior. Along with other institutions, they shape individual motives and behavior.

Evans (1995) has suggested that states lie on a continuum from "predatory" to "developmental." A predatory state is more than just the revenue maximizer that Levi (1988) identified. In this sort of state, the market has so penetrated all aspects of public life that almost anything is up for sale. Rentier behavior is the norm in both the public and the private sectors; thus productive investment is less likely. Where states fall on this continuum depends on the extent to which they impede or foster long-term entrepreneurial perspectives, which in turn depends on their bureaucratic cohesiveness and their authoritative mechanisms. These state capacities do not appear overnight. In developing countries they are built through the interaction of national political institutions with international markets and their own societies.

The historic construction of states—that is, how they became predatory or developmental—has not generally been the object of social science inquiry, but it is a central feature of this book, especially Chapters 4 and 5. Just as Cardoso and Faletto (1979), Kurth (1979), and O'Donnell (1973) demonstrated an "elective affinity" between patterns of delayed industrialization and different regime types, I have attempted to show that there is also an elective affinity between specific configurations of commodity exploitation and different degrees and patterns of stateness. In other words, whether states are predatory or developmental depends in large part on the origins of their chief revenues, especially the character of the leading sector from which they extract these revenues. More specifically, where mineral exploitation coincides with the beginning of modern state formation, as it did in every case discussed here except Norway, the dynamics of production for export will shape states in fundamental ways, creating specific structures of choice, uneven capacities, and birth defects that endure long past the moment of their creation. Thus it is no accident that Evan's (1995, 45–47) archetypical case of a predatory state is Zaire, a mineral producer exhibiting the same skewed patterns of jurisdiction and authority combined with a similar incapacity to transform the economy or social structure over which it presides. Nor is it an accident that the archetypical developmental states, Taiwan and Korea, have not been historically constructed around the exigencies of exploiting mineral wealth for export.

The main finding of this study of petro-states is that countries dependent on the same export activity are likely to display significant similarities in the capacity (or incapacity) of their respective states to guide development, even if their actual institutions are quite different in virtually all other respects. In other words, we should expect common patterns of "stateness" in countries dependent on the same leading sector as long as strong, coherent political institutions were not already in place prior to the development of this leading sector. This common "stateness" creates similar predilections for some types of activities and roles and for the avoidance of others.

A central corollary to this argument is that states dependent on different, broadly defined export sectors— mining, agriculture, manufacturing, or services—should exhibit different bundles of capacities and incapacities. It should be possible to identify different types of states with their own specific features, structures of taxation, patterns of social and institutional relations, and combination of development blessings and blunders just as I have done with the petro-state. Shafer (1994) has already begun this effort by demonstrating how different sectoral specializations shape the strategies adopted by states. Together our studies suggest that it is possible and fruitful to distinguish analytically certain central properties in "mineral" states, "agricultural" states, "manufacturing" states, and even "service" states. This categorization would permit a conceptual mapping of states in the developing world based on the interaction between economies and political institutions rather than simply on different types of commodities alone.

There are several potential objections to an approach of this sort. First, while the "modes of governance" of different sectors may indeed vary systematically (Schmitter 1990) and this may shape state capacities in predictable ways, as I have claimed, this sectoral logic may have only limited applicability. Because it is most persuasive in countries domi- nated by a single product, a past reality that is no longer the norm, it is difficult to see how particular products will continue to shape political and social institutions in the future, except in the area of mineral extrac- tion. As Evans (1995, 252) argues, "The degree of specialization for a 'sectoral determinist' argument to be plausible is increasingly hard to find."

Second, other types of states are unlikely to be molded as drastically as mineral states and especially petro-states. In virtually all its charac- teristics, this "commodity state" represents an extreme case—distinct even from other mining states. Only sixteenth-century Spain had the same highly exaggerated combination of features, and this similarity arises from the fact that gold, like petroleum today, was the main engine of economic development at the time. The petro-state is more depen- dent on a single commodity than any other state, and the exploitation of this commodity is more depletable, more capital-intensive, more en- clave-oriented, and more rent-producing than the exploitation of any other commodity. Other mining states may have these same features, but their impact is bound to be less overwhelming. Thus, if it is difficult to find pure sectors today, it is even more difficult to find ones that will approximate the extraordinary impact of petroleum.

Both arguments are compelling; nonetheless, they do not detract from the utility of the commodity approach. In the contemporary devel- oping world most states were constructed, at least initially, around ex- port commodities, and many continue to reproduce the same profile. Even those states that now preside over far more complicated patterns of sectoral development have retained some of the institutional residue, norms, competencies, and practices of a prior time. Furthermore, while

no other case is likely to match the strong effects identified in the petro-
state, the approach presented here is an important corrective to purely
political analyses that emphasize institutional arrangements alone or
to economic approaches that stress only factor endowments, rates of
investment, or patterns of trade. What *is* new is the growing understanding that these elements are intertwined. Policy choices taken in
specific historical contexts, and not simple factor endowments or institutions alone, determine whether good or bad fruits will be harvested
from raw-material rents.

Mapping the links between the acquisition of state capacities and
leading commodities should provide a more complete explanation than
we now possess for distinctive development trajectories. This exercise
has both theoretical and practical implications. In theory, it challenges
rational-choice and other approaches based on individualism and vol-
untarism by illuminating how choices are prestructured and how this
structuration is produced and perpetuated. As we have seen, dependence on a leading export commodity has a profound impact on con-
tractual relations, property rights, the relative importance of markets
versus states, the degree of internationalization of the economy, the opportunities for technological innovation, the relative power of organized interests, the structure of taxation, the prerogatives accorded different state agencies, and the symbolic content of the state. In
developing countries dependent on a single leading commodity policymakers acquire certain aims and goals, accept some values and paths
over others, and prefer utilizing some institutions rather than others
precisely because they operate in the incentive structure shaped by this
commodity. Thus, their choices are not "free." Their actions are shaped
by this setting through patterns that are taken for granted and that have
a reality existing prior to the preferences of actors.

This approach also challenges neoliberal assumptions that the state
is the culprit wherever and whenever poor development outcomes are
present. Institutional frameworks, North (1990, 96) has noted, are "the
critical key to the relative success of economies," a finding that has been
reiterated from Weber ([1921] 1968) to Wade (1990). Norway, the one
case that is not a petro-state, is eloquent testimony to the importance
of capable bureaucracies as the essential ingredient in adjustment and
transformation as well as the indispensable counterpart to private interests. If there is one clear lesson from the experience of oil exporters,
it is that developmental outcomes depend on the character of state

institutions. Markets are governed either badly or well, but they are always governed. Where public agencies are fiscally diversified, accountable and coherent, these markets are likely to be governed well.

Furthermore, this approach demonstrates that no transformation of the state is possible without a transformation of its private counterparts. The oil exporters illustrate how states and social structures are mutually constitutive; one does not exist logically or empirically prior to the other. Oil states defined private interests and were in turn defined by them. Together they coalesced into a thick rentier network that shaped the strategies of both states and private interests in a mutually beneficial (for them) but vicious development cycle. Reforming one part of the equation by constructing a coherent bureaucracy is not enough; indeed, it is not even possible because powerful oligopolistic interests will find myriad ways to block the formation of a state apparatus that cannot be successfully penetrated by them.

These theoretical findings have practical implications. The link between commodities and states reveals the weaknesses of present-day economic policy prescriptions based on neoliberal packages of structural adjustment, especially in oil-exporting countries. Because these countries are the epitome of Barzelay's (1986) "politicized market economies," economic rationality cannot be separated from political rationality. Prescriptions of the IMF, other international and U.S. agencies, and authorities in developing countries that are aimed solely at restructuring economies along free-market lines miss the point. In denying that economic restructuring is profoundly political, not just in terms of "political will," as international actors frequently claim, but also in terms of changing the political institutions that shape and give meaning to economic policymaking, they do not address the essence of the skewed stateness of these countries. Nor do they address the oligopolistic structure of the market that has been so carefully constructed and preserved by these skewed states.

On the contrary, the overriding neoliberal preoccupation with shrinking the jurisdiction of the state ignores the crying need for strengthening its authority. Predation is not simply a function of state size. Although the removal of regulations, price controls, tariff barriers, and the like may eliminate some of the arrangements that have fostered rentier behavior, there is no guarantee that a more minimalist state will not simply revert to new rentier arrangements in the future, especially if new booms occur. Nor is there any guarantee that rentier havens will not simply relocate elsewhere—for example via the privatization process, as the case of Mexico demonstrates. These policies, as they are presently constituted, may temporarily improve balance-of-payments performance, but they fail to place emphasis where it is really needed: enhancing domestic taxation, professionalizing civil services, prosecuting corruption, breaking up oligopolies, and democratizing polities. These are the actions that eventually will change the behavior of political and economic elites as well as ordinary citizens.

Finally, this approach should have some capacity to predict the future prospects of oil exporters. It has already proved useful in predicting the crisis of the Venezuelan state (Karl 1982, 1987), and it should be more widely applicable to the capital-surplus countries that were not included in this study. In Saudi Arabia, for example, past financial stability has been undermined by more than two decades of unrestrained spending, military purchases, and irregular banking practices. Despite its small population and huge reserves, which give it a substantial advantage over capital-deficient countries, more than $120 billion in financial reserves have almost vanished as spending has far outstripped the billions of dollars earned annually from the largest oil fields in the world. Nonetheless, Saudi policymakers continue to forge ahead with ambitious development plans, but now they are doing so on credit and in the face of a deficit that is 9.2 percent of their GDP, nearly twice the comparable U.S. figure. Reducing spending significantly does not seem to be an option because officials argue that "political and social considerations preclude a reduction in subsidies or increases in fees" to Saudi citizens (*International Herald Tribune,* August 23, 1993).

Thus already evidence indicates that oil has also transformed the states and regimes of capital-surplus countries in ways that trap their policymakers in spending sprees. If so, overspending combined with low oil prices will eventually turn them into the equivalent of capital-deficient countries. Only a prolonged fiscal crisis is likely to provoke change, and adjustment, when it comes, will be especially abrupt and severe. Without conscious intervention, even "one-crop" countries like Saudi Arabia and Libya are likely to face the deleterious combination of economic deterioration and political decay that has so marked their counterparts, but in these cases the international and geostrategic ramifications may be far greater.

As long as petroleum fulfills a fundamental need and yields a profit for powerful state and private interests, governments will choose to exploit it—and consider themselves fortunate. Oil exporters are then left confronting the simultaneous challenges of building more competitive and equitable economies, more stable regimes, and more capable states. In this respect, they are not very different from many of their non-oil counterparts. However, the route by which they have arrived at this point and the especially inflexible barriers to readjustment they confront are distinctive. These barriers present even more of a problem for adjustment than non-oil countries face. This is especially true if new booms should once again occur.

Lessons from the past suggest a perverse relationship between some forms of natural-resource endowment and successful state-building. History is replete with examples of the development failures of mining states. Spain benefited immensely from a gold and silver boom and subsequently became one of the poorest countries in Europe. Peru once had a tremendous guano boom and "bonanza development" through minerals, but it is now impoverished. Chile, too, had a boom in nitrates at the end of the nineteenth century, which led to the most ambitious development plan of its history and a subsequent plunge in its fortunes. Viewing Latin American reality through the prism of these mineral booms and busts, novelist Eduardo Galeano (1973, 19) has wryly noted that the continent's poverty was the consequence of its natural wealth. Conversely, just as Adam Smith once observed about the Tartars, Asian NICs may be rich precisely because they are resource poor. The need to overcome this poverty may have been one of the chief catalysts for building effective states.

This is the paradox of plenty. But it is not inevitable. Paradoxes can be resolved and development trajectories can be altered, even if it takes decades or sometimes centuries. There is nothing inescapable about the future repercussions of petroleum or any other commodity. As the reality of declining oil prices sinks in, perceptions about the role of oil in petro-states show some signs of change, and they should continue to do so—absent another boom. If policymakers are pushed, both domestically from below and internationally from above, to accompany this new economic wisdom with conscious efforts to build state capacity through diversified tax structures, professionalized civil services, and more representative and equitable institutions, they can begin gradually to break the vicious cycle of petro-development. If not, Pérez Alfonzo's warnings about "the devil's excrement" will ring increasingly true, and future generations may find that they would have been better off if no oil had been found at all.

Research Note

The study of oil-exporting countries is hampered by the poverty of relevant social science literature as well as by a lack of statistical data in some essential areas. Finding reliable statistics and economic studies is especially difficult for the period immediately following the 1973 and 1980 booms, the period of greatest interest for this study. In each of the five cases discussed (Venezuela, Iran, Nigeria, Algeria, and Indonesia), few (if any) serious studies are available to researchers on income distribution, the performance of state enterprises as a group, the extent of subsidies and tariff barriers, or patterns of corruption. As a result of the chaos produced by two booms, the annual reports of a number of government agencies either declined in reliability or failed to appear at all. After 1973 there were widespread discrepancies in figures on, for example, the national debt, steel production, the losses of state enterprises. Data collection is especially problematical for Iran after the revolution and for Algeria. The tables presented in the Statistical Appendix and throughout the book are drawn from the best sources of data available.

Some of the material presented in Part II is based on data gathered in Venezuela between 1978 and 1979 and in over fifty confidential interviews with government officials (including four former presidents), party leaders, businessmen, and foreign observers. Confidentiality was required because of the highly politicized atmosphere surrounding economic policy in this preelectoral period. I have continued to maintain this confidentiality, especially in light of Venezuela's current political turmoil. These interviews were supplemented by further discussions in 1983 and 1992. Interviews played an especially important role in understanding the Venezuelan case because, contrary to the situation in Mexico, Argentina, Brazil, Chile, and other Latin American countries, relatively little political or economic literature about Venezuela was published in the post-1973 period.

Finally, one indicator of the petro-state is institutional disarray. Administrative chaos in Venezuela in the late 1970s and early 1980s was often so great that it was difficult to find answers to relatively simple questions. For example, after the nationalization of petroleum I tried to discover which ministry had official responsibility for the newly formed oil company, Petróleos de Venezuela (PETROVEN), the most important state enterprise in Venezuela. Three different ministries—Planning, Mines and Hydrocarbons, and the Secretariat of the Presidency—claimed this role. PETROVEN, however, insisted that it was autonomous and that it submitted its accounts only to the president of the Republic. Eventually, the legal department of one of the foreign oil companies, responding to my pleas for clarification, discovered that Hydrocarbons and Mines did have formal oversight responsibility, although in practice PETROVEN presented its reports to the Secretariat of the Presidency (probably because it was headed by the president's favorite minister). Several weeks later, I received a call from the Ministry of Planning, asking me whether I had ever discovered where PETROVEN presented its accounts. "We need to know," I was told, "and we can't seem to find out."

Statistical Appendix

Full references for the sources listed in the following tables are given in the Statistical Appendix Citations.

TABLE A-1
PRICE OF SAUDI ARABIAN
RAS TANURA PETROLEUM
(U.S. DOLLARS PER BARREL)

1970	1.30
1971	1.65
1972	1.90
1973	2.70
1974	9.76
1975	10.72
1976	11.51
1977	12.41
1978	12.70
1979	17.26
1980	28.67
1981	32.50
1982	33.47
1983	29.31
1984	28.47
1985	27.99
1986	13.08
1987	16.94
1988	13.22
1989	15.70
1990	20.46
1991	16.54
1992	17.19
1993	14.96
1994	14.76

SOURCES: Figures for 1970–1984 are from International Monetary Fund, *International Financial Statistics Yearbook,* 1988, lines 456 and 299; figures for 1985 are calculated from International Monetary Fund, *International Financial Statistics,* April 1989, line 299 (indexed version); figures for 1986–1992 are from International Monetary Fund, *International Financial Statistics Yearbook,* 1993, line 466; figures for 1993–1994 are from International Monetary Fund, *International Financial Statistics Yearbook,* 1995, line 466.

NOTES: Since approximately 1988, the International Monetary Fund's *International Financial Statistics Yearbook* has not reported oil prices using this category. Because recent values are unavailable in the sources listed, figures from 1986 to 1994 are average prices for Dubai Fateh on the spot market.

TABLE A-2

TOTAL GOVERNMENT REVENUES (CONSTANT 1985 PRICES, BILLIONS) AND REAL RATE OF GROWTH OF TOTAL GOVERNMENT REVENUES (PERCENTAGE)

	Algeria[a]		Indonesia		Iran		Mexico[b]		Nigeria		Norway		Venezuela	
	Dinars	%	Rupiah	%	Rials	%	New Pesos	%	Nairas	%	Kroner	%	Bolivares	%
1970	22.7		3,830		2,429		2.1		4.4		77.5		63.2	
1971	22.9	0.9	4,604	20.2	3,198	31.7	2.4	11.8	8.6	96.3	86.9	12.1	71.4	13.0
1972	28.6	24.8	5,908	28.3	3,511	9.8	2.9	23.2	9.0	4.6	149.9	72.5	73.9	3.5
1973	30.8	7.5	7,034	19.1	3,960	12.8	3.5	19.5	9.8	8.9	157.8	5.3	83.3	12.7
1974	39.1	45.6	8,561	21.7	7,135	80.2	3.2	−8.6	15.5	58.2	163.4	3.5	152.3	82.8
1975			9,583	11.9	7,362	3.2	3.3	4.7	14.5	−6.0	168.9	3.4	144.5	−5.1
1976			10,793	12.6	7,614	3.4	4.2	26.3	14.9	2.7	186.3	10.3	129.4	−10.4
1977			11,685	8.3	7,485	−1.7	4.8	14.2	15.4	3.3	192.3	3.2	129.1	−0.2
1978			12,690	8.6	5,358	−28.4	5.4	11.6	11.7	−24.2	202.2	5.1	121.2	−6.1
1979			15,427	21.6	4,333	−19.1	5.5	2.0	15.3	30.8	177.6	−12.2	118.9	−1.9
1980			17,637	14.3	2,693	−37.8	6.8	23.0	18.5	20.7	175.1	−1.4	124.4	4.6
1981			19,661	11.5	2,922	8.5	6.9	1.9	10.3	−44.4	184.4	5.3	162.0	30.2
1982			17,412	−11.4	3,527	20.7	7.2	5.3	8.3	−19.4	183.2	−0.7	137.1	−15.4
1983			17,686	1.6	3,490	−1.0	8.1	11.3	7.6	−8.4	196.6	7.3	119.8	−12.6
1984			19,730	11.6	3,176	−9.0	7.5	−7.4	7.2	−5.3	199.6	0.5	114.2	−4.7
1985			20,347	3.1	2,964	−6.7	7.8	4.8	9.6	33.3	224.5	12.5	126.6	10.9
1986			21,324	4.8	1,664	−43.9	7.3	−7.0	8.1	−15.6	249.4	11.1	105.4	−16.7
1987			21,400	0.4	1,706	2.5	8.1	11.4	11.0	35.8	243.6	−2.3	99.3	−5.8
1988			18,360	−14.2	1,387	−18.7	8.1	0.4	8.7	−20.9	247.0	1.4	101.2	1.9
1989			21,314	16.1	1,762	27.0	8.9	9.3	10.1	16.1	242.8	−1.7	99.2	−2.0

Continued on next page

TABLE A-2 (continued)

	Algeria[a]		Indonesia		Iran		Mexico[b]		Nigeria		Norway		Venezuela	
	Dinars	%	Rupiah	%	Rials	%	New Pesos	%	Nairas	%	Kroner	%	Bolivares	%
1990			26,554	24.6	2,585	46.7	6.7[c]	−24.7	14.2	40.6	256.1	5.5	122.6	23.6
1991			26,182	−1.4	2,664	3.1			9.7	−31.7			138.5	13.0
1992			29,106	11.2	3,142	17.9			9.6	−1.0			114.8	−17.1
1993			27,207	−6.5	4,604	46.5			11.0	14.6			105.8[c]	−7.8

SOURCES: 1970–1989 figures for all countries except Nigeria are calculated from International Monetary Fund, *International Financial Statistics Yearbook*, 1993, lines 81, 81z, and 99bip. 1990–1993 figures and 1982–1993 Nigerian figures are calculated from International Monetary Fund, *International Financial Statistics Yearbook*, 1995, lines 81, 81z, and 99bip. Nigerian GDP deflators for 1970–1972 are from International Monetary Fund, *International Financial Statistics Yearbook*, 1990.

NOTES: Total revenue = government revenue + grants received (where listed). Conversion to constant prices: revenue (current)/GDP deflator (1985 = 1.00). Breaks in series in source occur as follows: Indonesia 1972, Iran 1989 and 1993; Mexico 1984, Norway 1972, and Venezuela 1983 and 1987. Significant figures were retained in calculating growth rates. Missing figures are not available in source.

[a] Constant 1980 prices.

[b] Precise for 1970s to only one or two significant figures because of poor precision in GDP deflator in source.

[c] Based on preliminary figures in source.

TABLE A-3

GOVERNMENT EXPENDITURES AND NET LENDING (CONSTANT 1985 PRICES, BILLIONS) AND REAL RATE OF GROWTH OF TOTAL GOVERNMENT EXPENDITURES AND NET LENDING (PERCENTAGE)

	Algeria[a]		Indonesia		Iran		Mexico		Nigeria		Norway		Venezuela	
	Dinars	%	Rupiah	%	Rials	%	New Pesos	%	Nairas	%	Kroner	%	Bolivares	%
1970	29.5		4,904		3,130		2.4		5.5		88.7		67.4	
1971	28.6	-2.9	5,563	13.4	3,500	11.8	2.6	6.4	8.2	50.5	96.7	9.1	70.0	3.9
1972	31.4	9.8	6,982	25.5	4,109	17.4	3.8	45.9	8.6	4.9	155.7	60.9	74.8	6.9
1973	39.6	26.0	8,159	16.9	4,065	-1.1	4.9	29.0	7.5	-12.3	161.5	3.8	77.6	3.7
1974	35.7	-9.8	9,346	14.5	6,435	58.3	4.3	-11.0	10.0	32.2	169.3	4.8	135.5	74.5
1975			11,533	23.4	7,308	13.6	4.7	8.3	1.4[c]	-85.8	183.2	8.2	138.0	1.9
1976			13,313	15.4	7,763	6.2	5.8	24.3	18.0	1,166.2	214.5	17.1	142.3	3.1
1977			12,949	-2.7	8,379	7.9	6.1	4.0	12.6	-29.8	226.5	5.6	149.4	5.0
1978			14,875	14.9	6,747	-19.5	6.4	5.9	7.3	-42.3	237.6	4.9	140.7	-5.8
1979			17,098	14.9	4,895	-27.4	6.8	5.4	10.2	39.8	206.3	-13.2	109.7	-22.1
1980			19,505	14.1	4,416	-9.8	8.1	19.6	3.9	-61.9	183.1	-11.2	124.2	13.3
1981			21,336	9.4	4,199	-4.9	9.9	22.4	7.3	87.4	175.5	-4.1	168.4	35.6
1982			19,030	-10.8	4,315	2.8	14.2	43.0	17.7	142.5	178.6	1.7	157.7	-6.3
1983			19,810	4.1	4,471	3.6	11.5	-19.0	14.2	-19.8	186.2	4.3	126.5	-19.8
1984			18,446	-6.9	3,811	-14.8	10.7	-6.4	10.0	-29.6	190.4	2.3	99.4	-21.4
1985			21,295	15.4	3,558	-6.6	11.8	9.9	12.7[b]	27.0	206.2	8.3	103.0	3.6
1986			24,945	17.1	2,781	-21.8	13.2	12.3	16.6[b]	30.7	231.8	12.4	115.1	11.7
1987			22,295	-10.6	2,670	-4.0	14.4	8.7	15.0[b]	-9.6	243.3	4.9	128.5	11.6

Continued on next page

TABLE A-3 (continued)

	Algeria[a]		Indonesia		Iran		Mexico		Nigeria		Norway		Venezuela	
	Dinars	%	Rupiah	%	Rials	%	New Pesos	%	Nairas	%	Kroner	%	Bolivares	%
1988			21,704	-2.7	2,554	-4.3	13.0	-9.8	15.6	4.0	247.9	1.9	142.6	11.0
1989			23,777	9.6	2,263	-11.4	11.4	-12.0	16.0	2.6	249.3	0.6	107.5	-24.6
1990			26,054	9.6	2,845	25.7	6.4[b]	-43.9	22.3	39.4	244.6	-1.9	116.8	8.6
1991			25,608	-1.7	3,022	6.2			20.7	-7.2			136.4	16.8
1992			29,788	16.3	3,383	11.9			20.0	-3.4			121.2	-11.1
1993			26,257	-11.9	4,648	37.3			26.2	31.0			112.7	-7.0

SOURCES: 1970–1989 figures for all countries except Nigeria are calculated from International Monetary Fund, *International Financial Statistics Yearbook*, 1993, lines 82, 83, and 99bip. 1990–1993 figures and 1982–1993 Nigerian figures are calculated from International Monetary Fund, *International Financial Statistics Yearbook*, 1995, lines 82, 83, and 99bip. Nigerian GDP deflators for 1970–1972 are from International Monetary Fund, *International Financial Statistics Yearbook*, 1990.

NOTES: Figures include government expenditures plus lending minus repayments (where reported). Conversion to constant prices: expenditures (current)/GDP deflator (1985 = 1.00). Breaks in series in source occur as follows: Indonesia 1972, Iran 1989 and 1993, Mexico 1972 and 1977, Nigeria 1984, Norway 1972, and Venezuela 1983 and 1987. Significant figures were retained in calculating growth rates. Missing figures are not available in source.

[a] Constant 1980 prices.

[b] Based on preliminary figures in source.

[c] Net lending only.

TABLE A-4
CREDIT TO THE PRIVATE SECTOR (CONSTANT 1985 PRICES, BILLIONS) AND REAL RATE OF GROWTH OF CREDIT TO THE PRIVATE SECTOR (PERCENTAGE)

	Algeria[a]		Indonesia		Iran		Mexico		Nigeria		Norway		Venezuela	
	Dinars	%	Rupiah	%	Rials	%	New Pesos	%	Nairas	%	Kroner	%	Bolivares	%
1970	21.9		3,128		2,265		1.4		4.2		137.6		53.1	
1971	26.1	19.5	4,281	36.9	2,379	5.0	1.6	8.9	5.0	18.7	146.2	6.3	54.9	3.4
1972	41.6	59.3	4,954	15.7	2,890	21.5	1.7	10.0	6.0	20.2	157.0	7.4	61.3	11.7
1973	44.8	7.6	7,228	45.9	2,978	3.0	1.8	7.9	4.1	-31.3	162.5	3.6	69.3	13.1
1974	35.9	-19.8	6,514	-9.9	2,402	-19.3	1.5	-21.5	3.4	-16.9	167.7	3.2	64.1	-7.4
1975	47.5	32.1	11,083	70.1	3,341	39.1	1.3	-8.8	4.8	42.1	177.9	52.2	97.6	6.1
1976	55.3	16.4	12,644	14.1	4,180	25.1	1.6	19.8	5.9	21.9	169.5	-4.7	127.5	30.6
1977	54.4	-1.7	12,309	-2.6	4,172	-0.2	5.0	212.6	7.8	32.8	182.8	7.8	140.3	10.0
1978	63.2	16.2	15,246	23.9			5.9	19.6	8.2	4.9	186.4	2.0	159.8	13.9
1979	65.4	3.5	13,554	-11.1	3,989		6.1	3.2	7.9	-3.4	162.2	-13.0	147.9	-7.4
1980	68.5	4.9	7,327	-45.9	3,777	-5.3	7.0	14.1	9.8	23.2	144.1	-11.1	130.0	-12.1
1981	76.5	11.7	8,641	17.9	3,198	-15.3	7.8	12.2	11.8	20.6	146.7	1.8	126.1	-3.0
1982	85.2	11.3	11,569	33.9	2,874	-10.1	6.1	-22.9	13.7	16.4	151.1	3.0	138.9	10.2
1983			12,468	7.8	3,151	9.6	4.6	-24.6	12.0	-12.3	161.7	7.0	137.7	-0.9
1984			15,529	24.6	2,862	-3.5	5.3	15.8	10.8	-10.1	188.9	16.8	113.5	-17.6
1985			18,104	16.6	3,045	6.4	5.2	-2.0	11.4	5.1	241.7	28.0	115.8	2.1
1986			22,864	26.3	3,009		5.0	-2.8	15.3	35.1	313.8	29.8	145.5	25.6
1987			25,656	12.2	2,842	-5.6	5.4	8.0	11.0	-28.1	358.7	14.3	148.1	1.8
1988			30,893	20.4	2,591	-8.8	5.0	-8.3	10.8	-2.4	368.6	2.8	158.9	7.3

Continued on next page

TABLE A-4 (continued)

	Algeria[a]		Indonesia		Iran		Mexico		Nigeria		Norway		Venezuela	
	Dinars	%	Rupiah	%	Rials	%	New Pesos	%	Nairas	%	Kroner	%	Bolivares	%
1989			43,744	41.6	2,845	9.8	7.8	57.1	8.2	−23.4	377.5	2.4	99.2	−37.5
1990			66,450	51.9	3,410	19.9	9.9	26.9	8.9	8.5	378.6	0.3	87.0	−12.3
1991			71,326	7.3	3,828	12.3	13.1	32.3	9.5	6.7	353.9	−6.5	107.6	23.7
1992			71,678	0.5	4,219	10.2	17.0	29.8			362.2	2.3	113.2	5.2
1993					4,046	−4.1	19.2	12.9			362.4	0.1	95.5	−15.6

SOURCES: 1970–1989 figures are calculated from International Monetary Fund, *International Financial Statistics Yearbook*, 1993, lines 32d and 99bip. 1990–1993 figures are calculated from International Monetary Fund, *International Financial Statistics Yearbook*, 1995, lines 32d and 99bip. Nigerian GDP deflators for 1970–1972 and Iran figures for 1984–1985 are from International Monetary Fund, *International Financial Statistics Yearbook*, 1990.

NOTES: Figures include credit by both monetary authorities and deposit money banks (commercial banks, etc.). Conversion to constant prices: credit (current/GDP deflator (1985 = 1.00). Breaks in series in source occur as follows: Indonesia 1980, Mexico 1977 and 1982, Norway 1976, Venezuela 1987. Significant figures were retained in calculating growth rates. Missing figures are not available in source.

[a] Constant 1980 prices.

TABLE A-5
MONEY SUPPLY (CURRENT PRICES, BILLIONS) AND REAL RATE OF GROWTH OF MONEY SUPPLY (PERCENTAGE)

	Algeria		Indonesia		Iran		Mexico		Nigeria		Norway		Venezuela	
	Dinars	%	Rupiah	%	Rials	%	New Pesos	%	Nairas	%	Kroner	%	Bolívares	%
1970	11.6		241		128		0.05		0.6		17.2		7.1	
1971	13.0	11.4	313	29.9	155	20.7	0.06	7.4	0.7	4.2	19.2	11.7	8.2	15.8
1972	16.8	29.3	471	50.5	214	38.3	0.07	17.2	0.7	11.5	22.4	16.6	9.7	17.8
1973	18.9	13.0	669	42.0	278	29.8	0.08	23.5	0.8	5.3	25.8	15.3	11.5	19.1
1974	24.3	28.6	940	40.5	382	37.2	0.1	20.2	1.6	105.1	28.9	11.9	16.9	47.4
1975	32.0	31.7	1,250	33.0	458	20.1	0.1	20.8	2.5	51.9	33.7	16.6	25.6	51.1
1976	41.1	28.5	1,601	28.1	668	45.8	0.2	19.5	3.7	51.6	32.4	-3.7	29.0	13.3
1977	48.6	18.2	2,006	25.3	822	23.1	0.2	31.6	5.4	45.3	37.0	14.1	37.4	29.0
1978	62.2	28.0	2,488	24.0	1,078	31.2	0.3	29.8	5.1	-5.9	40.2	8.6	44.1	17.7
1979	72.2	16.1	3,379	35.8	1,689	56.7	0.4	33.7	6.2	20.5	43.3	7.6	46.6	5.7
1980	84.4	16.9	5,011	48.3	2,258	33.7	0.5	32.1	9.2	50.1	45.6	5.3	54.5	17.2
1981	97.9	16.0	6,474	29.2	2,637	16.8	0.6	33.1	9.8	5.6	52.4	15.0	58.3	6.9
1982	125.3	28.0	7,120	10.0	3,293	24.9	1.0	62.4	10.1	3.1	58.8	12.3	60.8	4.3
1983	152.8	21.9	7,576	6.4	3,922	19.1	1.5	40.3	11.3	12.3	65.9	12.1	76.3	25.4
1984	180.4	18.1	8,581	13.3			2.3	60.0	12.2	8.2	82.0	24.4	96.7	26.8
1985	202.2	12.1	10,124	18.0	5,509		3.5	49.5	13.2	8.4	98.7	20.3	105.2	8.8
1986	204.8	1.2	11,631	14.9			5.8	67.2	12.7	-4.3	101.8	3.2	109.9	4.4
1987	223.9	9.3	12,705	9.2	6,462	17.3	12.6	118.1	14.9	17.7	152.6	50.0	122.6	11.6
1988	252.2	12.7	14,392	13.3	7,118	10.2	21.2	67.8	21.5	43.9	187.1	22.6	145.5	18.7
1989	250.0	-0.9	20,559	42.9	8,238	15.7	29.1	37.3	26.7	24.3	218.3	16.7	170.0	16.8

Continued on next page

TABLE A-5 *(continued)*

	Algeria		Indonesia		Iran		Mexico		Nigeria		Norway		Venezuela	
	Dinars	%	Rupiah	%	Rials	%	New Pesos	%	Nairas	%	Kroner	%	Bolivares	%
1990	270.4	8.2	23,819	15.9	9,729	18.1	47.4	63.1	34.5	29.6	237.6	8.9	269.3	58.4
1991	324.5	20.0	26,693	12.1	12,266	26.1	106.2	123.9	48.7	41.0	255.8	7.6	347.6	29.1
1992	377.0	16.2	28,801	7.9	14,081	14.8	122.2	15.1			323.3	26.4	375.5	8.0
1993	450.3	19.4			18,305	30.0	143.9	17.7			340.1	5.2	416.9	11.0
1994	505.7	12.3					145.4	1.0					991.4	137.8

SOURCES: 1970–1992 figures are calculated from International Monetary Fund, *International Financial Statistics Yearbook*, 1993, line 34. 1992 figures for Algeria, Iran, Mexico, Norway, and Venezuela are from International Monetary Fund, *International Financial Statistics*, August 1994. 1993–1994 figures are from International Monetary Fund, *International Financial Statistics Yearbook*, 1995, line 34. Iran figure for 1978 is estimated in International Monetary Fund, *International Financial Statistics Yearbook*, 1990.

NOTES: Breaks in series in source occur as follows: Algeria (1992), Indonesia (1980), Mexico (1977 and 1982), Nigeria (1973), Norway (1976, 1992), Venezuela (1987). Significant figures were retained in calculating growth rates. Missing figures are not available in source.

TABLE A-6
CURRENT-ACCOUNT BALANCES
(CURRENT PRICES, MILLIONS OF U.S. DOLLARS)

	Algeria	Indonesia	Iran	Mexico	Nigeria	Venezuela	Capital-Deficient Total
1970	−125	−310	−507	−1,068	−368	−104	−2,482
1971	42	−372	−118	−835	−406	−11	−1,700
1972	−126	−334	−338	−916	−342	−101	−2,207
1973	−445	−476	154	−1,415	−8	877	−1,313
1974	176	598	12,267	−2,876	4,897	5,760	10,822
1975	−1,658	−1,109	4,707	−4,024	42	2,171	111
1976	−882	−907	7,660	−3,409	−357	254	1,359
1977	−2,323	−51	2,816	−1,854	−1,012	−3,179	−5,603
1978	−3,538	−1,412	104	−3,171	−3,757	−5,735	−17,510
1979	−1,631	980	11,968	−5,459	1,669	350	7,877
1980	249	3,011	−2,438	−10,750	5,127	4,728	−73
1981	90	−566	−3,446	−16,061	−6,164	4,000	−22,147
1982	−183	−5,324	5,733	−6,307	−7.285	−4,246	−17,612
1983	−85	−6,338	358	5,403	−4,354	4,427	−589
1984	74	−1,856	−414	4,194	115	4,651	6,764
1985	1,015	−1,923	−476	1,130	2,566	3,327	5,639
1986	−2,230	−3,911	−5,155	−1,673	366	−2,245	−14,848
1987	141	−2,098	−2,090	3,968	−69	−1,390	−1,538
1988	−2,040	−1,397	−1,868	−2,443	−194	−5,809	−13,751
1989	−1,081	−1,108	−191	−3,958	1,090	2,161	−3,087
1990	1,420	−2,988	327	−7,117	4,988	8,279	4,909
1991	2,367	−4,080	−7,909	13,786	1,203	1,755	−20,450
1992	1,600	−3,679	−8,100	−22,811	2,267	−3,365	−34,088
1993	180[a]	−2,800	900[a]		1,320	−1,691	

SOURCES: 1970–1991 figures are from International Monetary Fund, *International Financial Statistics Yearbook*, 1993, line 77a.d., except figures for Iran 1989–1991, Mexico 1991–1992 and Nigeria 1991 from International Monetary Fund, *International Financial Statistics*, August 1992. 1992–1993 figures (except Mexico) are from Organization of Petroleum Exporting Countries, *OPEC Annual Statistical Bulletin 1993*, 1994, Table 7.

NOTES: Figures exclude exceptional financing. Missing figures are not available in source.

[a] Based on preliminary figures in source.

TABLE A-7

CURRENT-ACCOUNT BALANCES OF CAPITAL-DEFICIENT
AND CAPITAL-SURPLUS MEMBERS OF OPEC
(CURRENT PRICES, BILLIONS OF U.S. DOLLARS)

	Capital Deficient[a]	Capital Surplus[b]	Total OPEC
1970	−1.53	2.31	0.78
1971	−1.00	4.31	3.31
1972	−1.30	5.39	4.09
1973	0.06	6.72	6.78
1974	23.92	43.32	67.24
1975	4.23	27.96	32.19
1976	5.82	31.50	37.32
1977	−3.65	25.03	21.38
1978	−14.27	12.12	−2.15
1979	13.58	45.95	59.53
1980	11.06	93.30	104.36
1981	−5.68	58.24	52.56
1982	−11.00	14.70	3.71
1983	−5.89	−8.43	−14.32
1984	2.68	−3.85	−1.16
1985	4.35	3.20	7.55
1986	−14.96	−7.14	−21.37
1987	−5.95	−0.45	−6.40
1988	−11.92	−1.83	−13.76
1989	0.68	6.16	6.84
1990	12.24	8.02	20.26
1991	−6.58	−52.25	−58.83
1992	−11.41	−16.13	−27.54
1993[c]	−2.07	−12.71	−14.78

SOURCES: 1970–1989 figures are from Organization of Petroleum Exporting Countries, *OPEC Annual Statistical Bulletin 1992, 1993*, Table 7. 1990–1993 figures are from Organization of Petroleum Exporting Countries, *OPEC Annual Statistical Bulletin 1993, 1994*, Table 7.

NOTE: For consistency, all figures for individual countries are taken from the sources listed above and may not always correspond to figures in Table A-6.

[a] Algeria, Gabon, Indonesia, Iran, Nigeria, and Venezuela.
[b] Iraq, Kuwait, Libya, Qatar, Saudi Arabia, and UAE.
[c] Based on preliminary figures in source.

TABLE A-8
RATE OF GROWTH OF CONSUMER PRICES (CURRENT PRICES, PERCENT INCREASE OVER PREVIOUS YEAR)

	Algeria	Indonesia	Iran	Mexico	Nigeria	Norway	Venezuela
1970	6.6	12.3	1.7	5.2	13.8	10.6	2.5
1971	2.6	4.4	4.2	5.3	16.0	6.3	3.2
1972	3.7	6.5	6.4	5.0	3.5	7.5	2.8
1973	6.2	31.0	9.8	12.0	5.4	7.4	4.1
1974	4.7	40.6	14.2	23.8	12.7	9.4	8.3
1975	9.0	19.1	12.9	15.2	33.9	11.7	10.3
1976	8.9	19.9	11.3	15.8	24.3	9.2	7.6
1977	12.1	11.0	27.0	29.0	13.8	9.0	7.8
1978	17.2	8.1	1.7	17.5	21.7	8.2	7.1
1979	11.5	16.3	10.5	18.2	11.7	4.8	12.4
1980	9.5	18.0	20.6	26.4	10.0	10.9	21.5
1981	14.6	12.2	24.2	27.9	20.8	13.6	16.2
1982	6.7	9.5	18.7	58.9	7.7	11.4	9.6
1983	6.0	11.8	19.7	101.8	23.2	8.4	6.3
1984	8.1	10.5	12.5	65.5	39.6	6.3	12.2
1985	10.5	4.7	4.4	57.7	7.4	5.7	11.4
1986	12.4	5.9	18.4	86.2	5.7	7.2	11.5
1987	7.4	9.3	28.6	131.8	11.3	8.7	28.1
1988	5.9	8.0	28.7	114.2	54.5	6.7	29.5
1989	9.3	6.4	22.3	20.0	50.5	4.6	84.2
1990	16.6	7.8	7.6	26.7	7.4	4.1	40.7
1991	25.9	9.4	17.1	22.7	13.0	3.4	34.2
1992	31.7	7.5	25.6	15.5	44.6	2.3	31.4
1993	20.5	9.2	21.2	8.7	57.2	2.3	38.1
1994	29.0	8.5	31.5	7.0	57.0	1.4	60.8

SOURCES: 1970–1989 figures are from International Monetary Fund, *International Financial Statistics Yearbook*, 1993, Table 64 x. 1990–1994 figures are from International Monetary Fund, *International Financial Statistics Yearbook*, 1995, Table 64 x.

NOTES: Breaks in series in source occur as follows: Algeria 1982, Indonesia 1979 and 1983, Iran 1985, Nigeria 1975, 1977, and 1984, Venezuela 1984.

TABLE A-9
TOTAL EXTERNAL DEBT (CURRENT PRICES, MILLIONS OF U.S. DOLLARS)

	Algeria	Indonesia	Iran	Mexico	Nigeria	Venezuela	Capital-Deficient Countries[a]	Oil Exporters[b]	Oil Importers[b,c]	All LDCs[b]
1970	937	2,904	2,167	5,966	567	964	13,505	13,983	52,194	66,177
1971	1,233	4,101	2,906	6,416	651	1,304	16,611	16,897	60,651	77,548
1972	1,488	5,117	3,466	7,028	732	1,712	19,543	19,717	71,325	91,042
1973	2,932	6,534	4,492	2,999	1,205	1,891	26,053	25,793	83,634	109,427
1974	3,305	8,202	4,079	11,946	1,274	1,784	30,590	31,860	104,075	135,935
1975	1,477	10,363	3,833	15,609	1,143	1,494	36,919	41,477	120,552	162,029
1976	5,934	12,626	4,298	20,149	906	3,311	47,224	53,339	142,566	195,905
1977	8,632	14,512	6,170	25,227	985	5,301	60,827	69,626	171,899	241,525
1978	13,416	16,190	7,367	30,487	2,645	8,568	78,673	90,792	211,939	302,731
1979	16,029	16,418		34,668	3,952	12,128	83,195	106,537	252,888	359,425
1980	16,917	18,162	4,508	41,215	5,302	13,775	99,879			427,804
1981	16,072	19,481		53,232	7,591	15,118	111,494			
1982	14,853	21,721		59,651	10,282	17,391	123,898			560,667
1983	14,090	25,007		81,565	13,366	23,690	157,718			643,531
1984	13,338	26,073		86,022	12,690	27,389	165,512			684,491
1985	16,380	30,598	1,290	88,448	14,555	26,383	177,654			779,544
1986	19,482	36,395	2,413	90,921	19,686	32,763	201,660			882,381
1987	23,095	45,424	2,280	98,506	27,454	30,485	227,244			1,142,449
1988	24,421	46,746	2,055	86,529	28,074	29,464	217,289			1,091,601
1989	24,629	50,811	1,862	80,085	29,657	29,089	216,133			1,133,938

1990	26,432	58,326	1,797	81,816	31,936	28,159	228,466	1,206,118
1991	25,979	65,298	2,065	85,442	32,668	28,589	240,041	1,265,151
1992	25,495	70,239	1,730	81,743	26,809	29,628	235,644	1,305,097
1993	24,881	71,490	5,759	86,401	26,742	30,177	245,450	1,391,083
1994	28,103	79,391	16,005	92,843	28,479	30,475	275,296	1,522,570

SOURCES: 1970–1979: World Bank, *World Debt Tables 1988–1989*, 1988.
1980–1984: World Bank, *World Debt Tables 1989–1990*, 1989, vol. 2, except "All LDCs" 1980–1986 from vol. 1.
1985–1986: World Bank, *World Debt Tables 1993–1994*, 1993, vol. 2.
1987–1994: World Bank, *World Debt Tables 1996*, 1996, vol. 2, except "All LDCs" 1987 from World Bank, *World Debt Tables 1994–1995*, 1994 vol. 1, and 1988–1994 from World Bank *World Debt Tables 1996*, 1996, vol. 1.
Iranian figures: 1970–1971: World Bank, *World Debt Tables 1977*, 1977; 1972, 1974, 1976–1978: World Bank, *World Debt Tables 1982–1983*, 1983; 1973, 1975: World Bank, *World Debt Tables 1979*, 1979; 1980: World Bank, *World Debt Tables 1993–1994*, 1993.

NOTES: Figures are for long-term, outstanding, and disbursed debt, including public, publicly guaranteed, and private nonguaranteed debt; Iranian figures do not include private nonguaranteed debt (not available in source). Missing figures are not available in source.
[a] Includes the six countries listed, except Iran 1979 and 1981–1984.
[b] World Bank members only.
[c] Calculated as "All LDCs" minus "Oil Exporters."

TABLE A-10

TOTAL DEBT SERVICE (CURRENT PRICES, MILLIONS OF U.S. DOLLARS)

	Algeria	Indonesia	Iran	Mexico	Nigeria	Venezuela	Capital-Deficient Countries[a]	Oil Exporters[b]	Oil Importers[b,c]	All LDCs[b,d]
1970	44	165	318	1,300	96	121	2,044	2,212	6,655	8,867
1971	69	219	496	1,360	94	173	2,411	2,412	7,703	10,115
1972	189	300	861	1,530	95	267	3,242	1,999	8,962	11,961
1973	300	445	981	1,869	229	389	4,213	4,160	11,892	16,052
1974	709	696	1,571	2,123	192	586	5,877	5,260	14,520	19,780
1975	456	1,003	955	2,613	270	594	5,891	6,021	17,622	23,643
1976	773	1,340	873	3,346	400	454	7,186	7,543	18,458	26,001
1977	1,044	1,981	889	4,698	138	916	9,666	10,558	22,503	33,061
1978	1,488	2,830	1,057	7,163	149	976	13,663	15,010	32,537	47,547
1979	1,791	3,060		11,422	393	3,107	20,773	24,145	39,668	63,813
1980	3,854	2,809	963	9,351	772	4,441	22,190			75,815
1981	3,837	3,220		10,641	1,307	4,127	23,132			
1982	4,268	3,509		12,315	1,699	4,387	26,179			96,216
1983	4,462	3,658		12,991	2,173	3,754	27,038			90,794
1984	4,570	4,217		15,923	3,465	3,778	31,953			100,236
1985	4,870	5,057	412	14,454	4,067	2,778	31,656			107,085
1986	5,109	4,678	382	12,099	1,796	4,245	28,309			111,871
1987	5,381	6,662	252	11,088	1,066	4,598	29,047			141,561
1988	6,269	8,194	396	13,741	2,170	5,094	35,864			147,487
1989	6,853	9,218	168	13,349	2,087	3,196	34,871			141,274

1990	8,564	9,200	253	8,621	3,304	4,741	34,683	145,190
1991	9,011	10,297	225	10,477	2,917	2,772	35,699	142,924
1992	8,889	11,673	286	18,263	3,709	2,639	45,459	148,646
1993	8,762	13,428	564	18,510	1,441	3,283	45,988	161,535
1994	5,105	13,650	3,682	16,032	1,866	3,143	43,478	192,074

SOURCES: 1970–1979: World Bank, *World Debt Tables 1988–1989*, 1988.
1980–1984: World Bank, *World Debt Tables 1987–1988*, 1987, except "All LDCs" 1980–1986 from World Bank, *World Debt Tables 1989–1990*, 1989, vol. 1.
1985–1986: World Bank, *World Debt Tables 1993–1994*, 1993, vol. 2.
1987–1994: World Bank, *World Debt Tables 1996*, 1996, vol. 2, except "All LDCs" 1987 from World Bank, *World Debt Tables 1994–1995*, 1994, and 1988–1994 from World Bank, *World Debt Tables 1996*, 1996, vol. 1.
Iranian figures: 1970–1971: World Bank, *World Debt Tables 1977*, 1977; 1972, 1974, 1976–1978: World Bank, *World Debt Tables 1982–1983*, 1983; 1973, 1975: World Bank, *World Debt Tables 1979*, 1979; 1980: World Bank, *World Debt Tables 1993–1994*, 1993.

NOTES: Debt service is on long-term debt as listed in Table A-9; see notes to that table for details. Missing figures are not available in source.
[a] Includes the six countries listed, except Iran 1979 and 1981–1984.
[b] Only World Bank members.
[c] Calculated as "All LDCs" minus "Oil Exporters."
[d] Figure for 1981 not included in sources for 1980s figures (earlier sources not comparable). Significant break in series occurs between 1986 and 1987.

TABLE A-11
RATIO OF DEBT SERVICE TO EXPORTS

	Algeria		Indonesia		Iran		Mexico		Nigeria		Venezuela		Capital-Deficient Countries		Oil Exporters		Oil Importers		All LDCs	
	%	Index	%	Index	%	Index	%	Index	%	Index	%	Index	%	Index	%	Index	%	Index	%	Index
1970	3.28	100	13.88	100	15.67	100	44.29	100	7.16	100	4.27	100	17.52	100	18.22	100	14.11	100	14.95	100
1971	5.88	179	16.36	118	15.62	100	42.89	97	4.68	65	5.18	121	16.97	97	17.54	96	13.47	96	14.26	95
1972	11.66	355	16.33	118	21.85	139	40.09	91	4.10	57	7.81	183	19.13	109	18.51	102	12.85	91	13.92	93
1973	12.16	370	13.46	97	10.52	67	38.62	87	6.08	85	7.37	173	14.54	83	17.27	95	12.08	86	13.10	88
1974	12.61	384	9.32	67	7.19	46	33.34	75	1.91	27	4.90	115	9.28	53	10.35	57	11.19	79	10.95	73
1975	8.65	264	14.28	103	4.49	29	41.05	93	2.96	41	5.89	138	9.96	57	12.47	68	13.16	93	12.98	87
1976	12.95	394	15.27	110	3.43	22	46.45	105	3.66	51	4.38	102	10.46	60	13.55	74	11.98	85	12.40	83
1977	15.51	472	18.13	131	3.59	23	57.22	129	1.04	15	8.37	196	12.91	74	16.44	90	12.26	87	13.34	89
1978	20.88	636	25.02	180	6.26	40	62.83	142	1.29	18	8.99	211	19.77	113	21.90	120	15.27	108	16.89	113
1979	26.52	808	19.70	142			71.37	161	2.17	30	19.06	446	20.47	117	24.39	134	14.80	105	17.38	116
1980	25.76	785	12.65	91	7.73	49	42.25	95	2.78	39	19.98	468	18.23	104					17.52	117
1981	24.63	751	12.94	93			38.33	87	6.64	93	16.83	394	18.71	107						
1982	28.65	873	16.49	119			44.59	101	13.19	184	21.80	511	21.98	125					22.35	149
1983	31.82	970	18.40	133			45.28	102	20.00	279	21.65	507	24.01	137					21.55	144
1984	32.84	1,001	18.99	137			48.91	110	27.99	391	20.06	470	27.36	156					21.92	147
1985	34.61	1,055	25.12	181	2.76	18	48.64	110	30.08	420	16.16	378	28.87	165					23.85	160
1986	55.87	1,703	29.16	210	4.91	31	50.70	114	28.43	397	37.72	883	38.05	217					25.76	172
1987	52.81	1,610	35.22	254	2.04	13	36.80	83	13.64	191	35.69	836	31.47	180					20.14	135
1988	73.40	2,238	38.17	275	3.54	23	42.81	97	29.71	415	40.09	939	38.44	219					19.56	131
1989	65.35	1,992	36.04	260	1.21	16	35.21	79	24.31	340	20.47	479	31.12	178					17.11	114
1990	61.67	1,880	29.20	210	1.25	8	19.71	45	22.37	312	22.08	517	23.82	136					15.54	104
1991	69.17	2,109	30.57	220	1.15	7	22.92	52	21.74	304	14.92	349	24.80	142					15.71	104
1992	73.05	2,227	29.32	211	1.38	9	38.83	88	28.41	397	15.40	361	30.32	173					14.86	99
1993	78.54	2,395	31.80	229	2.92	19	36.99	84	12.59	176	18.98	444	30.36	173					15.34	103
1994	52.64	1,605	27.69	199	18.63	119	28.50	64	19.05	266	16.96	397	26.62	152					14.37	96

SOURCE: Calculated from Tables A-10 and A-16.
NOTES: For index columns, 1970 = 100. Last four columns are the ratios of the aggregate debt service to the aggregate exports for the appropriate category. See also notes for Tables A-10 and A-16.

TABLE A-12

STRUCTURE OF THE GROSS DOMESTIC PRODUCT, 1965–1993

| | As % of GDP | | | | Ratio of Tradeables to Nontradeables[b] $(A+C)/(B-C+D)$ | % Change in Ratio (1965–93) |
	Agriculture A	Industry B	Manufacturing[a] C	Services D		
Algeria						
1965	15	34	11	51	0.35	−8.6
1970	11	41	15	48	0.35	
1977	8	57	11	35	0.23	
1982	6	55	10	39	0.19	
1987	12	42	12	45	0.32	
1992	15	47	10	38	0.33	
1993	13	43	11	43	0.32	
Indonesia						
1965	56	13	8	31	1.78	−61.2
1970	45	19	10	36	1.22	
1977	31	34	9	35	0.67	
1982	26	39	13	35	0.64	
1987	26	33	14	41	0.67	
1992	19	40	21	40	0.68	
1993	19	39	22	42	0.69	
Iran						
1965	26	36	12	38	0.61	0.0
1970 not available in source						
1977	10	55	13	35	0.30	
1982 and 1987 not available in source						

Continued on next page

TABLE A-12 (continued)

	As % of GDP				Ratio of Tradeables to Nontradeables[b] (A+C)/(B−C+D)	% Change in Ratio (1965–93)
	Agriculture A	Industry B	Manufacturing[a] C	Services D		
1992	23	28	14	48	0.60	
1993[c]	24	29	14	47	0.61	
Mexico						−25.0
1965	14	27	20	59	0.52	
1970	12	29	22	59	0.52	
1977	10	36	28	54	0.61	
1982	7	38	21	55	0.39	
1987[d]	9	34	25	57	0.52	
1992	8	28	20	63	0.39	
1993	8	28	20	63	0.39	
Nigeria						−54.7
1965	54	13	6	33	1.50	
1970	41	14	4	45	0.81	
1977	34	43	9	23	0.75	
1982	22	39	6	39	0.39	
1987	30	43	8	27	0.61	
1992	37	38	n.a.	25	n.a.	
1993	34	43	7	24	0.68	
Norway						−51.2
1965	8	33	21	59	0.41	
1970	6	32	22	62	0.39	
1977	6	35	20	59	0.35	

1982	4	41	15	55	0.23	
1987	4	35	15	62	0.23	
1992[c]	3	35	13	62	0.19	
1993[c]	3	35	14	62	0.20	
Venezuela						
1965	6	40	n.a.	55	n.a.	
1970	6	39	16	54	0.29	−20.7
1977	6	17	n.a.	77	n.a.	(1970–93)
1982	6	42	16	52	0.28	
1987	6	38	22	56	0.39	
1992	5	41	16	53	0.27	
1993	5	42	14	53	0.23	

SOURCE: World Bank, *World Development Report*, 1979, 1980, 1984, 1985, 1989, 1993, 1994, 1995.

[a] A subset of B.
[b] Warning: This measure is a very simple one.
[c] Figures in source are for years other than those indicated.
[d] Estimated.

TABLE A-13

VALUE OF PETROLEUM EXPORTS (CONSTANT 1985 PRICES, BILLIONS) AND REAL RATE OF GROWTH OF PETROLEUM EXPORTS (PERCENTAGE)

	Algeria[a]		Indonesia[b]		Iran		Mexico		Nigeria[c]		Norway[d]		Venezuela	
	Dinars	%	U.S. Dollars	%	Rials	%	New Pesos	%	Nairas	%	Kroner	%	Bolivares	%
1970	11.4		4.7		2,319		0.03		4.8		1.5		64.6	
1971	3.8	−14.3	5.9	24.3	3,078	32.7	0.02	−20.0	8.4	75.3	1.3	−10.3	73.1	13.2
1972	14.1	44.6	8.4	42.3	2,996	−2.7	0.02	−25.0	10.3	22.3	2.2	70.8	68.9	−5.9
1973	17.0	20.6	11.1	32.5	3,120	4.2	0.02	−33.3	10.5	1.4	2.3	5.0	90.7	31.8
1974	29.3	72.7	24.4	119.4	7,068	126.5	0.05	150.0	19.8	89.3	6.1	162.2	152.7	68.3
1975	27.8	−5.4	22.1	−9.1	6,009	−15.0	0.1	190.0	14.3	−27.8	14.5	137.3	121.4	−20.5
1976	29.6	6.6	21.8	−1.3	6,465	7.6	0.2	44.8	16.8	17.2	22.6	56.0	121.7	0.2
1977	31.3	5.6	23.5	7.5	5,688	−12.0	0.5	121.0	17.5	4.2	22.2	−1.7	117.4	−3.5
1978	28.4	−9.2	21.6	−8.1	4,717	−17.1	0.7	48.7	11.7	−32.9	24.3	9.4	105.9	−9.8
1979	36.7	29.3	19.4	−10.0	3,290	−30.3	1.1	61.7	17.2	47.2	32.8	34.7	136.1	28.4
1980	48.5	32.2	21.8	12.2	1,767	−46.3	2.3	102.2	21.6	25.5	46.3	41.3	145.8	7.2
1981	48.4	−0.2	20.6	−5.6	1,435	−18.8	2.6	15.3	15.6	−28.1	45.9	−0.8	135.3	−7.2
1982			20.2	−1.8	2,102	46.5	4.5	72.4	11.4	−26.7	43.2	−5.9	109.5	−19.1
1983			15.4	−23.9	1,935	−7.9	4.6	1.6	8.8	−23.0	49.8	15.4	92.0	−16.0
1984			12.8	−17.0	1,205	−37.7	4.3	−5.5	9.2	4.7	57.6	15.6	93.0	1.1

1985	7.7	−39.8	1,420	17.8	3.8	−11.7	10.9	18.5	61.1	6.2	77.6	−16.6
1986	5.2	−32.6	407	−71.3	2.2	−41.1	8.5	−21.5	32.4	−47.0	52.2	−32.8
1987	5.1	−1.2	490	20.5	2.8	26.6	19.2	125.0	38.6	19.2	74.1	42.0
1988			351	−28.4	1.8	−35.9	16.0	−16.9	33.2	−14.1	71.6	−3.4
1989	3.6		358	2.0	1.9	2.0	21.5	34.3	56.0	68.7	114.2	59.7
1990	4.4	22.2					38.8	80.8			152.4	33.4
1991	3.6	−18.2					35.8	−7.7			132.1	−13.3
1992	3.4	−5.6					37.5	4.7			113.3	−14.2
1993	2.4	−29.4									104.4	−7.9

SOURCES: 1970–1989 figures are calculated from International Monetary Fund, *International Financial Statistics Yearbook*, 1993, lines 70a and 90bip, except Indonesia, line 70a.d, and Nigeria, line 70aa. 1970–1989 Mexican and Nigerian figures are from International Monetary Fund, *International Financial Statistics Yearbook*, 1990, and were converted to constant prices using GDP deflators from the 1993 edition, except Nigerian GDP deflators for 1970–1972 are from the 1990 edition. 1990–1993 figures are calculated from International Monetary Fund, *International Financial Statistics Yearbook*, 1995, lines 70a and 99bip, except Indonesia, line 70a.d, and Nigeria, line 70aa.

NOTES: Conversion to constant prices: revenue (current)/GDP deflator (1985 = 1.00). Breaks in series in source occur for Venezuela 1987. Significant figures were retained in calculating growth rates. Missing figures are not available in source.

[a] Constant 1980 prices.
[b] Figures include only crude petroleum and petroleum products.
[c] Figures include only crude petroleum.
[d] Figures exclude natural gas.

TABLE A-14
RATIO OF EXTERNAL DEBT TO GROSS NATIONAL PRODUCT

	Algeria		Indonesia		Iran		Mexico		Nigeria		Venezuela		Capital-Deficient Countries[a]		Oil Exporters		Oil Importers		All LDCs	
	%	Index	%	Index	%	Index	%	Index	%	Index	%	Index	%	Index	%	Index	%	Index	%	Index
1970	19.34	100	29.94	100	22.44	100	16.18	100	4.31	100	8.76	100	15.84	100	15.60	100	13.80	100	14.15	100
1971	23.50	122	41.61	139	23.85	106	15.79	98	4.38	102	10.91	125	17.53	111	17.28	111	14.64	106	15.14	107
1972	21.22	110	44.65	149	22.27	99	15.00	93	4.29	100	12.69	145	17.54	111	17.46	112	15.51	112	15.89	112
1973	32.59	169	38.72	129	17.90	80	15.73	97	6.29	146	11.58	132	18.13	114	18.69	120	14.57	106	15.37	109
1974	25.04	129	30.99	103	8.96	40	16.06	99	3.82	89	6.98	80	14.00	88	16.12	103	14.95	108	15.21	108
1975	29.05	150	33.07	110	7.41	33	17.16	106	2.84	66	5.41	62	14.35	91	17.48	112	14.80	107	15.40	109
1976	33.96	176	32.50	109	6.43	29	22.04	136	1.83	43	10.50	120	15.98	101	20.09	129	16.23	118	17.12	121
1977	41.79	216	30.50	102	7.45	33	29.99	185	1.75	41	14.65	167	18.56	117	24.43	157	17.21	125	18.81	133
1978	51.97	269	30.40	102	10.40	46	28.90	179	4.30	100	21.84	249	22.09	139	27.57	177	18.01	131	20.10	142
1979	49.85	258	31.13	104			25.16	155	5.12	119	25.15	287	23.90	151	26.50	170	18.18	132	20.04	142
1980	41.11	213	24.28	81	4.80	21	21.79	135	5.33	124	19.76	226	17.58	111					20.77	147
1981	37.31	193	21.78	73			22.10	137	8.17	190	19.23	220	20.46	129						
1982	33.85	175	24.10	80			36.41	225	11.21	260	22.37	255	26.52	167					26.61	188
1983	29.61	153	32.33	108			58.22	360	15.18	353	29.94	342	36.49	230					31.85	225
1984	26.25	136	32.27	108			51.83	320	13.96	324	48.59	555	37.21	235					33.45	236
1985	28.69	148	36.52	122	1.33	6	50.37	311	18.65	433	44.10	503	28.03	177					37.36	264
1986	31.35	162	47.40	158	1.14	5	74.68	462	50.86	1,180	55.48	633	35.37	223					41.22	291
1987	36.58	189	63.17	211	1.65	7	73.87	457	112.79	2,617	65.34	746	47.62	301					33.03	233
1988	43.01	222	55.20	184	1.64	7	52.14	322	96.44	2,238	49.07	560	41.75	264					28.72	203
1989	46.43	240	52.44	175	1.51	7	40.05	248	106.47	2,470	69.67	795	39.83	251					27.40	194

Year																
1990	45.72	236	53.41	178	1.51	7	34.31	212	109.60	2,543	59.70	682	38.01	240	26.53	187
1991	59.78	309	53.27	178	1.71	8	30.27	187	109.88	2,549	54.60	623	36.86	233	27.95	198
1992	55.78	288	52.84	176	1.58	7	25.17	156	98.92	2,295	50.60	578	33.74	213	27.99	198
1993	51.82	268	47.04	157			24.22	150	103.55	2,403	51.84	592	37.41	236	28.95	205
1994	69.87	361	47.26	158			25.44	157	87.21	2,023	52.94	604	39.09	247	29.76	210

SOURCE: Calculated from Tables A-9 and A-15.

NOTES: For index columns, 1970 = 100. Last four columns are the ratios of the aggregate debt to the aggregate GNP for the appropriate category. See also notes to Tables A-9 and A-15.

[a] Does not include data for Iran in 1979, 1981–1984, and 1993–1994.

GROSS NATIONAL PRODUCT (CURRENT PRICES, MILLIONS OF U.S. DOLLARS)

	Algeria	Indonesia	Iran[a]	Mexico	Nigeria	Venezuela	Capital-Deficient Countries[b]	Oil Exporters[c]	Oil Importers[c,d]	All LDCs[c,e]
1970	4,845	9,698	9,657	36,869	13,170	11,003	85,242	89,663	378,181	467,844
1971	5,247	9,856	12,183	40,641	14,859	11,954	94,740	97,803	414,395	512,198
1972	7,012	11,459	15,564	46,842	17,081	13,492	111,450	112,934	459,839	572,773
1973	8,996	16,873	25,091	57,222	19,169	16,331	143,682	137,972	573,842	711,814
1974	13,198	26,468	45,536	74,372	33,365	25,555	218,494	197,592	696,314	893,906
1975	15,413	31,334	51,707	90,959	40,303	27,641	257,357	237,286	814,537	1,051,823
1976	17,476	38,848	66,812	91,425	49,498	31,536	295,595	265,503	878,636	1,144,139
1977	20,657	47,588	82,834	84,121	56,298	36,189	327,687	284,961	999,041	1,284,002
1978	25,816	53,253	70,849	105,484	61,493	39,238	356,133	329,268	1,176,670	1,505,938
1979	32,153	52,740	85,491	137,790	77,165	48,219	433,558	402,025	1,391,348	1,793,373
1980	41,149	74,806	93,862	189,155	99,539	69,706	568,217			2,059,465
1981	43,071	89,427	107,009	240,877	92,960	78,601	651,945			
1982	43,883	90,125	133,392	163,815	91,715	77,735	600,665			2,107,054
1983	47,587	77,357	162,354	140,089	88,049	79,116	594,552			2,020,221
1984	50,806	80,794	168,286	165,962	90,891	56,366	613,105			2,046,231
1985	57,103	83,789	179,426	175,597	78,040	59,828	633,783			2,086,588
1986	62,135	76,789	211,726	121,745	38,710	59,049	570,154			2,140,492
1987	63,144	71,904	137,805	133,356	24,341	46,655	477,205			3,458,459
1988	56,778	84,681	125,466	165,966	29,110	58,513	520,514			3,800,659
1989	53,044	96,894	123,200	199,949	27,855	41,752	542,694			4,138,319

1990	57,811	109,209	119,290	238,432	29,138	47,164	601,044	4,545,984
1991	43,457	122,573	120,835	282,230	29,730	52,359	651,184	4,526,517
1992	45,708	132,938	109,400	324,740	27,101	58,554	698,441	4,662,614
1993	48,013	151,992		356,695	25,826	58,207	640,773	4,804,569
1994	40,220	168,000		364,952	32,655	57,560	663,387	5,115,410

SOURCES: 1970–1979: World Bank, *World Debt Tables 1988–1989*, 1988.
1980–1984: World Bank, *World Debt Tables 1989–1990*, 1989, vol. 2, except "All LDCs" 1980–1986 from vol. 1.
1985–1986: World Bank, *World Debt Tables 1993–1994*, 1993, vol. 2.
1987–1994: World Bank, *World Debt Tables 1996*, 1996, vol. 2, except "All LDCs" 1987 from World Bank, *World Debt Tables 1994–1995*, 1994, and 1988–1994 from *World Debt Tables 1996*, 1996, vol. 1.
Iranian figures: 1970–1984 calculated using national-currency GNP and exchange rates in International Monetary Fund, *International Financial Statistics Yearbook*, 1990, lines 99a and rf.

NOTE: Missing figures not available in source.
[a] Figures before 1985 may not be exactly comparable to other country figures; see source note.
[b] Includes the six countries listed, except Iran 1993–1994.
[c] World Bank members only.
[d] Calculated as "All LDCs" minus "Oil Exporters."
[e] Figure for 1981 not included in sources for 1980s figures (earlier sources not comparable). Significant break in series occurs between 1986 and 1987.

TABLE A-16
EXPORTS OF GOODS AND SERVICES (CURRENT PRICES, MILLIONS OF U.S. DOLLARS)

	Algeria	Indonesia	Iran[a]	Mexico	Nigeria	Venezuela	Capital-Deficient Countries[b]	Oil Exporters[c]	Oil Importers[c,d]	All LDCs[c,e]
1970	1,340	1,189	2,029	2,935	1,341	2,833	11,667	12,142	47,173	59,315
1971	1,173	1,339	3,176	3,171	2,010	3,339	14,208	13,752	57,167	70,919
1972	1,621	1,837	3,941	3,816	2,316	3,418	16,949	16,205	69,743	85,948
1973	2,467	3,306	9,326	4,840	3,764	5,279	28,982	24,089	98,441	122,530
1974	5,621	7,464	21,856	6,368	10,048	11,971	63,328	50,819	129,814	180,633
1975	5,270	7,025	21,289	6,365	9,130	10,092	59,171	48,296	133,876	182,172
1976	5,971	8,776	25,449	7,204	10,924	10,376	68,700	55,687	154,041	209,728
1977	6,733	10,926	24,793	8,210	13,277	10,947	74,886	64,223	183,578	247,801
1978	7,127	11,309	16,873	11,401	11,535	10,855	69,100	68,528	213,017	281,545
1979	10,525	15,536	25,007	16,003	18,100	16,305	101,476	98,984	268,101	367,085
1980	14,963	22,208	12,463	22,133	27,754	22,232	121,753			432,749
1981	15,581	24,878	11,188	27,765	19,675	24,519	123,606			
1982	14,899	21,274	22,296	27,618	12,880	20,122	119,089			430,576
1983	14,024	19,876	21,830	28,689	10,864	17,341	112,624			421,279
1984	13,928	22,205	16,884	32,555	12,381	18,834	116,777			457,340
1985	14,070	20,200	14,938	29,717	13,520	17,189	109,634			448,954
1986	9,144	16,043	7,778	23,864	6,318	11,253	74,400			434,267
1987	10,190	18,918	12,353	30,132	7,818	12,883	92,294			702,879
1988	8,541	21,469	11,176	32,097	7,304	12,705	93,292			753,932
1989	10,486	25,578	13,879	37,911	8,584	15,610	112,048			825,608

Year							
1990	13,887	31,508	20,197	43,738	14,771	21,476	145,577	934,331
1991	13,026	33,680	19,542	45,709	13,417	18,573	143,947	909,514
1992	12,168	39,815	20,714	47,031	13,056	17,137	149,921	1,000,099
1993	11,156	42,226	19,315	50,042	11,445	17,293	151,477	1,053,309
1994	9,698	49,296	19,765	56,258	9,795	18,534	163,346	1,179,903

SOURCES: 1970–1979: World Bank, *World Debt Tables 1988–1989*, 1988.
1980–1984: World Bank, *World Debt Tables 1989–1990*, 1989, vol. 2, except "All LDCs" 1980–1986 from vol. 1
1985–1986: World Bank, *World Debt Tables 1993–1994*, 1993, vol. 2.
1987–1994: World Bank, *World Debt Tables 1996*, 1996, vol. 2, except "All LDCs" 1987 from *World Debt Tables 1994–1995*, and 1988–1994 from *World Debt Tables 1996*, 1996, vol. 1.
Iranian figures: 1970–1984 calculated using national-currency exports and exchange rates in International Monetary Fund, *International Financial Statistics Yearbook*, 1990, lines 90c and rf.

NOTES: Missing figures are not available in source.
[a] Figures before 1985 may not be exactly comparable to other country figures; see source note.
[b] Includes the six countries listed.
[c] Only World Bank members.
[d] Calculated as "All LDCs" minus "Oil Exporters."
[e] Figure for 1981 not included in sources for 1980s figures (earlier sources not comparable). Significant break in series occurs between 1986 and 1987.

Statistical Appendix Citations

International Monetary Fund (IMF), *International Financial Statistics,* April 1989, 42(2). Washington, D.C., 1989.
———, *International Financial Statistics,* August 1992, 45(8). Washington, D.C., 1992.
———, *International Financial Statistics,* August 1994, 47(8). Washington, D.C., 1994.
———, *International Financial Statistics Yearbook.* Vol. 41. Washington, D.C., 1988).
———, *International Financial Statistics Yearbook.* Vol. 43. (Washington, D.C., 1990.
———, *International Financial Statistics Yearbook.* Vol. 46. Washington, D.C., 1993).
———, *International Financial Statistics Yearbook.* Vol. 48. Washington, D.C., 1995.
Organization of Petroleum Exporting Countries (OPEC), *OPEC Annual Statistical Bulletin 1992.* Vienna, 1993.
———, *OPEC Annual Statistical Bulletin 1993.* Vienna, 1994.
World Bank, *World Debt Tables.* Washington, D.C., 1977.
———, *World Debt Tables.* Washington, D.C., 1979.
———, *World Debt Tables 1982–1983.* Washington, D.C., 1983.
———, *World Debt Tables 1987–1988.* Vol. 2. Washington, D.C., 1987.
———, *World Debt Tables 1988–1989.* Vol. 3. Washington, D.C., 1988.
———, *World Debt Tables 1989–1990.* Vols. 1–2. Washington, D.C., 1989.
———, *World Debt Tables 1993–1994,* Vols. 1–2. Washington, D.C., 1993.
———, *World Debt Tables 1994–1995.* Vol. 1. Washington, D.C., 1994.
———, *World Debt Tables 1996.* Vols. 1–2. Washington, D.C., 1996.
———, *World Development Report.* New York: Oxford University Press, various years.

Notes

CHAPTER ONE:
THE MODERN MYTH OF KING MIDAS

1. Interview with Hector Hurtado, Minister of Finance of the Republic of Venezuela, Caracas, 1978.

2. Interview with Juan Pablo Pérez Alfonzo, former oil minister and founder of OPEC, Caracas, 1976.

3. This term originated with Becker (1983, 64), who argued that Peru's mineral resources could replace agriculture as the original source of large-scale industrial capital. In this development model, the Peruvian state would be able to exploit its dependence on minerals by maximizing returns from the mining sector, then redirecting the surplus to foster industry in other sectors. In oil countries, this same strategy is known as "sowing the petroleum." As we shall see below, this is precisely the reasoning of state planners in numerous mineral-producing countries. But it has proved false repeatedly for reasons that shall become clear, most especially in Peru, which in the early 1990s was devastated by the worst economic crisis in Latin America.

4. The Dutch Disease received its name from economists who examined the impact of North Sea gas production on the Dutch economy. They noted that the guilder, backed by strong export revenues from natural gas, appreciated rapidly against other currencies; the results were the exposure of Dutch industries to foreign competition, deindustrialization, and loss of employment.

5. Smith's observations were supplemented by those of David Ricardo and John Stuart Mill. Ricardo ([1817] 1973, 33–34) distinguished the rent of mines from the rent of agricultural lands and noted that the basis of rent of mines was "destructible." Mill ([1848] 1895, 30) developed the notion of diminishing returns in mining. Together these works became the genesis of a separate branch of economic theory, known as the theory of exhaustible resources.

6. Political economy has a variety of different interpretations and meanings.

Originated by seventeenth-century scholars attempting to make policy prescriptions about trade during the rise of mercantilism, it initially sought to illuminate the manner in which governments, producers, and consumers were operating in an economic system of complex mutual interdependence. On the origins of this approach, see Deane (1978). For an attempt to distinguish between Marxist and non-Marxist approaches, see the review by Moore (1989). For an emphasis on collective choices and the application of "economic reasoning" to political processes, see Staniland (1985), Rothchild and Curry (1978), Bates (1983), and North (1990).

7. The popularity of approaches based on the political economy of development, especially in the study of Latin America, is rooted in the central observation by dependence theorists that the development paths of Third World countries are fundamentally and distinctively determined by their incorporation into the world capitalist economy as exporters of primary products (Cardoso and Faletto 1969, Dos Santos 1970). Scholars contending that leading economic sectors have a fundamental impact on politics have offered "sectoral" explanations for cycles of regime instability in Argentina and Central America (O'Donnell 1978b, Reynolds 1978), differing modes of agrarian protest (Paige 1975), and patterns of labor relations in Latin America (Bergquist 1986).

8. Referred to as the "new staple theory" or "sectoral analysis," this approach is exemplified in some interesting work by Shafer (1994), who seeks to elaborate a general theory regarding the interaction of leading sectors and states in developing countries. Deyo (1981, 1989) offers a sectoral argument about the implications of the marginalization of labor in the East Asian newly industrialized countries.

9. An enormous literature exists on the 1973–1974 oil boom and its impact on the oil industry and the developed countries, but studies of the effect on specific exporters have been slow in coming. Important sources for individual-country studies of Algeria, Indonesia, Iran, and Nigeria are cited in Chapter 9. But few scholars have attempted to analyze these countries as a group. The works of Jahangir Amuzegar and Alan Gelb, listed in the Bibliography, are notable exceptions and have substantially influenced this study.

10. Rational-choice perspectives, for example, claim that social action can be reduced to statements about competing individuals, that people are self-interested and rational maximizers of their satisfactions, and that specific public policies can be understood as the result of a predictable maximizing process taking place within a fixed set of preferences. Once these preference structures are established, such choices can even be predicted through game-theoretic models of strategic interactions among policymakers at key junctures (Riker 1962, Buchanan and Tullock 1962).

11. The limited impact of rational-choice theories on the study of development has been noted by Moore (1989).

12. This approach implicitly underlies other studies attempting to explain various trajectories of national development, especially in Latin America. Some of the most important of these are Cardoso and Faletto (1969), Schmitter (1972), and O'Donnell (1973, 1978b). Only Collier and Collier (1991) explicitly utilize the concept of path dependence to examine the different trajectories

that result from the way the labor movement was initially incorporated into political life in Latin America.

13. Elisabeth Wood, personal communication, June 18, 1991.

14. I am grateful to Michael Shafer for this language.

15. Asset specificity essentially claims that the more specific an asset, the greater are the losses incurred by owners who are forced to reorient their activities. See, for example, Williamson (1975, 1985).

16. The definition of the state given here is the classic Weberian one. For regime and government I have elaborated on prior definitions, published and unpublished, that have been formulated by Philippe Schmitter (personal communication, 1982) and Collier (1979, 402). These definitions differ strikingly from certain ones offered by other scholars. Nordlinger (1981, 9), for example, argues: "The definition of the state must refer to individuals....Only individuals have preferences and engage in actions that make for their realization." In my view, Nordlinger is confusing state and government, which leads both to a reification of the state and a systematic underemphasis of the importance of the permanent apparatus and the institutions that limit policy choice. A definition of the state as a group of individuals occupying particular roles rather than as an administrative apparatus or legal order encourages the view that government leaders are relatively unconstrained by preexisting institutional arrangements.

17. Iraq is often put in either category, although it is usually considered a capital-surplus country. For this study it has been retained in this category, although the consequences of the war with Iran have led it to behave more like a capital-deficient exporter.

18. Egypt, Oman, Syria, Gabon, Cameroon, Ecuador, and Trinidad-Tobago do not appear in Table 1—though all belong to the category of capital-deficient countries—because their shares of world oil production are so small, as explained below.

19. Indeed, Elfeituri (1987, 283) notes that the ratio of oil exports to total exports for petroleum-exporting developing countries exceeded 90 percent after the second oil boom in 1982 for all but Algeria, Indonesia, and Kuwait.

20. These statistics are constantly revised as new oil is discovered or new technologies make possible the continued exploitation of older fields; thus there is considerable discrepancy in reserve and production figures in alternative sources, especially for Kuwait and Saudi Arabia. Reserve and production statistics from a 1973 contemporary source, *The Oil and Gas Journal,* have been used in Table 1 because they capture the perceptions of country actors at the time of the boom.

21. Mill argues that if a series of different units demonstrate a similar outcome, the characteristic or characteristics these different units have in common are the cause of the phenomenon. In essence, it is a search for invariance.

CHAPTER TWO: SPANISH GOLD TO BLACK GOLD

1. Pérez Alfonzo described the origins of the idea to form an organization of producer nations in an interview (Caracas, summer 1976): "The history of

the [oil] industry gave me the idea when I was in exile. After all, weren't the oil companies the first to organize the centers of production among themselves? I first understood the idea of prorating and controlling production when I was in the United States. I worked for the Texas Railroad Commission, the organization which controls the domestic production of fuels in the state. I immediately thought, if state regulation can do that for the companies, couldn't an international organization do that for our countries? And couldn't we gain more control?"

2. See the development plans of the oil exporters: for example, Government of Nigeria (1975), and Imperial Government of Iran (1976).

3. There are very few income-distribution studies of oil-exporting countries. On Venezuela, see Nissen and Mommer (1989), Musgrove (1981), or Bourguignon (1980b).

4. Note, however, that the ratios of debt to GNP and of debt service to exports remained relatively low because of the high growth rates of the exporters through 1980. These ratios changed as oil prices began to fall in 1981.

5. For more on the debt patterns of oil-exporting countries, see Karl (1983, 22, Table 8).

6. For the impact of debt rates and "great leaps" into foreign borrowing, see Dhonte (1979, 61) and Seiber (1982, 3–11).

7. For a brief description of the spate of nationalizations and new participation agreements in the early 1970s, and the debate over the relative merits of different formulas of cooperation with the oil companies, see Schneider (1983, 99–100, 168–169).

8. Some important works on Spain in this period are Vincens-Vives (1957), Elliot (1961, 52–75; 1963), Lynch (1965), Carande (1967), Braudel (1972).

9. This argument is made strongly in Anderson (1979, 69ff) and Wallerstein (1974, 166–167, 180ff).

10. For more on this system of credit, see Braudel (1972, 500–504), Vásquez de Prada (1978, 687–705), and Carande (1967).

11. *Memoria de la política necesaria, 1600*, cited in Wallerstein (1979, 195).

CHAPTER THREE:
THE SPECIAL DILEMMA OF THE PETRO-STATE

1. The extent of the state's intervention in the economy and its degree of centralization of power are two important measures of capacity in this approach. See Skocpol (1979), Evans, Rueschemeyer, and Skocpol (1985), Krasner (1978), Huntington (1968) for this interpretation of state capacity. The impetus behind this process of state expansion, intervention, and centralization of power is ascribed to various sources. First, state interventionism is seen as an effective means of resolving crises in the process of capital accumulation. The state needs to manage external capital and commodity flows, oversee the restructuring of specific industries, and undertake administrative planning in areas formerly regarded as private (Wright 1978, Habermas 1975). Second, the gradual achievement over many decades of social and political rights for pre-

viously excluded groups eventually translates into demands for public goods, social security measures, and economic interventions designed to promote employment and growth (Lipset 1960). Both political ideology and the organization of interests are contributory elements affecting the size and concentration of the public sector (Cameron 1978). The bureaucracy also has a strong self-interest in maintaining and expanding its resources, leading to the inevitable growth of bureaucratic agencies (Weber [1921] 1946, 224). Whatever the cause, however, this dual tendency toward expansion plus centralization is seen as generally enhancing the capacity of the state to act.

2. As Gourevitch notes (1978, 904), this type of strong-weak dichotomy encourages an inaccurate identification of the state with the executive branch alone and an emphasis on implementation at the expense of the prior and perhaps more critical stage of goal formulation. This form of reductionism cannot provide adequate explanations for government policies, the reasons why states move in one direction rather than another, their patterns and propensities to use leverage over particular groups in some ways and not others, or the general political orientation of the state.

3. The rationale behind this drive toward cooperation was demonstrated by Hotelling (1931), who argued that the price of exhaustible resources is different under pure competition, monopoly, and intermediate market structures assuming that all other conditions are equal. Under pure competition the market price is low and rises gradually at about the real rate of interest; resources are depleted at an early date. Under monopoly the initial price is relatively high and rises gradually at less than the real rate of interest; resources are depleted later. Because monopoly conditions, which are the most favorable, can seldom be maintained, there is a tremendous incentive to form a cartel or producers' group that can substitute cooperation for competition and thereby maximize prices in a manner approaching the monopoly model.

4. Krasner (1983, 2) defines these regimes as "sets of implicit or explicit principles, norms, rules, and decision-making procedures around which actor's expectations converge." I use quotation marks to distinguish the concept from its generally understood use in comparative politics: as the type of polity characterizing a country at a national level. For a critique of the "regime" terminology in international political-economy literature, see Strange (1983).

5. This was, however, a process of learning. Between 1900 and 1914, when competition between them was strong, oil prices fluctuated dramatically, ranging from a high nominal price of $1.19 per barrel in 1902 to $0.61 in 1911. Once the companies understood the destructive impact of competition on price trends, they jointly decided to ensure the orderly exploitation of petroleum through the Red-Line Agreement (1914) and the As-Is Agreement (1928). Prices began to climb steadily after the Red-Line Agreement, reaching $3.07 per barrel by 1920. See American Petroleum Institute (1971, 70–71).

6. For a description of events leading to the oil shock of 1973, see Schneider (1983), Vernon (1975), Blair (1976), and Stork (1975).

7. I am grateful to Michael Shafer for this point and for some of the language used in making it.

8. Led by Innis (1956; see also Baldwin 1966, Watkins 1963), staple theorists attempt to trace in detail how one thing leads to another in the development process through the requirements of the leading export commodity (the staple)—from transportation needs and patterns of settlement to entirely new economic activities tied to the elaboration of the staple itself.

CHAPTER FOUR: THE MAKING OF A PETRO-STATE

1. Centralization was no easy task given the power of local *caudillos*. "Venezuela is like a dry hide," tradition claims that Guzmán, the nation's leading state builder, once remarked. "If you step on one side, it jumps up at the other." Still, Guzmán succeeded in placating the *caudillos* by paying off their war debts and granting them almost absolute authority over municipal policy. He rarely interfered in their domains and in return demanded social peace. He also used subsidies and tax exemptions to control unruly local authorities. For the first time since independence, the central government was able to reduce military expenditures and began to concentrate on infrastructural development. For the epoch of Guzmán, who served as vice-president from 1863 to 1868 and as president during 1870–1877, 1879–1884, and 1886–1888, see Floyd (1976, 165–200).

2. As a result of the blockade of Venezuela by European powers the United States fundamentally revised its vision of Latin America, and legal doctrine regarding intervention was also substantially revised. An Argentine jurist, Luis Maria Drago argued that the collection of foreign debts by force violated the juridical equality of states and was itself illegal. Carlos Calvo, another Argentinean jurist, asserted that interventions, which were based purely on force and the will of an imperial country, could not form the foundations of a legal contract. The Calvo Clauses, which are inserted in contracts between governments and foreign firms today, require foreigners to settle legal disputes in the host country and prohibits them from asking for diplomatic assistance from their home government.

3. Their arrival in Venezuela was no coincidence; it was mandated by the worldwide scramble for black gold as well as changing political realities in other producing countries. Although studies carried out primarily by the Royal Dutch/Shell group had quickly indicated the likelihood of discovering oil in Venezuela, the oil companies sought especially to punish Mexico's nationalism and, in their view, insubordination (Vallenilla 1973). As a result, Mexican production, having reached a peak of 530,000 barrels per day in 1921, declined to 100,000 by 1930 and remained at that level until the nationalization of 1938, when exports virtually ceased (Hausmann 1981, 118).

4. McBeth (1983, 214) argues that Gómez sought to increase the return from the oil industry and also established an effective framework to control it. But as Balestrini (1974) point outs, Venezuela did not retain the same value from petroleum as Mexico, and other administrations were able to achieve far more than Gómez.

5. Within a short time, three U.S. companies (Standard of New Jersey, Stan-

dard of Indiana, and Gulf) controlled the bulk of the country's production; by 1931 over a hundred companies were operating in Venezuela (Brito Figueroa 1966, vol. 1, 434).

6. Considerable debate on this issue occurred inside the government. Gumersindo Torres, the Minister of Mines, favored the U.S. arrangement of leaving private landowners in charge of "their" resource, while Vicente Lecuna, president of the Bank of Venezuela, sustained the thesis that oil had to be the national patrimony of the state. The weakness of the landowning class and their precapitalist mentality meant that they did little to support Torres's position (Baptista and Mommer 1987, 4–7).

7. His many constitutional changes provide an eloquent record of evolving patterns of political authority: allowing a president to serve more than one term, removing all restrictions on the simultaneous holding of different offices, creating the offices of first and second vice-president (and filling them with his brother and his son), and then governing from his personal estate in Maracay (Donnelly 1975, 21ff).

8. When the nationalist minister Torres attempted to place restrictions on the oil companies by regulating the surface areas that could be exploited, the time span of leases, the taxes on surface use, the commercial value of the product, and company imports, his efforts were defeated in the Mining Code of 1918 and the Petroleum Code of 1922. Overruled by Gómez, who, in turn, was heavily influenced by U.S. Ambassador Preston McGoodwin, Torres was dismissed in 1921.

9. According to Aranda (1977, 92), Gómez's budgets show that between 1920 and 1930 his administration spent approximately 664 million bolívares in the Ministry of the Interior and the Ministry of War alone (where expenditures on budgetary items like penitentiaries increased sixfold) and less than one-tenth that figure on education.

10. These disagreements usually flared over Venezuela's exchange rate. The overvalued currency hurt agricultural exports but favored commercial interests importing cheap foreign goods. These disagreements led to the first act of state intervention in monetary matters with the convocation of the Convenio Tinoco in 1934. For a while, Venezuela had dual exchange rates (Malavé Mata 1974, 22ff).

11. The beginning of significant manufacturing activities is especially notable. The stagnation of agriculture, the huge growth in public-works projects paid for by petroleum, the creation of a small internal market, and the wartime disruptions in imports fostered a strong expansion of this sector between 1936 and 1944. In these years, for example, the production of sugar leapt 250.5 percent, food products 206 percent, and cement 318.4 percent (Aranda 1977, 114).

12. Migration flows that took over a century to accomplish in the advanced industrialized countries occurred in a mere twenty years in Venezuela. The proportion of the workforce engaged in agriculture declined rapidly—from 72 percent in 1920 to 44.1 percent by 1950 (Karlsson 1975, 34).

13. Mendoza was one of the first to grasp the new opportunities presented

by the war's disruption. He launched Vencemos and Protinal, two of the most prominent industrial concerns in present-day Venezuela, and became the country's leading industrialist. For an interesting and self-interested description of the Mendoza empire, see Empresas Mendoza (n.d.b).

CHAPTER FIVE: OIL AND REGIME CHANGE

1. I first used this classification for Venezuela's type of democracy in Karl (1987), and portions of this chapter are drawn from that article. Levine (1978) was the first scholar to emphasize the essential role that political pacts have played in the consolidation of democracy, and I have been influenced by his excellent work on the theme. However, Levine limits his discussion of pacts to the strictly political level and thus adopts a consociational perspective, while my own approach emphasizes their importance for substantive economic policies, bargains between capital and labor, and the organization and role of the state. Other scholars, notably Peeler (1985), have also adopted this consociational approach in noting the elite-bargained character of Venezuela's democracy. For more about how pacted democracies differ from those set up through force, reform, or revolution, see Karl (1990).

2. This is not to argue that petroleum-induced changes provide a sufficient explanation for the successful construction of a competitive party system. They do not. The combination of petroleum and political pacts is important for explaining the emergence of Venezuela's democracy, as I have argued elsewhere (Karl 1986). But petroleum is a central part of the explanation, and it is often ignored or underestimated by others—for example, Merkl (1981) and Martz (1966).

3. Details on the *trienio* can be gleaned from Martz (1966), Burggraaff (1972), Maza Zavala (1977), and Betancourt (1979).

4. Industrialization could also create an internal market and new jobs, and thus it could help to avoid a zero-sum class struggle by providing benefits for all Venezuelans (Acción Democrática 1962). Agrarian reform was also a key component of the party's plans for the future, as was gaining increased control over the oil companies, the symbols of foreign domination.

5. The results of this government stimulation were not negligible. Manufacturing output between 1945 and 1948 showed a 12.6 percent average yearly compounded increase. Production of beer, timber, and cement more than doubled, while leather and chemical production grew by more than 50 percent (Salazar-Carrillo 1976, 88).

6. Only the Iranians had trouble gaining such an agreement. In 1951, the Anglo-Iranian Oil Company failed to endorse the fifty-fifty formula, and Mossadegh responded by nationalizing Anglo-Iranian. Nationalization generated the combined hostility of Great Britain and the United States and led eventually to a CIA-staged coup to replace Mossadegh with Shah Reza Pahlavi, who returned Iranian oil to U.S. and British control (Stork 1975, 52).

7. The history of both the state-owned petrochemical plants and the steel plant was illustrative. Normal design and contracting procedures were by-

passed, resulting in expensive errors in the location and conception of the plants. The final costs of building SIDOR, the steel industry, were over three times the original bid, and technology problems halted production over and over throughout the 1960s (Dinkelspiel 1967). Construction of the Moron petrochemical complex took so long that its technology was obsolete by the time it was completed (Pérez Sainz and Zarembka 1979).

8. Like the entrepreneurs, the local Church hierarchy had benefited especially from military rule and was hostile to AD because of its secularizing, anti-Catholic, and reformist policies. But when Seguridad Nacional, the political police, detained a well-known opposition priest and harassed other important Church figures, the Church and the Christian Democratic Party (which had never been declared illegal) also moved into the opposition (Levine 1973, Herrera Campíns 1978).

Pérez Jiménez had initially been careful to please the armed forces. Yet the general's extraordinary level of corruption, combined with his total reliance on unpopular civilian ministers and his creation of a parallel military authority, alarmed younger officers. By December 1957, although Pérez publicly claimed to have the united support of the armed forces, distrust was so great that different divisions had begun to fight each other.

Pérez's former allies explained their change of heart in this way: "The economic structure of Venezuela cannot withstand the political chaos facing the country. The nation's patrimony is menaced and urgent protective measures must be taken to avoid a crash of commerce, industry, and banking. The return to normalcy can be contemplated only in a climate of security and guarantees, the free play of supply and demand, and equal opportunities to intervene in political and economic activity" (quoted in Stambouli 1979, 34).

9. These others included Comité de Organización Política Electoral Independienta (COPEI) party head Rafael Caldera, Union Républica Democrática (URD) leader Jovito Villalba, and Eugenio Mendoza. They had secretly met with Betancourt in New York prior to the downfall of Pérez Jiménez to discuss the composition and parameters of the new government. They agreed to abide by some formula of power sharing that would exclude the Communist Party.

10. Significant portions of these documents are reproduced in Herrera Campíns (1978).

11. The guerrilla movement was an explicit rejection of pact making and of the governing strategy of Betancourt. For the program of the MIR, see Rivas Rivas (1968).

12. There are a number of good studies of Venezuela's basic industries. See Dinkelspiel (1967), Dodge (1968), Esser (1976), Sánchez and Zubillaga (1977), and Bigler (1980).

13. Of a total of paid capital and reserves of 3,127 million bolívares in 1975, 86 percent was concentrated in the Banco de Venezuela, the Banco Nacional de Descuento, the Banco Unión, the Banco Industrial de Venezuela, and the Banco Mercantil y Agrícola—all, with the exception of the Banco Industrial, controlled by large, family-based economic groups (Superintendencia de Bancos, *Informe anual*, 1975).

Large industries are defined by CORDIPLAN as those employing over 100 workers.

14. The most notable change in social spending was in education, a particular boon to the middle class; education eventually encompassed a full 50 percent of all social spending in the democratic period—an astonishing change from the years of authoritarian rule.

15. Coppedge (1993) argues that AD's share of the vote declined an average of 8.6 percent following factional splits or conflicts over nominations for the presidency.

16. Article 109 of the 1961 Constitution is the juridical basis for this semi-corporatist arrangement. It is wonderfully vague and leaves state officials a great deal of leeway in organizing consultative bodies.

17. A technocratic style could appear to be nonpartisan and politically neutral, but as Rodwin's (1969) study of the CVG demonstrates, it contained an important bias. By focusing on technical rather than social problems, the CVG could divide production from distribution, a division that worked to the advantage of capital. Fedecámaras representatives promoted this same technical style in state commissions.

18. I have been especially influenced by Offe (1972, 1973b, 1974) in my discussion of selective mechanisms here.

19. Kelley (1977, 33) notes that entire ministries were apportioned among the parties with allocations based on electoral support.

Public contracts were often rewarded in return for contributing a certain percentage of gains to the governing parties. Although it is difficult to assess the extent of this practice, businessmen interviewed in Caracas in 1977–1978 generally confirmed that they had made party contributions and considered doing so to be an accepted business practice. The only two businessmen who agreed to give an estimate of their contributions claimed that donations to party coffers amounted to 5 percent of the contracts they had won.

20. According to the *Memoria y cuenta* (1959–1964) of the Labor Ministry, conflict petitions dropped from a high of ninety-one in 1960, the year of Betancourt's purge of union activists, to twenty-four by 1963. In the same period, the number of legal strikes dropped from thirty-six to nine.

21. The automobile industry gives an indication of the extreme distortions that arose: in 1971, fifteen assembly plants produced 140 models for the sale of only eighty thousand passenger cars, which were sold at prices over 80 percent higher than prices for imported cars (Esser 1976).

22. A list of the fifty-five countries can be found in the *World Development Report,* 1979, of the World Bank. The statistics here are based on my own calculations or those of Weeks and Dore (1982). Government studies of the time indicate that almost half of all children under five years of age suffered from some degree of malnutrition (Chossudovsky 1977a, 34).

CHAPTER SIX:
THE INSTANT IMPACT OF A BONANZA

1. Pérez's closest supporters, especially Governor of Caracas Diego Arria and Planning Minister Gumersindo Rodríguez, never tired of telling me about the president's extraordinary physical endurance during the campaign. For additional insights on the style of the candidates in 1973, see Martz and Baloyra (1978, especially 175–180) or Consuergra (1979).

2. For a comparison of Pérez's sweep with the victories of his predecessors, see Martz and Baloyra (1978, 225).

3. Born in the Táchira town of Rubio in 1922, Pérez grew up in the *andino* region that had once nourished Venezuela's most prominent *caudillos*. One of twelve children, he was a political activist from his youth, motivated perhaps by Gómez's jailing of his father. He joined the Partido Democrático Nacional, the forerunner of AD, when he was only fifteen. In 1941, he participated in the founding of AD, the only person present who was too young to sign the founding document. He held party posts throughout the 1940s and became a senator from Táchira in the 1946 elections. After the overthrow of President Rómulo Gallegos in 1948, he spent the next decade in prison and exile, following the "normal" career pattern of an AD professional politician and party bureaucrat. This sketch of Pérez's early career is based on Peña (1979) and Salinger (1978). For the best description of AD's Old Guard professional politicians, see Martz (1966).

4. This description of Pérez's later career is based on my interviews with him (Caracas, 1979) and on confidential interviews with two of his cabinet ministers.

5. When Betancourt became president in 1959, Pérez was appointed Deputy Minister of the Interior, and later Minister. Understood to be the heir apparent of AD's most important leader, he owed his primary allegiance to Betancourt rather than to the traditional party apparatus per se. Their commitment to each other was deep. Pérez always carried out the bidding of his mentor, even accepting the job of "chief cop" and putting down the guerrilla uprisings of the early 1960s. He may have expected the party's gratitude and a promotion for carrying out an unwanted and undesirable job but instead found himself abruptly shunted aside. When Betancourt tried to advance his protégé's candidacy during the 1963 elections, the attempt was rebuffed by a major faction of the party led by labor leader Raúl Leoni. Intent on curbing Pérez's influence, party leaders managed to isolate him from the centers of power during Leoni's presidency—a snub he would never forget. (Interviews with two cabinet members, Caracas, 1979.)

6. A former leader of the radical MIR and the guerrilla movement Pérez himself had fought to defeat, Rodríguez had recently reentered AD through Betancourt's campaign to recruit past members. But he was still out of favor with most of the Old Guard. That he, along with another former *adeco*, Roman Escovar Salom, should be awarded ministries over others who had remained loyal to the party was unforgivable to them. The choices of Carmelo Lauría—

the country's youngest bank president and a leader of Fedecámaras—as Minister of Development and Diego Arria—another member of the economic elite—as governor of Caracas were also the source of complaints. The information in this section was drawn from confidential interviews with two ministers and three leaders of the CEN (1978).

7. One planner for the steel industry in Ciudad Guayana (interview, 1978) recalled: "When we put in our initial request for SIDOR Plan IV, we were told by Caracas that is was too small, that we had to think big. So we expanded our plans and sent in a bigger budget request." Other planners in aluminum and petrochemicals interviewed gave similar reports.

8. This percentage was calculated from figures in CORDIPLAN (1976) as well as CORDIPLAN (1970), using the preliminary version of the 1976 plan. It is important to note, however, that the overall amount of expenditures in these areas increased significantly, even though their percentage share declined. Still, they represented only one-third of the investment planned for basic industry.

9. An exception was made for the petrochemicals industry, an act that later caused a considerable outcry, as Chapter 7 demonstrates. In the tertiary stages of petrochemicals, majority private control was permitted, which was justified by the technologically complex nature of production.

10. This poll was cited in my interviews with President Pérez and with CO-PEI congressional representatives Haydée Castillo and Eduardo Fernández (Caracas, 1979).

11. "Exposición de motivos de las medidas extraordinarias de la ley orgánica que autoriza al Presidente de la República para dictar medidas extraordinarias en materia económica y financiera," *Gaceta oficial,* 1974. For a supporting view, see Carlos Canache Mata, "Intervención en la Cámara de Diputados, April 14, 1975," in Canache Mata (1975).

12. The COPEI congressional whip, Eduardo Fernández, asked,"Does this international crisis affect Venezuela more than the other democratic countries? None others have asked for a suspension of Congressional guarantees; none others have given the head of state emergency powers. I haven't heard it said that the United States, with its galloping inflation, which is tearing apart that country, has asked the Congress to delegate its legislative functions" (Fernández, 1974).

13. In an attempt to prevent this, AD leaders insisted on several modifications of the Special Powers Act, such as a one-year duration and a congressional vigilance committee, which were subsequently adopted into law.

14. For these provisions, see "Ley orgánica que autoriza al Presidente de la República para dictar medidas extraordinarias en materia económica y financiera" (*Gaceta oficial,* no. 30.142, May 31, 1974.) Control of the FIV nominally lay in its General Assembly but in practice rested with the director, appointed by the president, and with Pérez himself. By the end of the first year, two members of the General Assembly charged that they had not met for over four months and that no year-end balance sheet had been presented to them (Fernández 1974, 144). The first director had resigned, and the second was under investigation for corruption by the attorney general.

15. See Decree 122 in *Decretos del presidente de Venezuela, Carlos Andrés Pérez* (1975, vol. 1) as well as the interview with Antonio Leidenz, Minister of Labor, in *Zeta,* no. 60, May 4, 1975.

16. See Decree 123 in *Decretos del presidente de Venezuela, Carlos Andrés Pérez* (1975, vol. 1). The pay raises were graduated so that anyone earning up to one thousand bolívares received a 25 percent increase while anyone earning closer to five thousand bolívares received only 5 percent.

17. This figure does not include the ministries, nonclassified positions, political appointees, or employees at the state or local level. In an apparent attempt to disguise the extent of bureaucratic growth, the administration did not take the regular census of public employees. It later cut the budget of the Oficina Central de Personel from 10.7 million bolívares in 1973 to 10.3 million bolívares in 1979. This may have been the only state budget item to drop during the oil boom in absolute terms. Because no census was taken, these figures are necessarily estimates. (Confidential interviews in the Dirección de Registro y Control, Oficina Central de Personel.)

18. From this point, employees *de confianza* began to include all division chiefs, people employed in any fiscal section and in reproduction of documents, and all secretaries in these areas as well. COPEI claimed that over eighty thousand people, mostly *copeyanos,* were fired because of the new law, and COPEI unsuccessful filed a law suit to stop its implementation. See "Reglamento de la ley contra despidos injustificados," *Gaceta oficial,* no. 30.604, January 22, 1975. Also see *El Nacional,* July 7, 1974, D1.

19. By "populist," I am referring to the elitist and authoritarian political experiences in Latin America that were characterized by their antioligarchic content, their antiimperialist rhetoric and assertion of national economic independence, their proindustrialization policies, their promotion of a certain degree of social justice, their emphasis on the role of the state in development, and their highly personalized leadership. Populism includes such diverse political movements and programs as Argentina under Juan Perón, Brazil during the first government of Getulio Vargas, and Mexico under Lázaro Cárdenas. For useful discussions of populism, see Ianni (1975), di Tella (1970), and Germani, di Tella, and Ianni (1973).

20. The law stipulated that companies must report all dismissals to a special tripartite commission representing the Ministry of Labor, management, and the Confederation of Venezuelan Workers (CTV). If the dismissal was contested and found to be unjustified, the employer would have to reinstate the employee with retroactive wages or pay double severance benefits and compensation for the lack of advanced warning—with the choice of options left up to the worker. Because the CTV and the Ministry of Labor were both controlled by AD and generally voted together, the tripartite commission almost always favored the employee.

21. The number of decrees was overwhelming indeed. COPEI Congressman Eduardo Fernández charged that Pérez, in less than a year, had produced "830 decrees and fifty-one commissions. I took an average: sixteen decrees a week. The Council of Ministers meets once a week. Each time that the Council of Ministers meets, it okays sixteen decrees and creates a commission. . . . I think

that this creates a situation of very profound confusion in the country" (Fernández 1974, 135).

22. See *Resumen,* no. 43, September 1, 1974, editorial. This same figure was quoted to me by a private polling agency in Caracas.

23. Between October 1974 and December 1977, only 23.2 percent of the total credits approved by the Industrial Credit Fund were channeled through the public sector. The rest went through private commercial banks (28.3 percent) and investment banks (48.5 percent). See the declarations of the president of the Fondo Crédito Industrial, Lincoln Garcia in *El Nacional,* August 8, 1978. The income on paid-in capital of the banks rose from 14.9 percent in 1970 to 31.9 percent in 1975 (Superintendencia de Bancos, *Informe anual,* 1975).

24. See the declarations of Development Minister Quero Morales in *El Nacional,* September 9, 1974, D9.

25. As *El Nacional* (September 10, 1974) editorialized, "Never in the history of democratic Venezuela has an opposition been so silent, so lukewarm, so *moorocoy* [turtle-like]."

CHAPTER SEVEN: THE POLITICS OF RENT SEEKING

1. Previous efforts to rationalize the state were also responses to economic crisis. In 1958, in the midst of high unemployment and capital flight, CORDIPLAN (the Office of Coordination and Planning) was established in the presidency as a mechanism for improving the public administration's ability to carry out the new democracy's ambitious program of import substitution. At the same time, the Commission on Public Administration was established, strongly influenced by ECLA in Chile. Over a decade later, the Caldera administration, confronting the first overt signs of the limitations to the import-substitution model, attempted to reform state agencies by upgrading CORDIPLAN and expanding the mandate of the Commission on Public Administration. For discussions of previous attempts to reform the public administration in Venezuela, see Friedman (1965), Betancourt (1956), Levy (1968), Tejera Paris (1960), Stewart (1977), Groves (1967, 1971), and Brewer-Carías (1970, 1975).

2. Together these entities are referred to in Venezuela as the decentralized administration and are distinct from the institutions of the central government—for example, the ministries. In this chapter we are concerned primarily with the state enterprises. These differ from autonomous institutes and are defined as firms that carry out activities of an industrial or commercial character. Any enterprise that is more that half owned by the state is considered a state enterprise.

3. See the annual reports of the Controlaría General de la República de Venezuela. For a comprehensive study, see Comisión de la Administración Pública (1972) and Brewer-Carías (1978). So great was the organizational chaos that at least sixteen state agencies could be involved in the construction of one house. Other administrators cited examples of two agencies building roads exactly parallel between the same two points and less than a mile apart. A simple permit could require up to ninety steps. Interviews with Antonio Casas González and Luis Enrique Oberto, former ministers of CORDIPLAN, 1979.

4. Interview with Alberto Quiros (1979). For more on the condition of the oil industry before nationalization, see Coronel (1983) and Randall (1987).

5. Banco Central de Venezuela, *Informe económico*, 1974, 1977, 1978. The magnitude of this change is statistically dramatic, but its significance should not be exaggerated. The nationalizations involved no real change in volumes of production, income received, or employment generated. These statistics do reveal, however, a qualitative change in the importance of state decisions for the functioning of the public and private economy. I am grateful to the late Manuel Rodríguez Trujillo for this point.

6. Reform proposals were made in 1960, 1961, and 1968, but they were never seriously implemented. For more on these early reforms, see Brewer-Carías (1977). For more information on the 1972 reforms, see Comisión de Administración Pública (1972) and Brewer-Carías (1970, 1975).

7. Pérez was grateful to Tinoco for drawing *perezjimenista* support away from COPEI during the 1973 elections and thus helping his election. But their relationship dated back to the Betancourt administration, when Pérez was Minister of Interior. According to Tinoco (interview, 1978), he convinced Pérez to refrain from a crackdown on the right in the early sixties. Nonetheless, the Old Guard of AD flatly ruled out Tinoco's participation as a minister because of his past ties with Pérez Jiménez; instead, Tinoco associates like Gumersindo Rodríguez and Diego Arria were given prominent roles in government, while he was handed the seemingly innocuous position of head of CRIAP.

By 1974, the coincidence in the views of the AD's populist president and the most articulate spokesman of conservative business interests was remarkable. Only the stated goals of the two men differed. Pérez claimed (interview, 1979) that administrative reform would enhance the power of the state and therefore lead to greater control over the private sector, a better distribution of income, and greater democratization. Tinoco (interview, 1978) believed that the appropriate reforms could finally institutionalize business participation in economic decision-making, insulate government decision-making from uncertain electoral outcomes, and increase the power of the private sector. In practice, this difference seemed to matter little. "We have the same ideas," Tinoco (interview, October 1978) said of his relationship with Pérez. "I have never agreed so wholeheartedly with a Venezuelan president before."

8. The CRIAP model was strongly influenced by the Instituto per la Ricostruzione Industriale and the Ministero delle Participazione Statale in Italy and by the Instituto Nacional de Industria in Spain, For an explanation of the differences between a presidentialist model and a ministerial model, see Mateo (1979, 138–143) and Boscan de Ruesta (1975).

9. This section is based on confidential letters and reports of the CRIAP to the Minister of Planning, interviews with Gumersindo Rodríguez and Pedro Tinoco, and the fourth version of the "Ante-proyecto de ley del sistema nacional de empresas del estado," 1974.

10. This version of the Organic Law of State Planning was published as CORDIPLAN (n.d). This discussion of the highly political and conflictive aspects of planning is based on three interviews with Gumersindo Rodríguez in 1978 and early 1979 as well as Rodríguez (1962, 1979, 1975, 1976b).

11. Pérez (interview, 1979) assessed the commission's usefulness thusly: "Business, labor, and the state...we could talk. This helped to create a better climate. By giving us a place to talk, we could arrive at understandings. It was an escape valve." For more on the commission, see Fedecámaras, Departamento Técnico (1978), and Pérez's speech to the XXXI Asamblea de Fedecámaras, May 10, 1975, in Presidencia de la República (1975–1978, vol. 1, 183).

12. As one AD leader explained (confidential interview, 1978), "Before, someone would pay a 5 percent commission on a contract, and it would not be much of a problem—5 percent of $100,000 is really only a few thousand dollars. But suddenly we were talking about contracts of millions of dollars, perhaps ten million like the Centro Simon Bolívar. So, we are talking about $50,000 or $100,000 for a minor middleman. Suddenly there is big money in a commission, not just the use of someone's summer home or his boat in Miami. Suddenly we would hear about millions of dollars getting handed around." Bankers claimed that the stakes were much higher, sometimes more than $1.5 million on one deal alone. In my private conversations with representatives of the trade and economics section of two foreign embassies, officials estimated that commissions could reach as high as 20 percent of a contract.

13. Marx's ([1852] 1970) description of the Bonapartist regime outlined the characteristics of the all-powerful executive. Weber ([1921] 1968, vol. 2, 283–284) discussed how this bureaucratic centralization tends to maximize the influence of capitalist interests in the state administration.

14. This group actually included more than twelve individuals, but the nickname has now become widely accepted in Venezuela's political folklore. The term was originally popularized in a denunciatory political tract by Duno (1975).

15. The ties between the president and the Apostles were forged largely during his bitter candidacy struggle, when Pérez's own isolation in AD and lack of control over the top party hierarchy convinced him of the necessity of establishing a power base separate from the party machine. Subsequently the prohibitive cost of the 1973 campaign—the first to employ foreign advisers and rely heavily on the media—increased the candidates' dependence on the large contributions of businessmen, while the absence of campaign disclosure laws encouraged the buying of favors.

16. The exact amount of government support is unclear. One source (Petkoff 1978) claims that the FIV provided 25 million bolívares in outright subsidies and 100 million in low-interest loans, and underwrote private bank loans for 320 million. Rodolfo José Cárdenas (Resúmen, no. 276, February 18, 1979) said that the owners of the plant put up 78 million bolívares, while various state agencies provided up to 631 million bolívares.

17. The plans called for the installation throughout the country of twenty new plants that would be able to exploit Venezuela's raw-materials advantage (El Nacional, March 29, 1975, D1).

18. Pentacom's vice-president was implicated in the well-known Kellogg scandal in the Venezuelan Petrochemical Institute, in which a series of irregularities led to operational problems that caused a monthly loss of $6 million. See the declarations of Carlos Canache Mata in Resúmen, February 2, 1975.

19. At the time, the Proceso Político research group essentially accepted the president's contention that a new bourgeoisie was being formed. In their view, this emerging class was characterized by its unwillingness to play a subordinate role to foreign capital, which was manifest in a strong nationalism; its willingness to form mixed enterprises with the state; its emphasis on industrialization rather than commerce; and its stress on technocratic criteria. (See Proceso Político 1978.) This argument is unconvincing, in my view, because the Apostles had strong ties to foreign capital; were generally more involved in commerce, banking, and construction than in manufacturing; evinced no unusually strong nationalist sentiment; and, while utilizing the rhetoric of efficiency, had been the beneficiaries of enormous subsidies and credits from the state.

20. The presence of this faction created a rather startling new situation, as one journalist remarked, in which "the president is governing with ex-*adecos* in the cabinet and with *adecos* in the opposition" (*Semana*, July 5–11, 1976, 7).

21. The warning was duly noted. As one COPEI leader explained (interview, October 1978), "They made it very clear from the beginning: if you go after this, . . . we will start opening up the kinds of things that went on during the Caldera administration."

22. AD leader Luis Piñerúa Ordaz's denunciation best describes the manipulation of state funds. In one example, Armando Brons had been the intermediary for obtaining foreign credits used by the Parque Central government housing. As director of administration for then Minister of the Treasury Tinoco, he had contracted short-term credits and received commissions from the negotiations with the banks. Later, after serving as director of Centro Simon Bolívar, the state agency in charge of Parque Central, he obtained a contract from the agency to carry out a feasibility study for close to $6 million. At the same time, he became financial adviser to the agency for a $3,750 monthly salary, auditor of projects for a $15,000 monthly salary, and auditor of a subsidiary for a fee of $5,000. In addition, as the financial consultant for the Banco Agrícola y Pecuario, the Banco Obrero, Fundacomún, and INOS—the four major debtors among the state enterprises—he received commissions on the loans he negotiated with the banks (Canache Mata, 1975, 43).

23. Privately, the top leaders of AD expressed their sentiments far more vehemently. In the words of one CEN leader (interview, November 1978), "When you put the proposed planning law together with the state-enterprise law—then you add Morales Bello's proposal to reelect Pérez—well it seemed that they were everywhere. There was a domain for Gumersindo [Rodríguez], a domain for Tinoco (for whom did you think the president of the state-enterprise system was going to be?). It meant economic totalitarianism. They were destroying our democracy. Yes, that is what I am saying: this president was destroying our democracy. . . . I didn't go into exile for this. I didn't watch my friends go to prison for this. I never would have voted for it. Never. I would have stood up in Congress and led a revolt in the party."

24. The oil nationalization, though not a focus of this study, has been studied extensively. See, for example, *Nacionalización del petróleo en Venezuela* (1982), Coronel (1983), and Randall (1987).

25. The Communist Party withheld its vote on one article because it was opposed to paying any compensation to the multinational corporations. The reservations of the private sector, which was most opposed to a provision prohibiting the formation of mixed enterprises in the nationalized industry, were a portent of things to come. Fedecámaras president and representative on the commission Alfredo Paul Delfino called the draft bill "inconvenient, punitive and restrictive" (El Nacional, August 18, 1974, A-1). In addition to his opposition to proscribing mixed enterprises, he was especially against provisions that permitted oversight by the Congress and party system.

26. For a careful rendering of this congressional debate, see El Nacional (June-August 1975).

27. Pulido Mora's resignation letter was widely publicized in political circles. This summary of his objections is drawn from a mimeo of that letter provided by the author.

28. Eventually, it was sent to the Tripartite Commission, where it languished for two years for modifications by the private sector, even though AD had the absolute majority necessary to pass it in Congress. Finally, it passed to Minister Lauría for more alterations, then died.

29. A party man, Piñerúa had been a member of AD since its founding, had been jailed and exiled, and later had served in virtually every party position from head of a local committee to secretary general. To Betancourt, the serious and uncharismatic adeco had other important qualities: absolute honesty, loyalty, and strong opposition to Pérez. One of the few cabinet members who had been unafraid to confront the president, Piñerúa had criticized the development plan and every budget put forward by the government. Deeply respectful of Betancourt, he represented the party founder well (interview with Rómulo Betancourt, 1978).

30. Lusinchi did everything possible to evoke the name and image of the president, even recalling Pérez's ebullient 1973 election through his slogan, "We will keep walking with Jaime." Arguing that his candidacy was "a protest against bad party government," he also called for direct and secret elections inside the party to replace the existing system, in which the members of the CEN selected the presidential candidate. This policy, when implemented, led to Piñerúa's victory with 62.5 percent of the vote (El Nacional, July 17, 1977, D1).

31. A study by Penniman (1980) reached the same conclusion.

32. Jawaharlal Nehru knew the dangers of this situation. He once declared, "Merely shouting from the house tops that everybody is corrupt creates an atmosphere of corruption. People feel they live in a climate of corruption and they get corrupted themselves. The man on the street says to himself: 'Well, if everybody seems corrupt, why shouldn't I be corrupt?' That is the climate sought to be created which must be discouraged." Quoted in Karanjia (1960, 9); cited in Myrdal (1968).

33. Ellner reviewed Venezuela's two leading newspapers, El Nacional and El Universal, during randomly selected months for each period and coded articles according to the sharpness of partisan rivalry, concentrating on three cate-

gories: criticism of the rival party for violating established norms, accusations that the rival party was attempting to undermine its adversary, and advocacy of interparty agreements.

34. In 1976, Comptroller General José Muci-Abraham was forced to resign when President Pérez refused to accept his recommendation to remove the director of the Instituto Nacional de Obras Sanitarias for blatant mismanagement. This resignation broke the tradition of placing a political independent in this post and permitting him wide authority, which had been respected by both parties since the *trienio* (Stambouli 1980, 66). In the future, the political neutrality of this state agency would be repeatedly threatened.

35. Functionaries in the Office of the Budget did not know whose authority they were under once the planning reform was announced. Although they were formally required to report to Finance Minister Hurtado, all understood that Rodríguez was a clear favorite of the president. While most stayed loyal to the Finance Ministry, others worked closely with Rodríguez. This division of the office affected morale and performance (confidential interview, Office of the Budget, 1978).

CHAPTER EIGHT: FROM BOOM TO BUST

1. This decline reflects a 250 percent increase in the production of non-OPEC oil between 1973 and 1990 (Odell 1992, 935–936).

2. In 1992 PETROVEN opened its doors to limited private investment from Venezuelan, U.S., and Japanese firms and began tentative bidding on its heavy-oil projects. This move created strong controversy in the Congress, adding to the difficulties of the Pérez presidency (*Financial Times,* July 2, 1992, 3).

3. This figure is overstated because it includes close to twenty billion bolívares of government monies owed to itself via the FIV, but it is an important indicator of the extent of borrowing.

4. Figures for 1978 from World Bank, *World Development Report,* 1980, Table 15; figures for 1986 from World Bank, *World Development Report,* 1988, Tables 18, 24; figures for 1988 from World Bank, *World Development Report,* 1990, Tables 18, 24. These figures are only for officially registered, long-term, external public debt and thus are considerably understated.

5. Detailed descriptions of these negotiations can be found in Mayobre (1985), Bigler and Tugwell (1986), and Alvarez de Stella (1988).

6. The number of CTV-led illegal strikes against the COPEI government reached a record high of 200 in Herrera Campíns's last year, then fell abruptly to 39 when AD resumed the presidency (Davis and Coleman, 1989, 255).

7. The debt agreement finally hammered out with the representatives of some 450 banks in September 1984 did not formally call for IMF supervision of the country's economic policies, making Venezuela the first Latin American country to negotiate a rescheduling agreement without IMF intervention. Nonetheless, because it committed the government to pay nearly $5 billion per year for twelve years to foreign bankers, it was not finally signed until February 26, 1986—a full year and a half after the initial accord had been reached. Even so,

it did not last. In April, as oil prices continued to drop, President Lusinchi avoided deregulation by invoking a contingency clause added to protect Venezuela from this very situation. "We were lent money on the basis of oil," he declared, "and we will pay on the basis of oil" (*LAER,* April 30, 1986, 9). A new rescheduling agreement was not signed with creditor banks for a full year, and, in the wake of strong protests against the high levels of debt service from party loyalists, it was soon set aside.

8. Public opinion polls demonstrate the high expectations accompanying the Pérez victory and the initially strong belief that conditions would improve under his rule. Fully 45 percent of those polled expected betterment of their situation by the end of the first Pérez government. This expectation is important for understanding the especially violent reaction to the austerity measures he would shortly implement. See Myers (1992). For another excellent treatment of Venezuelan perceptions of their economic situation, see Templeton (1992).

9. Hard lessons had been learned from his first term and from the diverse experiences of his closest political colleagues, Spain's Felipe González and Peru's Alan García. Pérez was disillusioned with the state and more open to market-oriented reforms as a means for solving Venezuela's problems (interview with President Pérez, Stanford University, 1991).

10. By the October 1991 party convention, the so-called orthodox, or anti-Pérez, faction of the party had won twenty-two of the twenty-six posts on the party's national executive committee. Prior to the convention, tensions ran so high between the two factions that violence broke out during a meeting of the party's electoral committee, leading to the shooting of three youths (*LAWR,* October 17, 1991, 3).

11. Some of the most important strikes were the strike of two hundred thousand teachers in November 1989, a "civic strike" organized by the radical labor party Causa-R in late 1991, and a twelve-hour general strike in November 1991. Rioting occurred in Maracaibo and Maracay in August 1990 and in Caracas in October 1991.

12. According to a Gaither Poll, commissioned and paid for by the government, only 26 percent of Venezuelans approved of the Pérez administration, while 64 percent expressed negative opinions (*El Nacional,* January 2, 1992, D1).

13. What became known as the Caso Recadi made past scandals like Pentacom look minor, as up to $8 billion "disappeared" through the blatant overinvoicing of imports, a scheme that took advantage of the three-tiered system of exchange rates. Investigations of the Lusinchi administration quickly spread to prominent local businessmen and employees of several leading foreign companies, including top executives from Ford, Colgate-Palmolive, and Procter & Gamble (*LAWR,* August 3, 1989, 5).

14. Immediately following the coup, Pérez announced increases in the minimum wage, sizeable reductions in petroleum and food prices, and increased government spending in the social arena—all of which meant higher expenditures at a time of lower world oil prices (*LAWR,* February 27, 1992, 2).

15. See, for example, the interview with general Alberto Muller Rojas in *Economía Hoy,* March 13, 1992.

16. Charges of corruption first became public in late 1992, when accusations of Pérez's illegal misuse of $17 million from a secret Interior Ministry fund through the last-minute use of a preferential exchange-rate system first surfaced. These charges were compounded when *El Nuevo País* published a series of internal documents of the Bank of Credit and Commerce International documenting the bank's contribution to Pérez's political campaign, accounts held by Venezuelan government agencies in the failed bank, and a transfer of funds by Cecilia Matos, the president's mistress, to an account in a U.S. bank (*LAWR*, October 15, 1992, 3). Later, in an impeachment bid, the attorney general asked the Supreme Court to rule whether sufficient grounds existed to initiate a court case against the president (*Financial Times*, May 7, 1993, 4).

CHAPTER NINE:
PETRO-STATES IN COMPARATIVE PERSPECTIVE

1. The lack of data is especially significant. Crucial indicators of the economies of these countries and especially of their "stateness" are not readily available. The reasons for the dearth of information vary. Because of the revolution in Iran records became scanty after 1976 and ceased to be available after 1978. Financial chaos in Nigeria was so great after 1976 that recordkeeping in certain critical areas stopped for several years. International organizations did not gather Algeria's statistics in the mid-1970s. Indicators of state disorganization are especially scarce, including information on the extent of administrative corruption (which is particularly difficult to compile), the duplication of agencies and tasks, and the proliferation and performance of state enterprises.

2. The countries studied were Bahrain, Saudi Arabia, Cameroon, Malaysia, Trinidad-Tobago, Venezuela, Nigeria, and Indonesia.

3. The ratio for Algeria, which performed better over this time period, fell shortly thereafter.

4. Indonesia joined OPEC in 1962, Algeria in 1969, and Nigeria in 1971; they thus had an institutionalized mechanism for sharing valuable lessons in dealing with the oil companies.

5. This decline was in part the result of the land reform carried out by the shah and financed by petrodollars. As late as 1959, the agricultural sector provided 33 percent of GNP, but by 1968, after the reform and its ensuing problems, its share declined to 23 percent (Kazemi 1980b, 32; also see Hooglund 1982 and Saikal 1980).

6. Exploration for oil began in the 1930s, but large-scale production did not occur until 1958, when huge deposits were discovered shortly after the beginning of the nationalist revolution. Because oil was found in the Sahara Desert, in the southern half of the country, which was populated only by Bedouins, facilities were not sabotaged, and operations continued at a low level (Quandt 1969, 92).

7. The Second Quadrennial Plan (1974–1977) authorized total investment four times greater than the previous plan had, increasing expenditures for industry by 246 percent and directing the lion's share of investments to iron and steel, fertilizer plants, and natural gas (which was intended to alleviate the

dependence on petroleum) (Rabhi 1979, 133; Raffinot and Jacquemot 1977; Gelb 1986, 69).

8. Between 1970 and 1982, the annual production of cocoa fell by 43 percent, rubber by 29 percent, cotton by 65 percent, and groundnuts by 64 percent. The share of agricultural imports in total imports increased from about 3 percent in the late 1960s to about 7 percent in the 1980s (Pinto 1987, 432).

9. These increases were from an extremely low base, however, because tax collection was virtually halted during the turmoil of the mid-1960s.

10. This policy stemmed from the political turmoil experienced after the Korean War, which resulted from Indonesia's inability to import rice; the policy was strengthened by the fears invoked by another shortage in 1972–1973.

11. One must be careful in this assessment because as Gillis (1983, 22) has noted, it is not possible to calculate the real costs of the Pertamina crisis in income maldistribution and reduced investment.

12. While non-oil exports plunged in Nigeria, Indonesia's trade in rubber, coffee, tea, and spices was maintained during the oil boom (Pinto 1987, 435).

13. In Nigeria, the Ajoakuota steel complex, the biggest industrial project in sub-Saharan Africa, was beset for years by cost overruns and was a constant economic drain on the country. Initially planned at a cost of $1.4 billion, after twelve years it had already cost more than $4 billion and is still not fully operational (*New York Times,* July 11, 1992, 3).

In Venezuela, bureaucratic delays and corruption tripled the construction costs of SIDOR, postponed needed financing, and "made nonsense out of feasibility studies" (Auty 1989, 366). Estimated break-even costs are 30 percent above those of an efficient producer.

14. Higley, Brofoss, and Groholt (1975, 254) note that in 1975 the central administration of the state consisted of fourteen departments and the prime minister's office. Each department had a political leadership consisting of the cabinet minister and an undersecretary. All other persons below this thin layer of politicians were civil servants. In 1970, they numbered 2,212.

15. According to Higley, Brofoss, and Groholt (1975, 255), 93 percent have university degrees, the majority as lawyers or economists. Olsen (1983, 126–129) reports that entry into this small elite is traditionally based on university achievement, not party affiliation. He also notes that civil servants are highly unrepresentative of the general population in terms of education.

16. Higley, Brofoss, and Groholt (1975, 253) note that investigatory bodies aimed at uncovering blunders or corrupt practices are notable only by their absence. They mention the single exception of an investigation of a coal-mine disaster in 1963. There is only one exception to the absence of high-level resignations as well—in 1949!

17. From his interviews with civil servants, Olsen (1983, 133) gives a description that fairly boggles the mind of a Latin Americanist: "They claim they will forward a proposal they think is professionally right even if they know that their superiors are against it. They say that official channels of authority and information should be followed, and they are strongly opposed to leakages to the public. There are norms of moderation in political participation."

18. Noreng (1980, 132–144) observes that there was an initial debate over

whether to create a new governing agency or to keep oil matters within existing government agencies. They were kept within existing agencies in order to avoid duplication or the creation of an agency that might become the advocate of the industry it was to control.

CHAPTER TEN:
COMMODITIES, BOOMS, AND STATES REVISITED

1. The phrase is Webb's (1952) from his controversial book *The Great Frontier*. He claimed that booms create exceptional institutions and belief systems because they are in themselves exceptional.

2. As Table A-12 shows, between 1982 and 1987 industry's contribution to GDP declined from 42 to 38 percent, agriculture stayed flat, and services jumped from 52 to 56 percent. Only manufacturing, where the government had made a big push, increased significantly, from 16 to 22 percent.

3. Venezuela, with only 4 percent of the region's population, accounted for more than 10 percent of its imports in these two "bust" years (Naím 1993, 12).

4. Productivity decreased 1.1 percent per year from 1975 to 1979, and 1.4 percent per year from 1983 to 1988 (World Bank 1991, cited in Naím 1993, 4).

Bibliography

GENERAL

Adelman, Irma, and Cynthia T. Morris, 1973. *Economic Growth and Social Equity in Developing Countries.* Stanford, Calif.: Stanford University Press.

Adelman, Morris Albert, 1972. *The World Petroleum Market.* Baltimore: published for Resources for the Future by Johns Hopkins University Press.

Alavi, Hamza, 1972. "The State in Postcolonial Societies: Pakistan and Bangladesh," *New Left Review,* no. 74 (July-August).

Alt, James, 1987. "Crude Politics: Oil and the Political Economy of Unemployment in Britain and Norway, 1970–85," *British Journal of Politics* 17 (April).

American Petroleum Institute, 1971. *Petroleum Facts and Figures, 1971.* Washington, D.C.

Amuzegar, Jahangir, 1982. "Oil Wealth: A Very Mixed Blessing," *Foreign Affairs* 60 (4).

———, 1983. "Oil Exporters' Economic Development in an Interdependent World." Occasional Paper 18. Washington, D.C.: International Monetary Fund (April).

———, 1986. "The IMF Under Fire," *Foreign Policy* (Fall).

Anderson, Charles W., 1967. *Politics and Economic Change in Latin America.* Princeton, N.J.: Princeton University Press.

Anderson, Lisa, 1986. *The State and Social Transformation in Tunisia and Libya.* Princeton, N.J.: Princeton University Press.

Attiga, Ali A., 1981a. "Economic Development of Oil Producing Countries," *OPEC Bulletin* (November).

———, 1981b. "How Oil Revenues Can Destroy a Country," *Petroleum Intelligence Weekly,* special supplement (October 19).

Auty, Richard M., 1989. "The Internal Determinants of Eight Oil-Exporting

Countries' Resource-Based Industry Performance," *Journal of Development Studies* 25 (3).

Auty, Richard M., and A. H. Gelb, 1984. "The Deployment of Oil Rents in a Small Parliamentary Democracy: The Case of Trinidad and Tobago." World Bank, Washington, D.C., mimeo (February).

Bachrach, Peter, and Morton Baratz, 1963. "Decisions and Non-decisions," *American Political Science Review* 57 (September).

Baer, Werner, 1972a. "The Economics of Prebisch and ECLA," *Economic Development and Cultural Change* 10 (2).

———, 1972b. "Import Substitution and Industrialization in Latin America," *Latin America Research Review* 7 (1).

Balassa, Bela, and Associates, 1971. *The Structure of Protection in Developing Countries*. Baltimore: Johns Hopkins University Press.

Baldwin, Robert E., 1966. *Economic Development and Export Growth: A Study of Northern Rhodesia, 1920–1960*. Berkeley: University of California Press.

Bank for International Settlements, 1982. *Statistics on External Indebtedness*. Paris: Organization for Economic Co-operation and Development.

Barzelay, Michael, 1986. *The Politicized Market Economy: Alcohol in Brazil's Energy Strategy*. Berkeley: University of California Press.

Bates, Robert H., 1981. *Markets and States in Tropical Africa: The Political Basis of Agricultural Policies*. Berkeley: University of California Press.

———, 1983. *Essays on the Political Economy of Rural Africa*. Cambridge: Cambridge University Press.

———, ed., 1988. *Toward a Political Economy of Development: A Rational Choice Perspective*. Berkeley: University of California Press.

———, 1989. "A Political Scientist Looks at Tax Reform." In Malcolm Gillis, ed., *Tax Reform in Developing Countries*. Durham, N.C.: Duke University Press.

Becker, Gary D., 1983. *The New Bourgeoisie and the Limits of Dependency: Mining, Class, and Power in "Revolutionary" Peru*. Princeton, N.J.: Princeton University Press.

Bergquist, Charles, 1986. *Labor in Latin America: Comparative Essays on Chile, Argentina, Venezuela, and Colombia*. Stanford, Calif.: Stanford University Press.

Blair, John, 1976. *The Control of Oil*. New York: Pantheon.

Bobrow, Davis B., and Robert T. Kudrle, 1976. "Theory, Policy and Resource Cartels: The Case of OPEC," *Journal of Conflict Resolution* (March).

Bosson, Rex, and Bension Varon, 1977. *The Mining Industry and the Developing Countries*. New York: Oxford University Press.

Buchanan, James M., Robert D. Tullison, and Gordon Tullock, eds., 1980. *Toward a Theory of the Rent-Seeking Society*. Economic Series 4. College Station: Texas A&M University Press.

Buchanan, James M., and Gordon Tullock, 1962. *The Calculus of Consent: Logical Foundations of Constitutional Democracy*. Ann Arbor: University of Michigan Press.

Cameron, David R., 1978. "The Expansion of the Public Economy: A Comparative Analysis," *American Political Science Review* 72 (December).

Canak, William L., 1984. "The Peripheral State Debate: State Capitalist and Bureaucratic Authoritarian Regimes in Latin America," *Latin American Research Review* 19 (1).

Cardoso, Fernando H., 1971. *Ideologías de la burguesía industrial en sociedades dependientes*. Mexico City: Siglo XXI.

———, 1973. "Associated Dependent Development." In Alfred Stepan, ed., *Authoritarian Brazil: Origins, Policies, and Future*. New Haven, Conn.: Yale University Press.

———, 1979. "On the Characterization of Authoritarian Regimes in Latin America." In David Collier, ed., *The New Authoritarianism in Latin America*. Princeton, N.J.: Princeton University Press.

Cardoso, Fernando H., and Enzo Faletto, 1969. *Dependencia y desarrollo en América Latina*. Mexico City: Siglo XXI. In English: Fernando H. Cardoso and Enzo Faletto, 1979. *Dependency and Development in Latin America*. Berkeley: University of California Press.

Carnoy, Martin, 1984. *The State and Political Theory*. Princeton, N.J.: Princeton University Press.

CEPAL, various years. *Informe económico de America Latina*. Santiago, Chile.

Chalmers, Douglas A., 1977. "The Politicized State in Latin America." In James M. Malloy, ed., *Authoritarianism and Corporatism in Latin America*. Pittsburgh: University of Pittsburgh Press.

Chaudhry, Kiren Aziz, 1989. "The Price of Wealth: Business and State in Labor Remittance and Oil Economies," *International Organization* 43 (1).

Chenery, Hollis, Montek S. Ahluwalia, C.L.G. Bell, John H. Duloy, and Richard Jolly, 1974. *Redistribution with Growth*. London: Oxford University Press.

Cohen, Stephen, 1977. *Modern Capitalist Planning: The French Model*. Berkeley: University of California Press.

Cohen, Stephen, and Charles Goldfinger, 1975. "From Permacrisis to Real Crisis in French Social Security." In Leon N. Lindberg, Robert Alford, Colin Crouch, and Claus Offe, eds., *Stress and Contradiction in Modern Capitalism*. Lexington, Mass.: Lexington Books.

Collier, David, ed. 1979. *The New Authoritarianism in Latin America*. Princeton, N.J.: Princeton University Press.

Collier, David, and Ruth Collier, 1991. *Shaping the Political Arena: Critical Junctures, the Labor Movement and Regime Dynamics in Latin America*. Princeton, N.J.: Princeton University Press.

Conybeare, John A. C., 1982. "The Rent-Seeking State and Revenue Diversification," *World Politics* 35 (1).

Corden, W. Max, 1982. "Booming Sector and Dutch Disease Economics: A Survey." Working Paper 079. Canberra: Faculty of Economics and Research, School of Social Sciences, Australian National University.

Corden, W. Max, and J. Peter Neary, 1982. "Booming Sector and Deindustrialisation in a Small Open Economy," *Economic Journal* 92 (368).

Crozier, Michael, Samuel P. Huntington, and Joji Watanuki, 1975. *The Crisis of Democracy: Report on the Governability of Democracies to the Trilateral Commission.* New York: New York University Press.

Dahl, Robert A., 1956. *A Preface to Democratic Theory.* Chicago: University of Chicago Press.

———, 1961. *Who Governs: Democracy and Power in an American City.* New Haven, Conn.: Yale University Press.

Danielsen, Albert, 1982. *The Evolution of OPEC.* New York: Harcourt Brace Jovanovich.

Dasgupta, P., and G. M. Heal, 1978. *Economic Theory and Exhaustible Resources.* Cambridge: Cambridge University Press.

David, Paul, 1985. "Clio and the Economics of QWERTY," *American Economic Review* 75 (2).

———, 1989. "A Paradigm for Historical Economics: Path Dependence and Predictability in Dynamic Systems with Local Network Externalities." Center for Economic Policy Research, Stanford University, Stanford, Calif. (March 6).

Davis, J. M., 1983. "The Economic Effects of Windfall Gains in Export Earnings 1975–1978," *World Development* 11 (2).

Deane, Phyllis, 1978. *Evolution of Economic Ideas.* Cambridge: Cambridge University Press.

Delacroix, Jacques, 1980. "The Distributive State in the World-System," *Studies in Comparative International Development* 15 (fall).

Deyo, Frederic C., 1981. *Dependent Development and Industrial Order: An Asian Case Study.* New York: Praeger.

———, 1989. *Beneath the Miracle: Labor Subordination in the New Asian Industrialism.* Berkeley: University of California Press.

Dhonte, Pierre, 1979. *Clockwork Debt.* Lexington, Mass.: Lexington Books.

Díaz-Alejandro, Carlos, 1965. "On the Import Intensity of Import Substitution," *Kyklos* 18 (3).

di Tella, Torcuato, 1970. "Populism and Reform in Latin America." In Claudio Veliz, ed., *Obstacles to Change in Latin America.* London: Oxford University Press.

Dos Santos, Teotonio, 1970. "The Structure of Dependence," *American Economic Review* 60 (2) (Papers and proceedings of the 82d annual meeting of the American Economic Association, New York City, December 28–30, 1969).

Dyson, Kenneth, 1980. *The State Tradition in Western Europe.* New York: Oxford University Press.

Eckstein, Harry, 1975. "Case Study and Theory in Political Science." In F. I. Greenstein and N. W. Polsby, eds., *Handbook of Political Science,* vol. 7. Reading, Mass.: Addison-Wesley.

Eisenstadt, S. N., 1964. "Breakdown of Modernization," *Economic Development and Cultural Change,* no. 12 (July).

Elfeituri, Attia Elmahndi, 1987. "Oil Price Changes and Economic Growth in Oil-Exporting Countries," *OPEC Review* (autumn).

Engler, Robert, 1961. *The Politics of Oil: A Study of Private Power and Democratic Directions.* New York: Macmillan.

Evans, Peter, 1979. *Dependent Development: The Alliance of Multinational, State, and Local Capital in Brazil.* Princeton, N.J.: Princeton University Press.

———, 1989. "Predatory, Developmental and Other Apparatuses: A Comparative Analysis of the Third World State," *Sociological Forum* (August).

Evans, Peter, 1995. *Embedded Autonomy: States and Industrial Transformation.* Princeton, N.J.: Princeton University Press.

Evans, Peter B., Dietrich Rueschemeyer, and Theda Skocpol, eds., 1985. *Bringing the State Back In.* Cambridge: Cambridge University Press.

Fagen, Richard R., 1978. "Equity in the South in the Context of North-South Relations." In Albert Fishlow, Carlos Díaz-Alejandro, Richard R. Fagen, and Roger D. Hansen, eds., *Rich and Poor Nations in the World Economy.* New York: McGraw-Hill.

———, ed., 1979. *Capitalism and the State in U.S.–Latin American Relations.* Stanford, Calif.: Stanford University Press.

Felix, David, 1956. "Profit Inflation and Industrial Growth: The Historical Record and Contemporary Analogies," *Quarterly Journal of Economics* 70 (3).

Finer, Samuel P., 1975. "State- and Nation-Building in Europe: The Role of the Military." In Charles Tilly, ed., *The Formation of National States in Western Europe.* Princeton, N.J.: Princeton University Press.

Frank, Andre Gunder, 1978. *World Accumulation, 1492–1789.* New York: Monthly Review Press.

———, 1979. "Economic Crisis and the State in the Third World." Development Discussion Paper 30. University of East Anglia, Norwich, England (February).

Frieden, Jeffry, 1991. *Debt, Development and Democracy: Modern Political Economy and Latin America.* Princeton, N.J.: Princeton University Press.

Friedrich, Carl J., 1968. *Constitutional Government and Democracy: Theory and Practice in Europe and America.* 4th ed. Waltham, Mass.: Blaisdell.

Galeano, Eduardo, 1973. *Open Veins in Latin America.* New York and London: Monthly Review Press.

Geithman, David T., 1974. *Fiscal Policy for Industrialization and Development in Latin America.* Gainesville: University of Florida Press.

Gelb, Alan, 1981. "Capital Importing Oil Exporters: Adjustment Issues and Policy Choices." Staff Working Paper 475. World Bank, Washington, D.C. (August).

———, 1984. "Adjustment to Windfall Gains: A Comparative Analysis of Oil-Exporting Countries." World Bank, Washington, D.C. (October).

———, 1986. "Adjustment to Windfall Gains: A Comparative Analysis of Oil-Exporting Countries." In J. Peter Neary, ed., *Natural Resources and the Macroeconomy.* Cambridge: MIT Press.

———, 1988. "Development Paths for Oil Exporters: Structure and Integration of Political Analysis." Mimeo CB43-08 080481. World Bank.

George, Alexander, 1979. "Case Studies and Theory Development: The Method of Structured, Focused Comparison." In Paul G. Lauren, ed., *Diplomatic History: New Approaches.* New York: Free Press.

Germani, Gino, Torcuato S. di Tella, and Octavio Ianni, 1973. *Populismo y contradicciones de clase en Latinoamérica*. Mexico City: Serie Popular Era.

Gerschenkron, Alexander, 1962. *Economic Backwardness in Historical Perspective*. Cambridge: Harvard University Press.

———, 1966. *Bread and Democracy in Germany*. New York: H. Fertig.

Gillis, Malcolm, ed., 1989. *Tax Reform in Developing Countries*. Durham, N.C.: Duke University Press.

Glezakos, Constantine, 1973. "Export Instability and Economic Growth: A Statistical Verification," *Economic Development and Cultural Change* 21 (July).

Gourevitch, Peter A., 1978. "The Second Image Reversed," *International Organization* 32 (autumn).

———, 1986. *Politics in Hard Times: Comparative Responses to International Economic Crises*. Ithaca, N.Y.: Cornell University Press.

Grindle, Merilee S., ed., 1980. *Politics and Policy Implementation in the Third World*. Princeton, N.J.: Princeton University Press.

Hablutzel, R., 1981. "Issues in Economic Diversification for the Oil-Rich Countries," *Finance & Development* 18 (June).

Hartshorn, J. E., 1967. *Oil Companies and Governments: An Account of the International Oil Industry in Its Political Environment*. London: Faber.

Hintze, Otto, 1975. "Military Organization and the Organization of the State." In Felix Gilbert, ed., *The Historical Essays of Otto Hintze*. New York: Oxford University Press.

Hirschman, Albert O., 1958. *Strategy of Economic Development*. New Haven, Conn.: Yale University Press.

———, 1965. *Journeys toward Progress*. New York: Doubleday, Anchor.

———, 1968. "The Political Economy of Import Substitution," *Quarterly Journal of Economics* 82 (1).

———, 1971. *A Bias for Hope: Essays on Development and Latin America*. New Haven, Conn.: Yale University Press.

———, 1977. "A Generalized Linkage Approach to Development, with Special Reference to Staples," *Economic Development and Cultural Change* 25 supplement.

———, 1979. "The Turn to Authoritarianism in Latin America and the Search for Its Economic Determinants." In David Collier, ed., *The New Authoritarianism in Latin America*. Princeton, N.J.: Princeton University Press.

———, 1981. *Essays in Trespassing: Economics to Politics and Beyond*. Cambridge: Cambridge University Press.

Hotelling, Harold, 1931. "The Economics of Exhaustible Resources," *Journal of Political Economy* 39 (April).

Hughes, Helen, 1975. "Economic Rents, the Distribution of Gains from Mineral Exploitation, and Mineral Development Policy," *World Development* 3 (11 and 12).

Huntington, Samuel P., 1968. *Political Order in Changing Societies*. New Haven, Conn.: Yale University Press.

———, 1975. "The United States." In Michael Crozier, Samuel P. Huntington, and Joji Watanuki, *The Crisis of Democracy: Report on the Governability of Democracies to the Trilateral Commission.* New York: New York University Press.

Ianni, Octavio, 1975. *La formación del estado populista en América Latina.* Mexico City: Serie Popular Era.

Innis, Harold, 1956. *The Fur Trade in Canada: An Introduction to Canadian Economic History.* Toronto: University of Toronto Press.

———, 1972. *Empire and Communications.* Toronto: University of Toronto Press.

International Monetary Fund, 1978. *Government Finance Statistics Yearbook.* Vol. 2. Washington, D.C.

———, 1984. *Government Finance Statistics Yearbook.* Vol. 8. Washington, D.C.

———, 1988a. *Government Finance Statistics Yearbook.* Vol. 12. Washington, D.C.

———, 1988b. *International Financial Statistics Yearbook.* Vol. 41. Washington, D.C.

———, 1990. *International Financial Statistics Yearbook.* Vol. 43. Washington, D.C.

———, 1993. *International Financial Statistics Yearbook.* Vol. 46. Washington, D.C.

———, 1995. *International Financial Statistics Yearbook.* Vol. 48. Washington, D.C.

———, 1996. *International Financial Statistics Yearbook.* Vol. 49. Washington, D.C.

Jabarti, Anwar, 1977. "The Oil Crisis: A Producer's Dilemma." In Ragaei El Mallakh and Carl McGuire, eds., *U.S. and World Energy Resources: Proceedings of the Third International Conference.* Boulder, Colo.: International Research Center for Energy and Economic Development.

Jessop, Bob, 1977. "Recent Theories of the Capitalist State," *Cambridge Journal of Economics* 1 (4).

Karanjia, R. K., 1960. *The Mind of Nehru.* London: Allen & Unwin.

Karl, Terry, 1982. "Democracy over a Barrel: Authoritarian Responses to Oil Shocks in Venezuela and Iran." Paper presented at the Tenth National Meeting of the Latin American Studies Association, Washington, D.C., March 3–6.

———, 1983. "The Paradox of the Rich Debtor: The Foreign Borrowing of Oil-Exporting Countries." Paper delivered at the Annual Meeting of the American Political Science Association, Chicago, September 1–4.

———, 1986. "Mexico, Venezuela, and the Contadora Initiative." In Morris J. Blachman, William M. LeoGrande, and Kenneth E. Sharpe, eds., *Confronting Revolution: Security through Diplomacy in Central America.* New York: Pantheon.

———, 1987. "Petroleum and Political Pacts: The Transition to Democracy in Venezuela," *Latin American Research Review* 22 (1).

———, 1990. "Dilemmas of Democratization in Latin America," *Comparative Politics* 23 (1).

Keohane, Robert, and Joseph Nye, 1977. *Power and Interdependence: World Politics in Transition.* Boston: Little, Brown.

Keynes, John Maynard, 1930. *A Treatise on Money.* Vol. 2. London: Macmillan.

Kingdom of Saudi Arabia, Ministry of Planning, [1980]. *Third Development Plan, 1400–1405/1980–1985.* Riyadh.

Klapp, Merrie G., 1982. "The State: Landlord or Entrepreneur?" *International Organization* 36 (3).

Kohli, Atul, 1987. "The Political Economy of Development Strategies: Perspectives on the Role of the State," *Comparative Politics* 19 (January).

Krasner, Stephen D., 1978. *Defending the National Interest: Raw Materials Investments and U.S. Foreign Policy.* Princeton, N.J.: Princeton University Press.

———, ed., 1983. *International Regimes.* Ithaca, N.Y.: Cornell University Press.

———, 1984. "Approaches to the State," *Comparative Politics* 16 (January).

———, 1988. "Sovereignty: An Institutional Perspective," *Comparative Political Studies* 21 (1).

Kremers, Jeroen J. M., 1986. "The Dutch Disease in the Netherlands." In J. Peter Neary, ed., *Natural Resources and the Macroeconomy.* Cambridge: MIT Press.

Kriesberg, M., 1965. *Public Administration in Developing Countries.* Washington, D.C.: Brookings Institute.

Krueger, Anne O., 1974. "The Political Economy of Rent-Seeking Economy," *American Economic Review* 64 (June).

Kubbah, Abdul, 1974. *OPEC: Past and Present.* Vienna: Petro-Economic Research Center.

Kurth, James R., 1979. "The Political Consequences of the Product Cycle: Industrial History and Political Outcomes," *International Organization* 33 (1).

Levi, Margaret, 1988. *Of Rule and Revenue.* Berkeley: University of California Press.

Levin, Jonathan, 1960. *The Export Economies.* Cambridge: Harvard University Press.

Lewis, Stephen R., 1982. "Development Problems of the Mineral-Rich Countries." Research Memorandum 74. Williams College Center for Development Economics, Williamstown, Mass.

Lindblom, Charles, 1977. *Politics and Markets: The World's Political Economic Systems.* New York: Basic Books.

Linden, Henry, 1988. "World Oil—An Essay on Its Spectacular 120 Year Rise (1859–1979), Recent Decline, and Uncertain Future," *Energy Systems and Policy* 2 (4).

Lipset, Seymour M., 1960. *Political Man: The Social Bases of Politics.* New York: Doubleday.

Malloy, James M., ed., 1977. *Authoritarianism and Corporatism in Latin America.* Pittsburgh, Pa.: University of Pittsburgh Press.

Mann, Michael, 1980. "State and Society, 1130–1815: An Analysis of English

State Finances." In Maurice Zeitlin, ed., *Political Power and Social Theory*, vol. 1. Greenwich, Conn.: JAI Press.

March, James G., and Johan P. Olsen, 1976. *Ambiguity and Choice in Organizations*. Bergen: Universitetsforlaget.

———, 1984. "The New Institutionalism: Organizational Factors in Political Life," *American Political Science Review* 78 (September).

Marx, Karl, [1852] 1970. "The Eighteenth Brumaire of Louis Bonaparte." In Karl Marx and Friedrich Engels, *Selected Works*, vol. 2. New York: International Publishers.

Marx, Karl, and Friedrich Engels, 1979. *Collected Works*. London: Lawrence and Wishart.

Massell, Benton F., 1970. "Export Instability and Economic Structure," *American Economic Review* 60 (September).

McNally, David, 1981. "Staple Theory as Commodity Fetishism: Marx, Innis and Canadian Political Economy," *Studies in Political Economy* (Ottawa), no. 6 (autumn).

Merkl, Peter, 1981. "Democratic Development, Breakdowns, and Fascism," *World Politics* 34 (1).

Michels, Robert, 1949. *Political Parties: A Sociological Study of the Oligarchical Tendencies of Modern Democracy*. Glencoe, Ill.: Free Press.

Mikdashi, Z[uhayr] M., 1972. *The Community of Oil-Exporting Countries*. Ithaca, N.Y.: Cornell University Press.

———, 1980. "Oil Exporting Countries and Oil-Importing Countries: What Kind of Interdependence?" *Millennium: Journal of International Studies* 9 (spring).

Miliband, Ralph, 1969. *The State in Capitalist Society*. New York: Basic Books.

Mill, John Stuart, [1848] 1895. *Principles of Political Economy*. London: Routledge.

———, [1843] 1967. *A System of Logic: Ratiocinative and Inductive*. Toronto: University of Toronto Press.

Moore, Barrington, 1966. *Social Origins of Dictatorship and Democracy*. Boston: Beacon Press.

Moore, Mick, 1989. "What and Where Is Political Economy?" *Journal of Development Studies* 25 (4).

Moran, Theodore, 1974. *Multinational Corporations and the Politics of Dependence: Copper in Chile*. Princeton, N.J.: Princeton University Press.

Murphy, K. J., 1983. *Macroproject Development in the Third World: An Analysis of Transnational Partnerships*. Boulder, Colo.: Westview Press.

Musgrave, Richard, 1987. "Tax Reform in Developing Countries." In David Newbury and Nicholas Stern, eds., *The Theory of Taxation for Developing Countries*. Oxford: Oxford University Press.

Myrdal, Gunnar, 1957. *Economic Theory and Under-developed Regions*. London: Duckworth.

———, 1968. *Asian Drama: An Inquiry into the Poverty of Nations*. New York: Pantheon.

Nankani, Gobind, 1979. "Development Problems of Mineral Exporting Countries." Staff Working Paper 354. World Bank, Washington, D.C. (August).

Neary, J. Peter, ed., 1986. *Natural Resources and the Macroeconomy.* Cambridge.: MIT Press.

Neary, J. Peter, and Sweder van Wijnbergen, 1986. "Natural Resources and the Macroeconomy: A Theoretical Framework." In J. Peter Neary, ed., *Natural Resources and the Macroeconomy.* Cambridge: MIT Press.

Nef, John U., 1937. "Prices and Industrial Capitalism in France and England, 1540–1640," *Economic History Review* 7 (2).

Nettl, J. R., 1968. "The State as a Conceptual Variable," *World Politics* 20 (July).

Nordlinger, Eric, 1981. *On the Autonomy of the Democratic State.* Cambridge: Harvard University Press.

Nore, Petter, and Terisa Turner, eds., 1980. *Oil and Class Struggle.* London: Zed.

North, Douglass C., 1981. *Structure and Change in Economic History.* New York: Norton.

———, 1990. *Institutions, Institutional Change and Economic Performance.* London: Cambridge University Press.

Odell, Peter, 1992. "Prospects for Non-OPEC Oil Supply," *Energy Policy* 20 (10).

O'Donnell, Guillermo, 1973. *Modernization and Bureaucratic Authoritarianism: Studies in South American Politics.* Berkeley: University of California Institute of International Studies.

———, 1977a. "Apuntes para una teoría del Estado." Document CEDES/G.E. CLACSO 9. Centro de Estudios de Estado y Sociedad, Buenos Aires.

———, 1977b. "Corporatism and the Question of the State." In James M. Malloy, ed., *Authoritarianism and Corporatism in Latin America.* Pittsburgh, Pa.: University of Pittsburgh Press.

———, 1978a. "Reflections on the Patterns of Change in the Bureaucratic Authoritarian State," *Latin American Research Review* 12 (1).

———, 1978b. "State and Alliances in Argentina 1956–1976," *Journal of Development Studies* 15 (1).

O'Donnell, Guillermo, and Philippe C. Schmitter, 1986. *Transitions from Authoritarian Rule: Tentative Conclusions about Uncertain Democracies.* Baltimore: Johns Hopkins University Press.

Offe, Claus, 1972. "Advanced Capitalism and the Welfare State," *Politics and Society* (summer).

———, 1973a. "The Abolition of Market Control and the Problem of Legitimacy," *Kapitalstate,* no. 1–2.

———, 1975b. "The Capitalist State and the Problem of Policy Formation." In Leon N. Lindberg, Robert Alford, Colin Crouch, and Claus Offe, eds., *Stress and Contradiction in Modern Capitalism.* Lexington, Mass.: Lexington Books.

———, 1974. "Structural Problems of the Capitalist State: Class Rule and the Political System." In Klaus von Beyme, ed., *German Political Studies,* vol. 1. Beverly Hills, Calif.: Sage.

Olson, Mancur, 1965. *The Logic of Collective Action.* Cambridge: Harvard University Press.

Osborne, Dale K., 1976. "Cartel Problems," *American Economic Review* (December).

Oszlak, Oscar, 1981. "The Historical Formation of the State in Latin America: Some Theoretical and Methodological Guidelines for Its Study," *Latin American Research Review* 16 (2).

Paige, Jeffery M., 1975. *Agrarian Revolution.* New York: Free Press.

Penrose, Edith, 1969. *The Large International Firms in Developing Countries: The International Petroleum Industry.* Cambridge: MIT Press.

———, 1988. "Defending the Price of Oil," *Energy Journal* 9 (1).

Petras, James, 1978. *Critical Perspectives on Imperialism and Social Class in the Third World.* New York: Monthly Review Press.

Poulantzas, Nicos, 1973. *Political Power and Social Classes.* Translated by Timothy O'Hagan. London: Sheed and Ward.

———, 1976a. "The Capitalist State: A Reply to Ralph Miliband and Laclau," *New Left Review,* no. 95 (January-February).

———, 1976b. *Classes in Contemporary Capitalism.* Translated by David Fernbach. London: New Left Books.

———, 1980. *State: Power and Socialism.* London: New Left Books.

Przeworski, Adam, 1979. "Some Problems in the Study of the Transition to Democracy." Working Paper 61. Wilson Center, Smithsonian Institution, Washington, D.C.

Przeworski, Adam, Michael Alvarez, José Antonio Cheibub, and Fernando Limongi, 1996. "What Makes Democracies Endure?" *Journal of Democracy* 7 (1).

Przeworski, Adam, and Henry Teune, 1970. *The Logic of Comparative Social Inquiry.* New York: Wiley.

Quick, Stephan A., 1980. "The Paradox of Popularity: 'Ideological' Program Implementation in Zambia." In Merilee S. Grindle, ed., *Politics and Policy Implementation in the Third World.* Princeton, N.J.: Princeton University Press.

Quijano, Aníbal, 1975. *Crisis imperialista en América Latina.* Caracas: UCV.

Rabe, Stephen G., 1982. *The Road to OPEC.* Austin: University of Texas Press.

Ragin, Charles C., 1987. *The Comparative Method.* Berkeley: University of California Press.

Reynolds, Clark Winton, 1965. "Development Problems of an Export Economy: The Case of Chile." In Markos Mamalakis and Clark Winton Reynolds, eds., *Essays on the Chilean Economy.* Homewood, Ill.: Irwin, 1965.

———, 1978. "Fissures in the Volcano? Central American Prospects." In Joseph Grunwald, ed., *Latin America and the World Economy: A Changing International Order.* New York: Sage.

Ricardo, David, [1817] 1973. *The Principles of Political Economy and Taxation.* London: Dent.

Riggs, Fred, 1964. *Administration in Developing Countries: The Theory of a Prismatic Society.* Boston: Houghton Mifflin.

Riker, William H., 1962. *The Theory of Political Coalitions.* New Haven, Conn.: Yale University Press.

Robinson, T.J.C., 1989. *Economic Theories of Exhaustible Resources*. London: Routledge.

Roemer, Michael, 1983. "Dutch Disease in Developing Countries: Swallowing Bitter Medicine." Paper presented at the Arne Ryde Symposium on the Primary Sector in Economic Development, University of Lund, Sweden (August 29–30).

Rose, Richard, 1974. "The Evolution of Public Policy in the European State." Paper presented at the Conference on Comparing Public Policies, Committee on Political Sociology, Polish Academy of Sciences, Warsaw (May).

Rothchild, Donald, and Robert Curry, 1978. *Scarcity, Choice and Public Policy in Middle Africa*. Berkeley: University of California Press.

Sampson, Anthony, 1975. *The Seven Sisters: The Great Oil Companies and the World They Made*. New York: Viking.

Saul, John, 1979. *The State and Revolution in Eastern Africa*. New York: Monthly Review Press.

Schmitter, Philippe C., 1971. *Interest Conflict and Political Change in Brazil*. Stanford, Calif.: Stanford University Press.

———, 1972. "Paths to Political Development in Latin America." In Douglas A. Chalmers, ed., *Changing Latin America: New Interpretations of Its Politics and Society*. New York: Academy of Political Science, Columbia University.

———, 1974. "Still the Century of Corporatism?" *Review of Politics* 36 (1).

———, ed., 1977. "Corporatism and Policy-Making in Contemporary Western Europe," *Comparative Political Studies* 10 (1).

———, 1980. "Speculations about the Prospective Demise of Authoritarian Regimes and Its Possible Consequences." Paper presented at the Wilson Center, Smithsonian Institution, Washington, D.C. (September).

———, 1981. "Interest Intermediation and Regime Governability in Contemporary Western Europe and North America." In Suzanne Berger, ed., *Organized Interests in Western Europe: Pluralism, Corporatism, and the Transformation of Politics*. Cambridge: Cambridge University Press.

———, 1988. "Democratic Consolidation of Southern Europe." Unpublished manuscript, European University Institute.

———, 1990. "Sectors in Modern Capitalism." In Renato Brunetta and Carlo dell'Aringo, eds., *Labour Relations and Economic Performance*. London: Macmillan.

Schmitter, Philippe C., John H. Coatsworth, and Joanne Fox Przeworski, n.d. "Historical Perspectives on the State, Civil Society, and the Economy in Latin America: Prolegomenon to a Workshop at the University of Chicago, 1976–1977." University of Chicago, mimeo.

Schmitter, Philippe C., and Wolfgang Streeck, 1981. "The Organization of Business Interests." *Discussion Papers*, IIM/LMP. 81/13. Berlin: WZB.

Schneider, Steven A., 1983. *The Oil Price Revolution*. Baltimore and London: Johns Hopkins University Press.

Schumpeter, J., 1939. *Business Cycles*. Vol. 1. New York: McGraw-Hill.

Seiber, Marilyn, 1982. *International Borrowing by Developing Countries*. New York: Pergamon Press.

Serafy, Salah el, 1980. "Absorptive Capacity, the Demand for Revenues and the Supply of Petroleum." Paper presented at the Seventh International Energy Conference, organized by the International Research Center for Energy and Economic Development of the University of Colorado (October 13).

Seymour, Ian, 1980. *OPEC: Instrument of Change*. London: Macmillan.

Shafer, D. Michael, 1994. *Winners and Losers: How Sectors Shape the Development Prospects of States*. Ithaca, N.Y.: Cornell University Press.

Shaffer, Edward, 1980. "Class and Oil in Alberta." In Peter Nore and Terisa Turner, eds., *Oil and Class Struggle*. London: Zed.

Skidmore, Thomas E., 1977. "The Politics of Economic Stabilization in Postwar Latin America." In James M. Malloy, ed., *Authoritarianism and Corporatism in Latin America*. Pittsburgh, Pa.: University of Pittsburgh Press.

Skocpol, Theda, 1979. *States and Social Revolutions*. Cambridge: Cambridge University Press.

———, 1985. "Bringing the State Back In: Strategies of Analysis in Current Research." In Peter B. Evans, Dietrich Rueschemeyer, and Theda Skocpol, eds., *Bringing the State Back In*. Cambridge: Cambridge University Press.

Skowronek, Stephen, 1982. *Building a New American State: The Expansion of National Administrative Capacities*. New York: Cambridge University Press.

Smith, Adam, [1776] 1937. *An Inquiry into the Nature and Causes of the Wealth of Nations*. New York: Modern Library.

Soutar, Geoffrey, 1977. "Export Instability and Concentration in the Less Developed Countries," *Journal of Development Economics* 4 (3).

Staniland, Martin, 1985. *What Is Political Economy?* New Haven, Conn.: Yale University Press.

Stobaugh, Robert, and Daniel Yergin, 1979. *Energy Future*. New York: Random House.

Stork, Joe, 1975. *Middle East Oil and the Energy Crisis*. New York: Monthly Review Press.

Strange, Susan, 1983. "*Cave! hic dragones:* A Critique of Regime Analysis." In Stephen D. Krasner, ed., *International Regimes*. Ithaca, N.Y.: Cornell University Press.

Streeten, Paul, 1979. "Development Ideas in Historical Perspective." In Albert O. Hirschman, Dudley Seers, Samir Amin, Stephen Graubard, and Herbert Holloman, eds., *Toward a New Strategy for Development*. New York: Pergamon Press.

Sweeney, James L., 1977. "Economics of Depletable Resources: Market Forces and Intertemporal Bias," *Review of Economic Studies* 44 (February).

Tait, Alan A., Wilfrid L. M. Gratz, and Barry J. Eichengreen, 1979. "International Comparisons of Taxation for Selected Developing Countries, 1972–76," *IMF Staff Papers* 26 (1).

Tanzi, Vito, 1987. "Quantitative Characteristics of the Tax Systems of Developing Countries." In David Newbury and Nicholas Stern, eds., *The Theory of Taxation for Developing Countries*. Oxford: Oxford University Press.

Terzian, Pierre, 1985. *OPEC: The Inside Story*. London: Zed.

Thoburn, John T., 1977. *Primary Commodity Exports and Economic Development*. New York: Wiley.

Tilly, Charles, ed., 1975. *The Formation of National States in Western Europe*. Princeton, N.J.: Princeton University Press.

Timmer, C. Peter, 1982. "Energy and Agricultural Change in the Asia-Pacific Region: The Agricultural Sector." Discussion Paper 140. Harvard Institute for International Development, Cambridge.

Tollison, Robert D., 1982. "Rent Seeking: A Survey," *Kyklos* 35 (4).

Tribe, Keith, 1977. "Economic Property and the Theorization of Ground Rent," *Economy and Society*, 6 (1).

Truman, David, 1951. *The Governmental Process: Political Interests and Public Opinion*. New York: Knopf.

Tufte, Edward R., 1978. *Political Control of the Economy*. Princeton, N.J.: Princeton University Press.

United Nations Conference on Trade and Development, 1982. *Trade and Development Report*. New York: United Nations.

Usher, Dan, 1981. *The Economic Prerequisite to Democracy*. New York: Columbia University Press.

Valenilla, Luis, 1975. *Oil: The Making of the New Economic Order*. New York: McGraw-Hill.

Van Nierkerk, A. E., 1974. *Populism and Political Development in Latin America*. Amsterdam: Roterdam University Press.

van Wijnbergen, Sweder, 1982. "Optimal Capital and the Allocation of Investment between Traded and Non-traded Sectors in Oil-Producing Countries." Development Research Department, World Bank, Washington, D.C.

———, 1984. "'The Dutch Disease': A Disease after All?" *Economic Journal* 94 (373).

Verba, Sidney, 1967. "Some Dilemmas in Comparative Research," *World Politics* (October).

Vernon, Raymond, 1975. "The Oil Crisis in Perspective," *Daedalus* 104 (1) (whole issue).

———, ed., 1976. *The Oil Crisis*. New York: Norton.

Wade, Robert, 1990. *Governing the Market: Economic Theory and the Role of Government in East Asian Industrialization*. Princeton, N.J.: Princeton University Press.

Watkins, Melville H., 1963. "A Staple Theory of Economic Growth," *Canadian Journal of Economics and Political Science* 29 (May).

———, 1977. "The Staple Theory Revisited," *Journal of Canadian Studies* 12 (5).

Webb, Walter Prescott, 1952. *The Great Frontier*. Boston: Houghton Mifflin.

Webber, Carolyn, and Aaron Wildavsky, 1986. *A History of Taxation and Expenditures in the Western World*. New York: Simon & Schuster.

Weber, Max, [1921] 1946. "On Bureaucracy." In H. H. Gerth and C. Wright Mills, eds., *From Max Weber: Essays in Sociology*. New York: Oxford University Press.

———, [1921] 1968. *Economy and Society*. 3 vols. New York: Bedminister Press.

Weeks, John F., and Elizabeth W. Dore, 1982. "Basic Needs: Journey of a Concept." In Margaret E. Crahan, ed., *Human Rights and Basic Needs in the Americas.* Washington, D.C.: Georgetown University Press.

Wildavsky, Aaron, 1974. *The Politics of the Budgetary Process.* 2d ed. Boston: Little, Brown.

Williamson, Oliver E., 1975. *Markets and Hierarchies: Analysis and Antitrust Implications.* New York: Free Press.

———, 1985. *The Economic Institutions of Capitalism.* New York: Free Press.

Wolf, Eric, 1969. *Peasant Wars of the Twentieth Century.* New York: Harper & Row.

World Bank, 1988. *World Debt Tables 1988–1989.* Vol. 3. Washington, D.C.

———, 1989. *World Debt Tables 1989–1990.* Vol. 2. Washington, D.C.

———, 1991. "Venezuela Poverty Study: From Generalized Subsidies to Targeted Programs." Report 9114-VE. Washington, D.C.

———, 1993. *World Debt Tables 1993–1994.* Vol. 2. Washington, D.C.

———, 1996. *World Debt Tables 1996.* Vol. 2. Washington, D.C.

———, various years. *World Development Report.* Washington, D.C.

Wraith, R., and Edgar Simpkins, 1963. *Corruption in Developing Countries.* London: Allen & Unwin.

Wright, Eric Olin, 1978. *Class, Crisis and the State.* London: New Left Books.

VENEZUELA

Abente, Diego, 1989. "The Political Economy of Tax Reform in Venezuela," *Comparative Politics* 22 (2).

Acción Democrática, 1962. *Tésis política.* Caracas: Departamento de Prensa y Propaganda.

———, 1978. *Acción Democrática y la reforma administrativa.* Caracas: Fracción Parlamentaria de A.D.

Alexander, Robert J., 1964. *The Venezuelan Democratic Revolution.* New Brunswick, N.J.: Rutgers University Press.

Allen, Loring, 1977. *Venezuelan Economic Development.* Greenwich, Conn.: JAI Press.

Alvarez de Stella, Ana, 1988. "Economic Crisis and Foreign Debt Management in Venezuela." In Stephanie Griffith Jones, ed., *Managing World Debt.* New York: St. Martin's Press.

Andrade Arcaya, Ignacio, n.d. *Un estado para el desarrollo.* Caracas: Colección Los Desarrollistas.

Aranda, Sergio, 1977. *La economía venezolana.* Bogota: Siglo XXI.

Araujo, Orlando, 1969. *Situación industrial en Venezuela.* Caracas: Universidad Central de Venezuela.

Asociación Pro-Venezuela, 1978. "Nueva concepción del estado." Caracas.

Azpurua Ayala, Enrique, 1974. "Carta de Enrique Azpurua Ayala a Pedro Tinoco." Comisión de la Administración Pública, Caracas (December 16).

Balestrini, César, 1974. *Los precios del petróleo y la participación fiscal de*

Venezuela. Caracas: Facultad de Ciencias Económicas y Sociales, Universidad Central de Venezuela.

Baloyra, Enrique, 1977. "Public Attitudes toward the Democratic Regime." In John Martz and David Myers, eds., *Venezuela: The Democratic Experience*. New York: Praeger.

Baptista, Asdrúbal, 1984. "Más allá del optimismo y del pesimismo: Las transformaciones fundamentales del país." In Moisés Naím and Ramón Piñango, eds., *El caso Venezuela: Una ilusión de armonía*. Caracas: Ediciones IESA.

———, 1991. *Bases cuantitativas de la economía venezolana 1830–1989*. Caracas: Ediciones María di Mase.

Baptista, Asdrúbal, and Bernard Mommer, 1987. *El petróleo en el pensamiento económico venezolano: Un ensayo*. Caracas: Ediciones IESA.

Betancourt, Rómulo, 1956. *Venezuela: Política y petróleo*. Mexico City: Fondo de Cultura Económica.

———, 1959. *Posición y doctrina*. Caracas: Editorial Cordillera.

———, 1979. *Venezuela: Oil and Politics*. Boston: Houghlin Mifflin.

Bigler, Gene, 1980. "State Economic Control versus Market Expansion: The Third Sector in Venezuelan Politics." Ph.D. diss., Johns Hopkins University.

Bigler, Gene, and Franklin Tugwell, 1986. "Banking on Oil in Venezuela." In Andrew McGuire and Janet Welsch Brown, eds., *Bordering on Trouble: Resources and Politics in Latin America*. Bethesda, Md.: Adler and Adler.

Blank, David Eugene, 1969. "Policy-Making Styles and Political Development: The Introduction of a System of Democratic Planning in Venezuela." Columbia University.

———, 1973. *Politics in Venezuela*. Boston: Little, Brown.

———, 1984. *Venezuela, Politics in a Petroleum Republic*. New York: Praeger.

Boesch, Andres, 1972. "Organization of Labor and Government under Conditions of Economic Scarcity." Ph.D. diss., University of Florida.

Bond, Robert D., 1975. "Business Associations and Interest Politics in Venezuela." Ph.D. diss., Vanderbilt University.

———, ed., 1977. *Contemporary Venezuela and Its Role in International Affairs*. New York: New York University Press.

———, 1992. "Why Venezuela Failed at Economic Reform," *VenEconomy* 10 (1).

Borja, Arturo, and Terry Karl, 1979. "La administración Carter y las relaciones Venezuela–Estados Unidos." In *Carter y América Latina*. Cuadernos Semestrales 5. Mexico City: CIDE.

Boscan de Ruesta, Isabel, 1975. "El Holding en la organización del sector económico público." Colección de Estudio Especiales de la Procuraduria General de la República, Caracas.

Bottome, Robert, and Carl Prunhuber, 1980. *Projections of the Venezuelan Economy: 1980–1984*. Caracas: Prunhuber/Bottome Asesores Económicos (October).

Bourguignon, F., 1980a. "La distribución del ingreso en Venezuela en el periódo 1968–1976," *Revista de Hacienda* (Caracas), no. 77 (January).

————, 1980b. "Oil and Income Distribution in Venezuela, 1968–1976." In J. de Bandt, P. Mandi, and D. Seers, eds., *European Studies in Development.* London: Macmillan.

Brewer-Carías, Alan Randolph, 1970. "El control de las actividades del estado en Caracas." Caracas.

————, 1975. *Cambio político y reforma del estado en Venezuela.* Madrid: Editorial Tecnos.

————, 1977. "Regimen jurídico de las empresas públicas en Venezuela." Caracas (January).

————, 1978. "Algunas ideas para un proyecto de estado contemporáneo en Venezuela: Ponencia en las jornadas sobre la democracia en Venezuela." Universidad Central de Venezuela and Ateneo de Caracas.

————, n.d. "La reforma de toda la administración pública por toda la administración pública." Caracas.

Brito Figueroa, F., 1966. *Historia económica y social de Venezuela.* 2 vols. Caracas: Universidad Central de Venezuela.

Burggraaff, Winfield, 1972. *The Venezuelan Armed Forces in Politics.* Columbia: University of Missouri Press.

Canache Mata, Carlos, 1975. *Defensa del gobierno en el parlamento.* Caracas: Publicaciones de la Secretaria General de Acción Democrática.

Carrillo Batalla, T. E., 1968. *El proceso presupuestario venezolano.* Caracas: Ediciones del Consejo Municipal del Distrito Federal.

Chossudovsky, Miguel, 1977a. *La economía política del desempleo.* Caracas: Instituto Latinoamericano de Investigaciones Sociales, Fundación Friedrich Ebert (December).

————, 1977b. *La miseria en Venezuela.* Valencia: Vadell Hermanos.

Clark, Robert, 1966. *Fedecámaras en el proceso de formulación de política en Venezuela.* Caracas: Comisión de la Administración Pública.

Combellas, T., 1973. "La actuación de Fedecámaras y la CTV ante la reforma tributaria," *Politeia* 2.

Consuerga, A., 1979. *CAP: Una campaña inolvidable: Promesas cumplidas.* Caracas: n.p.

Coppedge, Michael, 1993. *Strong Parties and Lame Ducks: Presidential Partyarchy and Factionalism in Venezuela.* Palo Alto, Calif.: Stanford University Press.

Cordido-Freytes, José Antonio, n.d. *La idea del desarrollo y la empresa contemporánea.* Caracas: Italgráfica s.r.l., Colección Los Desarrollistas.

Coronel, Gustavo, 1983. *The Nationalization of Venezuelan Oil.* Lexington, Mass.: Lexington Books.

Davis, Charles L., and Kenneth M. Coleman, 1989. "Political Control of Organized Labor in a Semi-consociational Democracy: The Case of Venezuela." In Edward Epstein, ed., *Labor Autonomy and the State in Latin America.* Boston: Unwin Hyman.

Decretos del presidente de Venezuela, Carlos Andrés Pérez. 1975. Vols. 1–9. Caracas: Centauro.

de la Plaza, Salvador, 1976. *Desarrollo económico e industrial básica.* Caracas: Universidad Central de Venezuela.

Dinkelspiel, John, 1967. "Administrative Style and Economic Development." Ph.D. diss., Harvard University.

Dodge, Stephen Charles, 1968. "The History of the Development of the Venezuela Guayana Region." Ph.D. diss., University of Minnesota.

Donnelly, Vernon Charles, 1975. "Juan Vicente Gómez and the Venezuelan Worker 1919–1929." Ph.D. diss., University of Maryland.

Duno, Pedro, 1975. *Los doce apóstoles.* Valencia: Vadell Hermanos.

El Año chucuto, 1975. Colección Parlamento y Socialismo. Caracas.

Ellner, Steven, 1984–1985. "Inter-party Agreement and Rivalry in Venezuela: A Comparative Perspective," *Studies in Comparative International Development* 19 (winter).

———, 1987. "The Venezuelan Petroleum Corporation and the Debate over Government Policy in Basic Industry, 1960–1976." Latin American Studies Occasional Paper 47. University of Glasgow.

Empresas Mendoza, n.d.a. *Cincuenta años de la Empresa Mendoza.* Caracas: Consejo de Coordinación de las Empresas Mendoza.

———, n.d.b. *Las Empresas Mendoza.* Caracas: Fundación Mendoza.

España, Luis Pedro, 1989. *Democracia y renta petrolera.* Caracas: Universidad Católica Andrés Bello.

Espinasa, Ramón, 1985. "El mercado petrolero mundial," *Revista SIC* (Caracas), no. 475 (May).

Espinasa, Ramón, and Bernard Mommer, 1991. "Venezuelan Oil Policy in the Long Run," *Energy* (East-West Center, Hawaii).

Esser, Klaus, 1976. "Oil and Development: Venezuela." German Development Institute, Berlin.

Ewell, Judith, 1984. *Venezuela: A Century of Change.* Stanford, Calif.: Stanford University Press.

Fagan, Stuart I., 1974. "The Venezuelan Labor Movement: A Study in Political Unionism." Ph.D. diss., University of California, Berkeley.

———, 1977. "Unionism and Democracy." In John Martz and David Myers, eds., *Venezuela: The Democratic Experience.* New York: Praeger.

Fedecámaras, 1974. *Informe final. XXX Asamblea Anual, San Cristóbal.* Caracas (June 24–29).

———, 1977. "Planificación concertada a nivel de las entidades federales." *Informe final. XXXIII Asamblea Anual. Maracay.* Caracas (July 10–16).

———, 1978a. "La concertación y el Desarrollo Económio y Social: La concertación como esquema fundamental del sistema democrático." *Boletín Informativo* 7 (June 15).

———, 1978b. "Planificación concertada regional y sub-regional." *Informe anual del XXIV Asamblea Anual de Fedecámaras.* Caracas (June 11–17).

Fedecámaras, Departamento Técnico, 1978. "La concertación en el Desarrollo Económico y Social." *Informe anual del XXIV Asamblea Anual de Fedecámaras.* Caracas (June 11–17).

Fernández, Eduardo, 1974. *La batalla de la oposición.* Caracas: Ediciones Nueva Política.

"Five Year Projection of the Venezuelan Economy, 1977–1981." 1977. Prepared for Citibank, Caracas (August).

Flores Díaz, Max, 1975. "Sentido y proyección de la política económica guber-
namental," *Nueva Ciencia* (Universidad Central de Venezuela), no. 1.
———, 1977. "Venezuela: La otra cara del desarrollo," *SIC* 40 (399).
Floyd, Mary, 1976. "Política y economía en tiempos de Guzmán Blanco: Cen-
tralización y desarrollo." In *Política y economía de Venezuela: 1810–1976*.
Caracas: n.p.
Friedman, John, 1965. *Venezuela: From Doctrine to Dialogue*. Syracuse, N.Y.:
Syracuse University Press.
Fuad, Kim, 1974. "CAP in the Saddle: Riding Hell for Leather," *Business Vene-
zuela* (Caracas), no. 31 (May/June).
Fuenmayor, Juan Batista, 1975. *Historia de la política contemporánea venezo-
lana, 1899–1969*. Caracas: Universidad Central de Venezuela.
García Araujo, Mauricio, 1975. *El gasto público consolidado en Venezuela*.
Caracas: Artegrafía.
———, 1979. "La situación económica venezolana." Caracas, mimeo.
———, 1982. "The Impact of Petrodollars on the Economy and the Public
Sector of Venezuela." Paper presented at the Tenth National Meeting of the
Latin American Studies Association, Washington, D.C. (March 4).
Gil Fortoul, José, 1942. *Historia constitucional de Venezuela*. 3d ed. Vols. 1–3.
Caracas: Las Novedades.
Gil Yepes, J. A., 1977. "Entrepreneurs and Regime Consolidation." In John
Martz and David Myers, eds., *Venezuela: The Democratic Experience*. New
York: Praeger.
———, 1978. *El reto de los elites*. Madrid: Editorial Tecnos.
Gilmore, Robert L., 1964. *Caudillism and Militarism in Venezuela, 1810–1910*.
Athens: Ohio University Press.
Godio, Julio, 1980. *História del movimiento obrero latinoamericano*. Caracas:
Nueva Sociedad; Mexico City: Editorial Nueva Imagen.
Groves, Roderick, 1967. "Administrative Reform and the Politics of Reform:
The Case of Venezuela," *Public Administration Review*, no. 4 (December).
———, 1971. "Administrative Reform and Political Development," *Develop-
ment and Change* 2 (2).
Hanson, James, 1977. "Cycles of Economic Growth and Structural Change
since 1950." In John Martz and David Myers, eds., *Venezuela: The Demo-
cratic Experience*. New York: Praeger.
Hassan, Mostafa, 1975. *Economic Growth and Employment Problems in Ven-
ezuela*. New York: Praeger.
Hausmann, Ricardo, 1981. "State Landed Property, Oil Rent and Accumula-
tion in Venezuela: An Analysis in Terms of Social Relations." Ph.D. diss.,
Cornell University.
Hein, Wolfgang, and Conrad Stenzel, 1973. "The Capitalist State and Underde-
velopment in Latin America: The Case of Venezuela," *Kapitalistate*, no. 2.
Hellinger Daniel, 1991. *Venezuela: Tarnished Democracy*. Boulder, Colo.:
Westview Press.
Herrera Campíns, Luis, 1978. "Transición política." In J. L. Salcedo Bastardo,
Luis Herrera Campíns, and Benito Raúl Losad, eds., *1958: Tránsito de la
dictadura a la democracia en Venezuela*. Caracas: Editorial Ariel.

Hessey, Roland, 1962. *La compañía de Caracas: 1728–1784*. Caracas: Banco Central de Venezuela.

Hurtado, Héctor, 1974. "Introducción a la memoria del año 1974." Caracas, pamphlet.

————, 1975, 1976, and 1977. "Discurso pronunciado ante la Cámara de diputados del Congreso de la República en ocasión de la presentación del presupuesto." Mimeo.

Karl, Terry, 1987. "Petroleum and Political Pacts: The Transition to Democracy in Venezuela," *Latin American Research Review* 22 (1).

Karlsson, Weine, 1975. *Manufacturing in Venezuela: Studies in Development and Location*. Stockholm: Alquist and Wiksell.

Kelley, R. Lynn, 1977. "Venezuelan Constitutional Forms and Realities." In John Martz and David Myers, eds., *Venezuela: The Democratic Experience*. New York: Praeger.

Kornblith, Miriam, 1989. "Deuda y democracia en Venezuela: Los sucesos del 27 y 28 de Febrero," *Cuadernos del CENDES* (Centro de Estudios del Desarrollo, Universidad Central de Venezuela), no. 10 (January-April).

Kornblith, Miriam, and Daniel Levine, 1995. "Venezuela: The Life and Times of the Party System." In Scott Mainwaring and Timothy R. Scully, eds., *Building Democratic Institutions: Party Systems in Latin America*. Stanford, Calif.: Stanford University Press.

Kornblith, Miriam, and Thais Maingon, 1985. *Estado y gasto público en Venezuela, 1936–1980*. Caracas: Ediciones de la Biblioteca, Universidad Central de Venezuela.

Kornblith, Miriam, and Luken Quintana, 1981. "Gestión fiscal y centralización del poder político en los gobiernos de Cipriano Castro y de Juan Vicente Gómez," *Politeia* (Instituto de Estudios Políticios, Universidad Central de Venezuela) 10.

La libertad económica y la intervención del estado, 1945. Series of conferences organized by the Partido Democrático Venezolano on September 5–22. Caracas: Tipografía La Nación.

La responsabilidad empresarial en el progreso social de Venezuela, 1963. Maracay: Seminario Internaciónal de Ejecutivos (February 17–21).

Las elecciones presidenciales, 1989. Caracas: Grijalba.

Levine, Daniel, 1973. *Conflict and Political Change in Venezuela*. Princeton, N.J.: Princeton University Press.

————, 1978. "Venezuela since 1958: The Consolidation of Democratic Politics." In Juan Linz and Alfred Stepan, eds., *The Breakdown of Democratic Regimes: Latin America*. Baltimore: Johns Hopkins University Press.

————, 1985. "The Transition to Democracy: Are There Lessons from Venezuela?" *Bulletin of Latin American Research* 4 (2).

Levy, Fred D., 1968. *Economic Planning in Venezuela*. New York: Praeger.

Lombardi, John, 1966. *Los esclavos negros en las guerras venezolanas de la independencia*. Caracas: Cultura Universitaria (October).

————, 1977. "The Pattern of Venezuela's Past." In John Martz and David Myers, eds., *Venezuela: The Democratic Experience*. New York: Praeger.

Magallanes, Manuel Vicente, 1973. *Los partidos políticos en la evolución histórica venezolana.* Caracas: Monte Avile Editores.

Malavé Mata, Héctor, 1974. *Formación histórico del anti-desarrollo en Venezuela.* La Habana: Casa de las Americas.

———, 1976. *Dialéctica de la inflación.* Caracas: Universidad Central de Venezuela.

Mann, Joseph, 1976. "Labor: The Honeymoon Is Over," *Business Venezuela,* no. 41 (January-February).

Marín, Amerigo, 1975. *Los peces gordos.* Valencia: Vadell Hermanos.

Martz, John, 1966. *Acción Democrática: Evolution of a Modern Political Party.* Princeton, N.J.: Princeton University Press.

———, 1977. "The Venezuelan Presidential System." In Thomas diBocco, ed., *Presidential Power in Latin American Politics.* New York: Praeger.

Martz, John, and Enrique Baloyra, 1978. *Electoral Mobilization and Public Opinion: The Venezuelan Campaign of 1973.* Chapel Hill: University of North Carolina Press.

———, 1979. *Political Attitudes in Venezuela: Societal Cleavages and Political Opinion.* Austin: University of Texas Press.

Martz, John, and David Myers, eds., 1977. *Venezuela: The Democratic Experience.* New York: Praeger.

Mateo, Ramón Martín, 1979. "Relaciones entre el gobierno y las empresas públicas a través de instituciones especializadas." In *Gobierno y empresas públicas en América Latina.* Buenos Aires: Ediciones Siap.

Mayobre, Eduardo, 1985. "The Renegotiation of Venezuela's Foreign Debt during 1982 and 1983." In Miguel S. Wionczek, ed., *Politics and Economics of External Debt Crisis: The Latin American Experience.* Boulder, Colo.: Westview Press.

Mayobre, José Antonio, 1970. *Las inversiones extranjeras en Venezuela.* Caracas: Monte Avila.

Maza Zavala, D. F., 1977. "Historia de medio siglo en Venezuela." In Pablo González Casanova, ed., *América Latina: Historia de medio siglo,* vol. 1. Mexico City: Siglo XXI.

Maza Zavala, D. F., Héctor Malavé Mata, Celio S. Orta, Orlando Araujo, Miguel J. Bolívar Chollet, and Alfredo Chacón, 1974. *Venezuela: Crecimiento sin desarrollo.* Mexico City: Editorial Nuestro Tiempo.

Maza Zavala, D F., Héctor Malavé Mata, and Héctor Silva Michelena, 1975. *Venezuela: Economía y dependencia,* 3d ed. Caracas: Fondo Editorial.

McBeth, B. S., 1983. *Juan Vicente Gómez and the Oil Companies in Venezuela 1908-1935.* New York: Cambridge University Press.

McClure, Charles E., 1991. "Income Tax Reform in Colombia and Venezuela: A Comparative History." Hoover Institution, Stanford, Calif.

McCoy, Jennifer, 1986. "From Party to State: Inducements, Constraints, and Labor in Venezuela." Georgia State University (September).

———, 1987. "State, Labor and the Democratic Class Compromise in Venezuela." Paper presented at the 1987 Meeting of the Southeastern Conference on Latin American Studies, Mérida, Yucatán, April 1-5.

Mendoza Acedo, Manuel, 1974. *Porque Eugenio Mendoza.* Caracas: Gráficas Arnitano.

Merhav, Meir, 1980. "Un perfil de la política industrial, 1980–1985." Caracas (February).

Mimob, Ney, 1973. *Los desarrollistas.* Caracas: Colección los Desarrollistas.

Mommer, Bernard, 1990. "Renta petrolera y distribución del ingreso." In Omar Bello Rodríguez and Hector Valencillo, eds., *La economía de la Venezuela contemporánea: Ensayos escogidos.* Caracas: BCV.

Movimiento al Socialismo, 1977. *Otro gobierno que fracasa: Un análisis del MAS para los venezolanos.* Caracas: G & T Editores.

Musgrove, Philip, 1981. "The Oil Price Increase and the Alleviation of Poverty: Income Distribution in Caracas, Venezuela, in 1966 and 1975," *Journal of Development Economics* 9 (2).

Myers, David J., 1973. *Democratic Campaigning in Venezuela: Caldera's Victory.* Caracas: Fundación La Salle.

———, 1992. "Perceptions of a Stressed Democracy: Inevitable Decay or Foundation of Rebirth?" Paper presented at the North-South Center Conference on Democracy under Stress: Politics and Markets in Venezuela, Caracas (November 9–11).

Nacionalización del petróleo en Venezuela: Tésis y documentos y documentos fundamentales, 1982. Caracas: Ediciones Centauro.

Naím, Moisés, 1993. *Paper Tigers and Minotaurs: The Politics of Venezuela's Economic Reforms.* Washington, D.C.: Carnegie Endowment for International Peace.

Naím, Moisés, and Ramón Piñango, eds., 1984. *El caso Venezuela: Una ilusión de armonía.* Caracas: Ediciones IESA.

Nissen, Hans-Peter, and Bernard Mommer, eds., 1989. *Adiós a la bonanza? Crisis de la distribución del ingreso en Venezuela.* Caracas: Instituto Latinoamericana de Investigaciones Sociales y Centro de Estudios del Desarrollo, Editorial Nueva Sociedad.

Njaim, Humberto, Ricardo Combellas, Eva Josko de Guerón, and Andrés Stambouli, 1975. *El sistema político venezolano.* Caracas: Instituto de Estudios Políticos, Facultad de Derecho, Universidad Central de Venezuela.

Nolf, Max, 1978. "Notas sobre el desarrollo industrial de Venezuela." Caracas.

Peeler, John A., 1985. *Latin American Democracies: Colombia, Costa Rica and Venezuela.* Chapel Hill: University of North Carolina Press.

Peña, Alfredo, 1978. *Democracia y reforma del estado.* Caracas: Editorial Juridica Venezolana.

———, 1979. *Conversaciones con Carlos Andrés Pérez.* Caracas: Editorial Ateneo de Caracas.

Penniman, Howard, 1980. *Venezuela at the Polls: The National Elections of 1978.* Washington, D.C.: American Enterprise Institute for Public Policy Analysis.

Pérez, Carlos Andrés, 1973. *Acción de gobierno.* Caracas: Acción Democrática.

———, 1974. "A circumstancias anormales, medidas extraordinarias." Special message presented at the Congreso Nacional. Caracas (April 29).

————, n.d. "Mensaje como candidato de Acción Democrática a la presidencia de la República." Caracas.

Pérez Alfonzo, Juan Pablo, and Domingo Alberto Rangel, 1976. *El desastre.* Valencia: Vadell Hermanos.

Pérez Sainz, Juan Pablo, and Paul Zarembka, 1979. "Accumulation and the State in Venezuelan Industrialization," *Latin American Perspectives* 6 (3).

Petkoff, Teodoro, 1978. *La corrupción administrativa.* Caracas: Ediciones Fracción Socialista.

Petras, James F., Morris Morley, and Steven Smith, 1977. *The Nationalization of Venezuelan Oil.* New York: Praeger.

Piñerúa Ordaz, Luis, 1975. "Intervención el Congreso Nacional de Luis Pinerua Ordaz, April 14, 1975." Caracas, mimeo.

Piñerúa Ordaz, Luis, and Carlos Canache Mata, 1976. "Dos años para el Porvenir." Fracción Parlamentaria de Acción Democrática, Caracas.

Política y economía en Venezuela, 1810–1976, 1976. Caracas: Fundación John Boulton.

Powell, John Duncan, 1971. *Political Mobilization of the Venezuelan Peasant.* Cambridge: Harvard University Press.

Presidencia de la República, 1975–1978. *Manos a la obra: Textos de mensajes, discursos y declaraciones del presidente de la República.* Vols. 1–4. Caracas.

————, 1975–1979. *Mensaje al Congreso de la República.* Caracas.

Proceso Político, 1978. *CAP: 5 años.* Caracas: Editorial Ateneo.

Programa de las Naciones Unidos para el Desarrollo, n.d. *Reforma administrativa en Venezuela, enero 1972–diciembre 1976.* Caracas.

Pro-Venezuela, 1973. *La política y los empresarios.* Caracas.

Pulido Mora, Iván, 1976. "Notas para el primer ajuste sistemático del V Plan de la Nación, 1976–1980," *Resumen,* no. 131 (May 9).

Quero Morales, Constantino, 1978. *Imagen-objetivo de Venezuela. Reformas fundamentales para su desarrollo.* 2 vols. Caracas: Banco Central de Venezuela.

Quintero, Rodolfo, 1966. *Sindicalismo y cambio social en Venezuela. Boletín bibliográfico, 2a época, año 2, no. 8.* Caracas: Facultad de Económica, Universidad Central de Venezuela.

————, 1972. *Antropología del petróleo.* Mexico City: Siglo XXI.

Randall, Laura, 1987. *The Political Economy of Venezuelan Oil.* New York: Praeger.

Rangel, Domingo Alberto, 1974. *Capital y desarrollo, la Venezuela agraria.* Caracas: Universidad Central de Venezuela.

————, 1977a. *Capital y desarrollo, el rey petróleo.* Caracas: Universidad Central de Venezuela.

————, 1977b. *La revolución de las fantasias.* Caracas: Ediciones Ofidi.

————, 1978. *Los mercaderes del voto: Estudio de un sistema.* Valencia: Vadell Hermanos Editores.

Ray, Talton, 1969. *The Politics of the Barrios in Venezuela.* Berkeley: University of California Press.

Rey, Juan Carlos, 1986. "Los veinticinco años de la constitución y la reforma del estado," *Venezuela 1986 2.*

————, 1989a. *El futuro de la democracia en Venezuela.* Caracas: Serie Estudios/Colección IDEA.

————, 1989b. *"Polarización electoral," "economía del voto," y "voto castigo" en Venezuela.* Caracas: Instituto Internacional de Estudios Avanzados, Unidad de Ciencia Política.

————, 1989c. "Continuidad y cambio en las elecciones venezolanas: 1958–1988." Instituto Internacional de Estudios Avanzados, Unidad de Ciencia Política, Caracas.

————, 1994. "La democracia y la crisis del sistema populista de conciliación." *Revista de Estudios Políticos* (Madrid).

Rivas Rivas, José, 1968. *Las tres divisiones de Acción Democrática.* Caracas: Pensamiento Vivo Editores.

Rodríguez, Gumersindo, 1962. "La planificación económica," *La República* (September 10).

————, 1975. "The Role of Planning in the Economic and Social Development of Venezuela." Speech delivered to the Venzuelan-British Chamber of Commerce, Caracas (February 19).

————, 1976a. *El desarrollo económico y la medicina social.* Caracas: Ediciones de CORDIPLAN.

————, 1976b. *El estado y la planificación del desarrollo en Venezuela.* Caracas: Ediciones de CORDIPLAN.

————, 1979. *El nuevo modelo de desarrollo venezolano.* Caracas: Corpoconsult.

————, 1988. *El primer gobierno de CAP: Era posible la gran Venezuela?* Caracas: Editorial Ateneo de Caracas.

Rodríguez, Miguel, 1985. *Auge petrolero, estancamiento y políticas de ajuste en Venezuela.* Papeles de trabajo, no. 8. Caracas: Ediciones IES

Rodríguez Gallad, Irene, 1974. *El petróleo en la historiografía venezolana.* Caracas: Universidad Central de Venezuela.

Rodwin, Lloyd, and Associates, 1969. *Planning Urban Growth and Regional Development: The Experience of the Guayana Program of Venezuela.* Cambridge: MIT Press.

Rourke, Thomas, 1941. *Gómez: Tyrant of the Andes.* New York: Morrow.

Salazar-Carrillo, T., 1976. *Oil in the Economic Development of Venezuela.* New York: Praeger.

Salcedo Bastardo, J. L., 1972. *Historia fundamental de Venezuela.* 4th ed. Caracas: Universidad Central de Venezuela.

Salcedo Bastardo, J. L., Luis Herrera Campíns, and Benito Raúl Losad, eds., 1978. *1958: Tránsito de la dictadura a la democracia en Venezuela.* Caracas: Editorial Ariel.

Salinger, Pierre, 1978. *Cuadernos venezolanas, viajes y conversaciones con CAP.* Barcelona: Editorial Seix Barral.

Sánchez, Covisa, and Oropeza Zubillaga, 1977. "Sistema de la economía mixta," *Resumen,* no. 196 (August 7).

Sanin, 1975. *Gracias a ti.* Valencia: Vadell Hermanos.

————, 1978. *Venezuela saudita.* Valencia: Vadell Hermanos.

Shoup, Carl, 1959. *The Fiscal System of Venezuela*. Baltimore: Johns Hopkins University Press.

Shugat, Matthew Soberg, 1989. "Venezuelan Electoral Institutions in Comparative Perspective." University of California, San Diego.

Silva, Carlos Rafael, 1976. "Bosquejo histórico del desenvolvimiento de la economía venezolana en el siglo XX." In *Venezuela Moderna*. Caracas: Fundación Mendoza.

Silva Michelena, Héctor, 1975. "Proceso y crisis de la economía nacional, 1960–1973." *Nueva Ciencia* (Caracas), no. 1 (January-April).

Silva Michelena, José A., 1971a. *The Illusion of Democracy in Dependent Nations*. Cambridge: MIT Press.

———, 1971b. "State Formation and Nation Building in Latin America," *International Social Science Journal* 23 (3).

Stambouli, Andrés, 1979. "La actuación política de la dictadura y la rechazo del autoritarianism." Paper presented at a meeting of the Latin American Studies Association, Pittsburgh.

———, 1980. *Crisis política: Venezuela, 1945–1958*. Caracas: Editorial Ateneo de Caracas.

———, 1981. "Los resultados de las elecciones nacionales de 1978 y de las municipales de 1979," *Politeia* 9.

Stewart, William, 1977. "Public Administration." In John Martz and David Myers, eds., *Venezuela: The Democratic Experience*. New York: Praeger.

Sullivan, William, 1976. "Situación económica y política durante el periodo de Juan Vicente Gómez." In *Política y economía en Venezuela 1810–1976*. Caracas: Fundación John Boulton.

Taylor, Philip B., Jr., 1968. *The Venezuelan Golpe de Estado of 1958: The Fall of Marcos Pérez Jiménez*. Political Studies Series 4. Washington, D.C.: Institute for the Comparative Study of Political Systems.

———, ed., 1971. *Venezuela 1969: Analysis of Progress*. Houston, Tex.: University of Houston Press.

Tejera Paris, Enrique, 1960. *Dos elementos de gobierno*. Caracas: Editorial Grafos.

Templeton, A., 1992. "The Evolution of Popular Opinion." Caracas.

Tennassee, Paul Nehru, 1979. *Venezuela, los obreros petroleros y la lucha por la democracia*. Madrid: Editorial Popular.

Tinoco, Pedro, 1973. *El estado eficaz*. Caracas: Colección Los Desarrollistas.

Torres, José Dimas, 1973. "The Politics of Planning in Venezuela." Ph.D. diss., Ohio State University.

Tugwell, Franklin, 1975. *The Politics of Oil in Venezuela*. Stanford, Calif.: Stanford University Press.

———, 1977a. "Petroleum Policy and the Political Process." In John Martz and David Myers, eds., *Venezuela: The Democratic Experience*. New York: Praeger.

———, 1977b. "The United States and Venezuela: Prospects for Accommodation." In Robert D. Bond, ed., *Contemporary Venezuela and Its Role in International Affairs*. New York: New York University Press.

Ugalde, Luis, 1976. "Momento político," *Revista SIC* (Caracas) 39 (388).
———, 1977. "40 años de desarrollo: 1938–1958–1978," *Revista SIC* (Caracas) 40 (399).
Uslar Pietri, Arturo, 1948. *Venezuela en el petróleo.* Caracas.
Valecillos, Héctor, 1973. "Sindicatos, distribución de ingreso y empleo: El caso de Venezuela," *Cuadernos de la Sociedad Venezolana de Planificación,* no. 108 (January-March).
Vallenilla, Luis, 1973. *Auge, declinación y porvenir del petróleo venezolano.* Caracas: Editorial Tiempo Nuevo.
———, 1975. *Oil: The Making of a New Economic Order: Venezuelan Oil and OPEC.* New York: McGraw-Hill.
Velásquez, Luis Corder, 1971. *Gómez y las fuerzas vivas.* Caracas: n.p.
Venezuela moderna: Medio siglo de historia, 1926–1976. Caracas: Fundación Eugenio Mendoza.

PUBLICATIONS OF GOVERNMENT AGENCIES

Banco Central de Venezuela, yearly. *Informe económico.* Caracas.
———, 1973. "La reforma administrativa en Venezuela." Caracas (November).
———, 1974. "Proyecto de reorganización para la Corporación Venezolana de Fomento." Caracas (November).
———, 1978a. "Declaraciones del fin de año del presidente del Banco Central." Caracas.
———, 1978b. *La economía venezolana en los ultimos 35 años.* Caracas.
———, 1979. "Ley de presupuesto." (Summary of 1979.) Caracas.
Comisión de la Administración Pública, 1972. *Informe sobre la reforma de la administración pública nacional.* 2 vols. Caracas: Imprenta Nacional.
———, n.d. "La Corporación Venezolana de Fomento y el sistema financiera nacional." Caracas.
Consejo Supremo Electoral, 1968. *Resultados electorales 1968.* Caracas.
———, 1988. *Resultados electorales 1988.* Caracas.
Controlaría General de la República de Venezuela, yearly. *Informe anual.* Caracas: Imprenta Nacional.
———, 1978. *Informe al Congreso Nacional 1977.* Caracas.
CORDIPLAN (Oficina Central de Coordinación y Planificación), various years. *Encuesta industrial.* Vols. 1–3. Caracas.
———, 1963. *Plan de la nación, 1963–1966.* Caracas.
———, 1966. *Plan de la nación, 1965–1968.* Caracas.
———, 1970. *Plan de la nación, 1970–1974.* Caracas.
———, 1976. *Plan de la nación, 1976–1980.* Caracas.
———, 1978–1982. *Projection of the Venezuelan Economy: 1978–1982.* Caracas.
———, 1979a. "Evaluación de los aspectos socioeconómicos en el périodo 1974–1978 y su relación con el V plan de la nación." Caracas (July).
———, 1979b. "Quinta mensaje al Congreso de la República." Caracas.
———, n.d. "Ante-proyecto de ley orgánica del sistema de planificación del estado." Chapter 1 of Title 2. Caracas.

Corporación Venezolana de Fomento. 1976 *La Corporación Venezolana de Fomento en sus 30 años.* Caracas.
Corporación Venezolana de Guayana. 1979. "Informe sobre Guayana." Confidential report on the Guayana Region. Caracas.
Fondo de Crédito Industrial, 1977 and 1978. *Informe anual.* Caracas.
Fondo de Inversiónes de Venezuela, yearly. *Informe anual.* Caracas.
———, 1978. *Report and Accounts 1978.* Caracas.
Gaceta oficial, various years. Caracas.
Gaceta oficial extraordinaria, various years. Caracas.
Memoria de hacienda, 1966, 1973–1977. Caracas.
Ministerio de Energía y Minas, 1977. *Petróleo y otros datos estadísticos, 1976.* Caracas (October).
Ministerio de Fomento, Dirección Estadística y Censos Nacionales, yearly. *Anuario estadístico de Venezuela.* Caracas.
———, 1976. *Encuesta nacional de hogares por muestro.* Caracas.
———, 1977. *Encuesta industrial,* vol. 4. Caracas.
Ministerio de Hacienda, various years. *Cuenta general de rentas y gastos públicos.* Caracas.
Ministerio de Hacienda, Dirección General de Finanzas Públicas, 1978. *Boletín estadístico,* no. 83. Caracas.
———, 1980. *Resúmen de la ley de presupuesto, 1973–1978.* Caracas.
Ministerio de Trabajo, various years. *Memoria y cuenta.* Caracas.
Oficina Central de Coordinación y Planificación: see CORDIPLAN.
Oficina Central de Estadística e Informática, Presidencia de la República, República de Venezuela, 1985. *Anuario estadístico 1982–83.* Caracas.
———, 1993. *Anuario estadístico 1992.* Caracas.
Oficina Central de Presupuesto, various years. *Informe anual.* Caracas.
Superintendencia de Bancos, various years. *Informe anual.* Caracas.

NEWSPAPERS, PERIODICALS, AND MAGAZINES

El Nacional (1973–1989) and *El Universal* (1973–1979), the two leading newspapers in Caracas, were a main source of information for the Venezuelan case study. To a lesser extent I also utilized the *Daily Journal* (1973–1979) (the local English newspaper), *El Diario de Caracas, Political Impact,* and the *Financial Times* and *International Herald Tribune.*

Venezuelan magazines provided additional material, especially *Resumen* (1973–1979), *Zeta* (1973–1992), and *Semana* (1973–1979).

The most important independent publication concerning the Venezuelan economy published locally is *VenEconomy,* which was formerly the *Monthly Report.* Other nongovernmental sources for the economy include a variety of confidential World Bank reports; *Business Venezuela,* the magazine of the Venezuelan-American Chamber of Commerce; and the *Quarterly Economic Review: Venezuela.* Finally, Datos, an independent public-opinion and market-research group, provided additional information. All these sources were utilized for the period 1973–1979.

Periodicals on Latin America were also consulted for the period 1973–1992.

These include *Latin America Weekly Report (LAWR), Latin American Monitor (LAM), Latin America Regional Reports Andean Group (LARR), Latin America Economic Report (LAER).*

ALGERIA

Amiar, Jamal, 1992. "In Algeria, the Agenda Is Violence, No New Ideas, and a War Economy." *Washington Report on Middle East Affairs* 11 (3).

Balta, Paul, 1981. *L'Algerie des algeriens, vingt ans après.* Paris: Editions Ouvrières.

Cubertafond, Bernard, 1981. "L'Algerie du President Chadli," *Politique Etrangère* 46 (1).

Entelis, John P., 1986. *Algeria: The Revolution Institutionalized.* Boulder, Colo.: Westview Press.

Etienne, Bruno, 1977. *Algerie: Cultures et révolution.* Paris: Editions du Seuil.

Grimaud, Nicole, 1976. "Une Algerie en mutation à l'heure de la charte nationale," *Magreb-Machrek,* no. 73 (July/September).

Horne, Alistair, 1977. *A Savage War of Peace: Algeria, 1954–1962.* London: Macmillan.

Leca, Jean, and Jean-Claude Vatin, 1975. *L'Algerie politique: Institutions et régime.* Paris: Presses de la Fondation Nationales des Sciences Politiques.

Mortimer, Robert A., 1993. "Algeria: The Clash between Islam, Democracy, and the Military." *Current History* 92 (570).

Nair, Kuider Sami, 1982. "Algeria 1954–1982: Social Forces and Blocs in Power," *Telos* 53 (fall).

Nelson, Harold D., ed., 1979. *Algeria: A Country Study.* Washington, D.C.: Foreign Area Studies, American University.

Quandt, W. B., 1969. *Revolution and Political Leadership: Algeria, 1954–1968.* Cambridge: MIT Press.

Rabhi, Mohammed, 1979. "External Debt: Comparative Analysis for Algeria and Venezuela—A Linear Quadratic Control Theory Explanation." Ph.D. diss., University of Texas, Austin.

Raffinot, Marc, and Pierre Jacquemot, 1977. *Le capitalisme d'état algerien.* Paris: Francois Manpero.

Zartman, William, 1984. "L'élite algerienne sous la presidence de Chadli Benjedid," *Maghreb-Machrek,* no. 106 (October/December).

PERIODICALS

L'Annuaire de l'Afrique du Nord.
Maghreb-Machrek.
Middle East Economic Digest.
Middle East Economic Survey.
New York Times.

INDONESIA

Arndt, H. W., 1977. "Survey of Recent Developments," *Bulletin of Indonesian Economic Studies* 13 (November).

———, 1984. *The Indonesian Economy: Collected Papers.* Singapore: Chopmen.

Balassa, Bela, 1981. *The Policy Experience of Twelve Less Developed Countries, 1973–1978.* Staff Working Paper 449. Washington, D.C.: World Bank (April).

Barnes, Philip, 1995. *Indonesia: The Political Economy of Energy.* Oxford: Oxford University Press for the Oxford Institute of Energy Studies.

Booth, Anne, ed., 1992. *The Oil Boom and After: Indonesian Economic Policy in the Soeharto Era.* New York: Oxford University Press.

Booth, Anne, and Peter McCawley, eds., 1981. *The Indonesian Economy during the Soeharto Era.* Kuala Lumpur: Oxford University Press.

Bowring, Philip, 1977. "Indonesia: Back to Real Priorities," *Far Eastern Economic Review* (September).

Carlson, S., 1977. *Indonesia's Oil.* Boulder, Colo.: Westview Press.

Dapice, David O., 1980. "An Overview of the Indonesian Economy." In Gustav F. Papanek, ed., *The Indonesian Economy.* New York: Praeger.

Dick, Howard, 1979. "Survey of Recent Developments," *Bulletin of Indonesian Economic Studies* 15 (March).

Gillis, Malcolm, 1983. "Economic Growth in Indonesia: 1950–1980." Discussion Paper 146. Cambridge: Harvard Institute for International Development (March).

Glassburner, Bruce, 1976. "In the Wake of General Ibnu: Crisis in the Indonesian Oil Industry," *Asian Survey* (December).

———, 1984. *ASEAN's 'Other Four': Economic Policy and Economic Performance since 1970.* Kuala Lumpur and Canberra: ASEAN-Australia Joint Research Project.

Kartadjoemena, H. S., 1977. *The Politics of External Economic Relations: Indonesia's Options.* Singapore: Institute of Southeast Asian Studies.

Macawley, P., 1975–1976. "Some Consequences of the Pertamina Crisis in Indonesia," *Pacific Affairs* (winter).

Mears, Leon A., 1984. "Rice and Food Self-Sufficiency in Indonesia," *Bulletin of Indonesian Economic Studies* 20 (August).

Nasution, Anwar, 1983. *Financial Institutions and Policies in Indonesia.* Singapore: Institute of Southeast Asian Studies.

Pinto, Brian, 1987. "Nigeria during and after the Oil Boom: A Policy Comparison with Indonesia," *World Bank Economic Review* 1 (3).

Sundrum, R. M., 1986. "Indonesia's Rapid Economic Growth: 1968–1981," *Bulletin of Indonesian Economic Studies* 22 (December).

Warr, Peter G., 1986. "Indonesia's Other Dutch Disease: Economic Effects of the Petroleum Boom." Working Paper in Trade and Development 6/2. Canberra: Research School of Pacific Studies, Australian National University.

IRAN

Bashiriyeh, Hossein, 1984. *The State and Revolution in Iran, 1962–1982*. London: Croom Helm.

Bernard, Cheryl, and Zalmay Khalilzad, 1984. *"The Government of God"— Iran's Islamic Republic*. New York: Columbia University Press.

Elm, Mostafa, 1992. *Oil, Power, and Principle: Iran's Oil Nationalization and Its Aftermath*. Syracuse, N.Y.: Syracuse University Press.

Fesharaki, Fereidun, 1976. *Development of the Iranian Oil Industry: International and Domestic Aspects*. New York: Praeger.

Frank, Lawrence P., 1984. "Two Responses to the Oil Boom: Iranian and Nigerian Politics after 1973," *Comparative Politics* 16 (April).

Graham, Robert, 1978. *Iran: The Illusion of Power*. London: Croom Helm.

Halliday, Fred, 1979. *Iran: Dictatorship and Development*. Harmondsworth: Penguin Books.

Hill, Lewis E., and R. Niknam, 1978. "American Treasure and the Price of Revolution in Iran," *Iranian Economic Review*, no. 5–6 (fall-winter).

Hooglund, Eric J., 1982. *Land and Revolution in Iran, 1960–1980*. Austin: University of Texas Press.

Imperial Government of Iran, 1976. *Fifth National Development Plan, 1973– 1979*. Teheran.

Kadhim, Mihssen, 1983. "The Political Economy of Revolutionary Iran," *Cairo Papers in Social Science* 6 (1).

Katouzian, Homa, 1981. *The Political Economy of Modern Iran: Despotism and Pseudo-Modernism, 1926–1979*. New York: New York University Press.

Kazemi, Farhad, 1980a. "The Military and Politics in Iran: The Uneasy Symbiosis." In Elie Dedourie and Sylvia G. Haim, eds., *Towards a Modern Iran: Studies in Thought, Politics and Society*. London: Frank Cass.

———, 1980b. *Poverty and Revolution in Iran: The Migrant Poor, Urban Marginality and Politics*. New York: New York University Press.

Looney, Robert E., 1982. *Economic Origins of the Iranian Revolution*. New York: Pergamon Press.

Mahdavy, Hossein, 1965. "The Coming Crisis in Iran," *Foreign Affairs* 44 (October).

———, 1970. "The Pattern and Problems of Economic Development in Rentier States: The Case of Iran." In M. A. Cook, ed., *Studies in the Economic History of the Middle East*. London: Oxford University Press.

Moghtader, Hushang, 1980. "The Impact of Increased Oil Revenue on Iran's Economic Development (1973–1976)." In Elie Dedourie and Sylvia G. Haim, eds., *Towards a Modern Iran: Studies in Thought, Politics and Society*. London: Frank Cass.

Nasri, Farzeen, 1983. "Iranian Studies and the Iranian Revolution," *World Politics* 35 (July).

Razi, G. Hosseign, 1987. "The Nexus of Legitimacy and Performance: The Lessons of the Iranian Revolution," *Comparative Politics* (July).

Saikal, Amin, 1980. *The Rise and Fall of the Shah*. Princeton, N.J.: Princeton University Press.

Walton, Thomas, 1980. "Economic Development and Revolutionary Upheavals in Iran," *Cambridge Journal of Economics* 4 (September).

Zonis, Marvin, 1983. "Iran: A Theory of Revolution from Accounts of the Revolution," *World Politics* 35 (July).

NIGERIA

Adejumabi, Said, and Abubakar Mowoh, eds., 1995. *The Political Economy of Nigeria under Military Rule (1984–1993)*. Harare: SAPES Books.

Ahmad Khan, Sarah, 1994. *Nigeria: The Political Economy of Oil*. Oxford: Oxford University Press for the Oxford Institute of Energy Studies.

Barber, Karin, 1982. "Popular Reactions to the Petro-Naira," *Journal of Modern African Studies* 20 (3).

Bienen, Henry S., and Mark Gersovitz, 1982. *Nigeria Absorbing the Oil Wealth*. London: Euromoney Publications.

Diamond, Larry, 1983. "Class, Ethnicity and the Democratic State: Nigeria, 1950–1966," *Comparative Studies in Society and History* 25 (3).

———, 1988. *Class, Ethnicity and Democracy in Nigeria: The Failure of the First Republic*. London: Macmillan; Syracuse: Syracuse University Press.

———, 1990. "The Failures of Nigeria's First and Second Republics and Their Lessons for the Third Republic." Paper presented at the Conference on Democratic Transition and Structural Adjustment in Nigeria, Hoover Institution, Stanford, Calif. (August 27–29).

Falola, Toyin, and Julius Ihonvbere, 1985. *The Rise and Fall of Nigeria's Second Republic: 1979–84*. London: Zed.

Frank, Lawrence P., 1984. "Two Responses to the Oil Boom: Iranian and Nigerian Politics after 1973," *Comparative Politics* 16 (3).

Freund, Bill, 1978. "Oil Boom and Crisis in Contemporary Nigeria," *Review of African Political Economy*, no. 13 (September-December).

Government of Nigeria, Federal Ministry of Development. 1975. *Third National Development Plan, 1975–1980*. Lagos.

Ihonvbere, Julius Omozuanvbo, 1983. "Oil Revenues, Underdevelopment and Class Struggles in Nigeria," *Scandinavian Journal of Development Alternatives* 2 (June).

Joseph, Richard, 1987. *Democracy and Prebendal Politics in Nigeria: The Rise and Fall of the Second Republic*. Cambridge: Cambridge University Press.

Nnadozie, Emmanuel U., 1995. *Oil and Socioeconomic Crisis in Nigeria*. Lewiston, N.Y.: Mellen University Press.

Olayiwola, Peter O., 1987. *Petroleum and Structural Change in a Developing Country: The Case of Nigeria*. New York: Praeger.

Pearson, Scott R., 1970. *Petroleum and Nigerian Economy*. Stanford, Calif.: Stanford University Press.

Pearson, Scott R., and J. Cownie, 1974. *Commodity Exports and African Economic Development*. Lexington, Mass.: Lexington Books.

Pinto, Brian, 1987. "Nigeria during and after the Oil Boom: A Policy Comparison with Indonesia," *World Bank Economic Review* 1 (3).

Schatz, Sayre P., 1984. "Pirate Capitalism and the Inert Economy of Nigeria," *Journal of Modern African Studies* 22 (1).

Struthers, John J., 1990. "Nigerian Oil and Exchange Rates: Indicators of 'Dutch Disease.'" *Development and Change* 21 (2).

Taylor, Lance, Kadir T. Yurukoglu, and Shahid A. Chaudry, 1986. "A Macro Model of an Oil-Exporter: Nigeria." In J. Peter Neary, ed., *Natural Resources and the Macroeconomy.* Cambridge: MIT Press.

Watts, Michael, ed., 1987. *State, Oil, and Agriculture in Nigeria.* Berkeley: Institute of International Studies, University of California.

Watts, Michael, and Paul Lubeck, 1983. "The Popular Classes and the Oil Boom." In William Zartman, ed., *The Political Economy of Nigeria.* New York: Praeger.

Zartman, I. William, ed., 1983. *The Political Economy of Nigeria.* New York: Praeger.

NORWAY

El Mallakh, Ragaei, Oystein Noreng, and Barry W. Poulson, 1984. *Petroleum and Economic Development: The Cases of Mexico and Norway.* Lexington, Mass: Lexington Books.

Elder, Neil, Alastair H. Thomas, and David Arter, 1982. *The Consensual Democracies? The Government and Politics of Scandinavian States.* Oxford: Martin Robertson.

Eliasson, Gunnar, 1983. "Microeconometrics and the Dynamics of Resource Allocation." *Microeconometrics, IUI Yearbook 1982–83.* Stockholm: Industrial Institute for Economic and Social Research.

Eliasson, Gunnar, Mark Shavefkin, and Bengt-Christer Ysander, eds., 1983. *Policymaking in a Disorderly World Economy.* Stockholm: Industrial Institute for Economic and Social Research.

Galenson, Walter, 1986. *A Welfare State Strikes Oil: The Norwegian Experience.* Lanham, Md., and London: University Press of America.

Higley, John, Karl Erik Brofoss, and Knut Groholt, 1975. "Top Civil Servants and the National Budget in Norway." In Mattei Dogan, ed., *The Mandarins of Western Europe.* New York and London: Wiley, Halsted Press.

Lind, T., and G. A. MacKay, 1980. *Norwegian Oil Policies.* London: C. Hurst.

Noreng, Oystein, 1980. *The Oil Industry and Government Strategy in the North Sea.* London and Boulder, Colo.: Croom Helm, ICEED.

Olsen, Johan P., 1983. *Organized Democracy: Political Institutions in a Welfare State: The Case of Norway.* Oslo: Universitetsforlaget.

———, 1988. "Political Science and Organization Theory: Parallel Agendas but Mutual Disregard." LOS-senter Notat 88/22. Norsk Senter for Forskning i Ledelse, Organisasjon og Styring, Oslo.

Petroleum Industry in Norwegian Society, 1973–1974. Parliamentary Report 25. Oslo.

Stinchcombe, Arthur L., and Carol A. Heimer, 1985. *Organization Theory and*

Project Management: Administering Uncertainty in Norwegian Offshore Oil. Oslo: Norwegian University Press (Universitetsforlaget).

NEWSPAPERS

New York Times clippings and index, 1970–1985, various articles. *Financial Times* clippings and index, 1980s. *International Herald Tribune* (1986).

SPAIN

Anderson, Perry, 1979. *Lineages of the Absolutist State,* London: Verso.
Braudel, Fernand, 1972. *The Mediterranean and the Mediterranean World in the Age of Philip II.* Vol. 2. New York: Harper Colophon Books.
Carande, Ramón, 1967. *Carlos V y sus banqueros.* Vol. 3. Madrid: Sociedad de Estudio y Publicaciones.
Chaunu, Pierre, 1959. *Seville et l'Atlantique, 1504–1650.* 8 vols. Paris: S.E.V.P.E.N.
Elliot, J. H., 1934. *American Treasure and the Price Revolution in Spain.* Cambridge: Harvard University Press.
———, 1961. "The Decline of Spain," *Past and Present,* no. 20.
———, 1963. *Imperial Spain: 1469–1716.* 2 vols. New York: Meridian Books.
———, 1970. *The Old World and the New, 1492–1650.* London: Cambridge University Press.
Hamilton, Earl J., 1934. *American Treasure and the Price Revolution in Spain, 1501–1650.* Cambridge, Mass.: Harvard University Press.
Larraz, José, 1963. *La época del mercantilismo en Castilla.* Madrid: Aguilar.
Lynch, John, 1965. *Spain under the Habsburgs.* London: Oxford Press.
Mauro, Frédéric, and Geoffrey Parker, 1977. "Spain." In Charles Wilson and Geoffrey Parker, eds., *An Introduction to Sources of European Economic History 1500–1800.* Ithaca, N.Y.: Cornell University Press.
Parker, Geoffrey, 1972. *The Army of Flanders and the Spanish Roa, 1567–1659.* Cambridge: Cambridge University Press.
Vásquez de Prada, V., 1978. *História económica y social de España, los siglos XVI y XVII.* Madrid: Confederación Española de Cajas de Ahorros.
Vincens-Vives, J., 1957. *História social y económico de España y América.* Vol. 2. Barcelona: Teide.
Wallerstein, Immanuel, 1974. *The Modern World System: Capitalist Agriculture and the Origins of the European World Economy in the Sixteenth Century.* New York: Academic Press.

Index

Text: 10/13 Sabon
Display: Sabon
Compositor, Printer, and Binder: Maple-Vail Book Mfg. Group